Transitioning From Globalized to Localized and Self-Reliant Economies

Ruchika Gupta
Amity University, India

Priyank Srivastava
Amity University, India

Shiv Ranjan
Amity University, India

M. Affan Badar
Indiana State University, USA

IGI Global
PUBLISHER of TIMELY KNOWLEDGE

A volume in the Advances in Finance, Accounting, and Economics (AFAE) Book Series

Published in the United States of America by
IGI Global
Business Science Reference (an imprint of IGI Global)
701 E. Chocolate Avenue
Hershey PA, USA 17033
Tel: 717-533-8845
Fax: 717-533-8661
E-mail: cust@igi-global.com
Web site: http://www.igi-global.com

Library of Congress Cataloging-in-Publication Data

Names: Gupta, Ruchika, editor. | Srivastava, Priyank, editor. | Ranjan, Shiv, editor. | Badar, M. Affan, editor.
Title: Transitioning from globalized to localized and self-reliant economies / Ruchika Gupta, Priyank Srivastava, Shiv Ranjan, M. Affan Badar, editors.
Description: Hershey, PA : Business Science Reference, [2022] | Includes bibliographical references and index. | Summary: "With the outbreak of COVID-19 which had a profound impact on global economic growth, this edited book contains contributions that explore the paradigm shift of how economies are moving more toward becoming self reliant"-- Provided by publisher.
Identifiers: LCCN 2021033600 (print) | LCCN 2021033601 (ebook) | ISBN 9781799887058 (hardcover) | ISBN 9781799887065 (paperback) | ISBN 9781799887072 (ebook)
Subjects: LCSH: Economic development--Technological innovations. | Manufacturing industries--Technological innovations. | Business logistics. | COVID-19 (Disease)
Classification: LCC HD82 .T72 2022 (print) | LCC HD82 (ebook) | DDC 338.9--dc23
LC record available at https://lccn.loc.gov/2021033600
LC ebook record available at https://lccn.loc.gov/2021033601

This book is published in the IGI Global book series Advances in Finance, Accounting, and Economics (AFAE) (ISSN: 2327-5677; eISSN: 2327-5685)

British Cataloguing in Publication Data
A Cataloguing in Publication record for this book is available from the British Library.

Advances in Finance, Accounting, and Economics (AFAE) Book Series

Ahmed Driouchi
Al Akhawayn University, Morocco

ISSN:2327-5677
EISSN:2327-5685

Mission

In our changing economic and business environment, it is important to consider the financial changes occurring internationally as well as within individual organizations and business environments. Understanding these changes as well as the factors that influence them is crucial in preparing for our financial future and ensuring economic sustainability and growth.

The **Advances in Finance, Accounting, and Economics (AFAE)** book series aims to publish comprehensive and informative titles in all areas of economics and economic theory, finance, and accounting to assist in advancing the available knowledge and providing for further research development in these dynamic fields.

Coverage

- Microeconomics
- Public Finance
- Applied Finance
- Applied Accounting
- Macroeconomics
- Interest Rates and Annuities
- Accounting Standards
- Entrepreneurship in Accounting and Finance
- Managerial Accounting
- Economics Geography

IGI Global is currently accepting manuscripts for publication within this series. To submit a proposal for a volume in this series, please contact our Acquisition Editors at Acquisitions@igi-global.com or visit: http://www.igi-global.com/publish/.

The Advances in Finance, Accounting, and Economics (AFAE) Book Series (ISSN 2327-5677) is published by IGI Global, 701 E. Chocolate Avenue, Hershey, PA 17033-1240, USA, www.igi-global.com. This series is composed of titles available for purchase individually; each title is edited to be contextually exclusive from any other title within the series. For pricing and ordering information please visit http://www.igi-global.com/book-series/advances-finance-accounting-economics/73685. Postmaster: Send all address changes to above address.

Titles in this Series

For a list of additional titles in this series, please visit: www.igi-global.com/book-series/advances-finance-accounting-economics/73685

Handbook of Research on Changing World Economic Order in the Post-Pandemic Period
Sushanta Kumar Mahapatra (IBS Hyderabad, The ICFAI Foundation for Higher Education, India) and Vishal Sarin (Lovely Professional University, India)
Business Science Reference • © 2022 • 470pp • H/C (ISBN: 9781799868965) • US $295.00

Handbook of Research on Developing Circular, Digital, and Green Economies in Asia
Patricia Ordóñez de Pablos (The University of Oviedo, Spain)
Business Science Reference • © 2022 • 521pp • H/C (ISBN: 9781799886785) • US $225.00

Handbook of Research on Climate Change and the Sustainable Financial Sector
Odunayo Magret Olarewaju (Durban University of Technology, South Africa) and Idris Olayiwola Ganiyu (University of KwaZulu-Natal, South Africa)
Business Science Reference • © 2021 • 573pp • H/C (ISBN: 9781799879671) • US $295.00

CSR and Management Accounting Challenges in a Time of Global Crises
Ionica Oncioiu (Titu Maiorescu University, Romania)
Business Science Reference • © 2021 • 278pp • H/C (ISBN: 9781799880691) • US $215.00

Impact of Global Issues on International Trade
Ahu Coşkun Özer (Marmara University, Turkey)
Business Science Reference • © 2021 • 291pp • H/C (ISBN: 9781799883142) • US $215.00

Handbook of Research on the Empirical Aspects of Strategic Trade Negotiations and Management
Nuno Crespo (ISCTE – Instituto Universitário de Lisboa, Portugal) and Nadia Simoes (ISCTE – Instituto Universitário de Lisboa, Portugal)
Business Science Reference • © 2021 • 446pp • H/C (ISBN: 9781799875680) • US $265.00

Handbook of Research on Financial Management During Economic Downturn and Recovery
Nuno Miguel Teixeira (Center for Research in Business and Administration, School of Business Sciences, Polytechnic Institute of Setúbal, Portugal) and Inês Lisboa (CARME, School of Management and Technology, Polytechnic of Leiria, Portugal)
Business Science Reference • © 2021 • 566pp • H/C (ISBN: 9781799866435) • US $295.00

IGI Global
PUBLISHER of TIMELY KNOWLEDGE

701 East Chocolate Avenue, Hershey, PA 17033, USA
Tel: 717-533-8845 x100 • Fax: 717-533-8661
E-Mail: cust@igi-global.com • www.igi-global.com

Table of Contents

Detailed Table of Contents

The COVID-19 pandemic brought an extraordinary disturbance regarding the worldwide economy and global trade, as creation and utilization downsized. Perhaps the best methodology for addressing this type of emergency is convenient, unspoiled information. An informed public is better established to use wise judgment including on cases recognized for trade. This is the situation, and a devoted page at WTO site has been created. This will provide present data related with trade information. The chapter discusses rising protectionism in course of the last half period, unexpected monetary crises created by the pandemic, disturbances regarding production network movement, and shocks related to market interest. Reporters worldwide have trumpeted the 'finish' of globalization.

The COVID-19 pandemic has raised serious questions about the applicability of international trade theories. International trade has now changed its shape due to this novel coronavirus. It is a fact that no country in the world follows one trade theory. They use multiple theories for their goods and services and will continue to do so. The future of international trade theories is suspected as to which theory will be employed or any new theory of international trade will emerge. Empirical evidence illustrates the emergence of regionalization as compared to globalization. In this context, trade theories will also adjust their forms and assumptions. Therefore, this chapter reconciles international trade theories with actual data, most notably COVID-19.

The world is currently experiencing a dramatic crisis that has not yet reached bottom. In Mexico, in the second quarter of 2020, there was a drop in the gross domestic product of 18.9% compared to the same quarter of 2019. In this context, the objective is to identify types of personal expenses in households located in Culiacán, Sinaloa, Mexico as of July 15, 2020. The main results were that most of the respondents' budgets spend according to their income, have had no problem paying their bank loans on time, would consider a fund for future contingencies, have not purchased health insurance, have not bought a computer or cell phone, among other issues analyzed. The main findings are oriented to the fact that the studied population has not acquired additional medical insurance despite the pandemic. It is also concluded that the population under study has become aware of having savings for contingency funds and that digital life still shows resistance in making personal financial decisions.

Higher education has the ability to contribute to global, national, and local growth. Institutions of higher education have played an important role in society throughout modern history, training the elite and making groundbreaking advances in science and the humanities. Education broadens people's perspectives on themselves and the world around them. It improves people's competitiveness and innovation while also encouraging entrepreneurship and technical advancement. This chapter will provide an insight on the role of higher educational institutes in economic development. The chapter will provide cross-country analysis and cases from different parts of the globe.

Technological progress is critical for improving manufacturing resilience and achieving self-sufficiency in any nation. The COVID-19 crisis has shown the importance of, as well as the threats associated with, our new industrial processes. Manufacturing's critical position in both industrialized and emerging economies has been shown by shortages of medical supplies and disruptions in basic goods. These delays and market fluctuations have also highlighted the pitfalls of focusing solely on a globalized distribution system characterized by fragmented supply chains, the separation of engineering and manufacturing, and just-in-time production. Although globalisation was the trend before the COVID-19 pandemic, several countries realized the dangers and began to look inward, focusing on developing local manufacturing capacities. In addition, the automotive sector has established itself as a cornerstone of post-COVID-19 recovery strategies.

Technology is widely acknowledged in economics as the primary source of economic development. Technological advancement enables more efficient production with more and superior products and services, which is essential for development. Technology encompasses a vast body of knowledge and instruments that make it easier to make efficient and creative use of economic resources to generate goods and services. Technological advancement is necessary for economic growth and development, and the more sophisticated the technology, the faster the local and global economies may improve. Globalization further fueled and results in increased importance of social and economic analysis and also necessitates coordinated development efforts using technology.

The pandemic has an impact on almost all sectors of people's lives, in the economic, political, and socio-cultural sectors. The government has implemented large-scale social restrictions (PSBB) as an effort to stop the spread of the COVID-19 virus. With the PSBB, it causes disruption to the hospital supply chain management. As a step to anticipate the hospital's impact on the PSBB, the hospital needs to evaluate the performance of supply chain management. The purpose of this chapter is to describe the performance evaluation of hospital supply chain management using a balanced scorecard approach. A new finding from this study is to measure the performance of hospitals experiencing various disruptions in their supply chain management caused by the COVID-19 pandemic with a balanced scorecard. The author concludes that measurements with the balanced scorecard approach can provide information about the performance of hospital supply chain management broadly in areas experiencing disruption due to the COVID-19 pandemic.

Natural or manmade disasters can bring havoc to the healthcare industry in terms of poor services, out of stocks, cost overruns, and loss of lives. Specifically, the aftermath of disasters can be brutal if not managed properly. The quicker the healthcare providers recover, the lesser the impact would be. A resilient system has the potential to reduce the recovery time significantly. Healthcare providers under emergency scenarios may realize out-of-stock situations for their critical medical supplies. The out-of-stock supplies potentially cause poor patient care including death. COVID 19 is an unfortunate example where critical medical supplies were completely out for many medical providers and that had a serious negative impact on healthcare service deliveries. Healthcare providers needed to replenish their supplies from the overseas manufacturing plants, or central distribution centers, or unaffected regional distribution centers. Most of the times healthcare authorities struggle to secure critical medical supplies from other distribution centers due to operational and transportation issues. Depending on the disaster condition, sometimes many health care providers are beyond reach due to damaged transportation networks. This is the perfect time to share critical medical supplies from unaffected regions. Proven techniques like operation research can alleviate this situation. There are very few works that have been done in the field of healthcare service deliveries in case of a disaster. This chapter discusses the modeling techniques using operations research to improve the service levels while minimizing unsatisfied demand in the natural disaster-affected zones.

Skills and information are the driving powers of financial development and social improvement of any

sector, which has remained stable at roughly 16%. To facilitate 'Aatmanirbhar Bharat', the government has brought in the product-linked incentive (PLI) scheme to encourage several sectors to increase their local manufacturing and supply chain base, among other things, to help India become self-reliant for high end products. These efforts will aid in the creation of jobs, the alleviation of stressed sectors, the assurance of liquidity, the boost of manufacturing, the energization of the real estate industry, and the assistance of farmers. The chapter aims to evaluate the Balance of Payment of India as structural growth country wise and sector wise growth of FDI in India as well as the 'Aaatmanirbhar Bharat' status and stimulus packages, which have been announced for sustainable growth of GDP during this pandemic situation.

Today's corporate landscape is undergoing a transformation process, and India is not untouched by these phases of transition as humans are replaced by computers and brick-and-mortar firms are substituted by e-commerce companies. In the midst of these shifts, issues such as labour dynamics have changed dramatically. One such consequence is the Gig Economy. With the gradual improvement in the labour market and the focus of government on localisation, it remains important to analyse the widespread influence of growing gig culture in making India a self-reliant economy. This chapter of the book therefore seeks to review the different components of the gig economy along with the advantages and disadvantages and how gig can contribute towards a localised and self-reliant Indian economy. The chapter also evaluates the regulatory framework of the gig economy in India. The chapter also proposes a conceptual model incorporating various pillars that could serve as an analytical framework for the rapidly increasing number of concepts and policy proposals.

From small companies to major enterprises, the COVID-19 pandemic put us all to test. While it has left us facing an unpredictable future, it also offers us the chance to create a self-sufficient and self-reliant India, or "Atma Nirbhar Bharat." The motivation towards a self-reliant India became stronger after the border conflict with China. Being dependent on China for both finished products and raw material, it is imperative for India to reduce this dependence. The "Atma Nirbhar Bharat" needs to be planned and executed as a nationwide program comprising several projects. Successful execution of this program needs to follow a systematic project management approach. This chapter tries to develop a blueprint for planning and execution of this program which is aimed at a self-reliant India.

In India, the land of farmers, where agriculture has always been the primary occupation of the people, more than 50% of the population is still engaged in agriculture and its allied sectors. However, over the years, a significant decline has been observed in the contribution by the agriculture sector towards India's GDP. This chapter aimed towards identifying the gap between the ratio of high inputs and low yields by portraying the various limitations in traditional Indian agriculture methods and how hydroponic agriculture is the need of the hour for the growth of Indian agriculture. Hydroponic agriculture or hydroponics, around the world, has proved to be an efficient and more productive method of agriculture than geoponics (i.e., the traditional agriculture practice carried out in the soil). Although bearing a large bouquet of advantages, there are some limitations associated with it as well. This chapter aimed at overcoming these limitations to enhance this novel approach of agriculture even further.

Foreword

World affairs have shifted and transformed in cyclic patterns in recent decades. The changes have been most noticeable in commerce, productive capacities, and economic infrastructure. As has been documented in engineering and manufacturing literature in recent decades, economies have morphed in various stages between efficiency, quality, flexibility, environment, globalization, miniaturization, reliability, effectiveness, and so on. Markets that have aggressively pursued globalization in the early 2000s have now realized that a reversed reengagement with localization is the new order of the present international enterprises. Of particular interest in the cycles of shifts is a focus on self-reliant economies. Until now, no book has addressed the changing landscapes in a structured and rigorous manner. It is, thus, a bold move by the editors of *Transitioning From Globalized to Localized and Self-Reliant Economies* to tackle the gap in the literature by assembling a high-powered collection of authoritative authors on the various pertinent chapters related to the theme of the book. The book is exactly what the market needs at this particular point in a pandemic-disrupted global supply chain.

From a systems integration perspective, a localized economy provides the best avenue for communities and nations to achieve self-reliance in the basic needs of commerce, production, and technological advancement. The chapters of the book include well-researched, articulated, and expertly-presented topics. Innovation and entrepreneurship for self-reliant and localized economy is one of the featured chapters of the book. Another chapter covers nationalism and populism as the driving forces of economic deglobalization, regionalism, and localism processes. Of particular topical relevance are the chapters dealing with post-Covid business environment. The workplace of the future will be marked different from the conventional setup we were previously used to seeing around the world. Due to pandemic response mandates around the world, transactions that had previously been targets of outsourcing are now being organized under self-reliant in-sourcing processes. Some of the chapters in the book addressing this emerging reality are entitled "Globalization and trade in post-covid world," "The new face of global trade in a post-pandemic world," "An exploratory study on personal finance in the context of covid-19." Other chapters in the book include "Role of higher educational institutes in developing self-reliant economies," "Role of technological innovations in improving manufacturing resilience in post-covid era: A cross country comparison," "Role of information technology and its perspectives in research and development of economy", "Evaluation of hospital supply chain performance during the covid-19 pandemic: Balanced score card approach," "Improving resiliency in healthcare service by minimizing unsatisfied demand." Workforce development is of utmost importance in any localized and self-reliant economy. For this purpose, this book has a chapter dedicated to the topic of "Skill proficiency and managerial role in different sectors from globalized to localized." Another chapter that caught my attention is on "Digitalization and Urbanization," which is very essential in supporting an economy that has transitioned from the global realm to the local realm. The book nicely rounds off with chapters on "Protection and promotion of Intellectual Property Rights for economic competitiveness and growth," "Sustainable GIG economy finance towards GDP of India," "Sustaining India's GIG economy in Industry 4.0: Regulatory framework and proposed model," "Implementing ATMA NIRBHAR BHARAT: A project management approach," and "Smart monitoring IOT-based system for hydroponic agriculture."

Overall, the book is an essential addition to the book collection of fervent followers of Industry 4.0. It contains guidelines, perspectives, analyses, research results, and technical models for transitioning from globalized and self-reliant economies. I strongly recommend the book all engineering, management, and business institutions, both private and public.

Adedeji B. Badiru
AFIT/EN, Air Force Institute of Technology, Wright-Patterson Air Force Base, USA

Adedeji B. Badiru *is a Professor of Systems Engineering and also SES-level Dean of the Graduate School of Engineering and Management at the Air Force Institute of Technology (AFIT). He has oversight for planning, directing, and controlling operations related to granting doctoral and master's degrees, professional continuing cyber education, and research and development programs for the US Air Force. He was previously Professor and Head of Systems Engineering and Management at AFIT, Professor and Department Head of Industrial Engineering at the University of Tennessee – Knoxville, and Professor of Industrial Engineering and Dean of University College at the University of Oklahoma, Norman. He is a registered professional engineer (PE), a certified Project Management Professional (PMP), a Fellow of the Institute of Industrial & Systems Engineers, and a Fellow of the Nigerian Academy of Engineering. He is also a Program Evaluator (PEV) for ABET. He holds a leadership certificate from the University Tennessee Leadership Institute. He has BS in Industrial Engineering, MS in Mathematics, and MS in Industrial Engineering from Tennessee Technological University, and Ph.D. in Industrial Engineering from the University of Central Florida. His areas of interest include mathematical modeling, project modeling and analysis, economic analysis, systems engineering modeling, computer simulation, and productivity analysis. He is a prolific author, with over 35 books, over 30 book chapters, over 130 Journal and magazine articles, and over 200 conference presentations. He is a member of several professional associations and scholastic honor societies. Professor Badiru, a world-renowned educator, has won several awards for his teaching, research, administrative, and professional accomplishments. Some of his selected awards include the 2009 Dayton Affiliate Society Council Award for Outstanding Scientists and Engineers in the Education category with a commendation from the 128th Senate of Ohio, 2010 ASEE John Imhoff Award for his global contributions to Industrial Engineering Education, the 2011 Federal Employee of the Year Award in the Managerial Category from the International Public Management Association, Wright Patterson Air Force Base, the 2012 Distinguished Engineering Alum Award from the University of Central Florida, the 2012 Medallion Award from the Institute of Industrial Engineers for his global contributions in the advancement of the profession, 2016 Outstanding Global Engineering Education Award from the Industrial Engineering and Operations Management (IEOM), 2015 Air Force-level Winner of the National Public Service Award from The American Society for Public Administration and the National Academy of Public Administration, 2013 Father D. J. Slattery Excellence Award, Saint Finbarr's College Alumni Association, North America Chapter, 2013 Award Team Leader, Air Force Organizational Excellence Award for Air University C3 (Cost Conscious Culture), 2013 Finalist for Jefferson Science Fellows Program, National Academy of Sciences, 2012 Book-of-the-Month Recognition for Statistical Techniques for Project Control from the Industrial Engineering Magazine, and the 2010 Industrial Engineering Joint Publishers Book-of-the-Year Award for The Handbook of Military Industrial Engineering. Professor Badiru is also the book series editor for CRC Press/Taylor & Francis book series on Systems Innovation. He has served as a consultant to several organizations around the world including Russia, Mexico, Taiwan, Nigeria, and Ghana. He has conducted customized training workshops for numerous organizations including Sony, AT&T, Seagate Technology, U.S. Air Force, Oklahoma Gas & Electric, Oklahoma Asphalt Pavement Association, Hitachi, Nigeria National Petroleum Corporation, and ExxonMobil. He has served as a Technical Project Reviewer, curriculum reviewer, and proposal reviewer for several organizations including The Third-World Network of Scientific Organizations, Italy, Social Sciences and Humanities Research Council of Canada, National Science Foundation, National Research Council, and the*

American Council on Education. He is on the editorial and review boards of several technical journals and book publishers. Prof. Badiru has also served as an Industrial Development Consultant to the United Nations Development Program. In 2011, Prof. Badiru led a research team to develop analytical models for Systems Engineering Research Efficiency (SEER) for the Air Force acquisitions integration office at the Pentagon. He has led a multi-year multi-million dollar research collaboration between the Air Force Institute of Technology and KBR Aerospace Group. Prof. Badiru has diverse areas of avocation. His professional accomplishments are coupled with his passion for writing about everyday events and interpersonal issues, especially those dealing with social responsibility. Outside of the academic realm, he writes motivational poems, editorials, and newspaper commentaries; as well as engaging in paintings and crafts. Professor Badiru is the 2020 recipient of the Lifetime Achievement Award from Taylor and Francis publishing group. He was also part of the AFIT team that led the institution's receipt of the 2019/2020 US Air Force Organizational Excellence Award.

Preface

In the last two decades, multinational corporations have taken advantage of globalisation by quickly expanding outside of their native markets. However, the advantages of global initiatives haven't been evenly distributed among nations, sectors, or trade systems. These inequalities, along with fundamental changes in the nature of products and services sold, have resulted in an increasing wave of worldwide uproars and clashes over value allocation in recent years. COVID-19 has dramatically exacerbated the reaction, so there's more to expect.

The outbreak of COVID-19 and resulting health crisis has shown a profound impact on global economic growth. The world economy is in its worst slump since World War II, causing disruptions in commercial activity, transport, supply chains, and other areas. Governments have reacted with lockdown measures and stimulus programs, although the scope of these efforts varies greatly between nations.

During the period, Global trade has transformed drastically and will only continue to do so as countries vote on export and import decisions based on global competition. Many countries have been compelled to reconsider multi-country trade deals as internal interests push and dictate them. All the major components of globalization have been deeply impacted by the pandemic:

Free Money Flow: The pandemic has had a significant influence on capital movement. Due to the lockout, cross-border movement was prevented.

Free Flow of Products and the Removal of Trade Barriers: According to data from the World Trade Organization (WTO), global commercial trade fell 9.2 percent in 2020 compared to the 2019 level. The movement of goods, especially capital goods, has been hampered.

People's Freedom of Movement: Prior to COVID-19, mass mobility took the shape of commerce, tourism, and travel. The notion of globalisation has been undermined by the limits imposed owing to the virus's infectious nature.

Technology Transfer: COVID-19 has increased the gap between countries with technical advances and those that do not.

More important than ever, it is imperative that self-reliant economies be investigated specifically in the post-COVID-19 era in order to understand the impacts made on international ties and trade agreements. This is the motivation behind this book.

ORGANIZATION OF THE BOOK

The book is organized into 17 chapters. A brief description of each of the chapters follows:

Chapter 1 reviews how innovation and entrepreneurship (I&E) would help create a self-reliant and localized economy. The chapter also looks at the importance of introducing entrepreneurship and innovation to an academic curriculum. By this approach, universities can reduce the gap of introducing the I&E concepts and use their synergies with the engineering technology course contents to create an innovative mindset, thereby creating a self-reliant and localized economy.

Chapter 2 analyzes the nationalism and populism as the driving forces of economic deglobalization and regionalism. The chapter provides the conceptualization that both globalization and deglobalization are two faces of the same coin, but with opposite driving forces. These driving forces of deglobalization lead to find regional and more local solutions to economic growth and social and environmental problems. The chapter further discusses the various issues and the implications of these issues.

Chapter 3 provides an overview of the disturbance caused by the COVID-19 pandemic regarding worldwide economy and global trade, as creation and utilization became downsized. The chapter emphasizes that the best methodology for addressing this type of emergency is convenient and unspoiled information. Informed public is better equipped to use wise judgment including cases dealing with trade. A devoted page at the WTO can provide updated trade related information, applicable agenda through the WTO officials, and impact of the infection upon fares and imports. The chapter also discusses about rising protectionism in course of the last half period, unexpected monetary crises created by the pandemic, disturbances regarding production network movement, and shocks related with market interest. Reporters from world-wide have trumpeted about the 'finish' of globalization.

Chapter 4 reviews how COVID-19 pandemic has raised serious questions about the applicability of international trade theories. The international trade has now changed its shape due to this novel coronavirus. It is a fact that no country in the world follows one trade theory. They use multiple theories for their goods and services and will continue to do so. The chapter discusses that it's uncertain as to which international trade theories will be employed in the future or any new theory of international trade will emerge. Empirical evidences illustrate the emergence of regionalization as compared to globalization. In this context, trade theories will also adjust their forms and assumptions. Therefore, this chapter reconcile international trade theories with actual data, most notably COVID-19.

Chapter 5 discusses the dramatic crisis the world is currently experiencing that has not yet reached its bottom. The objective is to identify types of personal expenses in households located in Culiacán, Sinaloa, Mexico as of July 15, 2020. The main results were that most of the respondents answered: spend according to their income, have had no problem paying their bank loans on time, would consider a fund for future contingencies, have not purchased health insurance, and have not bought a computer or cell phone among other issues analyzed. The main findings are oriented toward the fact that the studied population has not acquired additional medical insurance despite the pandemic. It is also concluded that the population under study has become aware of having savings for contingency funds and that digital life still shows resistance in making personal financial decisions.

Chapter 6 reviews the ability of higher education to contribute to global, national, and local growth. The chapter discusses how the Institutions of higher education have played an important role in society throughout modern history, training the elite and making ground breaking advances in science and humanities. This chapter also provides an insight on the role of higher educational institutes in economic development. To elaborate, the chapter provide cross country analysis and cases from different parts of the globe. The chapter states that education broadens people's perspectives on themselves and the world around them. It improves people's competitiveness and innovation while also encouraging entrepreneurship and technical advancement.

Chapter 7 discusses the role of technological innovations in improving the manufacturing resilience. The chapter focuses on cross country analysis in post Covid era. The chapter advocates that technological progress is critical for improving manufacturing resilience and achieving self-sufficiency in any nation. The COVID-19 crisis has shown the importance of, as well as the threats associated with, our new industrial processes. Manufacturing's critical position in both industrialized and emerging economies has been shown by shortages of medical supplies and disruptions in basic goods. These delays and market fluctuations have also highlighted the pitfalls of focusing solely on a globalized distribution system characterized by fragmented supply chains, the separation of engineering and manufacturing, and just-in-time production. Although globalisation was the trend before the Covid-19 pandemic, several countries realized the dangers and began to look inward, focusing on developing local manufacturing capacities.

Chapter 8 reviews the role of information technology and its perspectives in research and development of economy. The chapter discusses how technology is widely acknowledged in economics as the primary source of economic development as it enables more efficient production with more and superior products and services, which is essential for development. The chapter also focuses on how globalization further fuels and results in increased importance of social and economic analysis and also necessitates for coordinated development efforts using technology.

Chapter 9 describes the performance evaluation of hospital supply chain management using a balanced scorecard approach focusing on the COVID 19 pandemic situation. The chapter discusses the disruptions to the hospital supply chain management due to large scale social restrictions imposed by Government to stop the spread of virus. A new finding from this study is to measure the performance of hospitals experiencing various disruptions in their supply chain management caused by the COVID-19 pandemic with a balanced scorecard. The chapter concludes that measurements with the balanced scorecard approach can provide information about the performance of hospital supply chain management broadly in areas experiencing disruption due to the COVID-19 pandemic.

Chapter 10 provides an overview of the situation of healthcare industry during Covid 19 pandemic with regards to the medical supplies. Healthcare providers needed to replenish their supplies from the overseas manufacturing plant, or central distribution centers, or unaffected regional distribution centers. The most difficult situation that authorities face is the complexity of operating conditions where they had to work in order to supply medical items to the affected region from a central position. This chapter discusses the modeling techniques to improve service levels while minimizing unsatisfied demand in the natural disaster-affected zones.

Chapter 11 discusses the skill proficiency and managerial role in different sectors ranging from globalised to localised. The chapter states that skills and information are the driving powers of financial development and social improvement of any country. They have become more significant given the increasing speed of globalization. The chapter discusses the roles and duties of governments which have been redefined during last thirty years by the winds of progress achieved by globalization.

Chapter 12 discusses urbanization and digitalization with focus on construction industry. The chapter discusses the need of digitalization to stay modest. The chapter discusses the way new technologies are increasing rapidly and competitions racing fast. The chapter provides an overview of the factors leading to urbanization, impact of urbanization on community, challenges, and possible solution using advanced technologies.

Chapter 13 discusses and describes the importance of intellectual property rights (IPR). The chapter states that IPR has genuinely grown as an "intellectual currency," aiding in the advancement of global economic development, corporate prosperity, and creativity. In many fields of technology, intelligence, and culture, governments around the world are searching for ways to develop their economies, assist their people, and create national capabilities. This chapter also offers an empirical summary of how a successful intellectual property rights regime can support or impede economic growth.

Chapter 14 evaluates the Balance of Payment of India as a structural growth country wise, the sector wise growth of FDI in India, and the status of "Aatmanirbhar Bharat" and stimulus packages which have been announced for sustainable growth of GDP during this pandemic situation. The chapter provides an overview of the initiatives Government of India has brought in to help India become self-reliant for high end products. The chapter also discusses how these efforts aid in the creation of jobs, the alleviation of stressed sectors, the assurance of liquidity, the boost of manufacturing, the energization of the real estate industry, and the assistance of farmers.

Chapter 15 provides an overview of the Gig economy and analyzes the widespread influence of growing gig culture in making India a self-reliant economy. The chapter reviews different components of the gig economy along with its advantages and disadvantages, and how gig can contribute towards a localised and self-reliant Indian economy. The chapter also evaluates the regulatory framework of gig economy in India and proposes a conceptual model incorporating various pillars which could serve as an analytical framework for the rapidly increasing number of concepts and policy proposals.

Chapter 16 provides an overview of the self-sufficient and self-reliant India, or "Atma Nirbhar Bharat." The chapter discusses the present scenario and the factors necessitating the need. The "Atma Nirbhar Bharat" needs to be planned and executed as a nation-wide program comprising several projects. Successful execution of this program needs to follow a systematic Project Management approach. This chapter also suggests a blue print for planning and execution of this program.

Chapter 17 is aimed towards identifying the gap between the ratio of high inputs and low yields by portraying the various limitations in traditional Indian agriculture methods and how hydroponic agriculture is need of the hour for the growth of Indian agriculture. Hydroponic agriculture or hydroponics, around the world, has proved to be an efficient and more productive method of agriculture than geoponics i.e., the traditional agriculture practice carried out in the soil. Although bearing a large bouquet of advantages, there are some limitations associated with it as well. This chapter aims to overcome these limitations to enhance this novel approach of agriculture even further.

Ruchika Gupta
Amity University, India

Priyank Srivastava
Amity University, India

Shiv Ranjan
Amity University, India

M. Affan Badar
Indiana State University, USA

Chapter 1
Innovation and Entrepreneurship for the Self-Reliant and Localized Economy

Jaby Mohammed
https://orcid.org/0000-0003-0057-5077
Illinois State University, USA

Montasir Islam
Illinois State University, USA

ABSTRACT

Innovation and entrepreneurship (I&E) are two closely related words that go hand in hand in this era. Innovation is about applying creativity for different engineering/technology/service problems and producing unique solutions, while entrepreneurship is about applying the same to bring ideas to life by making them feasible to work. It is also about doing the business work. In this chapter, the authors review how innovation and entrepreneurship help create a self-reliant and localized economy. The chapter also looks at the importance of introducing entrepreneurship and innovation to an academic curriculum. By this approach, universities can reduce the gap of introducing the I&E concepts and use their synergies with the engineering technology course contents to create an innovative mindset, thereby creating a self-reliant and localized economy.

INTRODUCTION

Entrepreneurship is not only for entrepreneurs but for everyone. Sarasvathy and Venkataraman (2011) convincingly posit this as a trait that should live beyond the generalized predictor of startups' typical success or failure parameter. Similarly, regardless of how arcane the practice may seem and has been treated, it is high time entrepreneurship be decodified for the laymen. The authors also strongly suggest that anyone who invests in learning entrepreneurship can acquire its method, knowledge and pattern to

DOI: 10.4018/978-1-7998-8705-8.ch001

become proficient at it. Finally, that it is time to explore the notion how imperative it is to study what successful entrepreneurs do as daily actions instead of who they are or what their entrepreneurial lineage is.

According to Oviatt and McDougall (2005), the definition of entrepreneurship has continued to evolve combining ideas from risk-taking, opportunity exploiting, innovating to strategizing. The term "opportunity" has been coined quite frequently with entrepreneurship as entrepreneurs of all generations recognized, grasped, and exploited every chance of progress they would find along the journey of their creative endeavors. Indeed, it is fascinating how individuals excel at identifying, solving and capitalizing problems to make a difference in their lives and the community at large. Hence this phenomenon begs to stir up curiosity (Huber et al., 2014) and asks the respective audience: Can entrepreneurship be adeptly taught to others and help make the desired impact?

Evans-Obinna (2016) responds affirmatively and finds significant potential in entrepreneurship education leading to self-employment and sufficiency for sincere learners and implementers of the practice. The author's central tenet promotes early entrepreneurship education for consolidating personal skills, knowledge and motivation as initial ingredients for success. Furthermore, all these combined can assist individuals in being resourceful and confident in becoming self-supportive and sustaining in the long run. Proper entrepreneurship teaching can also instill a deep passion for making a difference in the students' lives while the persistence of opportunities may inculcate an exploratory mindset. The pedagogy of entrepreneurship can, however, convolute its understandings and applications in various educational settings. For a dynamic and impactful practice such as entrepreneurship, it is natural to expect behavioral differences within country borders. In general, entrepreneurship has shown to vary in concepts, implementation scopes and success criteria across different geography and demography (Oviatt & McDougall, 2005).

Being creative is key to success in any capacity and more so in running a business. "According to a recent IBM survey of chief executives around the world, it's the most sought-after trait in leaders today" (Kelly & Kelly, 2012; 116). It is thus encouraged to make people realize how important it is to persevere to be more creative. Academic institutions can do wonders in this regard and assist students in the pursuit of discovering their latent talents. With the work at the Stanford design school, Kelly (2012) further echoes similar thoughts corroborating that "The real goal of the school is to give students creative confidence ... the ability to do what one sets out to do, in her way, even while facing ambiguous circumstances." Kelly (2012) and Sternberg (2008) also advise individuals to possess entrepreneurship qualities which:

- Redefine problems in new ways to seek out solutions
- Take sensible risks and accept failure as part of the process
- Confront obstacles
- Tolerate ambiguity
- Continue to grow intellectually

Methods of international entrepreneurship can additionally extrapolate vast scopes of how the teaching of the practice can catalyze self-sustenance and personal development of individuals for competing in the modern economies. In addition, global trade, communications and businesses continue to profoundly shape the very pattern of entrepreneurship that is presently being taught and exercised. With the Covid-19 pandemic currently surging worldwide, the implications it has caused to date on communities are uniquely astonishing. Consequently, such a crisis calls for exploration, adaptation and survival of the global markets while everything is somewhat affected. This chapter of the book is primarily interested in looking at entrepreneurship and its applications through an academic lens that applies to students and practitioners alike in times of emergency, chaos and uncertainty.

BACKGROUND

Entrepreneurship in Higher Education

Entrepreneurship is defined as recognizing, identifying and choosing a set of opportunities with resource constraints (Evans-Obinna, 2016). It is also a process of creating value for the respective stakeholders considering all the associated risks and challenges. According to Evans-Obinna (2016), entrepreneurship education is a pedagogical template that aims to impart the necessary knowledge, guidance and skills to interested individuals in seeking entrepreneurial achievements. It can enable massive potential to the current proficiencies of the young generation and help create jobs (Premand et al., 2016). Strategic curricula with proper training by academic instructors can direct necessary willpower to the students of entrepreneurship. As a result, societies will benefit in a multitude of areas along with local solutions to local problems.

The positive effects of entrepreneurship in higher education have been further observed by Huber et al. (2014). It is identified how early age introduction of the practice in schools can make students acquire substantial interest in the subject matter and make them more willing to apply their knowledge in real life. Sharp increases in the number of entrepreneurship programs at academic institutions also show strong indications of the necessity for such education as early as at primary levels (Huber et al., 2014). With entrepreneurship being considered a key element to develop self-sufficient and employment skills worldwide (Premand et al., 2016), its applications by student practitioners appear to be more urgent than ever. The prospects of becoming entrepreneurial at a young age are hence providing ready opportunities for training institutions to design respective curricula accordingly and offer pragmatic models of associated skillset development (Huber et al., 2014).

Teaching entrepreneurship to university students continues to be a promising perspective in the current century. A good approach for improving entrepreneurship expertise is proven by encouraging critical thinking and improving confidence in creativity (Dimmit et al., 2019). The concept of critical thinking has been around for a long time in various forms. It goes back to Greek philosopher Socrates who used inquisitive questioning to examine ideas believed to be true but containing contentious logic. More recently, the term "critical thinking" has been introduced as a way of uncovering the truthfulness of an argument or point of view. Paul and Elder (2006) advanced the theory of critical thinking by adding to the notions of metacognition and problem-solving.

Self-Reliant Economy

Entrepreneurship plays a significant role in the growth of a country and leading it into prosperity. Like every developmental progress, a defining philosophy underlies its bedrock (Godfrey, 2003). Ineffective models yield outputs that fall below expectations and waste resources that could have been utilized elsewhere. Economic self-reliance, also termed ESR, instructs a different approach while addressing economic development in a more process-based way. According to Godfrey (2003), ESR is simply defined as the ability of an individual to foster productive capacities beyond basic needs. The author further recognizes

Figure 1. Role of entrepreneurship for a self-reliant economy

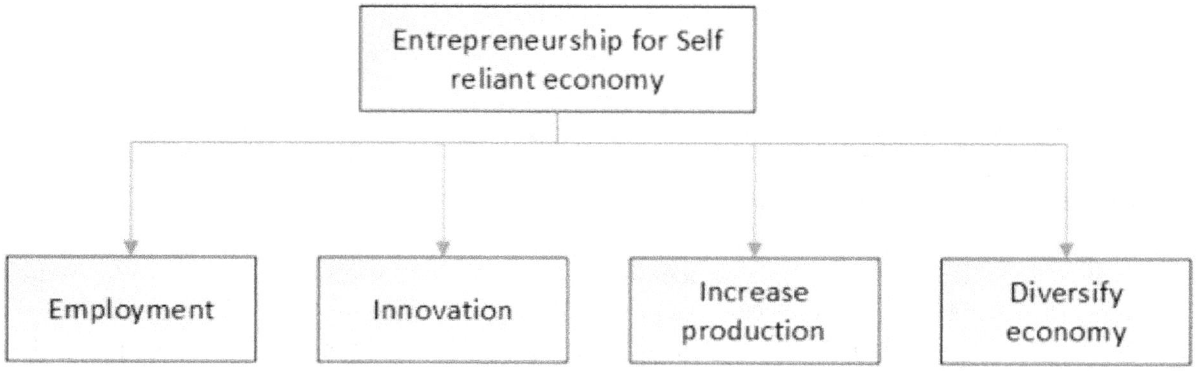

these basic needs as surplus resources in case-specific contexts. The idea of "basic needs" drastically differs in theme and ideology from a developed country to a developing one. Self-reliance consequently clarifies its nature of not being reliant on others but implies achieving a state where one's individual goals can be reached with solo effort and capacity (Galtung, 1976). Additionally, Galtung (1976) emphasizes that self-reliance characterizes a dynamic behavior paradigm encompassing an individual, community, and region. Figure 1 shows how entrepreneurship can help in sustaining a self-reliant economy.

Along with self-sustaining economies, self-reliant individuals exude more resilience and assertiveness during economic upheavals (Godfrey, 2003). These characteristics provide a sense of insurance to communities enabling them to accommodate more self-reliance in their members amidst any disruptions or adverse events. Such strength seamlessly helps to reach optimum human potential metrics. Godfrey (2003) stresses that these individuals become adept at exercising their talents, values and skills to the fullest with nurtured confidence. Self-reliance can thus be considered as a working recipe for looking out for opportunities in the surrounding just as entrepreneurs (Sarasvathy &Venkataraman, 2011). The innate entrepreneurial pursuit of opportunity creation through constantly innovating products and services indicates a culture of self-improvement, determination and growth (Evans-Obinna, 2016).

Additionally, with the right direction, this energy can be channeled to significant impact margins through facilitating entrepreneurship education and designing customized curricula for a more active and alert populace. University-level entrepreneurship programs have correspondingly shown to broaden the scope of how students acquire "self-start" knowledge and become self-reliant in the process (Vesper & Gartner, 1997). Four types of capitals have been found to drive economic self-reliance in an individual, namely Economic, Human, Institutional and Social capitals as shown in Figure 2.

Each of the four main categories mentioned is required for an individual to be self-reliant. The weightage between the categories will vary depending on the country's economic, demographic and social status. The author posits the impact drivers in the form of capitals as ingredients of a fluently working economic self-reliance:

- Institutional Capital
  - Tangible resources, physical infrastructures, education systems
- Social Capital
  - Community relationships, professional networks, civil organizations
- Economic Capital

Figure 2. Four types of capital driving ESR

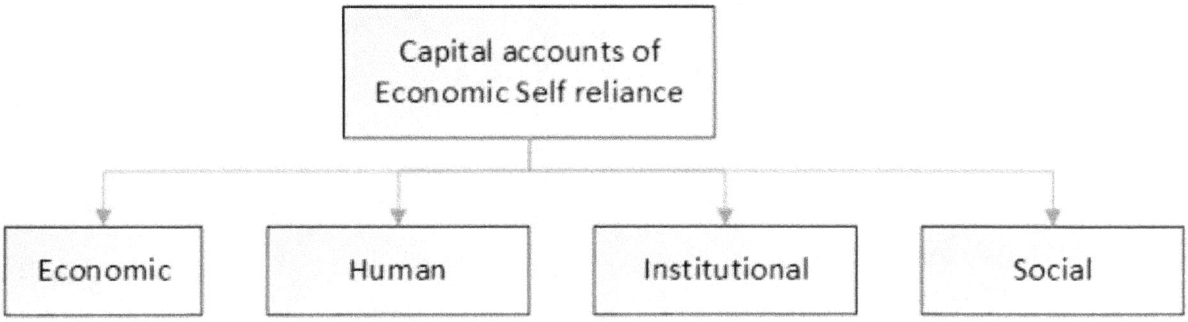

    - Purchasing power, cash investments, financial services
- Human Capital
    - Individual knowledge, health care, academic training

These ESR accounts clearly identify what activities, resources, enhancers and inhibitors are present in the economic system affecting the overall productivity. The multi-level and holistic development portfolio covering a wide range of criteria also indicates proficient economic self-reliance. The ESR model positions itself in differing from the traditional development thinking while explicitly dealing with the needs of the individuals in contributing towards a self-reliant climate (Godfrey, 2003).

The ESR also provides an ideal platform for individuals to reach their potential. Once the necessary skills are achieved, they can prepare to immensely benefit themselves and their respective communities. Institutional and economic capitals are the two tangible items in the list that form a solid foundation when applied in a developed socio-economic platform. Institutional capital also refers to society-based resources and often the community has a lot to offer there in terms of subsidies and tax breaks. On the other hand, economic capital is offered through loans and angel funds where the individual has easier access to the working capital. Finally, human and social capitals are the intangible items that constitute the knowledge of the individuals' processes and the network they live around.

RESULTS

Why Entrepreneurship Education is Necessary in Academia

Most corporate leaders acknowledge that the key to business growth is innovation, however, they are often challenged to lead and manage with that mentality. They find hurdles to build a creative co-working space and end up outsourcing important work to market research and development departments. Failure to deliver the desired innovation hurts the business internally and the employees' career aspirations by falling short of the potential to improve designated products and processes. Diversity in thinking and changing mindsets are at the foundation for building innovative cultures. Entrepreneurship provides the next stage of innovation when an innovator tries to combine all the resources within reach to develop a product or process to solve a problem cost-effectively. The recent global economies and employment trends show a substantial deficiency of the required skillsets in students for occupying relevant jobs in

Figure 3. Entrepreneurship characteristics

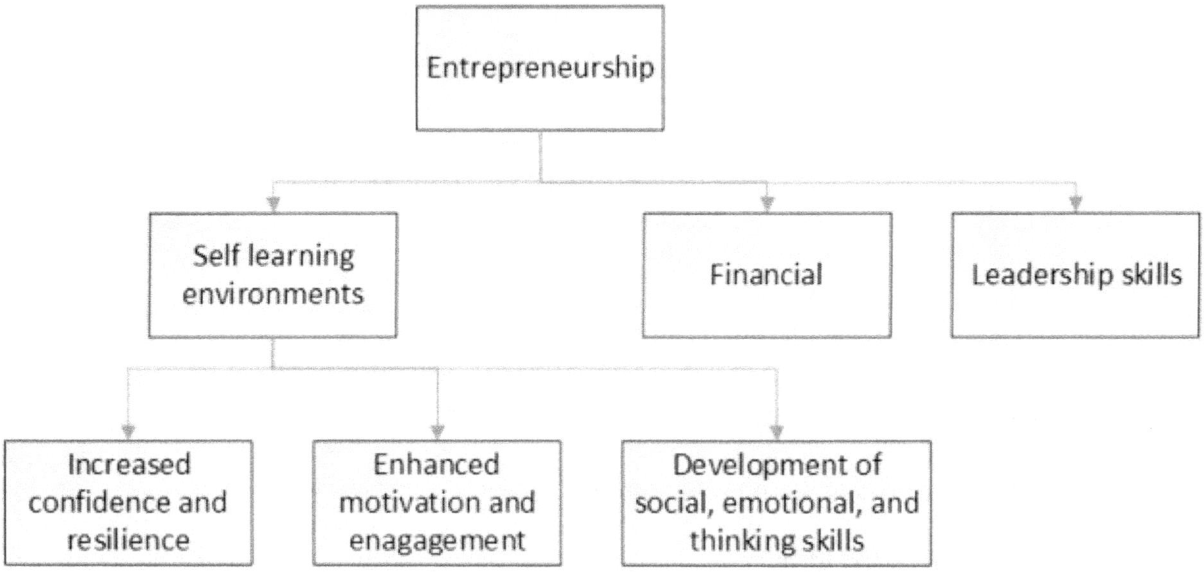

the market which vividly points to the students' inaccessibility to diverse ranges of learning facilities urging the necessities for inclusion of innovation and entrepreneurship curricula in higher education.

Additionally, there is a strong rationale for studying and teaching entrepreneurship at undergraduate and graduate levels. They impart essential life lessons through idea generation, prediction analyses and forecasting theories utilizing the available infrastructures and technologies. Innovative products and services are the driving forces to improve spatial and temporal inefficiencies in the economy (Shane, 2000) with unemployment being a significant economic issue around the world (Arrow, 1963). While university graduates struggle to find jobs that align with their academic backgrounds and qualifications (Kirzner, 1997), entrepreneurship education can assist in bridging the gap of market expectations and individual capabilities (Brown, 2003). Many universities are now becoming aware of the phenomenon and acquainting themselves with innovation courses to increase entrepreneurship lessons and encourage students to be self-employed instead of merely pursuing employment – to be job creators rather than job seekers.

One technique in deciding to become an entrepreneur starts by embracing the right temperament. Dweck (2015) claims that: "More and more research is showing that our brains constantly change with learning and experiencing and that this takes place throughout our lives." The author denotes this as a growth mindset as opposed to a fixed mindset. The author further argues: "In a growth mindset, people believe that their most basic abilities can be developed through dedication and challenging work – brains and talent are just the starting point." In a study Dimitt and Mohmmed (2019) similarly find best practices to teach entrepreneurship incorporated in the following concepts as shown in Figure 3, illustrating the various characteristics students develop during their academic coursework.

When students understand the growth mindset, they quickly realize, develop and apply new ideas from the classrooms in the outside world. One of the essential characteristics is that students consequently become critical thinkers. Evidence suggests that an impact of a creative learning environment (Davies, 2013) can make learners achieve higher confidence and resilience and improved motivation and engagement. Moreover, they develop social, emotional and thinking skills. Many innovation and entrepreneurship courses also target improving designs based on review meetings and enhancing creative thinking within the engineering design processes (Pasha Zaidi et al., 2015; Mohammed et al., 2016).

How Entrepreneurship Sustains Self-Reliant Economy

It is clear how entrepreneurship hones a collaborative climate to create employment and economic prosperity. Evans-Obinna (2016) emphasizes how the persistent pursuit of opportunity-seeking journeys can create innovative products and services. The continuous cycle of goods produced, transacted and consumed provides a proven track of healthy economic growth and progress. Businesses sustain over the long run when self-reliant and ambitious individuals work together to satisfy the needs and expectations of different stakeholders in the system (Evans-Obinna, 2016). Despite being risky, time-consuming and operationally expensive, innovation of any kind is necessary as a change-making agent in any stagnant situation (Costello & Prohaska, 2013). Self-reliance is a collective effort by motivating human resources capitalizing on inherent talents, skills, community relations and governmental administrations (Godfrey, 2003).

As a case in point, the BRICS (Brazil-Russia-India-China-South Africa) consortium is an example of self-reliance of a big consumer market being economically benefitted from the global trade. Due to a standstill economy after the massive urbanization in 1970s, the following decade experienced an international economic restructuring that led to trade access to many countries worldwide. With the BRICS countries shifting manufacturing facilities to developing countries in order to improve their economic conditions, unemployment as well as other associated economic situations have been drastically reduced, especially amongst the middle class. Subsequently, the contribution of the local economic development offered important lessons on how governments could increase the participation of the community for the economic growth of the nation resulting in changes to the operational structures. Figure 4 shows the strategies that have been used to revamp the economies with the first strategy being a regional planning component which many countries had adapted. Regional development programs ensued from the planning phase and implementation stage executed at the regional level and permeating into the national level. Location grants and loans have been further sanctioned and made readily available to interested parties who supported innovation and entrepreneurship while benefiting the community.

The next strategy after regional development has been termed improving the public support systems where removing the bureaucracy showed substantial improvements in the value of entrepreneurs as leaders in society who bring significant changes to the system. The public support systems are also put in place to establish and maintain a fluent network between different industries and government entities. Finally, sectoral interdependence where there is an interdependent social relationship amongst various sectors improving the overall growth of one leading to the betterment of the other.

Entrepreneurship: The Pandemic Response

The internet along with digitalization have clearly disrupted how economies normally operate. In today's world, consumers are abundantly dependent on digital devices for their day-to-day activities - from setting an alarm, ordering food to receiving news. Contemporary companies like Uber, Netflix and Airbnb are leading the way for pioneering disruptive business models with opportunities discovered in the modern realm of digitalization. The ongoing Covid-19 has further demonstrated how consumers could limit

Figure 4. Strategies to promote economy

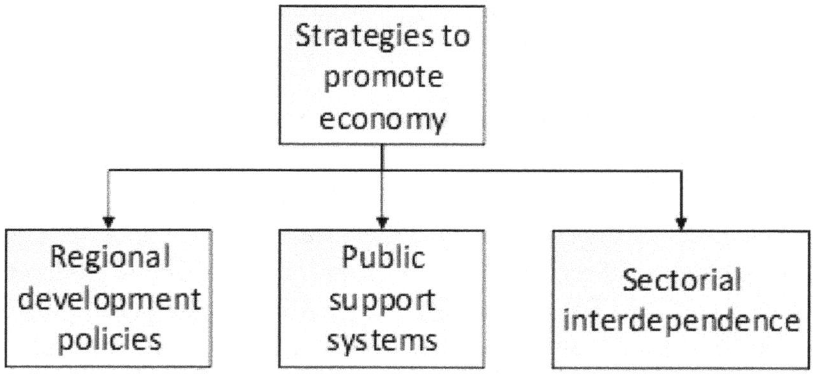

mobility and stay connected to the home creating a plethora of opportunities to numerous challenges. The pandemic undoubtedly unraveled massive numbers of everyone's daily activities and practices worldwide and put all of them under emergency settings. From healthcare, education, commerce, travel and government administration, to name a few, it affected everyone, everywhere and in every industry possible. Entrepreneurship is no exception as it clearly took its share of hit by Covid-19. However, it is also enduring the global setback with the uncertainties despite catastrophic events unfolding internationally while the deadly pandemic ravages on (Maritz et al., 2020).

Worldwide entrepreneurial personality, education, opportunity and innovation have vastly impacted during such challenging circumstances. Li-Ying and Nell (2020) point out how crises catalyze motivations for fundamental innovation, creation and implementation of initiatives catering to the needs of time. The covid-19 has utterly exposed deficiencies in many business spheres and one way to minimize the adverse effects is the pursuit of innovation and entrepreneurship. Uncertain times such as the pandemic also create ripe opportunities for academic institutions and research organizations to step up and invite learners and impart entrepreneurship teaching to assist them in navigating this sudden human calamity (Maritz et al., 2020). Ratten (2020) rightly cautions on the international chaos that Covid-19 has caused and stresses the entrepreneurial outlook that can revive businesses worldwide. With unique problems, the pandemic simultaneously presented opportunities to solve and salvage struggling economies. Critical external conditions like the previous viral catastrophes have also influenced adaptations of drastic measures (Maritz et al., 2020). The authors bring forth the immense contributions of entrepreneurship in customizing adequate products and services and other timely societal necessities.

Contrastingly, Covid-19 has enabled business opportunities by creating, expanding and substituting customer demands (Maritz et al., 2020) which is often undertaken by businesses via creating new avenues and pioneering innovations according to the need of time. For example, due to social distancing measures worldwide, businesses quickly adapted to enabling flexible formats of their actual operations. Transitioning businesses online, working limited shifts and meeting customer expectations over the phone have become the new normal. Many entities resorted to tapping the pandemic by expanding on their current offerings. One prevalent example is the academic institutions going from an in-person template to a completely online learning environment. A similar approach has also been carried out by most workplaces globally by adjusting to the sensitive Covid-19 requirements of health and personal wellbeing. This further became possible by modifying the entire product-service lines in alignment with

Figure 5. Disruptions with covid-19 pandemic

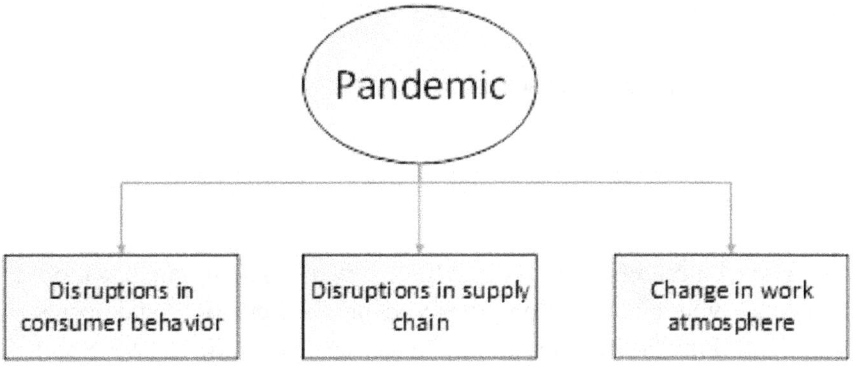

the shifting market demands during the pandemic and its changing consumer ecosystems (Maritz et al., 2020). Figure 5 shows the drastic changes and anomalies in consumer behavior, supply chains and living as well as the work environment. From spending more time indoors than usual, shopping online to shipping commodities home, the consumer buying patterns along with storage of goods have all been changed during Covid-19.

The disruptions of the supply chains have evidently been exposed. The large economy of the United States that previously depended on foreign goods has taken a big hit due to the pandemic which forced it to identify and explore reliable local supply chains to fulfil its domestic needs. With everyone's living and working environments disrupted, consumers needed more quick innovations to patch up with the unfolding situation opening grounds for innovative products and services. Online grocery platform Instacart and meeting service Zoom are two stark examples amongst many others that revamped and leveraged their business models during Covid-19. The response of entrepreneurship to the pandemic is also postulated by Li-Ying and Nell (2020) in different verticals of diverse business operations triggered by the pandemic. To elaborate, the authors investigate two specific dimensions to assess and understand the desperate business circumstances revolving around Covid-19. The first dimension focuses on the business value chain that is impacted by the change in customer-buyer purchase patterns; sudden halt in buying goods and shift from in-person to online modes. Moreover, added factors such as regional lockdowns and border closures highly affected the otherwise normal consumer behaviors of the pre-pandemic phase. The airline industry, for instance, faced a significant double blow with oil supply shortage and passenger decline at the same time during the peak of Covid-19 (Li-Ying & Nell, 2020).

As put forward by Li-Ying and Nell (2020), the second dimension concerns the widely popular innovation and entrepreneurship framework by Austrian economist Schumpeter. The robust mechanism explains the dynamic functions of how startups and incumbent firms innovate competitively. One is "creative destruction" - innovative individuals armored with modern technologies vying to capture markets with new solutions, and another "creative accumulation" - established firms continuously investing and acquiring advanced technologies to shun new market entrants. The authors finally combined the two dimensions and developed a unique "opportunity landscape" model for innovation and entrepreneurship to address the pandemic. The model proposes four specified agile strategies to respond to the volatile Covid-19 business environment:

- Newcomer - Rapidly adapting technologies
- Reorganizer - Assimilating both newcomers and technologies
- Option Maker - Providing quick alternatives
- Consolidator – Accumulating in-house resources

CONCLUSION

Exercising innovation and entrepreneurship in real life is always challenging. It is more so in the unprecedented Covid-19 climate where many of previously recognized practices and norms are continuously evolving every day. From human lifestyle, global businesses, education to governance, all spheres of civic engagements are getting tested and tried in search of a working formula towards sustainability and growth. Economies worldwide need stability and performance through opportunity creation, steady employment generation and adequate survival mechanisms. In critical times such as Covid-19, it is more imperative than ever to be resonant, adaptive and self-reliant, especially when the global supply chains are experiencing fundamental changes and challenges in operational volumes (Veselovská, 2020).

While the world economies are brought to a grinding halt exposing their vulnerabilities, the need for local economies to step up and keep striving becomes urgent. This is where academic institutions come in with their already established pedagogical outreach in entrepreneurship education for a massive student populace. As a result, they can immensely contribute in bringing back economic activities to the native markets and beyond. Research shows how new possibilities in career paths as entrepreneurs have significantly increased over time (Nurmi & Paasio, 2007), and the innate creative capacities that entrepreneurship provides along with independence to initiate and work. From the very first entrepreneurship course taught by Myles Mace in 1947 at Harvard University in the United States till date, entrepreneurship has impacted the academic infrastructure through more than 2200 courses, 44 referenced journals at some 1600 schools with about 277 endowed positions (Katz, 2003). Additionally, according to Katz (2003) the progress of entrepreneurship in academia has been gauged by three vital parameters:

- Growth in courses
- Growth of publications
- Growth of infrastructural elements

The natural tendency of entrepreneurs to search for opportunities and exploiting them (Sarasvathy & Venkataraman, 2011) has been observed to be an acquired conventional wisdom while it being a central point of a vast academic research interest. This practice in turn becomes a virtuous cycle where experienced entrepreneurs implement their learned co-creation expertise to generate adequate influence and prowess for others to follow and exercise. Stories of entrepreneurial actions and accomplishments are similarly spread across continents. Evans-Obinna (2016) finds exemplary necessity of tailor-made entrepreneurship education policy in Nigeria offered through the state and federal level institutions such as technical colleges, vocational schools and polytechnics. The author also draws direct correlations between self-reliant economic development and entrepreneurship education as both go together with youth empowerment and employment. Nurmi and Paasio (2007) further identify entrepreneurship learning at universities in Finland to garner promising attention in creating working models for influencing societal and regional impacts. With such an approach the universities are expected to step up in playing major roles in innovation and economic growth within the country and around the European Union at large.

Theories covered in the book chapter clearly show how innovation and entrepreneurship can help revive localized economies. The pressing commercial and socio-economic situations hampered by the pandemic can be tackled through self-reliance, entrepreneurship education and new business procedures. Innovative products and services have repeatedly proven how a dedicated workforce with adequate coordination and information can turn around crises quickly and efficiently. Proper entrepreneurship education and training facilitated locally and administered by academic institutions can benefit in the challenging and changing times of Covid-19.

REFERENCES

Arrow, K. J. (2003). *Uncertainty and the welfare economics of medical care (American economic review, 1963)*. Duke University Press.

Brown, P. (2003). The opportunity trap: Education and employment in a global economy. *European Educational Research Journal*, *2*(1), 141–179. doi:10.2304/eerj.2003.2.1.4

Costello, T., & Prohaska, B. (2013). 2013 trends and strategies. *IT Professional*, *15*(1), 64–64. doi:10.1109/MITP.2013.5

Davies, D., Jindal-Snape, D., Collier, C., Digby, R., Hay, P., & Howe, A. (2013). Creative learning environments in education—A systematic literature review. *Thinking Skills and Creativity*, *8*, 80–91. doi:10.1016/j.tsc.2012.07.004

Dimmitt, N. J., Mohammed, J., & Moore, D. (2018). Innovative Approaches to Education: Increasing Creative Confidence and Critical Thinking Skills. *ICPESS (International Congress on Politic, Economic and Social Studies), 4*.

Dweck, C. (2015). Carol Dweck revisits the growth mindset. *Education Week*, *35*(5), 20–24.

Evans-Obinna, R. N. (2016). Entrepreneurship education for self-reliance and economic development in Nigeria. *International Journal of Vocational and Technical Education Research*, *2*(2), 9–14.

Galtung, J. (1976). Trade or development: Some reflections on self-reliance. *Economic and Political Weekly*, 207–218.

Godfrey, P. (2003). *Toward a Theory of Economic Self Reliance (ESR)*. Marriot School of Management. Brigham Young University.

Huber, L. R., Sloof, R., & Van Praag, M. (2014). The effect of early entrepreneurship education: Evidence from a field experiment. *European Economic Review*, *72*, 76–97. doi:10.1016/j.euroecorev.2014.09.002

Katz, J. A. (2003). The chronology and intellectual trajectory of American entrepreneurship education: 1876–1999. *Journal of Business Venturing*, *18*(2), 283–300. doi:10.1016/S0883-9026(02)00098-8

Kelley, T., & Kelley, D. (2012). Reclaim your Creative Confidence. *Harvard Business Review*, *90*(12), 115–118. PMID:23227579

Kirzner, I. M. (1997). Entrepreneurial discovery and the competitive market process: An Austrian approach. *Journal of Economic Literature, 35*(1), 60–85.

Li-Ying, J., & Nell, P. (2020). Navigating opportunities for innovation and entrepreneurship under COVID-19. *California Management Review, 63*(1).

Maritz, A., Perenyi, A., De Waal, G., & Buck, C. (2020). Entrepreneurship as the unsung hero during the current COVID-19 economic crisis: Australian perspectives. *Sustainability, 12*(11), 4612. doi:10.3390u12114612

Mohammed, J. (2021). Introducing Entrepreneurship and Innovation in a Manufacturing Design Course. *2021 ASEE Virtual Annual Conference Content Access.*

Mohammed, J., & Hatakka, M. R. H. (2016). Enhancing Multiple Thinking through the Engineering Design Process. *2016 ASEE International Forum.*

Nurmi, P., & Paasio, K. (2007). Entrepreneurship in Finnish universities. *Education + Training, 49*(1), 56–65. doi:10.1108/00400910710729884

Oviatt, B. M., & McDougall, P. P. (2005). Defining international entrepreneurship and modeling the speed of internationalization. *Entrepreneurship Theory and Practice, 29*(5), 537–553. doi:10.1111/j.1540-6520.2005.00097.x

Pasha-Zaidi, N., Afari, E., Mohammed, J., Cubero, S., Shoukry, A. M., & El Sokkary, W. (2015). Gender-based teams: Perceptions of team satisfaction and effectiveness among engineering students in the United Arab Emirates. *International Journal of Engineering Education, 31*(4), 953–966.

Paul, R., & Elder, L. (2006). *Thinker's Guide to the Art of Socratic Questioning*. Foundation Critical Thinking.

Premand, P., Brodmann, S., Almeida, R., Grun, R., & Barouni, M. (2016). Entrepreneurship education and entry into self-employment among university graduates. *World Development, 77*, 311–327. doi:10.1016/j.worlddev.2015.08.028

Ratten, V. (2020). Coronavirus and international business: An entrepreneurial ecosystem perspective. *Thunderbird International Business Review, 62*(5), 629–634. doi:10.1002/tie.22161

Sarasvathy, S. D., & Venkataraman, S. (2011). Entrepreneurship as method: Open questions for an entrepreneurial future. *Entrepreneurship Theory and Practice, 35*(1), 113–135. doi:10.1111/j.1540-6520.2010.00425.x

Shane, S., & Venkataraman, S. (2000). The promise of entrepreneurship as a field of research. *Academy of Management Review, 25*(1), 217–226. doi:10.5465/amr.2000.2791611

Sternberg, R. (2008). The WICS Approach to Leadership: Stories of Leadership and the Structure and Processes that Support Them. *The Leadership Quarterly, 19*(3), 360–371. doi:10.1016/j.leaqua.2008.03.008

Veselovská, L. (2020). Supply chain disruptions in the context of early stages of the global COVID-19 outbreak. *Problems and Perspectives in Management, 18*(2), 490–500. doi:10.21511/ppm.18(2).2020.40

Vesper, K. H., & Gartner, W. B. (1997). Measuring progress in entrepreneurship education. *Journal of Business Venturing*, *12*(5), 403–421. doi:10.1016/S0883-9026(97)00009-8

Chapter 2
Nationalism and Populism as the Driving Forces of Economic Deglobalization, Regionalism, and Localism Processes

José G. Vargas-Hernández
https://orcid.org/0000-0003-0938-4197
Instituto Tecnológico Mario Molina, Unidad Académica Zapopan, Mexico

ABSTRACT

The aim of this chapter is to analyze nationalism and populism as the driving forces of economic deglobalization processes and regionalism. The analysis departs from the assumption that the economic deglobalization processes respond to more complex dynamic forces created by the economic, financial, and the most recent sanitary crisis that blocks the continuity of economic globalization. Moreover, at the center of the analysis is the conceptualization that both globalization and deglobalization are two faces of the same coin, but with opposite driving forces. These driving forces of deglobalization lead to regional and more local solutions to economic growth and social and environmental problems.

INTRODUCTION

During the first half of the 20th century, Europe suffered a destruction induced by nationalism and militarism. Initially, globalization processes were reduced to European countries that had democratic political structures, but there was awareness of expanding the participation of other countries that were stable constitutional democracies. Since 1945, internationalism has been promoted with economic cooperation systems supported by the Brettton Woods agreements and the emerging global governance institutions such as the General Agreement on Tariffs and Trade, as well as the Marshall Plan and the United Nations.

Western economic nationalism provokes tensions that lead to a trade war and that leaves the global space to the east to take the leadership of the processes of globalization that promote a new global concept. However, this connectivity becomes the medium of contagion. The impact has been reflected

DOI: 10.4018/978-1-7998-8705-8.ch002

in the resurrection of the nationalist entrepreneurial spirit that promotes the return of companies. The growing phenomenon of nationalism is manifested in different versions with identity religions, including eurocentrism, Brexit, America First, etc., which tend to undermine multilateralism and paralyze the World Trade Organization. The health crisis reaffirms the doctrine of America First as the way for companies and thus jobs to return to the United States. Globalization is widely criticized for its negative effects and loss of valuation, it has fueled nationalist and populist movements.

The processes of globalization have had devastating effects from the 2008-09 financial crisis on the jobs of workers in various sectors of the industry. The answer has been commercialism, nationalism and populism. Since 2010, nationalisms and populisms have resurfaced with force, trends in proximity trade are expanding, sustainability emerges as a concern for achieving an ecological balance between the exploitation of resources, productive activities and the effects on socio-ecosystems. For some years now, nationalist and populist governments have been promoting the reproduction of productive activities.

This paper first analyzes the implications of nationalism and populism on the economic deglobalization processes as the result of the most recent economic, financial and health crisis, leading to more regional and local alternatives to give continuity to the economic globalization. Finally, a discussion on the implications of these issues is offered.

NATIONALISM AND POPULISM

The growing phenomenon of nationalism is manifested in different versions with identity religions, including eurocentrism, Brexit, America First, etc., which tend to undermine multilateralism and paralyze the World Trade Organization. The health crisis reaffirms the doctrine of America First as the way for companies and thus jobs to return to the United States.

Until now, the manifestations of the deglobalization processes are nationalist dynamics that, under the allegation of the principle of sovereignty, oppose international agreements and treaties through the construction of physical and tariff barriers to their national borders. Both populism, nationalism and commercialism can be threats. The old and emerging middle classes are those who consume the most with objectives that are different and that serve as an argument for populism, despite that egalitarianism as well as excessive inequality are obstacles.

Populism slows down the processes of globalization rather than correcting it, with a return to the areas of influence of the great economic powers. Nationalist deglobalization is regressive and not progressive that tends to continue interactions and interrelations with the international community of nations in a creative way to achieve a balanced relationship between the different local and international levels of the economy.

Not only do nationalist and populist governments oppose the deepening of globalization processes, but also other more open governments that demand that globalization be controlled without control. Popular discontent has turned into pressure from social movements with nationalist sentiments, the rise of ultra-nationalist and xenophobic parties.

The processes of globalization were considered as an unavoidable and irreversible phenomenon to form a community that required a reduction of nationalism to delegate powers inherent to sovereign power to give rise to the formation of international organizations capable of making mandatory, binding decisions and subject to a regime international rights and sanctions. The resurgence of nationalism is a form of reaction and rejection of the current processes of globalization to demand the annulment of local communities, their history, local traditions and customs, and the resurgence of religious and cultural ties and values that traditionally unite groups. and communities.

The expanding economic globalization has brought also devastating negative effects on increasing levels of pollution in one part of the world that leads to extreme climate change and weather events and destruction of the eco systems and biodiversity. The negative effects of the processes of economic globalization have increased inequalities and economic and social inequality that are used as an argument to devalue globalization due to the emergence of new nationalist and populist movements.

The new globalizing institutions must face the challenges before nationalist and populist options roll back progress. If the processes of deglobalization intensify and are confined within the borders of the national states, and in the best of cases, regionally, they offer the opportunity to grow and develop with the implementation of their own model that require a revision internal competition systems to accelerate internal growth.

DEGLOBALIZATION

Economic and commercial history shows that intense periods of globalization are followed by periods of deglobalization based on the closing of the borders to international trade and the nationalist sentiment that is based on giving priority to the national before, to the foreign, both in economic matters, commercial, financial, tourist, etc. The global economy is in a process of deglobalization, manifested in the slowdown or reversal of the prevailing economic order since the second half of the 20th century, in such a way that communications, interactions and interdependencies have reached a level of exacerbation or rejection. The deglobalization process represents the end of the traditional forms of global economic and commercial relations.

The term deglobalization is a neologism coined to refer to the slowdown and reduction of the advance of the processes of economic globalization. The neologism deglobalization has been created to signify a step back that the processes of economic globalization are taking with their ebbs that reduce the commercial, financial and migratory exchanges of people and labor. However, the networks that facilitate transnational financial operations remain intact while labor has always had interruptions in its flows for its global displacement.

The processes of economic globalization reached their peak to initiate a return to globalization processes with a specific location, also known as deglobalization. Walden Bello and Focus on the Global South, coined the term deglobalization with a positive connotation by setting the objective to restructure the world economic and political system to strengthen national and local economies (Bello, 2005). Deglobalization refers to the reverse process of globalization in which the economy, society, politics and culture are regionalized. The beginning of a deglobalization phase is underpinned by a regionalization of the economies. Deglobalization is an impulse from the geopolitical situation of crisis management that intensifies economic policy and accelerates trade wars between the main powers.

Deglobalization processes involve the movement ralentization of goods, inputs, materials, premium services, as well as people, information and ideas, as in the cases of tourism activities and higher education. Deglobalization processes present some characteristics that seem to be evident motivated more by political reasons than economic, social or technological. Deglobalization processes are characterized by a slowdown and reduction of the functions of international and supranational institutions that are in charge of regulating economic, commercial, financial, political, and personal relations, ideas that are carried out between the nations. Financial deglobalization marks a recovery of the national sovereignty of the countries that had already given part of the globalization processes.

The phenomena of raletization and economic deglobalization mark a period of reversal of globalization processes that have a high impact on economies that produce raw materials and inputs. Deglobalization is a process of weakening the economic, commercial and financial interdependence between nations. The processes of economic deglobalization can be defined as a decrease in the economic, commercial, financial, people and ideas interdependence among all the countries of the world.

The KOF index developed by the Swiss Economic Institute in 1979 measures deglobalization with indicators of exports, investments, migration, geopolitics and culture. The index has shown a constant increase in the processes of globalization, especially in the eighties with the connection of world stock markets, the dissolution of the USSR and the end of the Cold War, which motivated Fukuyama to declare the end of history in 1992. However, the globalization and deglobalization processes have been promoted and steered by the great economic and political powers to pursue their own local priorities and benefits. The demise of the World Trade Organization (WTO) concerning the trade governance is one of the relevant point to bring downward pressure towards deglobalization.

The evidences suggest that globalization is giving way to a period of deglobalization in trade and foreign direct investment (FDI) began in 2007-2008, after more than two decades of integration and increasing flows in the global market, and since then the restrictions are increasing. Deglobalization is not a new phenomenon because it had already manifested itself since the economic-financial crisis of 2008 with the fall of Leman Brothers.

The evidence that suggests that a period of deglobalization has been entered is presented (Witt, 2016) by suggesting that trade globalization flows began to decline between 2007 and 2010, while the globalization of foreign direct investment flows began to decline between 2007 and 2011 (Witt, 2019). Some analyses on economic deglobalization trend are focusing on the evidences of free flows of trade, finances and movements of people since the economic and financial crisis of 2008-2009. The trend towards the economic deglobalization of trade, financial, foreign investment and migration flows that reinforce the trend towards isolationism.

The trend of deglobalization processes that began with the financial economic crisis of 2008-09, continues with the arrival of Trump to the US government, which anticipates a change in the international economic integration processes that take shape and deepen with the coronavirus health crisis. Deglobalization as a phenomenon that was already observable before the health crisis and that is accelerating with it. The advance of a period of deglobalization intensifies with the health crisis of the pandemic having an impact and sequelae in shocks to aggregate demand and supply.

In addition, this period of deglobalization is more pressured by the economic and financial crises that broke out in 2008-2009 and has deepened with the health crisis of the corona virus pandemic. The global health crisis has deepened the already existing economic, political and social crisis that will not be able to be rescued by China like the previous financial crisis of 2008-2009.

Deglobalization is a phenomenon that has occurred several times throughout the history of the world economy, although it currently has different characteristics and due to the fact that commercial and financial activities have slowed down since 2013. The term deglobalization was coined by Walden Bello in his book Deglobalization: Ideas for a New World Economy

The analysis of trends on the uncertainty of global economic development confirms an open regionalism marked by the North American-Chinese tension and the traumatic Brexit and driven by deglobalization processes under the assumption that it is preferable to have close allies with more reliable and solid economies and with more stable regulatory frameworks. Some relevant deglobalization political movements are the start point Brexit referendum in 2016, the movement of Trump in the United States in 2016 and Bolsonaro in Brazil, in 2018, and other minor movements that provide evidence of confrontation between people and the globalization processes (James 2018; Inglehart and Norris, 2016). The de-globalization processes integrated to politics induces a shift in strategies, structures and behaviors in international business (Witt, 2019).

The implications for the trade war between China and US on the WTO moves toward further deglobalization of trade. WTO demise is becoming increasingly dysfunctional a turning point for trade towards deglobalization, which brings some pressure for global growth. The United States has declared trade war on various partners and China in particular, while the UK has pulled out of the European Union after 47 years. Both events question the integration of the global economy and open the possibilities for processes of economic deglobalization. The major economies were open and integrated into the world economy. The peak of globalization processes was reached with the trade war between the United States and China to initiate a return through a process of national localization also known as deglobalization.

The strategic competition between the two great economic powers, US and China has become increasingly hostile relationship between the largest economies fostering the deglobalization tendency with further consequences in trade, finances and technology, with implications of a trade war, as well as other additional deglobalization forces. In 2016, the United States and China launched a trade tariff war that, if it continues, could lead to the risk of a debilitating crisis of a chaotic deglobalization overreaction that can deepen the problems.

Before the emergence of the coronavirus health crisis, deglobalization was already a trend. The economic decline deepened by the health crisis is the beginning of a sustained deglobalization that slows the world economy and affects geo-economics and geopolitical changes. The uncertainty generated by the health crisis of the pandemic can lead to negative reactions to the behavior of human beings expressed in less liberal traits that can manifest themselves in the new deglobalization project (Bremmer, 2013).

The tendency towards nationalist retreat in the face of economic globalization processes has deepened with the health crisis of the pandemic and has accelerated the deglobalization processes with the consequent recovery of the regulatory functions of the State. Insourcing such as the return of factories to the country of origin and robotization are two of the trends that have been accompanying the deglobalization processes as a direct impact of the health crisis of the pandemic.

The public policies that emanate from national governments in response to the health crisis of the pandemic are very different, depending on the country in question, and they range from bailouts to large companies and banks, payment of salaries or a part of them, etc., which in many cases are dysfunctional and lead to more political and national tensions. These processes of deglobalization tend to concentrate wealth and create higher levels of poverty

This situation of deglobalization gives rise to a paradox because the risks are global, such as the increase in economic and social inequalities, demographic and migratory imbalances, climate changes, the emergence of technologies that are disruptive, while solutions are taken to local levels where social, political and cultural activities take place. van Bergeijk (2010) analyses comprehensively the drivers and risks of desglobalization. Any excess in the deglobalization processes can generate more risks and damages than benefits to economies, especially the most advanced ones. If somebody overreacts to deglobalization processes, they can do more harm than good. However, deglobalization also poses economic risks for all countries, but more so for the more advanced ones.

The sharp drop in international credits (Financial Times, April 24, 2020) is explained as part of a long process of globalization. Credit, banking and financial deglobalization affects more the financing flows of emerging economies, which in the case of Latin America report a withdrawal of 4 percent of GDP according to Corsetti & Marin (2020) and Davis (2020).

The current global economic and financial crisis is the total sum of domestic crisis and does not offer local solutions which have to be looked for each nation, therefore the deglobalization tendency is to look for local solutions to a global crisis. Among the characteristics of the current one the globalization process indicates the increase in market volatility of financial products and currencies that increases the risk margins and uncertainty of exports and imports, the impoverishment of the middle classes due to the maintenance of competitiveness at the cost of salary reductions, and the limitations that emerging economies have to sustain economic growth despite the free trade policies adopted.

The current processes of deglobalization weaken cross-border and inter-state commercial and financial relations that, if not properly reordered, will introduce new, more chaotic problems that can significantly reduce real global GDP, affecting all advanced and developing economies.

The decentralization of policies and the growing externalities result in a deglobalization of macroeconomic and financial configurations, unlike territorial approaches focused on the deglobalization of financial entities and at the universal level through a binding international treaty that stabilizes the international financial system and avoid regulatory arbitrage and deglobalization of finances.

The decrease has been shown to have secondary effects on employment, among others. Another of the dysfunctional effects of deglobalization processes is the decrease in remittances as unemployment increases. Deglobalization processes go beyond the economic and are located in other areas such as higher education to be trapped in national borders.

Furthermore, it is difficult for the deglobalization processes to last due to the existing interconnections between the countries of the world and the now digital relationships created by economic, commercial, financial, scientific, technological and educational exchanges, etc. Physical deglobalization is encouraged by digital globalization and adopts technology to accelerate the production of food, medicine and other important commodities for regional consumption. Digital globalization encourages sectors such as business, tourism and education. The digital economic transformation transform spaces and times towards deglobalization.

Deglobalization processes have shown the deficiencies and risks that the economic globalization model has, such as the outsourcing of strategic production systems in a multilateral system in crisis. Defenders of globalization focus on minimizing the effects of disruption brought about by the period of deglobalization and aim to create the foundations for more sustainable processes with strategies that maintain the balance between efficiency, resilience and greater aversion to risk.

The direct effects of deglobalization processes are manifested in a greater increase in production and distribution costs, which affect the efficiency of companies and require a strategic change. All the changes that come with the deglobalization processes are certain to occur, but what cannot be determined is how deep and in what dimensions they will be. While some analysts believe that deglobalization will increase the well-being of the population, others consider that it will reduce well-being.

THEORETICAL APPROACH

The processes of economic deglobalization for the 21st century require a conceptual theoretical framework that facilitates the analysis of variables such as cooperation and integration and dimensions of development strategies through which the international community carries out negotiations to redesign a way of globalization more closely related between the socio-ecosystem and humanity.

With the processes of deglobalization, history comes into contradiction with the centripetal integrating forces. Deglobalization processes are an inverse phenomenon to globalization, it is a return to the era of nationalisms due to the failure to develop the international community based on values, ideas and a culture that are shared by local communities. The global interaction and interdependence of the economy, society and politics become forces with a more regional or local centrifugal orientation, a return to the territory of national states. Deglobalization re-embeds the economy and the market in society and not a society that continues to be governed by the market economy.

Deglobalization is a backlash against globalism supported by mixed with nationalism and market segmentation, which has been considered a transition towards globalization 2.0 as the new kind. Globalization 2.0 promotes economic integration through infrastructure of large regions instead of the populist deglobalization driven by different nationalistic issues moving towards the nation states. Deglobalization processes are a transition between economic globalization and post-globalization whose only alternative is to decrease, slow down and retract. Findlay and O'Rourke in Power and Plenty. Trade, War and the World Economy, argues that the world system has expansive stages of economic globalization processes followed by stages of deglobalization that are determined by geopolitics rather than geo-economics.

The nation state is receiving demands from citizens to take back control responding to the failures of the economic and financial globalization to fulfill the promises. Populist governments, from the right and from the left, have taken advantage of this discontent and providing a compelling rallying cry and to heat the desglobalization pressure. Deglobalization represents a new paradigm that presents the extreme right in a nationalist version of deglobalization that excludes immigrants and racial minorities.

Deglobalization is backed by backlashes against globalization that threaten the international order constructed in the second half of the twentieth century. The deglobalization movements around the world can be framed in the complex system theory which signals all the interdependencies among the local economies when there is a need to reduce these complex interrelationships.

Economic ideas and theories about globalizing and deglobalizing dynamics enter into contradictions and conflict, as in the case of free trade, if the results achieved in economic growth are considered, while there are economies that have grown their GDP per capita, there are others that they have not grown. According to Witt (2019) the deglobalization theories from political science are liberalism and realism both of which lead to different expectations. While liberalism visions economic visions, realism sees economic blocs.

The principle of deglobalization processes based on a logic of a construct of rigorous empirical data on the limitations of globalization processes based on multinational companies operating in a global economy and market. Decisions on the location of operations must consider the patterns of survival or investment in deglobalization processes, such as political and military patterns. Direct investment has slowed down with a direct consequence of accelerating deglobalization. The economic decisions submitted to the political deliberation of the national states advance towards processes of economic and financial deglobalization.

The dynamics of the deglobalizing processes affect each of the nations in different ways as the trend is accentuated because they have very different internal challenges and commitments in relation to the exercise of global governance. The trend of economic deglobalization moves towards the regionalization or location of production, distribution and consumption, with an emphasis on local companies and markets. Deglobalization processes are not uniform or global in the same way that globalization was because it was not fully accepted by non-governments of countries with autocratic political systems that have no affinity with the promoted values. The zero-polar world, predicted by Bremmer (2013), is the characteristic world order of deglobalization processes in which there would be no national or international power to face the challenges of world leadership.

Populist governments have had difficulty inserting themselves into globalization processes with very limited progress, which is why they are now promoting deglobalization. Many of these governments only participated nominally according to their historical-political contexts.

Deglobalization processes are the result of the globalization crisis due to cultural modifications introduced to secular values, such as, for example, intolerance expressed in norms towards certain intellectual expressions and manifestations. The excess of globalization has led to an opening of cultural values treated in normative terms such as gender.

REGIONALISM AND LOCALISM

Regionalization focuses on regions and are less interconnected than globalization. From the business corporation's perspective, it means to develop goods and services considering the habits of people living in these regions.

In the 1970s some national economies opened up by adopting the development of free trade policies and world exports increased between the different regions of the world. The economic and ðnancial crisis of 2008 and 2009 brought negative effects to regions of developed economies contributing to some drawback in the globalization processes and connected to economic recession. The period of decline in international commercial, financial and people flows began in the years prior to 2020 after the health crisis, mainly due to the risks posed by dependence on the provision of supplies from international geographic locations. What the health crisis has done is to deepen this trend towards regional and local production.

The current situation of the global economy is only comparable in magnitude of the impact of the crisis of the thirties of the last century and there is no region that escapes this economic shock that threatens all national economies. This situation requires the generation of support mechanisms to mitigate the impact of the crisis.

Globalization can be seen as the result of regional collective action and transnational co-operations between economic regions (Balme 1996) that leads to interstate international relations system in the context of regionalism (Ibarra and Letamendia 1999). The development of economic regionalism as part of the process of economic de-globalization is based on the promotion of regional and local alliances to enhance technological and organizational capacities for the production, distribution and consumption of satisfiers with high levels of regional content and with an orientation responsible for information management and the new challenges of sustainable development.

Globalization has benefited some countries or regions more economically than others, while it has promoted constitutional democracy and the recognition of rights and freedoms, as well as an increase in the level of education. The globalization of economic agents allows international reach and extraterritorial coverage in a process that encompasses all areas of economic competition that includes all countries and does not exclude any region (Berumen 2002: 350).

The globalization processes in the digital age are transformed and are moving towards a stage of more regional fragmentation under a new multilateral international trade model. This new multilateralism requires a profound revision or the creation of new existing institutions and regulations to build a new world order with greater capacities to regulate the new balances of power. World global cities globalization of economies play a relevant role in advanced producer and financial services increasing international interconnectedness of the corporate governance structures at the regional, national and international levels (Friedmann 1986: 70, 73 ff.; Sassen 1991: 127 ff.; Beaverstock, Smith and Taylor 2000: 125 ff.; Derudder, Taylor and Witlox et al. 2003: 876 ff.; Taylor 2004: 175 ff.; Robinson 2005: 757 ff.; Hanssens, Derudder and Taylor et al. 2010: 2 ff.; Lüthi, Thierstein and Goebel 2010: 115 ff.; Sassen 1991: 65 ff.).

Economic globalization is driving economic growth with disproportioned benefits to individuals, regions and nations, bringing some negative non homogenous consequences such as income inequalities. Despite the multiple benefits, the ongoing economic globalization processes has brought complicated financial crisis, growth of unemployment, social unrests and environmental sustainability problems. Still, the global economy is going into a large-scale continues transformation processes towards different type of globalization from which all the stakeholders participating may benefit.

However, the economic globalization has not fulfilled the expectations promised for all, so that, with the exception of some, it has not delivered the expected benefits. It has been accompanied by risks, especially when the prevailing logic is to obtain the maximum benefit in economic rationality to produce in some regions of the world where cheap resources abound and then commercialize in other regions of the globe, without any sanitary controls. These effects have not been as expected and have motivated a transition towards more regional and local economic processes.

However, researchers sustain that globalization had surfaced some atypical tendencies in this wave (Karunaratne, 2012; Miskiewicz, Ausloos, 2010, Swiss Economic Institute, 2014, and Zehra2011). The world economy is immersed in a process of regression of flows of goods and services, investments and people that have the tendency to regionalize after a hectic period of growth of global interdependence and interaction.

Economic globalization has increased the transnational economic integration through changes on the mobility of economic factors that have had a high impact on regional development and territorial consequences in investment and development of regional industries and firms. These changes affect the international competition and transform the socioeconomic conditions and the political processes. This situation is giving space to regional-local public policies to design a new economic, social, political and environmental scenario structured multilevel and polycentric forms of governance to influence development without challenging the power of nation states (Hooghe 1996; Keating and Jones 1985; Le Galès and Lequesne 1998).

Intra-regional trade relative to global trade in goods has increased in the last 7 years, reflecting the increase in consumption in emerging markets. This trend is reflected in the production activities that are located in neighboring countries inserted in the international flows of production, distribution, trade and consumption of goods and services.

The new global economic shift towards valorization of more local production and supply channels instead of the cost structure, centered on more personal service and sustainable values and principle, based on new disruptive technologies with regional value and new patterns of consumer behavior. The new phases of the globalization processes must converge in those constitutive elements that articulate all the economic, social, environmental, political, cultural elements at all levels: World, regional, national, local, community and individual.

Global international, regional and national financial centers are always in closed interrelated and in interconnected relationships with one another (Parr and Budd 2000: 605 ff.; Taylor 2004: 110 ff.; Harrschar-Ehrnborg 2002; Poon, Eldredge and Yeung 2004; Merki 2005; Cassis 2006). Clustering of financial services in financial centers in urban systems requires knowledge-intensive activities and economies of scale and scope at the global, international, regional or national levels of business operations (Porteous 1999: 3 ff.; Lo and Schamp 2001: 27; Schmidt/Grote 2005: 1 ff.; Schamp 2009: 89 ff.; Parr/Budd 2000: 605 ff.; Taylor 2004: 110 ff.; Harrschar-Ehrnborg 2002; Poon, Eldredge and Yeung 2004; Merki 2005; Cassis 2006).

The processes of reconfiguration of globalization require new alternatives, initiatives and structures for world and regional integration that promote harmonious development in multiple dimensions, in such a way that national states maintain their sovereign decisions in the face of globalization without ceasing to be functional to the world system. The alternative has been the creation of regional and bilateral free trade agreements.

Economic globalization processes are required to reach global consensus to be redesigned involving the connections between the economic systems and market impacted by socioeconomic and cultural issues, regional and local specificities, collaborative networks. A more rational globalization process must be based on the formation and integration of an international community capable of sharing values, ideas, traditions, customs, etc., that is, the creation of a more global culture while respecting the differences and diversity of regional and local cultures.

DISCUSSION

The great Western economic powers have played a preponderant role in the deglobalization processes to configure a new global order. However, the winners of the current globalization processes have been the countries known as the BRICS with China at the forefront, who may become the losers of the deglobalization processes or in the reversal of the globalization process. The deglobalization process represents the end of the traditional forms of global economic and commercial relations. Deglobalization represents a limited period in the integration of international economic relations and globalization. International cooperation aimed at maintaining prosperity and global peace is weakened by the effects of deglobalization with the reduction of the activities of the international commercial and financial systems.

The most recent stage of the processes of economic globalization is different from the previous stages due to the speed and scale of exchanges and interactions that entail other processes with negative effects with the spread of enormous risks such as the rapidity of the overwhelming contagion of the coronavirus pandemic that can accelerate the deglobalization processes of the world economy. The deglobalization process limits the circulation of goods, services, finances and people that during intense globalization only had sanitary limitations.

The processes of economic globalization have been inclined towards globalization rather than deglobalization of the economy. Globalization was intended to replace the nation states in a perverse and coercive manner and what it has achieved is a response from the populist and nationalist movements that have prevented it from deepening and that have supported the processes of deglobalization. The processes of deglobalization that are so contradictory are manifestations of new configurations of a new phase of the processes of globalization with expressions that are more exclusive, brutal and pathologically dangerous for the harmonious economic growth, inclusion and social justice, as well as the environmental sustainability of all countries.

The deglobalization of economic processes means decrease or withdrawal, it is a transition period towards a post-global period with a strong energy component. Deglobalization processes imply a decrease in commercial and financial exchange activities, movements of people and ideas with well-determined impacts on socio-ecosystems that can degrade nature. On the contrary, deglobalization processes should contribute to improving the conditions of economic growth, social development with inclusion and social justice, and environmental sustainability, which benefit individuals and communities more than multinational and transnational organizations.

The non-existence of a project and a model of deglobalization processes based on geopolitics that is based on institutions that are not entirely democratic, limits the scope to achieve economic growth, social development and environmental sustainability of the nation states. In the phase change of globalization processes to deglobalization processes, the national state recovers its functions in the face of the existence of a cosmopolitan international institutional community that was going to solve the problems. The reality has reached the international organizations formed by the nation states. The national state is responsible for intensifying rather than contracting international economic relations.

The tendency towards deglobalization, the concepts of urban development and politics have been re localized shifting towards more functionalist concepts such as creative cities and integrating of diversity and social justice. The distances between the localities in a context of deglobalization acquire a determining role to influence the regions and countries transversally, where those most addicted to energy abundance are the ones that suffer the most. Deglobalization processes must face the profound changes that globalization produced in the economic, social, political, social and cultural transformations that affect all aspects of individual and social life.

Proponents of globalization need to be more pragmatic in managing gradual and orderly processes of partial de-globalization so that they can lay the foundations for relaunching more sustainable and inclusive globalization processes. Deglobalization processes require the redesign of a more economic, social and environmental sustainable development based on more rebalanced investments and re-invigorated technology, science and innovation. The new development model that results from the deglobalization processes must adjust to the promotion of economic decisions from the spaces of the national state to factories and businesses, which are promoting equality, inclusiveness and social justice and fostering interrelationships between the economy, society and environmental socio-ecosystems.

Finding a balance between the processes of globalization and deglobalization that allows growth and evolution, reducing the gaps of economic, social, political, cultural inequality and the recovery of local identities. Economic globalization has been identified as a generator of economic and social inequalities, which have motivated anti-globalization movements that propose the beginning of a period of economic deglobalization within the framework of the 2030 agenda to point out a period of regression in international economic interrelations. between States, and the influence exercised by multinational companies to focus on national sovereignty with the detriment of the international standards imposed by international organizations and treaties for economic cooperation and integration.

In the case of Mexico, the entry into force of the T-MEC coupled with the trend of deglobalization accelerates the processes that can encourage and benefit the development of Mexican companies. Mexico has the opportunity to take advantage of deglobalization trends as a partner of the T_MEC commercially integrated with the United States and Canada. The coronavirus health crisis demonstrates the relevance of proximity to the North American market in order to have more certainty in ensuring the provision of supplies for production.

The model of the deglobalized world moves away from the other possible world of the anti-globalizers. An alternative deglobalization process must be centered on populations and nature. However, the current processes of deglobalization do not offer alternative solutions and can aggravate the imbalances and contradictions that can lead to scenarios that increase social vulnerability with more inequality and injustice. The socio-political arguments are more supportive of deglobalization processes, such as avoiding the increase in inequalities with a better distribution of benefits, promoting inclusive mechanisms in technological changes and advances. Otherwise, there will continue to be discontent movements, social upheavals, trade wars, etc.

Deglobalization processes can be presented in scenarios of their future development. A first scenario is one of soft changes that do not modify the structures of international institutions but that focus on regulating distortions to free trade, as well as the conditions imposed on developing countries.

The deconstruction of globalization processes, known as deglobalization, has to be for a better reconstruction that truly integrates humanity through economic, political and social change, and does not disintegrate. This change requires weakening the hegemony of the system of globalizing institutional powers, delegitimizing its ideology and its rules.

REFERENCES

Balme, R. (1996). *Les politiques du néo-régionalisme: action collective régionale et globalisation*. Paris Economica.

Beaverstock, J. V., Smith, R. G., & Taylor, P. J. (2000). World-City Network: A New Metageography? *Annals of the Association of American Geographers, 90*(1), 123–134. doi:10.1111/0004-5608.00188

Bello, W. (2005). *Deglobalization: Ideas for a New World Economy*. Zed books.

Berumen, S. (2002). *Economía internacional*. Editorial Continental, Ciudad de México.

Bremmer, I. (2013). *Every Nation for Itself. What Happens When No One Leads the World*. Portfolio / Penguin.

Cassis, Y. (2006). Capitals of capital – a history of international financial centres, 1780-2005. Cambridge.

Corsetti, G., & Marin, E. A. (2020). *A Century of Arbitrage and Disaster Risk Pricing in the Foreign Exchange Market*. CEPR Discussion Paper No. 14497.

Davis, S. (2020). *Emerging-Market Economies Face COVID-19 and a 'Sudden Stop' in Capital Flows*. Federal Reserve Bank of Dallas. Retrieved from https://www.dallasfed.org/research/economics/2020/0414

Derudder, B., Taylor, P. J., Witlox, F., & Catalano, G. (2003). Hierarchical Tendencies and Regional Patterns in the World City Network: A Global Urban Analysis of 234 Cities. *Regional Studies, 37*(9), 875–886. doi:10.1080/0034340032000143887

Financial Times. (2020, Apr. 24). US Banks Pull Back from Lending to European Companies. *Financial Times.*

Friedmann, J. (1986). The World City Hypothesis. *Development and Change, 17*(1), 69–83. doi:10.1111/j.1467-7660.1986.tb00231.x

Hanssens, H., Derudder, B., Taylor, P. J., Hoyler, M., Ni, P., Huang, J., Yang, X., & Witlox, F. (2010). The changing geography of globalized service provision, 2000-2008. The Service Industries Journal. doi:10.1080/02642069.2010.503887

Harrschar-Ehrnborg, S. (2002): *Finanzplatzstrukturen in Europa: Die Entstehung und Entwicklung von Finanzzentren. Academic Press.*

Hooghe, L. (Ed.). (1996). *Cohesion policy and European integration: building multi-level governance.* Oxford University Press.

Ibarra, P., & Letamendia, F. (1999). Los movimientos sociales. In M. Caminal (Ed.), *Manual de Ciencia Política.* Tecnos.

Inglehart, R., & Norris, P. (2016) *Trump, Brexit, and the rise of populism: economic have-nots and cultural backlash.* HKS Faculty Research Working Paper Series RWP16-026.

James, H. (2018). Deglobalization: The rise of disembedded unilateralism. *Annual Review of Financial Economics, 10*(1), 219–237. doi:10.1146/annurev-financial-110217-022625

Karunaratne, N. D. (2012). The Globalization Deglobalization Policy Conundrum. *Modern Economy.*, *3*(4), 373–383. doi:10.4236/me.2012.34048

Keating, M., & Jones, B. (Eds.). (1985). *Regions in the European Community.* Oxford University Press.

Le Galès, P., & Lequesne, C. (1998). *Regions in Europe.* Routledge.

Lo, V., & Schamp, E. W. (2001). Finanzplätze auf globalen Märkten – Beispiel Frankfurt/Main. *Geographische Rundschau, 53*(7/8), 26–31.

Lüthi, S., Thierstein, A., & Goebel, D. (2010). Intra-firm and extra-firm linkages in the knowledge economy: The case of the emerging mega-city region of Munich. *Global Networks, 10*(1), 114–137. doi:10.1111/j.1471-0374.2010.00277.x

Merki, C. M. (Ed.). (2005). *Europas Finanzzentren. Geschichte und Bedeutung im 20.* Jahrhundert.

Miskiewicz, J., & Ausloos, M. (2010). Has the World Economy Reached Its Globalization Limit? Physica A, 389(4), 797-806. DOI: .physa.2009.10.029 doi:10.1016/j

Parr, J. B., & Budd, L. (2000). Financial Services and the Urban System: An Exploration. *Urban Studies (Edinburgh, Scotland), 37*(3), 593–610. doi:10.1080/0042098002131

Poon, J. P. H., Eldredge, B., & Yeung, D. (2004). Rank Size Distribution of International Financial Centers. *International Regional Science Review, 27*(4), 411–430. doi:10.1177/0160017604267629

Porteous, D. J. (1999). The Development of Financial Centres: Location, Information Externalities and Path Dependence. In R. Martin (Ed.), Money and the space economy (pp. 95–114). Academic Press.

Robinson, J. (2005). Urban geography: World cities, or a world of cities. *Progress in Human Geography, 29*(6), 757–765. doi:10.1191/0309132505ph582pr

Sassen, S. (1991). The global city. Academic Press.

Schamp, E. W. (2009). Das Finanzzentrum – ein Cluster? Ein multiskalarer Ansatz und seine Evidenz am Beispiel von Frankfurt/Rhein-Main. *Zeitschrift für Wirtschaftsgeographie, 53*(1-2), 1–2, 89–105. doi:10.1515/zfw.2009.0006

Schmidt, R. S., & Grote, M. (2005). *Was ist und was braucht ein bedeutender Finanzplatz?* Working Paper Series Finance and Accounting 150, Department of Economics, Johann Wolfgang Goethe-University Frankfurt.

Swiss Economic Institute. (2014). *Press Release, KOF Index of Globalization: Switzerland no Longer Among the Top Ten.* Zurich: SEI. Available from: http://globalization.kof. ethz.ch/media/filer_public/2014/04/16/press_ release_2014_en.pdf

Taylor, P. (2004). *World City Network: A global urban analysis.* doi:10.4324/9780203634059

Van Bergeijk, P. A. G. (2010). *On the Brink of Deglobalization.* Edward Elgar. doi:10.4337/9781849805803

Witt, M. A. (2019). De-Globalization: Theories, Predictions, and Opportunities for International Business Research. *Journal of International Business Studies, 50*(7), 1053–1107. doi:10.105741267-019-00219-7

Witt, M. A., & Jackson, A. (2016). Varieties of Capitalism and institutional comparative advantage: A test and reinterpretation. *Journal of International Business Studies, 47*(7-2), 778-806.

Zehra, N. (2011). The Realist State and Deglobalization. Policy Perspectives, 2.

KEY TERMS AND DEFINITIONS

Economic Deglobalization: Is the process of decreasing economic interdependence and economic integration between certain units throughout the world, typically nation-states. This term is widely used to describe periods in history when economic trade and investment between countries declines.

Localism: Local quality as belonging to a place or a territory.

Nationalism: Political doctrine and movement that claim the right of a nationality to reaffirm its own personality through political self-determination. Special attachment to one's own nation and how much it belongs to.

Populism: Political tendency that claims to defend the interests and aspirations of the people. Tendency or fondness for what is popular in all areas of the life of peoples and people.

Regionalism: Doctrine or political tendency that defends that the government of a State must consider the way of being and the aspirations of each region.

Chapter 3
Globalization and Trade in the Post-Covid World

Anjuli Deepak Gupta
Pacific University, India

Muskan Nagi
Gulf University, Bahrain

ABSTRACT

The COVID-19 pandemic brought an extraordinary disturbance regarding the worldwide economy and global trade, as creation and utilization downsized. Perhaps the best methodology for addressing this type of emergency is convenient, unspoiled information. An informed public is better established to use wise judgment including on cases recognized for trade. This is the situation, and a devoted page at WTO site has been created. This will provide present data related with trade information. The chapter discusses rising protectionism in course of the last half period, unexpected monetary crises created by the pandemic, disturbances regarding production network movement, and shocks related to market interest. Reporters worldwide have trumpeted the 'finish' of globalization.

INTRODUCTION

A few observers have blared about "end" regarding globalization with wake related to rising protectionism throughout last half period, unexpected monetary stays created by pandemic, and result interruptions of production network action all throughout the planet. Reality, however, is related to organizations as well as investors participated into trade, transmission and offer regarding products, administrations, innovation along with finance and globalization was about become stop. Without a doubt, situation drastically moved in the period of 1990s, and chiefs should be deft and lithe in navigating the new climate, which is as of now in a condition of motion (Sudhakar, 2014). Indeed, later advancements in the worldwide trade climate including green structures, computerized conventions and provincial organizations offer an impression not of downfall regarding globalization, yet rather, worldwide business might resemble in post-pandemic period.

DOI: 10.4018/978-1-7998-8705-8.ch003

This conveys about ramifications, regarding manufacturing and industrial periods related with the creation of products have fundamentally helped public income about homegrown lines. Moreover, cut-throat fare of these merchandise to unfamiliar business sectors has additionally added to both homegrown just as worldwide monetary development. Looking past merchandise, cross-line trades of administrations (like travel, IT, and legitimate and proficient administrations), just as streams of finance as well as trades about people resources consists integral parts regarding globalized trade landscape, basic creating trade, benefit, and collecting outputs.

With eventual fate of business approaching for equilibrium, what's coming up at business leaders as well as investors? Regarding some, businesses as those along with predominantly homegrown deals fundamental having frequently depended at course regarding globalization with request to make riches, at last converting into increasing monetary development with work. Though ongoing business pressures-just like responses from governments related with coastal creation considering pandemic indeed end up being the finish of the multi-decade interaction of globalization as far as we might be concerned?

Presently, we may tell that we are negotiating about an alternate shade with discontent regarding social orders-especially articulated within cutting edge economies by which course regarding globalization is frequently accused: by increasing homegrown income type inequality. While worldwide business has increased about billions of individuals as neediness and pointedly decreased at inequality with respect to worldwide stage (like as among China, West along with southeast Asia and West) income, abundance, as well as opportunity inequality become consistently increasing within nations like US, UK, Italy.

Policymakers as well as trade pioneers about these nations consists choice regarding authorize homegrown answers for stand up to a portion of these cultural difficulties, that needs the drawn out mindset and skyline with execution. Though we will look, these arrangements may impart to introducing business sector and developing kind economies that contains experienced unfavorable shocks related with income because of pandemic (Kumar, 2009).

By the by, in spite of the potential for homegrown arrangements, a few chiefs have thought that it is both tasteful just like politically environment advantageous as point of finger regarding fault about different nations. Increasing income age as well as financial headway in consideration of Japan, like, turned into an objective of fury within certain circles in the US during the last part of the 1980s and mid 1990s. More as of late, regarding US as well as across Europe, about some extremist legislators and observers having regularly focused regarding monetary achievement create by sure gatherings (like foreigner specialists, or explicit nations) with reasonable causal parameter about disintegration of homegrown working section (Brahma, 2018).

OBJECTIVES

1. To discuss about globalization.
2. To study the impact on trade during COVID at global scenario.
3. To examine the trade scenario in post COVID world.

LITERATURE REVIEW

On the inventory side, medical problems are reñected in decreased movement in all neighborhood financial areas, including tradable areas like manufacturing. In particular, mortality and bleakness are customary reasons for the deficiency of useful labor force at whatever point the scholarly community attempts to determine the effect of a medical problem. Analyzing the effects of the Spanish influenza, Correia, Luck, and Verner (2020) distinguished discouraged work supply through self-segregation measures, limitations on versatility, ailment, and increased mortality as the main points of contention impacting nations' stockpile limit. Also, the investigation by McKibbin and Fernando (2020) on the effect regarding pandemic, recognizes the fall about complete work supply, an ascent in danger premium, and increment in expenses regarding creation at all areas as main inventory side effects.

Likely great striking effect related to present pandemic is monstrous interruptions at international business as well as worldwide worth chains. As per Baldwin and Freeman (2020), problem of output at most "globalized" economies with respect to manufacturing areas finding "triple hits":

- Direct stockpile interruptions hindering creation because illness was centered around globe manufacturing and spreading quick related to another industrial nations.
- Production network disease amplifying immediate stock issues related to manufacturing areas about less-influenced countries locate this harder as well as much costly by securing vital imported type of industrial receiving at hard-hit countries, as well as accordingly with one another.
- Demand disturbances because of: a) macroeconomic related drops in total demand (for example downturns); b) keep a watch out buy delays by buyers; and c) investment-delays with respect to organizations.

Considering demand pattern, most prompt business effect of Covid has become abrupt flood regarding worldwide demand with respect to pandemic related clinical supplies, that surpassed present homegrown creation stages in this way output regarding import demand and time increasing costs. Fare limitations considered by introducing significant economies deal with deficiencies further prompted cost enhancement as per World Bank, might be, like, 20.5% regarding situation about clinical veils.

GLOBALIZATION

Investment by MNCs helps nations by providing new positions and abilities for nearby individuals however it might likewise have an adverse consequence because of increased rivalry for neighborhood businesses and the way that many benefits from unfamiliar possessed firms are removed from the host country. Many assistance area businesses like banks, have set up call places in nations where there are high quantities of English-speaking laborers, eg India. This implies that they can profit from modest work and 24 hour administration arrangement. Diverse time regions imply that telephone lines and client assistance can work for more (Singh, 2011).

Globalization is explained like interaction with innovation along with data and correspondence innovation transformation in the period of 1990s-empowered quicker exchange periods and cycles regarding trades with cash, capital streams, and merchandise along with individuals all throughout planet. Though this transmissions regarding business worked with standards, legal entities, systems, and arrangements with governing business - like WTO at worldwide stage, and provincial arrangements like ASEAN (Chaudhary, 2015).

Lamentably, exactly the same worldwide interconnectedness which worked with abundance creation and financial freedoms additionally had a clouded side, which showed all through the 1990s and 2000s. Worldwide and transnational dangers like international psychological oppression (e.g., the assaults of 9/11); ecological debasement; digital assaults; pandemics; illegal exploitation; with financial imbalance and emergencies ricocheted in world. These dangers may spring up at one locale, and exactly same channels which encouraged 'brilliant side' regarding globalization-effectively spread within topographies.

Such transmissions related with business worked with standards, legal bounding, systems with settlements of governing business, for example, WTO at worldwide stage with arrangements like ASEAN considering provincial stage. At the public stage, making regarding streamlined commerce regions additionally worked with simplicity of business: like shipping container may travel with consistent coordinations hall in UAE at Port Jebel Ali to Dubai Airport at the period of four hours only (Pradhan, 2018).

In present environment, we may tell that we are working with an alternate shade in consideration of discontent within social orders-especially articulated within cutting edge economies that regarding globalization is regularly accused: increasing homegrown income imbalance. Though worldwide business has lifted in terms of billions of individuals out of destitution and forcefully decreased imbalance worldwide stage.

By and by, a few chiefs have thought that it is both acceptable just politically helpful at point considering finger at fault with different nations. Increasing income age as well as financial headway regarding Japan, like, turned into an objective of fury about certain spheres regarding US ABOUT last part of the 1980s and mid 1990s. All the more as of late, some extremist government officials and analysts have demonstrated regarding monetary advantages create by definite gatherings (like outsider laborers) like reasonable causal parameter for disintegration regarding homegrown working section (Gupta, 2008). Despite with reasons for homegrown inequality as well as social uneasiness, legislators carried on against business with manners as follows as under:

- Ructions against merchandise: As of late, a few nations have zeroed in on the equilibrium of trade in merchandise (or the lopsidedness) as an approach to diminish imports or to coastal creation. Taxes turned into the arrangement instrument of decision as a method of addressing such uneven characters, however when executed, have had blended outcomes. Information shows that endeavors to help homegrown creation of labor and products includes some significant pitfalls: straightforwardly, for the administrations, organizations and shoppers.
- Restrictions on portability: Reactions regarding tension felt about worldwide business have not become restrict in consideration of products. States consists additionally varying at confine migration, vowing regarding shield homegrown laborers as an apparent burden. Note that curtailing portability likewise includes some significant pitfalls-during pandemic limitations, the quick decrease about traveler horticultural specialists in OECD nations become added the quick ascent regarding food costs, that have arrived at long term high.

ANALYSIS

The Covid-19 pandemic has definitely influenced lives and livelihoods. Simultaneously, it has additionally disturbed financial exercises all through the world. Specifically, worldwide merchandise trade streams diminished by 7% in 2020. There are a few measurements to the pandemic that are probably going to influence international trade: its immediate wellbeing sway and related conduct changes; the results of governments' activities to forestall the spread of the infection; and the effect of the pandemic in third nations.

The pandemic creates impact on diversely at social orders along with economies regarding nations, including in Africa, depending on quantity related to international traveler appearances and reliance at international trade with investment, and not least regarding timing and thoroughness in consideration of government suggested preventive factors.

Different systems considered for utilization for determining effect related with pandemic about world's economies. UNCTAD at 2020, like, exhibits that EU, about effect related at USD 15.6 billion at business streams, US, along with 5.8 billion dollars, Japan along with 5.2 billion dollars, became absolute greatest affected economies. Examination, about restricted check just at present moment and direct impacts of COVID upon business, accepts that the supply interruptions were restricted at China and stockpile limit regarding remainder as world becomes consistent. At this modality, financial areas as well as nations generally presented as an interruption regarding China's fares with intermediate inputs are dissected by quantify about level of provided nation's fares at every organization that is powerless against supply disturbance in China.

Also, this tracked down that regarding worldwide situation, in case world's GDP downs at two percent underneath baseline regarding developing nations as GDP fall about 2.5 percent, and industrial nations at 1.8 percent. About intensified this type of situation, downfall would be twofold with respect to correlation. Under intensified worldwide situation, worldwide GDP became decline about would reach 3.9 percent, considering districts generally integrated for trading as the travel industry business assumes the major part regarding economy with respect to greatest GDP misfortunes. Nations of SSA along with MENA, were most un-influenced with these two situations, considering expected GDP loss about 3 percent.

INTERPRETATION

Possibilities regarding fast recuperation with respect to world business have improved like merchandise business expanded fast than anticipated at second fifty percent at last year. According to current gauges from WTO, as volume considering world merchandise trade has relied upon increase about eight percent in the period of 2021 as wake considering having down fall about 5.3 percent in the period of 2020, continuing returning back considering pandemic-induced breakdown that became reach as far down as possible related to second quarter considering last year.

Business development should about ease return at four percent in the period of 2022, and effects related to pandemic will continue to be felt with speed regarding extension would be any case leave trade beneath with its about pre-pandemic trends.

Generally sure transient consideration worldwide business is defaced from provincial differences, continued with issues regarding administrations business, and lagging vaccination schedules, especially to helpless countries. COVID sustains to represent best danger with standpoint for business, as current rushes related to infection might undoubtedly undermine any expected recuperation.

"The solid bounce back in worldwide trade since the center of last year has mellowed the blow of the pandemic for individuals, businesses, and economies," WTO Director-General conveyed. "Keeping international business sectors open will be fundamental for economies to recuperate from this emergency and a fast, worldwide and fair vaccine carry out is an essential for the solid and sustained recuperation we as a whole need."

"Ramping up creation of vaccines will permit businesses and schools to resume all the more rapidly and assist economies with getting in a good place again. Yet, insofar as huge quantities of individuals and nations are avoided from adequate vaccine access, it will smother development, and hazard reversing the wellbeing and monetary recuperation worldwide," she conveyed.

"Manufacturing vaccines requires inputs from various nations. One leading COVID-19 vaccine includes 280 parts sourced from 19 unique nations," she said. "Trade limitations make it harder to increase creation. The WTO has assisted keep with trading flowing during the emergency. Presently, the international local area should use the force of trade to expand admittance to life-saving vaccines."

1. Significant Economies Recuperate at 2020 Fall

As per report regarding import and fare patterns at portion regarding world's significant trading type of economies exhibit that couple of special cases, trade about significant economies recuperated as down in the period of 2020.

In any case, enormous increment are because of low level in the period of 2020, and business in a large number related with significant economies was at under 2019 midpoints. Pattern of more grounded recuperation regarding products comparative with administrations is normal to every significant economies.

This exhibits that China, India as well as South Africa fared generally best compared to another significant economies at Q1 in the period of 2021. China's fares, specifically, enrolled a solid increase from 2020 midpoints as well as comparable to pre-pandemic stages. Interestingly, trades regarding Russia remained good under the period of 2019 midpoints.

2. Trade Recuperation Abides Lopsided

Business and Trade recuperation abides lopsided, as report explained, particularly amid developing nations, for sending out regarding East Asia rebounding significantly quicker. EAE becomes additionally behind at recuperation of business amid developing nations. At the point when business figures at EA regarding developing economies are barred, South-South business abides beneath midpoints.

Report exhibits that at Q1 in the period of 2021, worth regarding fares abide underneath midpoints with respect to nations with economies experiencing significant change, at Middle East, SA and Africa. Albeit South America's fares enhanced comparative with Q1 in the period of 2020, they remained under 2019 midpoints. This searches that at Q1 in the period of 2021, worth regarding merchandise imports along with fares regarding developing nations was generously higher contrasted and Q1 in the period of 2020 and Q1 in the period of 2019 (Approx 16%).

Additionally, at Q1 in the period of 2021, business continued with bounce back not just in areas identified with COVID, like drugs, correspondence and office hardware, yet additionally another as minerals with agrifood. Interestingly, energy area continued as falling down behind and international business at transport gear remained well underneath midpoints.

3. More Trade Development Expected up to 2021

Report conjectures that business will continue expanding in the period of 2021, as development expected at remain solid regarding second fifty percent of year.

"Trade development is relied upon to remain more grounded for East Asia and created nations, while as yet lagging for some different nations," report conveyed.

General conjecture at the period of 2021 exhibits increment about sixteen percent from absolute bottom in consideration of 2020 (at nineteen percent for merchandise and eight percent for administrations). Worth regarding worldwide business with respect to labor and products is conjecture approaching approximately $6.6 trillion at Q2 in the period of 2021, comparable year-over-year increment about thirty one percent comparative with absolute bottom of the period of 2020 and three percent comparative with pre-pandemic degrees regrading 2019.

"All things considered, monetary boost bundles, especially in created nations, are relied upon to emphatically uphold the worldwide trade recuperation all through 2021," the report says. "The worth of worldwide trade ought to likewise ascend because of positive patterns across product costs." In any case, uncertainty remains regarding how trade examples will be molded consistently.

CONCLUSION

While trade strains have saturated restricting investments in basic areas within certain nations, China has really diminished its 'negative rundown' for unfamiliar organizations to invest in mainland China, within areas including oil and gas, the car industry, and urgently for some US and European banks, financial administrations.

Indeed, some US banks have invested billions of dollars in China all through 2020, and have pushed toward full responsibility for adventures on the ground in mainland China. In the abundance the executives space, one French organization has additionally taken larger part responsibility for adventure on the ground with a mainland Chinese business accomplice. Considering that mainland Chinese resources are set to fourfold in development within the following decade, a portion of the world's most productive organizations find this increased market access too tantalizing to even think about resisting. Indeed, one may contend that the tethering of US and European financial administrations to Chinese abundance may really keep the US and China from a full-scale decoupling.

Note that in thinking about the potential for trade in financial administrations across the globe, entertainers are not restricted to the US and China. Singapore is one country which has charged both customary just as new players in banking and in fintech. By creating an administrative sandbox wherein organizations can innovate within the boundaries a wellbeing net executed by the controllers, banks, tech, and even ride share organizations have utilized Singapore as a lab and a launchpad for growing businesses in fintech and financial inclusion. Singapore has likewise purported its intention to turn into a center of advanced network, adequately fostering computerized passageways with different nations within Asia and Latin America, where their organizations can take part in cross-line exchanges within common understandings of information security and online business guidelines.

Commendably, within some high level economies, COVID-19 alleviation measures have catalyzed the execution of strategies, including those intended to address housing reasonableness and admittance to childcare, that are intended to battle fundamental income inequality. As nations change from help to recuperation, and strategy producers weigh up possibilities for bolstering homegrown work, it's a given that demand for some positions within tradeable administrations is verifiably associated with the suitability of fare markets.

Along these lines, the capacity to underpin and reestablish trade attaches with exchange, for example, that as of late directed between the US and the EU-is integral to sustainable homegrown development. Also, in the domain of non-tradable administrations, imaginative strategies to incentivize corporate and private investment in reskilling, upskilling and learning for working are totally basic - fundamentally, segueing from investing in fixed money to human resources. Amplifying intensity and improving efficiency in both tradable and non-tradable areas can likewise be upgraded by infrastructure spending and investment, in hard and delicate areas.

In the domain of non-tradable administrations, inventive strategies to incentivize corporate and private investment in reskilling, upskilling, and learning for working are totally basic - fundamentally, segueing from investing in fixed money to human resources.

REFERENCES

Baldwin & Freeman. (2020). Supply Chain Contagion Waves: Thinking Ahead on Manufacturing 'Contagion and Reinfection' from the COVID Concussion. In *The COVID concussion and supply-chain contagion waves*. voxeu.org

Bohra. (2011). Foreign Direct Investment in India's Service Sector: An Analysis. *Conference: Energizing Economies through Business and Technology Excellence, 4*(1), 23-30.

Brahma, M., & Gupta, R. (2018). Impact of National and International Institution on the Behavior of Indian Stock Market in Indian Economy. *International Journal of Creative Research Thoughts*, *6*(2), 833–838.

Chaudhary. (2015). Globalization and Education. *Globus Journal of Progressive Education, 6*(1), 1-6.

Correia, S., Luck, S., & Verner, E. (2020). Fight the Pandemic, Save the Economy: Lessons from the 1918 Flu. The Economic Historian. economic-historian.com

Gupta, R. (2008). Information Security: An Economic Perspective. In Business and Competitive Dynamics. Macmillan India Limited.

Jayant. (2018). Impact of Agriculture and FDI Inflows in Different Sector. *Globus: An International Journal of Management & IT, 10*(1), 1-3.

Kumar, P. (2009). Convergence of Rural Marketing Strategies and Trends in Developing Economics. *Globus An International Journal of Management and IT*, *1*(1), 61–66.

McKibbin, W., & Fernando, R. (2020). The Economic Impact of COVID-19. *Economics in The Time of COVID-19*, 45-51.

Naveen & Agarwal. (2016). Social Media & Academic Performances: An Empirical Analysis. *Cosmos An International Journal of Art & Higher Education*, *5*(2), 5–7.

Pradhan & Anup. (2018). Problems Facing Indian Economy. *Cosmos An International Journal of Art & Higher Education*, *7*(1), 12–15.

Rao & Raja. (2018). Mutual Fund Industry and Market Scenario of India. *Globus An International Journal of Management & IT*, *9*(2), 1-3.

Singh, A. (2011). Foreign Direct Investment (FDI) In India Service Sector (A Study of Post Liberalization). *International Journal of Economic Research*, *2*(2), 10–18.

Sudhakar, S. (2014). Growth of Retail Industry in India. *Globus An International Journal of Management & IT*, *6*(1), 1–4.

Yadav, A.,, & Dwivedi, P. K. (2016). Model Based on the Utilization of Utilitarian Documentation. *Cosmos An International Journal of Management*, *5*(2), 1–3.

KEY TERMS AND DEFINITIONS

ASEAN: Association of Southeast Asian Nations.

EA: East Asian Economies.

Economic Growth: Increase in the production of economic goods and services, compared from one period of time to another.

MENA: Middle East and North Africa.

SA: South Asia.

SSA: Sub-Saharan Africa.

Chapter 4
The New Face of Global Trade in a Post-Pandemic World

Muhammad Irfan Khan
Jinnah University for Women, Pakistan

Syed Imran Zaman
Jinnah University for Women, Pakistan

ABSTRACT

The COVID-19 pandemic has raised serious questions about the applicability of international trade theories. International trade has now changed its shape due to this novel coronavirus. It is a fact that no country in the world follows one trade theory. They use multiple theories for their goods and services and will continue to do so. The future of international trade theories is suspected as to which theory will be employed or any new theory of international trade will emerge. Empirical evidence illustrates the emergence of regionalization as compared to globalization. In this context, trade theories will also adjust their forms and assumptions. Therefore, this chapter reconciles international trade theories with actual data, most notably COVID-19.

INTRODUCTION

The term "globalization" was first coined by an American journalist Theodore Levitt which economist Kinichi Ohmae further disseminated in 1988 in a study of the global strategies of multinational firms. This term delineates the international process of strengthening the goods, information and production requirements movements, particularly capital and financial instruments. Many are motivated to consider that globalization is simply an advanced phase of the development of capitalism. Globalization and capitalism are very much connected. As such, for Robinson (2004), the five-hundred-year process of capitalist expansion constitutes the definition of globalization, with the current period distinguished as being qualitatively and quantitatively different from its predecessors.

DOI: 10.4018/978-1-7998-8705-8.ch004

Capitalism is considered an economic system where the property is owned and controlled by private actors as per their interests and demand, fix prices in markets liberally to satisfy society's best interests. The same still exists as the economic system almost in all countries of the world.

Like all past crises, the current pandemic situation of COVID-19 has exposed several vulnerabilities concerning international trade (Aylor et al., 2020). The pandemic also illustrates a massive exogenous change to the global system (Buckly, 2020). Policymakers, academicians and practitioners have begun predicting the future of international trade more regional than global, forecasting the phenomenon of de-globalization. They argue that the global supply chain will shrink, and countries will start building up resilience. Economic prosperity for a country is very much dependent on international trade.

On January 24, 2019, The Economist showed that

The new world will work differently. Globalization will lead to deeper links within regional blocs. Supply chains in North America, Europe and Asia are sourcing more from closer to home. In Asia and Europe, most trade is already intra-regional, and the share has risen since 2011.

On December 10, 2020, The Financial Times showed that

The plausible future is not that international exchange is going to die. However, it is likely to become more regional and more virtual.

Regional trade was already at work before the COVID-19 pandemic. After the financial crisis of 2008, the year 2019 reached its lowest level of international trade. At the same time, neighboring countries started trade of goods and services which increased from 10% to 18% over the last two decades. This opens a new question of impacting international trade because of COVID-19 or the past crisis (Baldwin & Tomiura, 2020). The World Trade Organization explains that regional trade agreements have increased from less than 100 to 500. Based on reciprocal trade agreements, partner countries are now trading with each other, which increases the pie of regional trade.

The debates remains unanswered about the future of international trade. Is it a new phenomenon about the scope of regionalization? Is it the end of globalization? Is it the start of a new form of globalization? These answers are open for all researchers, policymakers and practitioners to find.

Although the prediction of regionalization is strong, international trade theories still exist. No one can deny the importance of these theories, which shows that theories will remain there but with their modified forms. One may alter the existing theories and design a new theory, stating the transition from globalization to localization. Fontaine (2020) stated that there would be a significant shift in corporation strategies and managerial thinking to avoid risk, nationalism, and protectionism in a post-pandemic world.

Before discussing the future of international trade, we must focus our attention on discussing some of the terminologies used in international trade perspectives. The theories of international trade will be discussed then in order to refresh our understanding of them.

GLOBALIZATION, INTERNATIONALIZATION, LOCALIZATION

Globalization, internationalization and localization all seem similar, and in fact, they are often used interchangeably. However, minor differences distinguish them. Recognizing the distinctions is critical for anybody charged with assisting a business in "going global" — and ensuring their marketing message resonates worldwide.

Scholars developed the acronym GILT (globalisation, internationalisation, localization, and translation) to refer to the practices that companies engage in when they diversified enough outside national boundaries. We will compare and contrast globalisation, internationalisation, and localization, highlighting some of the major drawbacks associated with each.

Gobalization: What is It?

Globalization is defined as any action that brings together the people, cultures, and economies of other nations. Globalization is a business phrase that refers to the processes through which companies strengthen their ties to their international consumers. This encompasses all aspects of doing business in diverse national markets, from product creation to marketing.

Examples of Globalization

If you're still uncertain, consider the following corporate globalisation examples: Online marketplaces such as eBay and Amazon make it simple to purchase goods from companies and people worldwide. Even goods sold at conventional brick-and-mortar shops like Target often travel through several countries on their way to their final destinations. Consumer gadgets, for example, are often obtained from India's raw resources, manufactured in China, and then marketed in the United States. Numerous multinational food companies, such as McDonald's, have operations in dozens of countries. McDonald's, for example, has franchises in over a hundred countries, and customers around the globe are acquainted with the brand and emblem.

Netflix is available in over 190 countries and tailors its content offerings, including subtitles and programmes in regional languages, to each market. Nike's immediately recognisable "swoosh" emblem is instantly recognisable across the world and in every language. Nike has partnered with players from a range of sports and nations, using their sponsorships to drive Nike's global growth.

Globalization has a plethora of advantages for businesses and consumers alike. Global connection has significantly benefited the world economy over the past few decades, increasing global GDP from $89.6 trillion in 2010 to a predicted $149 trillion in 2021. Globalization occurred along with the twentieth century's most transformative technologies, such as international air travel and the Internet.

The growth of globalisation also means that there has almost likely never been a better moment to convert a small firm into a multinational one. There are many possibilities for businesses to expand, ranging from greater access to a global talent pool to an expanded amount of data available for positioning a company. With increased ease of entry into new markets, there are also more product niches to exploit—and more consumers to entice.

On the other hand, true globalisation requires significant planning. Localizing and internationalising your product are critical stages in this process. While both localisation and internationalisation are synonymous with globalisation, they have significant distinctions. These will be discussed in more detail in the following sections.

What is Corporate Globalization

Corporate globalisation is the process through which national economies become more intertwined with the global economy via technological advancements, trade and investment laws, and privatisation. These policies lower trade and investment obstacles, weakening nation states' and communities' democratic control over their economic issues. The process is accelerated by big companies' aggressive lobbying of governments, which use the notion of comparative advantage, the aim of international competitiveness, and the growth model to maximise profits. It is taking place gradually, at the cost of social, environmental, and labour reforms, as well as growing inequality for the vast majority of the world's people.

It is critical to distinguish between a worldwide flow of technology, ideas, and information intended towards rebuilding sustainable local communities (what we call supportive internationalism) and the globalisation process. The latter is essentially the gradual removal of obstacles to the flow of commodities and money via international trade regulations developed by and for big business. It sets one country against another, one community against another, and one worker against another. That is the goal, since such a structure and procedure are needed to maximise profit. Internationalism is defined as the worldwide movement of ideas, technology, information, culture, money, and commodities to sustain and reconstruct local economies. Its main goal is not to save money, but to work together for the greater benefit.

Linguistic clarity is essential because globalisation proponents and beneficiaries exploit the apparent advantages of such constructive international flows to excuse the destructive process of corporate globalisation. Typically, this deceptive strategy is backed with the promise that the development of globalisation would eventually benefit the people.

What Exactly is Internationalization?

When it comes to internationalisation, making goods and services as flexible as feasible is a key part of the plan. This often necessitates consulting with specialists in the field. The phrase "i18n," which alludes to the term's character count of 18, is often used to abbreviate internationalisation.

Most products that are meant to be used by a global audience go through an internationalisation process. For example, IKEA's furniture assembly instructions exclude all English in favour of schematics and pictures, internationalising their product. Despite this, cultural neutrality is frequently a goal when developing products that need translation. Naturally, it's a lot simpler to say than accomplish.

Numerous issues arise as a result of software and electronics industry internationalisation. In most Western European languages, the ASCII character encoding is adequate. Russian, Chinese, Hindi, and Korean, which all use non-Latin alphabets, need bigger character encodings like Unicode. Providing assistance with hardware devices: Because not all hardware devices are available everywhere, software developers must take this into consideration. An application's user interface must be able to display text in each language in which it is available if it is translated into several languages. Most definitions state that businesses must first go global before becoming local when localising their goods. Internationalisation vs. localization will be discussed in detail in the next section

What Exactly is Localization?

The process of tailoring a product to a certain market is known as localization. This is more often the case after a company's internationalisation. Globalisation produces a product that is flexible to many different audiences in many different nations, but localization turns that product into something that is highly relevant to a certain market.

By placing a focus on the local, the practise of localization works to offset the effects of globalisation. If the situation calls for it, the term "local" may refer to either a part of the nation-state or a regional grouping of nation-states. Strategies for localization provide local and national governments greater economic authority. If community cohesiveness is improved, poverty and inequality are reduced, and livelihoods and social infrastructure are enhanced while environmental protection is enhanced as well, then the crucial feeling of security will be increased.

In fact, the new localist focus on global assistance and trade laws supports these, not restricting the flow of information, technology, commerce and investment, management and legal frameworks that enable localization. These transfers are also necessary for a smooth shift from globalisation to localization to take place. A new economic and legal framework will allow individuals, community organisations and companies to diversify their local economies without returning to authoritarian state control.

To reiterate what we said before, McDonald's operates about 30,000 locations in over 100 countries. Its globalisation may be seen in its rapid growth throughout the globe. The company develops a menu that takes regional preferences and traditions into consideration. This approach exemplifies internationalisation.

Kosher food and drinks are available at several McDonald's locations in Israel, which are open only on Sabbath and Jewish festivals. In India, where a large portion of the population abstains from beef and pig eating, McDonald's has also established a meat-free restaurant. The worldwide brand identity of McDonald's has been preserved in both instances, while adjusting its goods and services to local markets. This is an illustration of how something may be localised.

Local to Global

Governmental roles and obligations have been redefined during the last three decades as a result of globalization's winds of change. However, given the intricacy of globalization's interactions across many domains, globalisation governance has emerged as a challenging task. The three primary areas were economic (related to liberalisation), political (related to democracy), and cultural (related to universalization) contacts, with war and diplomacy included in the political exchanges. Globalization has altered the nature, context, and scope of threats, in addition to a variety of other issues. Conflicts between fragmentation and integration, as well as between localization and globalisation, have grown increasingly apparent during the past decade. In recent years, nationalist and protectionist movements have clashed directly with globalisation forces, blurring the line between global and local. For large businesses, the choice between building and/or maintaining manufacturing and research and development facilities in many locations across the globe versus doing so locally has become increasingly difficult.

There has been much debate over the last two months on the potential impact of COVID19 on globalisation itself. Apart from trade wars/barriers, the importance of new restrictions has been highlighted. National and local self-sufficiency has been a major facilitator of subsistence and economic activities in some areas throughout these trying times. The decentralisation of industrial and commercial activities has been emphasised as an early lesson. Migration as a result of a lack of opportunities in one's native location, particularly from rural to metropolitan regions, has exacerbated response issues while substantially increasing new and additional unemployment.

Global vs. Local

Societies and economics have never been closer or more linked than now, and the coronavirus has highlighted those linkages even more. After the rise of populism and protectionism, which has been followed, to some degree, by Brexit, globalization now confronts its greatest threat. Is globalization 5.0 a possibility? The new coronavirus is causing extraordinary levels of worldwide malfunction. If difficulties were to be anticipated globally in the beginning due to its effect on the Chinese economy and disruption in the supply chain, the global economy and people's lives across the globe are now in jeopardy. Due to the epidemic, the Organization for Economic Cooperation and Development (OECD) predicts that the global economy will expand at its weakest rate since 2009. The forecasted growth rate of 2.9 percent has been reduced to 2.4 percent. In the event of a longer-lasting and more intense coronavirus epidemic in Asia-Pacific, Europe, or North America, the OECD predicts that global growth will fall to 1.5 percent in 2020. This forecast is now getting closer to being a reality. The stock market is being severely impacted. Since the epidemic started, markets in London, New York, and Tokyo have seen significant declines. On March 16, Wall Street saw its most significant one-day drop since 1987's Black Monday.

The epidemic has given a severe setback to an already troubled globalization process. This is demonstrated by a reduction in the flow of people and commodities, the closure of the EU; trade restrictions; and mistrust of outsiders. Global supply networks have been disrupted, and the ensuing economic crisis will reduce global commerce. As the fragility of the global supply chain was recently revealed, the legacy of the crisis may be an attempt by several countries to bring manufacturing back home. Although this should be a period of collaboration, nation-states and their choices will determine the degree of cooperation. In many European and Asian nations, turning inward was already part of the conversation. With the current crisis, I anticipate these tendencies to gain even more traction. There are many indications of a reaction against globalization.

There has never been a time when the globe is so interconnected. Innovation has created many worldwide opportunities for both big and small companies during the past 15 years. This new technical advancement, on the other hand, brings with it a host of new issues. Globalization and localization are two terms that must be distinguished from one another if you want to be successful in business today. Any business plan must be adjusted based on the culture of the target market.

It takes time and effort to break into a new market, from creating a market entrance plan to establishing a strong client base. As in the case of Asia or South America, the launch of a brand in a new market requires careful preparation. This can help you avoid mistakes and work through any linguistic, cultural, or legal issues that may arise. In order to select and execute the most successful methods without sacrificing your brand or image, you need more knowledge about your target customers.

Understanding your adversary is the first step toward a successful growth into emerging markets. If you are unable to differentiate between globalisation and localization, developing a cohesive plan and preparing your business for many markets will be difficult.

When done properly, extending your business into emerging nations may open up many opportunities for growth for your company. Consider the following critical differences when considering globalisation, internationalisation, and localization.

THEORIES OF INTERNATIONAL TRADE

Voluntary interchange of goods, services, assets or money between two people or entities is a concept of trade. International trade is a notion of this interchange between individuals or entities in two different nations. International trade theories are various theories to explain international trade, as depicted in figure 1.

Figure 1. International trade theories. Source: Author

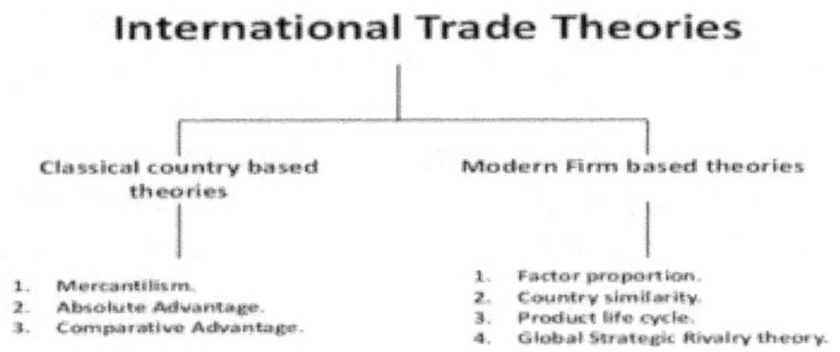

CLASSICAL OR COUNTRY-BASED TRADE THEORIES

Mercantilism

This economic system primarily concentrates on exports of goods and services, accumulating silver, and improving a country's wealth and control. This economic system assumes all individuals of society to be nationalistic and should be in the control of the administration. Furthermore, if any condition arises, they would restrain individuals from purchasing wealthy merchandise to avoid the wastage of a large number of resources and wealth.

It was the dominant ideology in all Europe from the 15th to 18th century, which replaced the Feudal economic system. The center of mercantilism was France and England. Mercantilists designed various policies at that time, including high tariffs, limiting wages, maximizing domestic resources, monopolizing the market, and many more to enhance exports and minimize imports. Adam Smith was the first scholar who rejected the concept of mercantilism and provided logical reasons to reject it.

Criticism

The system was criticized and rejected for many reasons. Some of the intense criticism is as follows.

It heavily focuses on accumulating money, gold and silver. It was the fact that gold and silver were considered wealth in the Mercantilism economic system due to limited availability. Scholars believe that money is only a medium of exchange and cannot be treated as wealth.

Mercantilism also did not emphasize the balance of trade. It only focuses on imports and does not motivate countries to become importers. How is it possible for all countries to become exporters without being importers?

State regulation for all commercial and economic activities was another criticism. This system mainly focuses on agriculture as the only productive activity, emphasizing commerce and manufacturing. Adam Smith and several French scholars were included to criticize it.

Absolute Advantage

In the context of international trade, the idea of absolute advantage was first coined by the Scottish economist Adam Smith in 1776 in response to Mercantilism economic system. He rejected mercantilism and argued that countries' absolute advantages in different commodities might simultaneously help gain imports and exports, building the unhampered international trade. He assumed that labor cannot move from one country to another country and that a country can benefit from a lower cost of production in any commodity compared to the cost of the same commodity in another country.

With this point of view, he argued that a country should import goods from abroad to be efficiently manufactured as this permits the importing country to employ its resources in its productive, efficient industries. He posed that technology is the central determinant in international trade between the two countries.

Criticism

It assumes that bilateral trade can take place only between two countries and in two commodities. Over time, when the needs and requirements of human beings started increasing, the idea of multilateral trade came into being, and the theory of absolute advantage was challenged.

Comparative Advantage

David Racardo coined the comparative advantage theory of international trade in 1817 to elucidate why international trade among countries exists. He argued that countries might enhance their overall consumption through exports of goods in which it enjoys comparative advantage while importing other goods, subject to the condition that there are differences in labor productivity between the two counties.

Comparative advantage is defined in terms of being more cost-efficient than another country.

It is generally argued that world output may be increased if countries apply the principles of comparative advantage.

MODERN FIRM-BASED THEORIES

As opposed to country-based international trade theories, university professors developed firm-based theories after World War II. Unfortunately, country-based theories could not address firms level variables like technology, quality, customer loyalty, and other product and service factors.

Country Similarity

Steffan Linder pioneered intra-industry trade in 1961 and coined the phrase. Customers in equivalent phases of development may have similar preferences, according to Linder's theory. Firm-based research also suggests that companies start out by creating for the local market's needs first. Exporting companies often find markets with similar customer inclinations to those in their native country. According to Linder's theory, manufactured goods are exchanged most of the time between countries with per capita incomes that are about similar, and there is also a lot of trade within industries themselves. Consumers' decision-making and purchasing behaviours are heavily influenced by the repute of the brands and goods they're considering.

Product Life Cycle

In the 1960s, Raymond Vernon, a Harvard Business School professor, created the idea. According to the idea, a product goes through three different stages:

1. New Product.
2. Maturing Product.
3. Standardized Product.

The concept presupposed that newly created products would be entirely produced in the country in which they were conceived. The theory was perfect for shedding light on the 1960s industrial supremacy of the United States. The United States was the world's biggest manufacturer in a number of areas after World War II.

Additionally, the concept has been used to illustrate the completion of the personal computer (PC) product cycle. The personal computer was a new idea in the 1970s. Throughout the 1980s and 1990s, it was refined into a mature product. The product has reached a level of standardisation, with the bulk of manufacture and production occurring in low-cost countries such as Asia and Mexico.

Global Strategic Rivalry

Global Strategic Rivalry Theory emerged in the 1980s as a consequence of research conducted by Paul Krugman and Kelvin Lancaster. The concept put an emphasis on multinational corporations and their attempts to acquire a competitive advantage over other multinational corporations operating in their industry. Businesses will confront global competition in their respective industries, and they must develop competitive advantages in order to survive. The acute ways in which companies may maintain a competitive advantage are referred to as the industry's entry barriers. The phrase "barriers to entry" refers to the challenges encountered by a new company while trying to enter an industry or a new market. Firms may seek to minimise entry barriers via a variety of strategies, including economies of scale, research and development, and ownership of intellectual property rights.

Porter's National Competitive Advantage

The development of different theories of international commerce compelled several academics to dig further. In 1990, Michael Porter was one of those who created a new paradigm for defining national competitive advantage.

National Competitive Advantage thesis highlighted an industry's ability for innovation and upgrading, which results in a nation's competitiveness in that industry. His thesis centred on elucidating why certain nations are more competitive than others in any given sector. He identified four key variables that are inextricably connected.

1. Domestic market capabilities and resources
2. Demand conditions in the domestic market
3. Domestic suppliers and industries that complement one another
4. Characteristics of domestic firms.

EFFECT OF COVID-19 ON ECONOMY AND TRADE

Since the start of the COVID-19 pandemic in March 2020, the global economy has been in shambles due to the ensuing health and economic shocks. To cope with the epidemic, governments across the globe placed severe restrictions on people's mobility, foreign travel, and the transfer of products and services to reduce the danger to health and safety. As a result, many companies and organizations have been forced to close or operate at reduced capacity, and the consequences can be seen worldwide. Whether it is the news of considerable losses in the aviation sector, millions of people losing their jobs, or tiny businesses going out of business forever, the effect of the novel coronavirus on our global economy is massive. Figure 2 shows the international trade pattern from 2006 to 2021.

Several nations have become too reliant on their trade partners and fail to satisfy domestic consumer needs to make things worse. When nations participate in international conflicts, the trade imbalance and over-reliance issue becomes even more troublesome. Consider the current trade conflict between Australia and China. China has slapped an 80% tax on Australian barley imports in response to Canberra's demand for an independent inquiry into the origins of the COVID-19 epidemic. This will cost Australian farmers an estimated AU$500 million each year. In reaction to Beijing's decision, Australia has vowed to file an appeal with the World Trade Organization (WTO), believing that this is a bullying and coercion strategy designed to compel Australia to reconsider its demand for the coronavirus investigation.

CAN GOVERNMENTS BECOME DOMINANT?

Scholars generally agree that national governments will be the dominating player. According to academics, in the short run, the crisis strengthens governments in most nations because they take on greater responsibility and delve deeper into the lives of their people. It may also play an essential part in revitalizing the economy, as witnessed in the United States. On the other hand, it may call into question the state's ability to resolve the issue. Similarly, national unity discourses that diminish political differences and other contentious topics would strengthen administrations. As shown by the slanging match between the US and Chinese governments, the crisis is rapidly becoming a competition of political systems, and so far, China's social controls seem to be more successful than the somewhat chaotic and overburdened health systems of other nations. This will likely lead to many other nations wanting to imitate China — but probably not in Europe, where privacy concerns are considerably more significant.

Figure 2. Global Trade Trends. Source: UNCTAD secretariat calculations based on UNCTADSTAT and IMF data

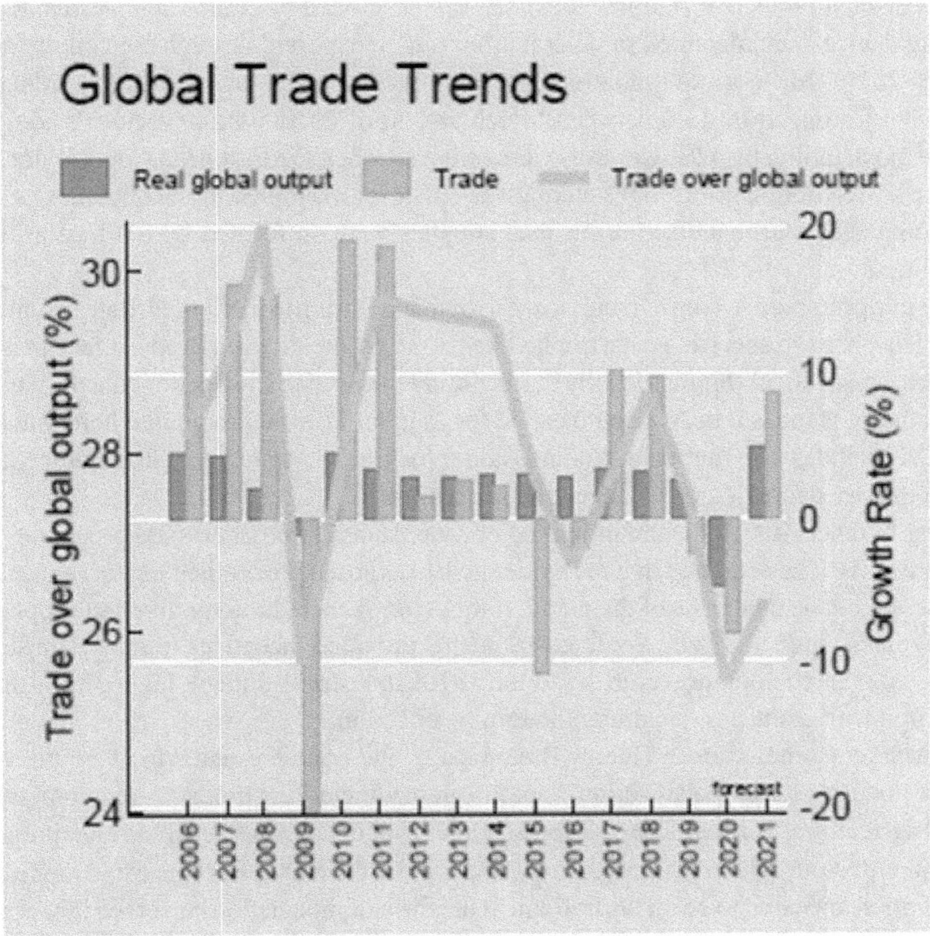

Examples from Europe

Economic liberals have exploited catastrophes to get unpalatable economic changes through. While it is true that catastrophes may cause a country's policies to shift, it is much more frequent for crises to have the opposite effect. Public expenditure and government authority tend to grow in reaction to a crisis, a terrorist attack, war, economic depressions, and even pandemics. Furthermore, there is human logic: when we are threatened, we want protection from the government. This also applies to trade protection, as the current epidemic exemplifies. It has been dubbed "disaster protectionism."

Consider Europe's first reaction to the epidemic. To keep the virus out, the European Union closed its external borders in March 2020, just as Europe had become the worldwide epicenter of the illness. For a while, commerce slowed to a halt, impacting the availability of food, labor, and hand sanitizers throughout the continent. Pfizer and BioNTech would not have been able to transport genetic material over the Atlantic Ocean to create the first effective Covid-19 vaccine if they had not had corporate aircraft access.

Meanwhile, additional barriers were constructed inside the union, restricting free movement and occasionally preventing people from returning to their home nation after losing employment during lockdowns. Personal protective equipment exports are prohibited in France and Germany. France also began seizing devices manufactured in other nations and transported through the country by third parties in March 2020. Due to these limitations, internal EU commerce in the medical products required to treat Covid-19 dropped by 13% between March and April 2020, with oxygen treatment equipment suffering the most, falling by 42%. Controls were removed when the European Commission intervened, but other export restrictions were reinstated at the EU level, banning shipments unless a license was acquired. Companies that manufacture medical supplies were suffocated by red tape at a time when supply timeliness was critical.

The epidemic prompted strong demands to return manufacturing to the United States. Some lawmakers wondered, "How can we survive a catastrophe like this if we do not even produce face masks, surgical gloves, and pharmaceutical supplies locally?" According to German Chancellor Angela Merkel, most of this manufacturing is located in Asia, who called for "a pillar of local production here as well" in April 2020. Stella Kyriakides, the European Commissioner for Health, shared a similar sentiment: "we need to guarantee that we decrease our reliance on other nations."

According to others, the epidemic prompted new demands for broader trade protection — not only in medical products. They claimed that the epidemic had exposed how reliant nations and supply chains are on businesses on the other side of the world: if these suppliers reduced or diverted supplies, wouldn't our assembly lines come to a halt? Some governments provided incentives to repatriate supply chains and develop national champions, reverting to the 1970s industrial strategy. Figure 3 illustrates import and exports trends of countries, including the European Union.

Internal Market Commissioner Thierry Breton said, "the issue presented to us by this crisis is that we may have gone too far in globalization," not just in medicines and protective equipment, but also in industry and agriculture. Furthermore, as a foreshadowing of the policies he would later propose, Breton, said, "I am sure that our relationship with the world will be different after this catastrophe." Moreover, just as the solution appeared to be on the horizon in the form of inoculations invented through worldwide collaborative efforts and the global data flow, the EU fallen victim to vaccine patriotism, raising the possibility of prohibiting exports of vaccines manufactured within the union and even trying to threaten a physical border between Ireland and Northern Ireland for a brief instant.

When the international collaboration was most required, Europe's image as a champion of free markets and the rule of law in international affairs was harmed. Developing nations who have opened their economy to the EU are now doubting the EU's future reliability as a provider of critical medical equipment. Pharmaceutical firms wonder whether they should move to smaller nations where there is no motive to obstruct exports.

This was, unfortunately, a foregone conclusion. In times of crisis, societies often respond with a fight-or-flight response. We choose conflicts with some and create scapegoats of others, whether immigrants, neighboring nations, or pharmaceutical corporations. Some politicians prefer to hide behind walls, while others want to hide behind trade obstacles. When the danger was predators and roaming bandits, instinctively hurrying to protect the perimeter may have made sense. However, in a complex global economy, when the resources needed to address social issues are dispersed throughout the globe, we must not target foreigners. Furthermore, when the shared adversary is a virus, wouldn't it be preferable to collaborate with outsiders to get more information and develop better solutions? Moreover, wasn't it the EU's spiritual foundation?

Figure 3. Imports and exports trends of major economies. Source: UNCTAD calculation based on national statistics. Year-over-year growth rate. Excludes intra-European Union trade

Import and Exports trends of major economies

Imports	January	February	March	April	May	June	July	August	September
Brazil	-1	5	11	-15	-11	-20	-35	-29	-25
China	-7	-10	-1	-14	-17	3	-1	-2	13
European Union	-3	-7	-12	-26	-28	-12	-15	-10	-2
India	0	4	-28	-60	-51	-48	-30	-26	-20
Japan	-5	-13	-1	-3	-25	-14	-21	-21	-14
Republic of Korea	-5	1	0	-16	-21	-11	-12	-16	1
Russian Federation	4	2	-2	-20	-13	-4	-13	-11	-3
South Africa	-3	-4	-17	-38	-40	-43	-39	-31	-15
United States	-4	-4	-7	-21	-25	-13	-8	-5	0

Exports	January	February	March	April	May	June	July	August	September
Brazil	-19	-1	5	-9	-15	-5	-3	-11	-10
China	-22	-10	-7	3	-3	1	7	9	10
European Union	-2	-3	-8	-31	-32	-9	-10	-9	3
India	-1	4	-34	-61	-35	-12	-10	-13	4
Japan	-4	0	-8	-19	-27	-25	-18	-15	-3
Republic of Korea	-7	4	-2	-26	-24	-11	-7	-10	7
Russian Federation	-2	-18	-20	-33	-36	-26	-28	-32	-14
South Africa	10	6	-1	-61	-28	-6	-14	-3	10
United States	0	2	-9	-29	-36	-24	-15	-15	-9

DIFFERENT APPROACHES IN GLOBALIZATION, LOCALIZATION AND INTERNATIONALIZATION CONTEXT

Globalization (G11n)

This mostly relates to your business's plan for growing outside national boundaries. It encompasses the procedures that teach you about international and domestic law, how to create a global business environment, and how to effectively collaborate with international partners. Globalization is identical with internationalisation and localization, since it encompasses any attempt to grow your company.

Localization (L10n)

Localization (L10n) is the act of tailoring your product to regional markets via the addition of a more local tone and feel. It entails more than just translating your text. To develop a product that meets people' expectations, it is necessary to consider factors such as culture, religion, and local preferences. Localization entails altering many aspects of your product, such as currency, time format, colours, and symbols, as well as any other characteristic that may seem strange to your target audience. As can be seen, each of globalisation, internationalisation, and localization has its own distinct characteristics. Each of these ideas, however, is important when approaching developing markets. By missing any stage, you risk falling behind and jeopardising your ability to build a strong worldwide brand.

A Few Words about Internationalization (I18n)

Internationalization (I18n) is the process of creating a product that is localizable as part of a business's worldwide strategy. This involves designing and creating a market-specific website, game, application, software, or other product. This is a collection of technological characteristics that make it easier to adjust your product to the preferences of a new audience. Internationalization is a necessary step prior to localisation. Consider the ways in which an i18n manager may assist you in obtaining the finest results.

Is There a Difference between Localizing for Asia and Localizing for Europe?

True and false. Translation and localisation for Asian nations is challenging due to the substantial cultural variations across target markets. We're discussing countries that operate according to their own set of laws, which may be confusing to Westerners at times. In nations such as China and India, international investors continue to encounter significant limitations. As a result, you may need local partners to assist you in strengthening your market presence. Additionally, tailoring your product and promotion to any of these nations is challenging since you are selling to individuals with varying values, beliefs, and consumption patterns.

It takes longer to translate into simplified Chinese or Hindi than it does to translate into German or Spanish. You'll need to work with indigenous experts and linguists to ensure that the correct information is delivered without hurting indigenous customs. For instance, across Asia, colours, iconography, and symbols all have their own distinct meanings. You will be unable to grow into Asia if you break local laws. On the other hand, each market's localization follows the same procedures. To achieve globalisation, your product must remain internationally compatible. Whether you're entering Germany, Italy, or China, you'll need a well-thought-out strategy and a product that adapts to the local market.

Last Words on Globalization vs. Localization

Understanding the distinction between globalisation and localization, as well as their relationship to internationalisation, may assist you in developing a consistent worldwide strategy. These lengthy and complex phrases convey a simple message: think globally, act locally. To achieve effective translation, you must strike a balance between your worldwide brand and the regionally targeted versions. It is simpler when dealing with countries that have a similar cultural history, but becomes more challenging when dealing with nations that hold different views on life.

Identifying reliable partners and solutions – such as a translation management system – to assist you with your internationalisation campaign may help expedite the process and improve the return on your marketing expenditures. Collaborating with specialists who are intimately acquainted with target markets may help you create a great first impression, regardless of whether you're localising an app, software, game, or other product.

The Top Emerging Markets to Watch in 2020

As your company grows into new nations, you become a part of a developing infrastructure that enables you to have a worldwide presence and diversify your client base. Not all markets, however, are a suitable match for your business. Depending on the business and intended audience, some nations may be more beneficial than others. Analyze prospective markets and focus on those with a high chance of purchasing your goods or services.

If you already have a small international following, keep track of where your existing audience comes from. It's a great way to choose where to begin developing your business. Conduct an in-depth analysis of each target market–create customer profiles, assess competitors, and make educated guesses about how cultural differences, taxes, and financial regulations will impact your business.

Do You Have What it Takes to Localize for Asia?

To begin, it is better to have a small number of nations. In 2020, India, Brazil, Thailand, and China seem to be the developing markets that investors are most interested in. Three of these nations are in Asia, which means you should be prepared to sell to individuals with a diverse range of religious and cultural views. You'll need to adjust your brand and goods to a market with few or no ties to the West. China, for instance, has the world's second largest economy and is the world's largest trader. By 2030, up to 70% of the country's population will be urban middle-class–people with significant buying power who adore the Western world but have strong connections to indigenous culture. Thailand has been awarded the "best nation in which to establish a company" for the second year in a row, after 2016 and 2017. The local economy is expanding steadily, resulting in low unemployment and inflation.

India is another Asian nation that is quickly growing. By 2020, the local economy will be worth $5.6 trillion. The consumer industry is worth $1.2 trillion at the moment, suggesting that businesses of all sizes have room to expand. India has the ability to substantially boost your income and firmly solidify your worldwide position with a well-executed localization plan. Entering any of these areas (or even Brazil) requires a well-thought-out plan. Local people are resistant to change unless regular marketing attempts in their native languages are made. To capture a significant portion of the market, your product, website, and marketing approach must be localised.

FUTURE OUTLOOK

The purpose of this chapter is to reconcile international trade theories with actual data, most notably COVID-19. Theories just assist academics, economists, governments, and business leaders in comprehending how to develop, manage, and control international commerce. Often, these ideas contradict actual events.

Typically, nations lack absolute advantages in a number of manufacturing and/or service sectors. Likewise, this is true of the elements of production. America has an abundance of arable land that may be used to grow a variety of agricultural goods. Additionally, there is no difficulty in obtaining capital. Although its labour market is not the cheapest in the world, it is one of the most advanced. These advantages in the factors of production resulted in the United States being the world's most powerful and wealthy economy. Nonetheless, the United States imports a large number of goods and services because its consumers spend their wealth on their needs and desires, and the majority of these goods and services are now manufactured in countries other than the United States that have sought to create comparative advantages through low labour, land, or manufacturing costs.

By 2023, bilateral commerce between the United States and China will be less than it was in 2019. By 2023, the EU's trade with China would be decreased, while trade with India will be flat (Aylor et al. 2020).

As a result, it remains unclear which international trade theory is dominating globally. In practise, businesses and governments use a combination of these ideas to deduce patterns and formulate a plan. These ideas have developed significantly during the last five hundred years. They will continue to evolve and adapt as new drivers of international commerce become apparent.

CONCLUSION

The chapter discussed the importance of international trade with respect to the COVID-19 pandemic. The globalization tends to an end has become a debatable topic. The world has witnessed the importance of regionalization which is hitting the importance of international trade with reference to globalization. International trade theories need to be revisited specially, in this pandemic situation. Which international trade theory is or will be dominant need to be studied. Is there any chance of emerging a new international trade theory is also questionable.

REFERENCES

Aylor, B., DeFauw, M., Gilbert, M., Knizek, C., Lang, N., Koch-Weser, J., & McAdoo, M. (2020). *Re-drawing the map of global trade*. Boston Consulting Group. https:// www.bcg.com/publications/2020/ redrawing-the-map-ofglobal-trade

Baldwin, R., & Tomiura, E. (2020). Thinking ahead about the trade impact of COVID-19. Economics in the Time of COVID-19, 59–72.

Blecker, R. (1999). *Taming Global Finance: A Better Architecture for Growth and Equity*. Economic Policy Institute.

Buckley, P. J. (2020). The theory and empirics of the structural reshaping of globalization. *Journal of International Business Studies, 51*(9), 1580–1592. doi:10.105741267-020-00355-5 PMID:32836503

Fontaine, R. (2020). Globalization will look very different after the coronavirus pandemic. *Foreign Policy*. https:// foreignpolicy.com/2020/04/17/globalization-trade-war-aftercoronavirus- pandemic/

Hines, C. (2000). *Localization—A Global Manifesto*. Earthscan.

International Society for Ecology and Culture. (1999). *From Global to Local—Resisting Monoculture, Rebuilding Community*. ISEC.

Lang, T., & Heasman, M. (2003). *Food Wars: The Battle for Mouths*. Minds and Markets.

Levitt. (1983). *The Globalization of Markets. Harvard Business Review Ohmae Kinichi (1988). Beyond national borders.* Kodansha International.

Mander & Goldsmith. (Eds.). (1996). *The Case Against the Global Economy*. San Francisco: Sierra Club Books.

McMichael, P. (2000). The Power of Food. *Agriculture and Human Values, 17*(1), 21–33. doi:10.1023/A:1007684827140

Norberg-Hodge, Merriªeld, & Gorelick. (2002). Bringing the Food Economy Home: Local Alternatives to Global Agribusiness. London: Zed Press.

Princen, T. (2002). Distancing: Consumption and the Severing of Feedback. In T. Princen, M. Maniates, & K. Conca (Eds.), *Confronting Consumption*. MIT Press. doi:10.7551/mitpress/2097.003.0008

Robinson. (2004). A theory of global capitalism: Production class, and state in a transnational world. *International Journal on World Peace, 21*(2), 81-86.

United Nations Conference on Trade and Development. (2020). *Trade Trends under the COVID-19 Pandemic*. United Nations.

Wairdel, L. (2002). *Coffee with Pleasure: Just Java and World Trade*. Black Rose.

Chapter 5
An Exploratory Study on Personal Finance in the Context of COVID-19

José G. Vargas-Hernández
https://orcid.org/0000-0003-0938-4197
Instituto Tecnològico Mario Molina, Unidad Acadèmica de Zapopan, Mexico

ABSTRACT

The world is currently experiencing a dramatic crisis that has not yet reached bottom. In Mexico, in the second quarter of 2020, there was a drop in the gross domestic product of 18.9% compared to the same quarter of 2019. In this context, the objective is to identify types of personal expenses in households located in Culiacán, Sinaloa, Mexico as of July 15, 2020. The main results were that most of the respondents' budgets spend according to their income, have had no problem paying their bank loans on time, would consider a fund for future contingencies, have not purchased health insurance, have not bought a computer or cell phone, among other issues analyzed. The main findings are oriented to the fact that the studied population has not acquired additional medical insurance despite the pandemic. It is also concluded that the population under study has become aware of having savings for contingency funds and that digital life still shows resistance in making personal financial decisions.

INTRODUCTION

The present investigation arises from the need to know how spending is being oriented in the families of Culiacán, Sinaloa, Mexico, in the current macroeconomic context, which is not positive. The annual percentage variation in the first quarter 2020 in the United Mexican States was -1.28% and in Sinaloa it was -0.67%. Likewise, the quarterly indicator of state economic activity, base 2013, for Sinaloa is the percentage variation compared to the previous quarter of -0.2% and the percentage variation compared to the same quarter of the previous year is of -0.9%. Then, Mexico has had the worst drop in the Gross Domestic Product in the second quarter of 2020, at -18.9% compared to the quarter of the previous year,

DOI: 10.4018/978-1-7998-8705-8.ch005

comprising a drop in secondary activities of -26%, tertiary 15.6% and primary -0.3%, this, according to data published by the National Institute of Statistics and Geography (INEGI, 2020).

In relation to the economic effects of Covid-19, based on the survey on the expectations of specialists in private sector economics in June 2020 published by the Bank of Mexico, annual GDP growth is expected by 2020 be -8.8. % and for 2021 of 2.80%. Regarding the behavior of household income and expenditure published in 2018 in the National Survey of Household Income and Expenditure (ENIGH), of the INEGI, they show that in Mexico the average quarterly current income per household is higher than the expenditure quarterly average current, being 49,610 pesos and 31,913 pesos respectively.

Likewise, in Sinaloa, the income is 55,474 pesos and the expense is 32,643. In addition, according to data from the ENIGH in Mexico as well as in Sinaloa, where the most is spent on food, beverages, and tobacco, followed by transportation, acquisition, maintenance, accessories and services for vehicles, communications, later education services, educational articles, entertainment items and other entertainment expenses. The item of expenditure that is spent the least is in health.

Thus, the objective of this research is to identify types of personal expenses in households located in Culiacán, Sinaloa, Mexico as of July 15, 2020.

LITERATURE REVIEW

Finance is defined as the art and science of managing scarce financial resources, by individuals or legal entities with the objective of making decisions about income generation and application of cash expenses; and the percentage of expenses with respect to their income, the percentage of savings, and investment, framed these in the principle of maximization of wealth. Likewise, the purpose of personal finances is to achieve the well-being of the individual and for companies it is the generation of profits, how they are applied in the same business or if they are distributed among the partners. Finance management is mainly directed to the analysis and control of cash flows, considering the inflows and outflows of money, to generate solvency and face credit obligations and acquire assets to meet the established goals (Gilman & Sutter, 2016).

The purpose of personal finances is to analyze weekly, biweekly, or monthly consumption habits that allows establishing an action plan on these habits according to the priorities that are been set up. This is achieved with a "budget that determines how much you have and how much you can spend and save while maintaining balance" (Rodríguez-Raga, 2017, p. 7). Personal finances are also known as family finances, that is, it deals with the way in which money is earned to acquire their assets, how they save and interact in the financial system. The purpose is to support families to achieve financial security, some contextual issues are financial education, ability, and well-being. (Dew, 2016). For Chiodi in 2020, he asserts that what can be more controlled in personal finances are the outflows of money or expenses, compared to the inflows of cash. He recommends that each spending decision be taken long enough to evaluate.

An analysis of the state of the art on personal finance was carried out by López-García in 2016. The main finding was that the most relevant topic is the budget, this is the basis of adequate personal financial management. This tool makes it possible to determine the financial situation in each time, plan and manage the strategies to achieve compliance and define the control and evaluation mechanisms.

It is worth mentioning that Figueroa-Delgado (2009) also proposes that a budget be made of all income and monthly expenses, so as not to spend more than necessary. First, it is necessary to identify where the income comes from and what it is spent on. Usually the income in a family is wages, pension or retirement payments, interest or dividends and others. Expenses can be fixed or variable expenses. The former can be rent, mortgage, taxes, insurance, child care, elderly care, car payments, loans. Variable expenses for example are savings, utilities, food, transportation, gasoline, car maintenance, education, personal expenses, and entertainment. (p. 137).

Likewise, personal financial planning for Rojas-López, et al., 2017, deals with a dynamic process of activities oriented to action plans to satisfy currently and future needs of the individual. Its components are asset and investment management, indebtedness, cash income and expenses, commodities and cash management, risk management and insurance, tax and retirement, and succession. The budget consists of listing the income and expenses in a period, allowing to have control of expenses, identify potential problems before their occurrence and that they become unmanageable, adequately plan the future and thus be able to achieve personal goals of short, medium, and long term. All this is achieved with a budget of expenses lower than income and a rational management of debts, which allows to live with greater flexibility and peace of mind. Although savings are not really an expense, they play a central role in budgeting (Guthrie & Nicholls, 2015).

A key aspect is to have control of expenses, which can be divided into mandatory and unnecessary. The first correspond to those necessary to be able to lead a normal life, among which are the payment of the house (mortgage or rent), food, public services, transport, social security, and cleaning supplies. The latter are related to whims and cravings, which, although we should not completely avoid them, if it is necessary to have control over them, cited by (Villada, et al., 2018, p. 44). Thus, the financial statement on cash flow is another that can be applied in personal finance. A cash flow is the variation and cash equivalent, which results in the changes between increases and decreases in operating, investment, and financing activities (Duque-Sánchez, 2015, p. 74). It should be noted that this cash flow applied in organizations can be transferred to a family, for example the variations are the increases and decreases of investments or assets such as houses, land, cars, as well as financing or debts acquired for these investments.

In relation to operational activities, they are weekly, biweekly, or monthly expenses in relation to food, clothing, security, gasoline, water services, electricity, telephone, among others. Some other relevant personal finance topics according to Zapata-Lambraño (2020) are, first of all, thinking about personal goals that involve the management of financial resources, defining savings objectives, not falling into misleading or flashy offers, education and financial advice are essential, when making a financial decision think it over carefully, keep the money in a safe place until you know what will be done, future forecasts, do not make emotional panic purchases, define goals and meet them, do not be influenced by anyone outside on financial decisions, manage the cash on a budget, don't lend money, don't buy brands, and take responsibility for all financial decisions.

The topic of personal finance is underdeveloped in academia and therefore in scientific research. However, there are a variety of blogs and applications that can be useful when making decisions, among them, for example, they are published in CONDUSEF (National Council of Users of financial services) in the case of Mexico. Likewise, an investigation was carried out by Hoffmann, & Otteby, in 2017, who found that the use of blogs could be a positive alternative of financial education for advice on personal finances and efficient decision-making.

Finally, it should be mentioned that in relation to how to make decisions in pandemic contexts such as the current one, Amat (2020), affirms in his work that the measures when in a crisis, is to rescue people, companies and sectors most affected and vulnerable; recognize the strengths of the staff and above all efficiently manage the cash flow and profit margin; This has an impact on economic reactivation and job creation.

MATERIALS AND METHODS

The study presented is exploratory, on how they decided on their personal finances in this context of the covid-19 pandemic. A survey was applied using Google forms, shared through social networks to the contacts of the person in charge of this study, and it was addressed to heads of household from June 29 to July 15, 2020. The instrument consisted of 48 research variables that were related to some elements of personal finances assumed as family expenses. It is presented in Table 1 the questions that were applied with the number of the respective variable.

The survey items compiled an exploratory study on personal finance elements exposed by Figueroa-Delgado in 2009, who classifies a matrix of expenses as urgent, which can be important and not important; as well as non-urgent, in the same way, important and not important. It should be mentioned that items with non-urgent and non-important aspects of expenses were not made, which are, for example: expensive clothes, expensive housing, luxurious cars, since it was not considered relevant to know if the respondents made this type of expenses in this lockdown. Now, based on some of these expenses raised by the cited author, some variables and their respective items are observed. (see Table 2). These were presented with frequency tables in the results section.

On the size of the sample, the total of the statistical sample was calculated based on the total of households in the city of Culiacán, Sinaloa, Mexico, being N = 244,754 to solve the statistical formula in the Decision Analyst STATS 2.0 software. The total of the statistical sample is of 384 households (Figure 1.)

The reliability of the instrument was calculated using Cronbach's Alpha, in SPSS 24.0. 488 surveys were processed. The result was 0.676, (see table Nº 3), this result is considered as a moderate evaluation attitude, according to, (Robinson, Shaver & Wrightsman, 1991). Likewise, Hair, et al. (2008), consider that a Cronbach's alpha "can drop to 0.6 in exploratory research" (pp. 105-106), which justifies the alpha 0.676, since this research is exploratory. Table 3. Calculation of Cronbach's Alpha

RESULTS

The way of making decisions about personal finances is framed on the principle of doing more with less, under this gaze the scarce resources in a home or in an organization are managed. It is observed in Table 4 that 67.8% of the respondents are men; the age of those who responded to the form is 34.9% of those between 40 and 50 years old, as well as 30% of those over 50 years of age.

It is observed in Table 5 in which the general considerations are grouped that teleworking from home is present in the sample studied, since 56.3% are working from home in this context of a pandemic. In relation to the fact that if they consider that the government is doing what is pertinent to address the health contingency, it is observed that 63.5% of those surveyed do not believe that the government will do what is concerned to face it. Likewise, the results of the survey show that 80% make a budget according to their income, that 63.5% do not spend more than they earn, 87.1% make a purchase planning through a list and 61.8% can save. There are coincidences with the proposals of Figueroa-Delgado, 2009, Gitman

Table 1. Variables and items of the survey

V	Items	V	Items
	Sex	v24	Have you paid your car insurance in a timely manner?
	Age	v25	Do you think the government is doing what is necessary to face this health crisis?
v1	Do you budget for expenses in your home?	v26	During confinement at home, did you, or your spouse, require medical services?
v2	Is the expense budget according to your income?	v27	Have you had the need to contract a new loan in a banking institution?
v3	Do you think you spend more than you earn per month?	v28	Have you had the need to take out a new loan at a pawn shop?
v4	Do you maintain or keep a fund of money for household expenses contingencies?	v29	Have you bought any computers or accessories during home confinement?
v5	After this confinement experience, do you think that from now on you would consider saving money for a contingency fund?	v30	Have you bought any cell phones or accessories during home confinement?
v6	Do you have a retirement and retirement savings fund?	v31	Did you buy medicines as a reserve during the quarantine?
v7	Have you reduced your personal care expenses?	v32	Did you buy food as a reserve during the quarantine?
v8	Have you increased cleaning and hygiene expenses at home?	v33	Have you paid for your water, electricity, and gas services, in a timely manner during the quarantine?
v9	Have you ever needed to use your bank credit card more often?	v34	Have you paid for television, landline, and cell phone services, in a timely manner during the quarantine?
v10	Have you bought non-essential products recently?	v35	Have you taken advantage of vacation package deals to travel soon?
v11	Do your children study in private schools or colleges?	v36	Have you purchased non-essential products and / or services online?
v12	Have you complied with the tuition payment in a timely manner during confinement?	v37	Do you work from home?
v13	Do you currently pay a credit for the purchase of a car for personal use?	v38	How often do you buy food at restaurants?
v14	If the previous question is yes, have you been behind in payments?	v39	Do you usually buy your food at the supermarket?
v15	Have you been busy delaying the maintenance service for your car due to lack of money during this period of confinement?	v40	What time do you go to the supermarket?
v16	Have you negotiated with the banking institutions about any grace period support to pay your credit cards or commercial loans?	v41	What day of the week do you go to the supermarket?
v17	Have you covered the monthly payments of your credits in a timely manner?	v42	Do you make the purchase in the supermarket by attending a list of necessary items at home that you previously make? That is, do you carry your shopping list?
v18	The house where you live is: own, rented, or loaned?	v43	According to your buying habits, how do you make your decisions?
v19	Do you pay a mortgage on your house?	v44	Do you buy all your food at the supermarket (Walmart, Ley, Soriana, others)?
v20	Have you had trouble paying the amount of your mortgage or rent in the last three months?	v45	Do you buy your meat and dairy at local butchers?
v21	Have you purchased any major medical insurance during this stay-at-home period?	v46	Do you buy vegetables and fruits, in greengrocers at the market or in small stores?
v22	Before quarantine, did you have any insurance for major medical expenses?	v47	What kind of medicines have you bought?
v23	Have you paid your insurance for major medical expenses in a timely manner?	V48	Do you consider that your family can save?

Source: Prepared by author

& Zutter, 2016, López-García, 2016 and Rodríguez-Raga, 2017, who argue about the importance of

Table 2. Research variables and item number variables items data: sex and age

Variables	Items
Data: Sex and age	
General considerations	v1, v2, v3, v25, v37, v42, v48
Important and urgent expenses: Housing, rent or mortgage, utilities, food, tuition, health.	v8, v11, v12, v18, v19, v20, v26, v31,, v32, v33, v34, v39, v40, v41, v43, v44, v45, v46, v47
Important and non-urgent expenses: Emergency funds, Savings for future situations, Insurance, Retirement, and retirement fund.	v4, v5, v6, v21, v22, v23, v24, v35
Unimportant and urgent expenses: excessive expenses in technology, and communications, consumption of credit card, high expenses in personal care, non-essential expense.	v7, v9, v10, v13, v14, v15, v16, v17, v27, v28, v29, v30, v36, v38

Source: Prepared by the author, based on Figueroa-Delgado, (2009).

Figure 1. Number of households in the different municipalities of the state of Sinaloa.
Source: INEGI. Tabulated from the Intercensal Survey (2015) retrieved from (https://www.inegi.org.mx/programas/intercensal/2015/default.html)

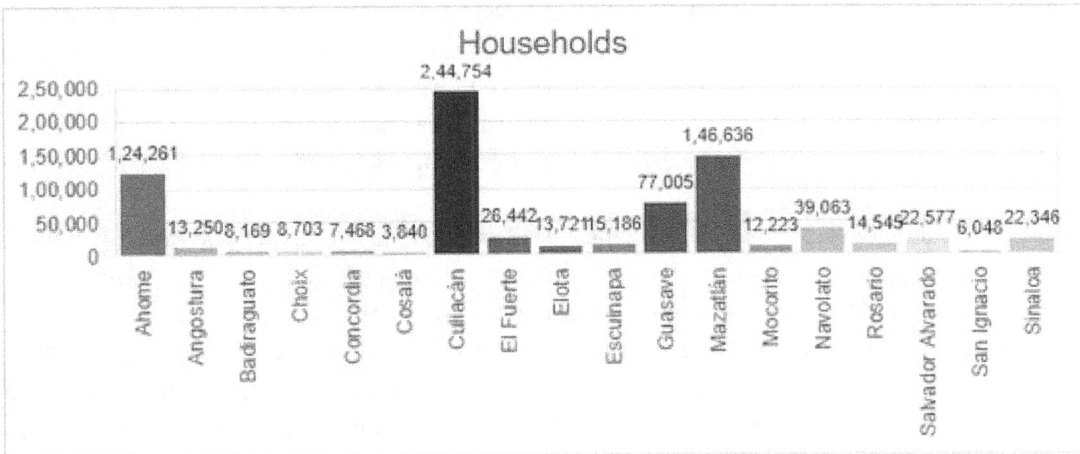

Table 3. Calculus of Alfa de Cronbach

Statistics of reliability	
Alfa de Cronbach	**Number of elements**
.676	48

Source: Own elaboration

Table 4. Description of the respondents

	Between 20 and 30 years	Between 30 and 40 years	Between 40 and 50 years	More than 50 years	Male sex	Female sex
Age/sex	13.3%	21.8%	34.9%	30%	67.8%	32.2%

Source: Prepared by the author

Table 5. General considerations

They make a budget: 83.5% they make a budget; 16.5% do not do it
Budget according to income: 80% budget according to income; 20% do not budget according to income.
They spend more than they earn: 36.5% they spend more than they earn; 63.5% do not spend more than they earn.
Government actions in the face of a pandemic: 63.5% believe that the government does not do what is necessary to face a pandemic; 36.5% consider that the government does what is necessary to face a pandemic.
Teleworking: 56.3% are doing teleworking; 13.5% are going to their office every day; 16.1% do teleworking and go to their office; 14.1% do not work
They use a shopping list: 87.1% use a shopping list; 12.9% do not use a list.
Saving capacity: 61.8% consider that they have saving capacity; 38.2% do not have

Source: Own elaboration.

keeping a budget and planning personal expenses according to income.

Important and urgent personal expenses are rent or housing fees; public services, administration; market, schools, health, and gasoline (Figueroa-Delgado, 2009, p. 138). In this exploratory study, some questions were applied in the survey to learn about this type of expenditure in households located in Culiacán, Sinaloa, Mexico. As can be seen in Table 6, that 83.5% of household spending decision-makers have their own house, have paid the public water, electricity, and gas services on time, and have covered the payment of telephone and television, cleaning and hygiene expenses have also increased. In this context of a pandemic, it is shown that only 7.8% of those surveyed have made purchases via the internet.

The food shopping preference is also 71.2% made in butchers and 74.5% in local greengrocers. Only 21.8% buy the cheapest; 64.7% did buy reserve food during the analyzed period. In addition, 9.4% have had problems with paying tuition; Lastly, 46.5% have bought a reserve of medicines and 73.9% did not require medical services.

The important and non-urgent expenses in the classification matrix of expenses exposed by Figueroa-Delgado, (2009), are: "pension savings, basis for home purchase, emergency fund, automobile savings, insurance, leisure savings and others (holidays) and taxes" (p.138).

It is observed in Table 7 that the respondents affirm in relation to this type of expenses in this pandemic context, that 55.3% have a contingency fund, and 93.5% would consider having one in the future. However, 93.5% of the respondents did not consider it urgent to have insurance for major medical expenses during the analysis period. Finally, 96.5% have not been interested in taking advantage of offers to travel in the future.

Finally, in this analysis of frequencies of the applied Google form, according to the classification matrix of non-important and urgent expenses, such as excessive expenses in technology and communications, credit card consumption, high expenses in personal care (Figueroa- Delgado, 2009, page 138), the following according to Table 8: regarding personal care expenses, 71.2% have decreased this type of expenses during this pandemic context. Regarding that, if they have borrowed more in this time with the use of credit cards, it is observed that 62.4% have not done so. They have not required 58% to request a grace period to pay their debts, nor have they had 59.6% problems to pay their credit on time. Similarly, 92.9% have not needed new loans either in banks or 94.3% in pawn shops.

The people who keep control of family expenses in the surveyed households, 62.4% have not bought non-essential products, neither have 59.8% of those consulted via the internet. Similarly, the frequency of buying food in restaurants is occasionally 44.1%.

Table 6. Important and urgent expenses

Housing, rent or mortgage
Increase in cleaning and hygiene expenses: 83.5% has increased; 16.5% has not increased
Own house, rented or loaned: 83.5% have their own house; 10.2% rented 6.3%; house loaned
Pay a mortgage: 32.4% pay a mortgage 46.3%; do not pay a mortgage; 21.4% does not apply.
Public services
Paid on time for water, electricity, and gas: 88.6% did pay on time; 11.4% did not pay on time.
Paid on time for television, landline, and cell phone: 84.5% did pay; 15.5% did not pay
Food
Bought reserve food: 64.7% did buy; 35.3% did not buy
Shopping at the supermarket: 77.1% go to the supermarket; 7.8% asked for it online; 13.3% go directly and ask for it online; 1.8% I do not go to the supermarket.
Time that go to the supermarket; 52.2% during the morning; 14.9% noon; 32.9% from 4 in the afternoon onwards
Day to go to the supermarket: 18% from Monday to Wednesday; 5.7% Thursday to Friday; 19.8% Saturday and Sunday; 50.4% don't have a day to go; 6.1% always ask at home.
Shopping habits: 21.8% buy the cheapest; 19.4% buy quality regardless of price; 17.6% buy brands 46.1% all the above.
You buy everything in the supermarket: 30.4% yes they buy everything in the supermarket; 54.7% almost everything; 14.9% do not buy everything in the supermarket.
Purchases in butchers: 71.2% do buy in butchers; 28.8% do not buy in butchers.
Purchases in greengrocers: 74.5% do buy in greengrocers 25.5%; do not buy in greengrocers Tuition
Your children study in schools: 31.8% yes; 47.3% no; 21% does not apply.
Complied with the tuition payment: 34.7% yes; 9.4% no; 55.9% does not apply.
Health
Required medical services: 9.4% in public hospitals; 13.5% in private hospitals; 3.1% both; 73.9% did not require medical services.
Bought medicines by reserve: 46.5% did buy reserve medicine; 53.5% did not buy.
Types of medicines bought: 13.3% patent; 20.2% generic; 47.5% the previous two; 19% have not bought medicines

Source: Prepared by author

DISCUSSION

The methodology used was exploratory, to identify the types of personal expenses in the homes located in Culiacán Rosales, Sinaloa, Mexico as of July 15, 2020 from the theory of personal finance; For this, 488 surveys were applied electronically through the google form shared on social networks, the research instrument consisted of 48 items applied to the heads of the family as of June 29. Derived from the context of the pandemic, the surveyed families have directed their personal expenses, increasing products for cleaning and hygiene in the home, reducing personal care expenses and purchases of non-essential products; as well as the acquisition of food for reservation. They also develop budgets and can save.

Important and urgent expenses were covered in the first place according to the classification given by Figueroa-Delgado, (2009), from mortgage expenses, rent, payment of public services, food, tuition,

Table 7. Important and non-urgent expenses

Emergency funds
Accounts with a contingency fund: 55.3% yes; 44.7% do not have a contingency fund.
Would you consider a contingency fund in the future? 93.5% yes; 6.5% no.
Savings for future situations.
You have taken advantage of offers to travel in the future: 3.5% yes; 96.5%; have not taken advantage.
Insurance
Have you purchased major medical insurance? 6.5% yes; 93.5% no.
You already had insurance for major medical expenses: 24.5% yes; 75.5% no.
You have paid the medical expenses insurance on time: 25.7% yes; 8% no; 66.3% does not apply

Source: Prepared by author.

Table 8. Unimportant and urgent expenses

Excessive spending on technology and communications
You pay credit for car: 28.4% yes; 71.6% no; If yes, have you fallen behind in credit: 8.2% yes; 26.3% no; 65.5% does not apply.
You have delayed car maintenance: 25.9% yes; 50.8% no; 23.3% does not apply.
Have you bought a computer or accessories? 19.8% yes; 80.2% no.
Have you bought a cell phone or accessories: 19.4% yes; 80.6% no.
Credit card consumption
Have you used your card more during this pandemic? 37.6% yes; 62.4% no.
You requested a grace period for your credits: 19% yes; 58% no; 22.9% does not apply.
You have paid your credit on time: 59.6% yes; 17.8% no; 22.5% does not apply.
You have had problems in the payment of the mortgage in this confinement: 10.2% yes; 41.8% no; 48% does not apply.
You have needed new credit: 7.1%; 92.9% no.
You have taken out credit at a pawn shop: 5.7% yes; 94.3% no.
Have you reduced your personal care expenses? 71.2% yes; 28.8% no.
Non-essential expenses
You have bought non-essential products 37.1% yes; 62.4% no.
You have purchased non-essential products online 20.8% yes by Amazon; 21.8% by Mercado Libre; 0.2% yes by eBay; 14.9% yes through the company's website; 59.8% no.
Frequency of purchase in restaurants
1% daily; 8.2% no more than 3 times a week; 26.3% only on weekends; 7.5% every fortnight; 44.1% occasionally; 12.9% did not buy.

Source: Prepared by author

and health. They agree with the cited author, in relation to the purchase of insurance and contingency funds, most of those surveyed consider them important, but not urgent. But not so important and urgent expenses, since most of the respondents have not considered excessive expenses of technology and communications, credit card consumption, high expenses in personal care and non-essential expenses, for example 82.8% have not acquired new cell phones or accessories, have not borrowed more, and 62.4% have not bought non-essential products.

CONCLUSION

The people surveyed who oversee making decisions about types of family expenses report that, derived from the context of the pandemic, they have now considered having savings for contingency funds. They maintain that they develop budgets to control their finances. There are important coincidences with what was stated by Aguilar (2020) and Cardona (2020), since they advise those who see their income diminished due to the pandemic, make financial plans, and prioritize expenses on food, prescription drugs, transportation to move food and medicines, try to save, not go into debt, and negotiate with credit institutions in case of debt. Spend in a measured way and only what is mandatory. For those who do not have a change in their income, that is, who receive their salaries regardless of the situation, they recommend not suspending their obligations, likewise, creating and strengthening their emergency fund.

Some research affirms that digital life begins in this context Covid-19 and that it will come to stay, however, in the families analyzed they still do not make digital purchases to a greater extent. Finally, it is worth mentioning that some future research is aimed at improving the design of the applied research instrument, for which it is recommended to calculate the factor analysis and reduce factors or items. Likewise, include data on professional profiles and levels of financial education in the information collection, since López-Salido (2020) observes that 63% of the Americans surveyed with a university level have done work from home and have been less affected in their finances personal in the current context.

Another future topic is to carry out an analysis on the importance and urgency of certain expenses such as insurance for major medical expenses in times of uncertainty. Finally, develop the financial education line to identify investment alternatives for family savings.

REFERENCES

Aguilar Pacas, G. (2020). Finanzas en familia y Coronavirus (COVID-19). *Realidad Empresarial*, (9), 51. doi:10.5377/reuca.v0i9.10070

Amat, O. (2020). *La botella medio llena*. Profit Editorial.

Banxico. (2020). *Encuesta sobre las expectativas de los especialistas en economía del sector privado.* Recuperado de https://www.banxico.org.mx/publicaciones-y-prensa/encuestas-sobre-las-expectativas-de-los-especialis/encuestas-expectativas-del-se.html

Cardona, J. F. (2020, Abril 22). *Finanzas personales*. Recuperado de https://www.youtube.com/watch?v=Jddhe_15OIQ

Chiodi, A. (2020). Compás financiero personal. *Descubre las finanzas desde lo básico e intuitivo hasta su sorprendente lado humano y pon los números a tu favor.* CONDUSEF, Conduguía, Finanzas Personales. Recuperado de (https://www.condusef.gob.mx/documentos/299734_Conduguia_finanzas_personales_y_familiares2018.pdf

Dew, J. P. (2016). Family Finances. In C. L. Shehan (Ed.), *Encyclopedia of Family Studies.* doi:10.1002/9781119085621.wbefs038

Duque Sánchez, A. (2015). Estado de flujos de efectivo: Aplicación de razonamientos algebraicos y de la NIC 7. *Cuadernos De Contabilidad*, *16*(40). Advance online publication. doi:10.11144/Javeriana.cc16-40.efea

ENIGH. (2018). *Encuesta Nacional de Ingresos y Gastos en los Hogares*. Recuperado de https://www.inegi.org.mx/contenidos/programas/enigh/nc/2018/doc/enigh2018_ns_presentacion_resultados.pdf

Figueroa Delgado, L. O. (2009). Las finanzas personales. Revista EAN. *Núm.*, *65*, 123–144.

Gitman, L. J., & Zutter, C. (2016). Principios de administración financiera (décimo cuarta edición. ed.). Pearson.

Guthrie, C. P., & Nicholls, C. M. (2015). The Personal Budget Project: A practical introduction to financial literacy. *Journal of Accounting Education, Elsevier*, *33*(2), 138–163. doi:10.1016/j.jaccedu.2015.04.002

Hair, J. F., Anderson, R. F., Tatham, R. L., & Black, W. C. (2008). *Análisis Multivariante*. Editorial Pearson Prentice Hall.

Hoffmann, A., & Otteby, K. (2017). Personal finance blogs: Helpful tool for consumers with low financial literacy or preaching to the choir? *International Journal of Consumer Studies*, *42*(2), 241–254. doi:10.1111/ijcs.12412

INEGI. (2020). *Estimación oportuna del PIB trimestral.* Recuperado de https://www.inegi.org.mx/temas/pibo/

INEGI. (2020). *México en cifras*. Recuperado de https://www.inegi.org.mx/app/areasgeograficas/

INEGI. (2020). *Sistema de Cuentas Nacionales de México.* Recuperado de https://www.inegi.org.mx/temas/itaee/

López García, J. C. (2016). *Las finanzas personales, un concepto que va más allá de su estructura. Estado del arte periodo 2006-2016 en Pereira, EAFIT.* Tesis Digitales. Universidad EAFTI Facultad de Ciencias Administrativas, Programa de Maestría en Administración, MBA. Disponible en https://repository.eafit.edu.co/bitstream/handle/10784/11784/LopezGarcia_JuanCarlos_2017.pdf?sequence=2

López Salido, D. (2020). Tribuna invitada. Confinamiento, mercado laboral y finanzas familiares. In *Aspectos económicos de la crisis del COVID-19: Boletín de seguimiento no. 2* (pp. 4–8). FEDEA.

Robinson, J.P., Shaver, P. R., & Wrightsman, L.S. (1991). Criteria for Scale Selection and Evaluation. *Measures of Personality and Social Psychological Attitudes, 13.*

Rodríguez-Raga, S. (2017). *Finanzas personales, su mejor plan de vida.* Bogotá: Universidad de los Andes, Facultad de Administración: Ediciones Uniandes.

Rojas-López, M. D., Maya-Fernández, L. M., & Valencia, M. E. (2017). Definición de un modelo para la planeación financiera personal aplicado al caso colombiano. *Revista Ingenierías Universidad de Medellín, 16*(31), 155–171. doi:10.22395/rium.v16n31a8

Villada, F., López-Lezama, J. M., & Muñoz-Galeano, N. (2018). Análisis de la Relación entre Rentabilidad y Riesgo en la Planeación de las Finanzas Personales. *Formación Universitaria, 11*(6), 41–52. doi:10.4067/S0718-50062018000600041

Zapata Lambraño, G. C. (2020). *Manual de finanzas personales.* Tesis Digitales. Universidad Cooperativa de Colombia Facultad de Ciencias Económicas, Administrativas y afines programa administración de empresas. Medellín. Disponible en http://hdl.handle.net/20.500.12494/18393

Chapter 6
Role of Higher Educational Institutes in Developing Self-Reliant Economies

Nidhi Agarwal
Integrated School of Education, INMANTEC, Ghaziabad, India

Jocelyn B. Hipona
Far Eastern University, Philippines

ABSTRACT

Higher education has the ability to contribute to global, national, and local growth. Institutions of higher education have played an important role in society throughout modern history, training the elite and making groundbreaking advances in science and the humanities. Education broadens people's perspectives on themselves and the world around them. It improves people's competitiveness and innovation while also encouraging entrepreneurship and technical advancement. This chapter will provide an insight on the role of higher educational institutes in economic development. The chapter will provide cross-country analysis and cases from different parts of the globe.

INTRODUCTION

India's distinguished IInd President, Hon'ble Dr. S. Radhakrishnan, Chairman, UEC in the period of 1948-49 following significance related to higher instruction as lift country by devastating in consideration of neediness as well as underdevelopment with original prologue regarding Commission report:

"The most significant and critical change required in training is to change it, to try to relate it to the life, necessities and desires of individuals and in this way make it the incredible instrument of social, monetary and social change vital for the acknowledgment of the public objectives. For this reason, instruction ought to be grown to expand efficiency, accomplish social and public combination, speed up the cycle of modernisation and develop social, good and otherworldly qualities."

DOI: 10.4018/978-1-7998-8705-8.ch006

These can be considered amazing information, that likewise reverberate with Preamble related to UNESCO's Constitution: "That the wide dispersion of culture and the training of humankind for equity and freedom and harmony are key to the nobility of man that harmony should in this way be established, in the event that it isn't to fizzle, upon the scholarly and good fortitude of humankind."

Founding guiders consistently featured significance related to tertiary schooling and regardless of asset crunch, fabricated educational institutions for sociologies just like clinical universities and India's presently celebrated Institute of Technology (IIT). It was anything but a simple assignment. In the period of 1947, after Independence of the country, compelled by passing up about Industrial Revolution on account regarding pioneer term, had the helpless nation at an immense populace and disturbing ignorance rates especially ladies.

Overall 'mantra' related with World Bank as well as Breton Woods organizations, staffed at previous pilgrim civil servants, was to constrain developing nations to put their assets just in essential and optional schooling, empowering the individuals who could stand to profit by college training to do as such in the nation of their previous colonialists. Dr. Mahmood Mamdani, Professor, Columbia University, and creator of 'Higher Education, the State and the Marketplace' says: "The World Bank made a front facing attack on African Universities in 1986, exhorting the Vice Chancellors that it would bode well to close colleges in free Africa and have its human asset needs prepared in Universities in the West."

This was trailed by what Mamdani characterized as 'contingent guide'. The endeavor was to empower a 'mind channel' with the outpouring of public savvy people toward the West since no chances were accessible in the nation of origin.

Tertiary training is working with the retention of the constructive outcomes of globalization and empowering India as foster the trillion or more economy by the profoundly qualified and wide public ability foundation (Sharma, 2017).

As far as India is concerned that if it is no more peculiar regarding higher instruction. Significance related to training was all around perceived in nation. 'Swadeshe pujyate raja, vidwan sarvatra pujyate' regarding Sanskrit basically signifies: "A lord is regarded distinctly in his own country, however one who is learned is respected all through the world." First University of world was set up in the period of 700 BC and University of Nalanda was already implicit about fourth century BC, an incredible accomplishment and commitment of antiquated India with aim of instruction. Nalanda presently considered as potential UNESCO World Heritage site. This is noted that Science and innovation with respect to old and archaic India consisting every one of significant parts of people's information as well as exercises. The various Indian researchers, for example, Charaka and Susruta, with Aryabhata, and various others create original commitment for information related to numerous assorted regions like math, stargazing, physical science, science, clinical science and medical procedure (Kumar, 2015).

Quality affirmation in higher instruction is the first concern of India's approach plan. Present auxiliary training needs on get ready alumni with new abilities, a wide information base with scope related to capabilities by entering the more intricate and associated (Sharma, 2013 ; Jalla, 2017 ; Sharma, Anand 2014). This has the requirement significant investment as quality is concerned with multi-dimensional idea. Frameworks regarding responsibility and accreditation alongwith vigorous administrative system are fundamental for the way toward maintaining and developing the quality. This must be a part of worry, everything being equal. Greatness will move from great quality establishments and proper administration modules. Higher instruction related with India has encountered the uncommon extension joined through broadening with respect to area. Impromptu development with respect to area presents difficulties for improving and looking after quality (Jaiswal, 2016 ; Navdeep, 2017).

As a proportion of value affirmation, India set up accreditation offices in 1994. The establishments of higher instruction should move toward the accreditation offices to get their foundation or program certify. Accreditation was willful and subsequently just couple of establishments are licensed in country. Issue should consider to tend as direly.

This country consists voyage far as Swami Vivekananda depicted such countless periods prior at 'The Essence of India'. He conveyed: "The longest night is by all accounts dying, the appearing body seems, by all accounts, to be stirring and a voice is coming to us - away back where history and even practice neglects to peep into the agony of the past, India, this homeland of our own is arousing! None can oppose her any longer; never is she resting any longer; no outward powers can hold her back any more. India that will be, the future India, should be a lot more prominent than old India."

ROLE OF HIGHER EDUCATION INSTITUTES IN SOCIETY

"India's predetermination is being molded in four dividers" is the first and significant assertion of the report of instruction commission which was submitted to the focal government in the year 1966. The individuals from schooling commission headed by Dr. D. S. Kothari were of the firm assessment that the educational institutes were the focuses where future society can be molded. What's more, the focal government took drives, based on proposals of schooling commission 1966, to get changes training and in educational organizations so they will end up being the focuses of socio-affordable change. The interaction of progress in instruction and educational foundations has been proceeding till this date.

The students subsequent to finishing their schooling according to their decision emerge from the educational foundations of higher training are required to accept some position, including business, according to their advantage and capacity. In the event that the educational establishments assume their legitimate part in conferring quality training with qualities and morals, society will get great human asset. Also, great human asset will build up business associations which will give labor and products to the general public to fulfill its requirements and the fulfilled society will uphold the business. Along these lines society and organizations can acquire practical development future since both are interrelated and reliant on one another. Anyway molding the fate of business and society relies more upon the training framework and educational establishments of a country (Navdeep, 2016 ; Brar, 2017).

India has the third biggest higher schooling framework on the planet, after the US and China, as per the World Bank. The higher training framework in India has filled in an exceptional way, especially in the post-freedom period and the Universities have consistently been a central part in a worldwide framework progressively determined by information, data and thoughts.

Clearly we live in when information is always imperative to our social orders and economies, in a universe of quickly circling capital and individuals and of progressive correspondence innovations. In such a period, we see that information is supplanting different assets as the primary driver of monetary development, and schooling has progressively become the establishment for singular success and social portability. Indeed, somewhat recently alone, admittance to higher schooling has improved as more IITs, IIMs and focal and state-level colleges have been set up. Notwithstanding, one should see that this multiplication has likewise raised worries about an awkwardness among greatness and incorporation.

Perceiving the above certainty, the Universities have begun to play out various jobs, such as making new information, procuring new capacities and delivering a wise human asset pool, through testing educating, exploration and augmentation exercises to adjust both the need and the interest. We should investigate a portion of these Indian Universities and how they're forming the understudies for a superior future in the country.

In the greater part of the Indian Universities today, we see a huge change in the manner in which they work. They're ceaselessly incorporating various subjects and working together with various organizations to bring the best for their understudies. We should simply investigate the investigation of humanities, it's seeing a gigantic change in India as well as across the world. While subjects like comic books, movies, and style history are authentic and far reaching in different nations from the 1980s, a similar field is presently gradually getting in India, with an extraordinary spotlight on assisting understudies with getting a new line of work in these new fields.

According to the new measurements in India, upwards of 75-100 million youngsters are relied upon to go onto the Indian work market in the five-year term of the following government. India's Human Resource Development Minister has expressed that India needs 800 new establishments of higher instruction by 2020 to raise the age investment rate-the level of school-age populace took on organizations of higher training-from 12.4% to 30%.

THE SIGNIFICANCE OF HIGHER EDUCATION

By and large, the College Board thinks about the functional advantages of higher instruction in the 21st century to include:

Monetary: As the Bureau of Labor Statistics details uncover, individuals with some type of higher schooling bring in more cash and have a lower likelihood of joblessness.

Wellbeing: Gainful business and a positive capital remove the pressure factors related with monetary instability. Accordingly, you are likelier to carry on with a more joyful and better existence with some type of school added to your repertoire.

City Contribution: People with beneficial business and monetary assets regularly reward the local area. At the point when you acquire well and your organization grows, you are bound to provide for a noble cause and become associated with charitable effort.

Self-Improvement: People with professions will in general lead more organized lives and have a more grounded awareness of certain expectations, attributes that fill in as strength-developers in different everyday issues.

Better Correspondence: Most positions include some type of composed or verbal correspondence. In that capacity, you will for the most part improve in the two territories during your school and expert profession.

Acknowledgment of Interests: As with a great many people, the more you learn, the likelier you are to track down your actual interests throughout everyday life. Through the training interaction, you can investigate the different aspects of a forthcoming field and discover your qualities.

More Noteworthy Feeling of Control: The regiments of training can impart you with the order needed in the expert world. By figuring out how to adhere to complex directions and fulfill exacting time constraints, you will be more ready for the afflictions of the commercial center.

Feeling of achievement: Each time you complete a school task or occupation task, it's the result of your ability and difficult work.

ECONOMIC COMPETITIVENESS IN COUNTRY

In the previous few decades the monetary rivalry between nations has escalated. Practically every state tries to turn into a persuasive and significant player of worldwide monetary relations and assume its legitimate position at the world financial market to forestall the significant dangers that globalization involves (Agarwal et al, 2017 ; Mishra, 2017). Regardless of whether there are a few questions that states/countries actually contend, it stays the case - as when a market is open it isn't just ventures that contend. As ambitious is just conceivable under certain state overseeing conditions, hence at the large scale level we have the proof of rivalry between states - for the assets (like speculations, oil), for the climate ("green advancements"), and so forth Experience of the world financial emergency has shown that the most defenseless against outer stuns are nations with low degrees of public seriousness. Thus, the subject of intensity (its evaluation, upgrading strategies) is extremely significant and significant for the future improvement of any state.

Globalization and Seriousness: Synergetic Turn of Events

During the new many years globalization has become the trademark pattern of the worldwide economy; its multi-dimensional execution is in economies of scale and dynamism of the worldwide development of merchandise, administrations and elements of creation, data, and innovation. From one perspective, this interaction speeds up the intermingling of public economies; on the other it prompts expanded highway and interlocked inconsistencies and expanded rivalry between subjects of worldwide monetary relations at provincial, sub-local and worldwide levels.

Globalization is a target interaction pointed basically at carrying out the prerequisites of worldwide rivalry and making quantitative and subjective changes in the serious climate of the nations with both positive and adverse consequences. To start with, it supports the requirement for another monetary framework dependent on market economy and subsequently realizes the part of rivalry as a rule; second, it adds to the strengthening of rivalry; and third, it directs a serious rivalry, and therefore, changes the cutthroat relationship.

The undeniable degree of public rivalry decides expanding openings for the fascination of speculation inwards, innovation move, extending market presence and marking of new exchange contracts for any country. On the other hand, low evaluations and audits fill in as pointers of underestimation by the legislatures of specific nations and the requirement for the inciting of an improved public climate. This can push the organizations to battle for business sectors (Singh et al 2020 ; Chaudhary 2015).

THE MOST COMPETITIVE: MOVERS AND SHAKERS

The world's top nations dominate in numerous fields-however there must be one. In 2019, Singapore wins the desired "most aggressive economy" title, with a 84.8 score on the GCI. The country's created foundation, wellbeing, work market, and monetary framework have all moved it forward-trading with the U.S. (83.7) for the best position. Be that as it may, more should be possible, as the report notes Singapore actually needs press opportunity and shows a low obligation to manageability.

Finland (80.2) and Canada (79.6) are outstanding ways out from this best 10 rundown throughout the long term. In the interim, Denmark (81.2) vanished from the rankings for a very long time, however figured out how to move back up in 2018.

Another point of view on the most aggressive economies is to take a gander at how nations charge inside districts, and how these locales contend among one another.

Center East and North Africa (MENA) has the most extensive hole in seriousness scores-Israel (76.7) scores over twofold that of least fortunate performing Yemen (35.5). Curiously, the MENA locale showed the most advancement, developing its middle score by 2.77% between 2018-2019.

The tightest hole is really in South Asia, with simply a solitary digit contrast between India (61.4) and Nepal (51.6). Be that as it may, the locale likewise became the slowest, with just 0.08% increment in middle score longer than a year.

Across all locales, the WEF tracked down that East Asia's 73.9 middle score was the most noteworthy. Europe and North America were not a long ways behind with a 70.9 middle score. This is reliable with the way that the most aggressive economies have all come from these districts in the previous decade.

As every one of these nations race towards the wilderness-an ideal state where efficiency development isn't compelled-the report takes note of that intensity "doesn't suggest a lose-lose situation". All things considered, any nations are fit for improving their profitability as per the GCI measures.

The principle justification the assortment of meanings of seriousness is its intricacy, composite character, and the precise idea of itself as a classification. We attempted to consider public intensity from the situation of its synergetic impact with globalization and reasoned that it generally showed up under the globalization of exchange and contributing. The more nations are available to global exchange, the more significant and sound for them is the serious level and its lists. We applied the numerical strategy to test our speculation, and approved our unique suppositions.

The model's evaluation showed that the best method to influence the public intensity level is to change the country's volume of unfamiliar exchange balance. We utilized the bunch investigation procedure to think about the agglomerations of states as per their degree of seriousness. The aftereffects of group investigation of 36 nations test apportioned five principle homogeneous bunches of nations.

By having this data while leading comparative investigation consistently every nation can undoubtedly foster its own public technique, see its accomplices and contradictors in a similar group and in adjoining bunches, and keep an appropriate "solid powerless" guides strategy toward arrive at the undeniable degree of monetary turn of events and supportability. Furthermore, the pushing of public "catches" - like unfamiliar exchange balance volume assurance - can "turn on" global state powers - like intensity level increment.

ROLE OF HIGHER EDUCATIONAL INSTITUTES IN DEVELOPING SELF RELIANT ECONOMIES

Training is one of the central spaces of Atmanirbhar Bharat. The proposed changes could prompt a positive change in the nature of training. Presently, despite the fact that we live in a time of online instruction, computerized availability is an issue. Likewise, as indicated by a Deloitte and GiveIndia report, there is an intense deficiency of qualified instructors. While all that instructors can't generally arrive at the grassroots, advanced substance can.

Schooling has a vital task to carry out in making India self-reliant and prosperous and the new National Education Policy has been presented with this unbiased, Prime Minister Narendra Modi said on Saturday. Tending to the country on India's 74th Independence Day from the defenses of the Red Fort, the executive said the NEP tries to fortify exploration and development in the nation to help it progress in a serious world.

"Instruction has a significant task to carry out in making India self-reliant, glad and prosperous. With this evenhanded, we have had the option to give the country another training strategy after more than thirty years," Modi said. "This will shape the India of the 21st century. We will before long have residents who shape another India, ones who are worldwide residents yet know and comprehend their foundations. The new instruction strategy additionally centers around innovative work to make India a key innovative work objective for the world," he said.

"The strategy lays exceptional accentuation on the National Research Foundation since advancement is significant for the nation's advancement. Just when we fortify advancement and exploration will our nation stay cutthroat and push forward. The more development is reinforced in the country the more advancement it will make in a serious world," he added.

Endorsed by the public authority a month ago, the NEP replaces the 34-year-old National Policy on Education outlined in 1986. It is pointed toward preparing for groundbreaking changes in school and higher training frameworks to make India a worldwide information superpower. The head administrator likewise underlined the chance introduced by the COVID-19 pandemic for the instruction area as online classes.

Eventual Fate of Education is a Self-Adequate Arrangement

Edtech plans to break the 'plant model' that has been continued in India since days of yore. The current instruction framework comes up short on the degree for personalization or customization of training, as the understudies are seen as a group rather than people. Edtech goliaths exploit the various necessities of assorted controls, just as understudies, and plan appropriately to make it a profitable instructing learning experience for the understudies. The instructive relationship can be reproduced and amplified through EdTech in light of the fact that it has the data transfer capacity to zero in on singular exhibitions of understudies in higher training also. While excess in content and obsolete instructing strategies are a major concern, it is important that these two will change consequently when EdTech is embraced by the majority. The Edtech area should adjust simpler open devices and a comprehensive methodology to turn into the eventual fate of India's schooling framework.

Another Benchmark has been set through NEP

The NEP has introduced itself to the majority as a progressive advance for the administration, conveyance and financing of training. It is a mammoth endeavor which predicts itself as one of the world's best training frameworks. Opportunity and adaptability are two key mainstays of self-dependence which it proposes to alter to suit the necessities and desires of current culture. It is a significant change as far as effect as the understudies from the dread and disarray of picking streams. The cultural pressing factor relating to the choice of a stream will not be an issue for understudies any longer. Best of all, the understudies will be furnished with an adaptable scope of subjects to look over, permitting them the chance to seek after their inclinations by clubbing Maths, Science and Arts. The occupation in center school is setting up the pinion wheels by embedding the seed of self adequacy into them.

Study hall correspondence has been coordinated towards competency based getting the hang of, reinforcing self-reliant instruction in India. We as compatriots of this all encompassing country need to get it and entertain ourselves more into such practices. With a multi-channel way to deal with battle these issues, presently TV channels can run educational substance for classes 1 to 12. This will be enhanced by radio and digital recordings. With this, the grassroots organization of government schools ought to be seen more as 'learning zones' instead of 'preparing establishments'. Edtech organizations can contribute by modifying the substance to the neighborhood setting. As per a KPMG report, around 50 lakh understudies will be hoping to select higher training foundations in this scholarly season alone, so permitting organizations to give online degrees was a much-anticipated change. Pacing up with the created nations, hereon understudies from the remotest and least fortunate of foundations will approach the best learning content. Besides, what we need is limit working for guardians and educators to draw in with this new type of learning. The impending NEP needs to structure these changes further.

These changes must be seen past the showy behaviors of learning on telephone, TV, and over the radio. India needs to take part in a profound, primary change in the schooling framework, as opposed to inconsistent declarations and budgetary distributions for us to call this a triumph.

Self-Dependence is the Route Forward

With the pandemic affecting schools and universities, educational foundations have started to think out-about the-crate to address the difficulties of computerized learning, and to make societies where inventive reasoning is propelled and sustained. They likewise need to get ready understudies for a quickly changing position market and make them self-reliant. To succeed, colleges too should be in any way self-reliant. Here is how they are getting along this.

New measurement to the hatchery business model: In the pre-COVID period, scholarly organizations zeroed in on preparing their understudies in abilities needed in bigger organizations. In any case, Atmanirbhar Bharat has moved the concentration to miniature, little and medium endeavors (MSMEs). Disregarding this area would be a lost chance. In developing countries across the world, MSMEs have drawn in with the scholarly community by putting resources into exploration and advancement, a relationship that can profit the two foundations and industry. Development, a significant target: With the assistance of cutting edge Artificial Intelligence and IoT, Indian colleges have responded to the call of discovering inventive answers for the issues raised by COVID-19. Maintainable business: Industry depends on scholarly world to prepare the ability needed for the working environment and to guarantee long lasting learning. Our educational institutes have started following the "Experiential University" model to guarantee that the understudies are work and industry-prepared.

CONCLUSION AND SUGGESTIONS

In the pre-Covid-19 period, scholastic establishments had placed consideration on preparing their understudies in abilities that are needed in bigger organizations. In any case, with Atmanirbhar Bharat the drive has carried the nation's concentration to MSMEs, one of the key main thrusts towards self-adequacy. MSMEs establish 80% of the labor force. Disregarding this area would be a lost chance. In developing countries, MSMEs have drawn in with the scholarly world by putting resources into exploration and advancement - a relationship that advantages the two foundations and industry. Understudies should be prepared likewise for occupations that will be popular later on.

Innovation as the Target

Colleges have responded to the call of discovering creative answers for the issues raised by Covid-19. With the assistance of AI and IoT, colleges are attempting to change a town into a savvy city so the occupants of the town can likewise benefit of the multitude of offices that will empower them to develop.

Making Business Reasonable

It is unavoidable for the business to depend on scholarly community to access and prepare the sort of ability needed to flourish later on work environment and to guarantee deep rooted learning. It has been assessed that more than 12 million Indians prepare work each year, yet the dismal part is that not every person is very much familiar with the requirements of the organization. Our institutes should follow the 'experiential college' model, which may be one of the responses to the test of an exceptionally evolved schooling framework.

Ideas

- Good Governance: there is a critical need of good administration in the colleges, foundations, self-ruling bodies and the legislatures for making the higher schooling pertinent to make great work power.
- Optimization Existing Resources: there has been wide contrast in limit use of HR in existing organizations of higher schooling. The HR in helped schools and state colleges are either underutilized or failing to meet expectations where as hundred percent pay is being paid to them according to VIth pay commission. What's more, the HR in non-allowed schools and in private colleges are either over used or being abused by underpayment of pay. Drives should be taken from every one of the partners including the administrations to utilize existing assets
- Optimum utilization of existing foundation: around 50% of the absolute schools/establishments are situated in country zones where enrolment of understudies is some time less 50% of their admission. What's more, subsequently infrastructural assets are being stayed unused.
- Economic Sustainability: the legislatures rather opening all the more new Universities and new model schools, should help monetarily to the current schools and foundations, based certain rules, to turn out to be financially practical.
- Relevance and Quality Enhancement: the focal government has effectively intended to speed up net enrolment proportion (GER) from existing 14% to 20 percent by 2020. A large number of rupees are being spent on this through different systems. This monetary asset, government ought to spend for improving educational principles of present schooling and existing educational organizations
- Strict Implementation of Regulations: the legislatures, both state governments and focal government, have been making different guidelines which are applicable and implementable. There is earnest need of carrying out them appropriately with fair methodology

- Reforms in alliance framework: connection arrangement of schools to colleges by and large has become quite recently a custom and at times it has gotten protracted. Changes are needed in this framework with the goal that straightforwardness and convenient fulfillment is being gotten

Molding the eventual fate of Business and Society relies more upon the schooling framework all in all and higher instruction specifically and the foundations of higher training. Present higher schooling framework is needed to be improved and the foundations engaged with this framework must be made more straightforward insect responsible to the general public. There is pressing need of making educational social obligation (ESR) among the establishments of higher schooling to make better society which at last may bring about forming the eventual fate of business.

REFERENCES

Agarwal, Sharma, & Tyagi. (2017). Role of Education in Meeting Challenges of Globalization. *Globus An International Journal of Management & IT, 9*(1), 1-3.

Agarwal & Pundir. (2017). A Study of Personality Traits of B. Ed. Students. *Learning Community-An International Journal of Educational and Social Development, 7*(2), 127-131.

Agarwal, N., & Kumar, P. (2009). Reflection on the new Innovations for maximizing the learning in Teacher of Mathematics. *International Journal Educational Herald, 382*, 41.

Bayero, Ibrahim, & Safiyan. (2020). Effect Of Entrepreneurial Education And Attitude On Entrepreneurial Intention Among Graduating Students Of The Nigerian Universities: A Conceptual Framework. *Cosmos Journal of Engineering & Technology, 10*(2), 1–12.

Brar, D. S. K. (2017). Transforming Education System: A Futuristic Perspective. *Globus An International Journal of Management & IT, 8*(2), 1–3.

Chaudhary. (2015). Globalization and Education. *Globus Journal of Progressive Education, 6*(1), 1-6.

Jaiswal, S. (2016). Quality Assurance in Teacher Education. *Globus Journal of Progressive Education, 6*(2), 1–4.

Kumari & Kumar. (2015). A Study On Value Education Quality In Dynamic World. *Globus An International Journal of Management & IT, 7*(1), 1-3.

Navdeep. (2016). A Study On Changes in Learning and Teaching Process in Today Environment. *Globus An International Journal of Management & IT, 8*(1), 1-3.

Navdeep. (2017). A Study of ICT in Various Aspects in Quality Education. *Globus An International Journal of Management & IT, 9*(1), 1-4.

Pradhan & Goel. (2017). A Study on Empowering Education and Globalization. *Globus Journal of Progressive Education, 7*(2), 1–5.

Ram. (2017). A Study on Teacher Performance Assessment for Quality Education. *Cosmos An International Journal of Art & Higher Education, 6*(2), 21–23.

Sharma. (2017). Technology, E-Learning and Social Media with Reference to Academic Achievement. *Cosmos An International Journal of Art & Higher Education*, *6*(1), 7–8.

Sharma, A. (2014). A Study of Total Quality Management: Its Legacy, Importance and Implementation In Educational Institutes. *Globus Journal of Progressive Education*, *4*(2), 1–5.

Sharma, R. K. (2013). An Abstract of Quality Assurance in Higher Education: For World Class Institution. *Globus Journal of Progressive Education*, *3*(1), 1–5.

Singh, G., Gupta, R., & Agarwal, N. (2020). Economic Re-Engineering: Covid-19. *International Journal on Emerging Technologies, 114*, 1–5.

Chapter 7
Role of Technological Innovations in Improving Manufacturing Resilience in the Post-Covid Era:
A Cross-Country Comparison

Ekansh Agarwal
NMIMS, Mumbai, India

Ramatu Ussif
University of Education, Winneba, Ghana

ABSTRACT

Technological progress is critical for improving manufacturing resilience and achieving self-sufficiency in any nation. The COVID-19 crisis has shown the importance of, as well as the threats associated with, our new industrial processes. Manufacturing's critical position in both industrialized and emerging economies has been shown by shortages of medical supplies and disruptions in basic goods. These delays and market fluctuations have also highlighted the pitfalls of focusing solely on a globalized distribution system characterized by fragmented supply chains, the separation of engineering and manufacturing, and just-in-time production. Although globalisation was the trend before the COVID-19 pandemic, several countries realized the dangers and began to look inward, focusing on developing local manufacturing capacities. In addition, the automotive sector has established itself as a cornerstone of post-COVID-19 recovery strategies.

INTRODUCTION

Manufacturers who manage and prosper in periods of transition all share one trait: they are resilient. Resiliency entails more than just being able to function and survive in the current circumstances. It also

DOI: 10.4018/978-1-7998-8705-8.ch007

entails creating more efficient procedures and activities in the future. This is becoming increasingly essential for manufacturers as the industry strives for economic recovery and competitiveness (Gupta, Alok 2019 ; Dev, Utkarsh 2020). Manufacturers require digital innovation to operate in a robust, secure, and sustainable manner. Data is an asset for manufacturers, and companies may use IoT or Industrial IoT, analytics, AI, and digital twins to increase resiliency.

The COVID-19 problem has highlighted the importance of, as well as the hazards involved with, our existing manufacturing processes. Manufacturing's critical significance in both advanced and emerging economies has been highlighted by shortages of medical equipment and interruptions of key goods. These shortages and supply interruptions have also highlighted the difficulties of depending only on a worldwide production system characterized by complicated supply chains, the separation of innovation and manufacturing. The COVID-19 emergency has also uncovered the weaknesses of people, social orders and economies, requiring a reevaluation of how financial and social exercises are coordinated. The emergency calls for solid reactions dependent on fortitude, co-activity and obligation. Social economy associations (affiliations, co-agents, shared associations, establishments and social undertakings), whose plans of action are worked around such standards can help to reshape the post-emergency economies and social orders.

Advancement doesn't happen in a vacuum yet rather expands on existing abilities and items. With regards to fast technological change, an association's upper hand is exceptionally subject to its dynamic abilities. This alludes to the association between the abilities inner to the firm and those produced by the setting inside which the company's exercises happen. A manufacturing framework that depends on a serious level of specialization in the manufacturing cycle (super-specialization) along supply chains makes divisions inside manufacturing between R&D, plan exercises and get together. Numerous organizations have offshored significant pieces of their creation, yet endeavoured to hold high worth creation exercises like plan and exploration. This prompts a reformist crumbling of nations' and firms' mechanical centres and may bargain their capacity to make and advance. Modern lodges are pertinent to steady area explicit advancement, yet additionally to cross-sectoral problematic development, transforming across areas in a way that is hard to foresee. By isolating manufacturing from the remainder of the worth chain, we hazard missing out on the exchange of significant unsaid information, in this manner harming any possibilities of startling and the most extreme innovations.

The COVID-19 emergency has uncovered the delicacy of isolating R&D and manufacturing measures. Where manufacturing is inserted in the neighbourhood and provincial organizations, economies have had the option to react quickly and adjust to the new real factors made by the pandemic, especially locales with organizations that have had the option to move abilities to the creation of various merchandise. Take the case of the creation of PPE kits. Producers in nations, for example, Turkey and China have had the option to adjust better because they created modern lodge with a blend of manufacturing limits, admittance to raw materials and significantly to information, just as quality confirmation and normalization capacities.

The pandemic has also featured the upgraded resilience of those economies with a more adjusted industry blend and uncovered new freedoms offered by nearby and provincial manufacturing. Makers, grassroots drives and fab labs have merged their innovation and skill to create PPE, segments and COVID-19 clinical consideration hardware, for example, mechanical pull siphons and ventilators. Such firms can advance, react to changes quickly and exhibit that joint effort is not a lose-lose situation yet a positive one, where communication across broadened networks prods development and adjusts innovation and assets in new phenomenal manners.

SIGNIFICANCE OF THE ENVIRONMENT IN MANUFACTURING

The current worldwide manufacturing model, in general, depend on straight creation frameworks, which are exceptionally inefficient and contaminating. The separation among creation and utilization frameworks has likewise had significant ecological outcomes, moving weights of utilization towards creation and extraction focuses and obscuring the comprehension of the ramifications of current utilization designs. The adverse consequences of manufacturing alluded to as 'externalities', are once in a while completely valued by purchasers since the results, which regularly happen in agricultural nations and rising economies, stay both out of the picture and therefore irrelevant for western buyers.

Global supply chains make it exceptionally dangerous to follow the manufacturing cycle from asset extraction to preparing crude materials, the vehicle of merchandise and the result. While new advances, for example, block-chain may give a financially savvy and dependable arrangement, their utilization is still a long way from standard. The natural and social effects related to every one of the periods of the cycle, particularly when manufacturing happens in unregulated conditions or under laxer conditions, is much harder to represent.

Likewise, since essential asset ventures bring about ecological effects that are lopsided to the related added esteem, it further reinforces the case for more limited worth chains and re-use and reusing of made products. Taking everything into account, the dichotomic model of manufacturing makes divisions among creation and utilization, which lessens the permeability and (financial) discernibility of utilization. The entirety of this has major worldwide ramifications.

Manufacturing has procured its place as a pillar of the recuperation procedures of post-COVID-19 economies. The new ordinary expects us to reevaluate how we create and burn-through and to reveal more insight into manufacturing and its part in tough different economies. Truth be told, a cooperative connection among utilization and creation cycles will be vital to a feasible future. We propose four principle empowering influences for different, strong and manageable manufacturing in a future post-COVID-19 world based on advancement and circularity.

TECHNOLOGICAL ADVANCEMENT

Technological development is another or improved item or interaction whose technological attributes are essentially not the same as in the past. Carried out technological item innovations are new items (item innovations) or cycles in the application (measure innovations) that have been brought to showcase. The item or interaction is viewed as a development on the off chance that it accomplishes determining benefits for the venture concerned; these need not be new according to the perspective of different organizations or the market.

Kinds of Innovation

It is striking the number of individuals who are under the bogus suspicion that organizations are either imaginative or not. This is a very polarizing and oversimplified point of view that doesn't consider the various sorts of innovations that organizations can and do seek after. For this post, we should separate development into two measurements: Technology and Market, which gives us the accompanying 4 sorts of advancement:

- Incremental Innovation
- Disruptive Innovation
- Architectural Innovation
- Radical development

Significance of Technological Innovation

- Technological development is the driver of serious accomplishment in numerous ventures
    - New items procure the most (generally state-of-the-art, bleeding-edge tech)
    - Product innovations assist firms with securing overall revenues by offering new interesting highlights - separated
    - Process innovations help make manufacturing more productive
    - Advances in data innovation have empowered quicker advancement: CAD - > fast plan and more limited creation time
- The importance of development and advances in data innovation has lead to:
    - Shorter item life cycles (since items are getting old quicker) item outdated nature
    - More quick new item presentations
    - Greater market division

The Role of Technology in Innovation

Innovation has an impact on advancement, yet not in the way that numerous individuals think. For the regular individual, innovation has no worth all alone. To have an effect, it must be properly applied to tackle explicit issues or meet certain objectives as characterized by your business or your client. To boost the worth of that distinction, it's fundamental to apply simply the littlest measure of innovation to the spaces that remain to profit by it (Kenge, Khan 2020).

Such a large number of individuals like innovation for the good of its own. They become involved with extravagant devices, spec sheets, and list items. They feel that having innovation is inventive all by itself. This isn't accurate. Advancement possibly happens when you use innovation to offer a genuine or saw the benefit to your client (Gupta et al. 2020).

There are two essential uses for business innovation: to meet the norm (site) and to make something new that pushes the business ahead (advancement). Regardless, the utilization of innovation ought to be driven by the requirements of the business and the client.

The state of affairs case is essentially the cost of affirmation. Each organization nowadays needs a site. It truly doesn't increase the value of your organization, however, you need it to work together. The best organizations are those that utilization innovation to help and improve their market differentiators.

MANUFACTURING RESILIENCE

The term Resilience got mainstream in the seventies and by and large depicts the capacity to react to aggravations. In various controls, resilience is utilized pretty much consistently, albeit the term aggravation can have broad implications.

In manufacturing, resilience refers to the ability to produce a consistent quality product at a fair cost and in a reasonable amount of time despite disruptions and risks. Customers want product customization and on-time delivery, yet the manufacturing business is beset with uncertainty from a variety of sources. Natural and man-made disruptions affect products and businesses, varying from shortages of materials, components, and energy to inconsistencies in supply chains and operations. Climate change and pollution have sparked interest in infrastructure, transportation, energy, and water resiliency on a global scale. Manufacturing requires a comprehensive approach to understanding and modeling resilience as a basis of economic activity. It is not enough to believe that material shortages and comments, as well as natural catastrophes (such as earthquakes), are the only variables affecting resiliency; rather, a thorough examination of all present and new manufacturing inputs is required (Kusiak, 2020).

A recent article in the Harvard Business Review puts out a three-step strategy for manufacturing executives to build resiliency:

- List down your suppliers (including those farther up the supply chain),
- Undertake a vulnerability assessment, and
- Build emergency plans that take into account both the costs and advantages.

Technology is equally important. Consider smart manufacturing, also known as Industry 4.0, which entails the digitization of the manufacturing process across the value chain, as well as data analytics to enable real-time choices. Professionals have the first lead, which translates to supply or demand shock resilience.

MANUFACTURING RESILIENCE AND INDUSTRY 4.0 TECHNOLOGIES

Resilience is bolstered by Industry 4.0, which provides real-time insight over raw materials, labor, and products. Even before the pandemic, manufacturers' processes were already being transformed by Industry 4.0 technology. Technology haves and have-nots are now adopting at different rates. However, in after the pandemic, the role of Industry 4.0 becomes even more essential. Players who use digital services are better placed to ride the wave since they ran faster as well as further during the crisis than their competitors.

Increased automation and technology, predictive maintenance, better optimization of process improvements, and, most importantly, a new level of efficiency and responsiveness to consumers not before conceivable are all benefits of digital technology. The manufacturing industry has a fantastic chance to enter the fourth industrial revolution by developing smart factories. Analyzing massive quantities of big data generated from industrial sensors enables real-time view of production assets and can give tools for doing predictive maintenance to reduce downtime.

Smart manufacturing (Industry 4.0) is based on a number of technologies (5G, blockchain, sensor technology, augmented reality, digital twins, and so on), and companies that use these technologies are stepping up their efforts in the face of the present crisis. Artificial intelligence (AI) and machine learning, such as deep learning, are being used to quickly find new medical therapies and vaccinations, for example. Machine learning was employed by the UK firm Benevolent AI to discover existing medicines (such as Eli Lilly's rheumatoid arthritis treatment baricitinib) that might be successful in treating COVID-19 patients, allowing for faster human trials.Machine learning (ML) and artificial intelligence

(AI) may be used to continuously monitor and analyze production plans. Augmented reality (AR) may help with difficult assembly and maintenance of industrial equipment, as well as speed up training for assembly duties.

Interconnectivity is critical to the smart factory's network design. Data gathered in real time from factory sensors, devices, and machines may be ingested and used right away by other manufacturing assets, as well as shared across other components in the enterprise system platform, such as enterprise resource planning (ERP) and other business and management software.

While looking for manufacturing resilience, companies should think about three areas where digital technology may assist right away:

- Improving insight and communication: Implementing off-the-shelf internet technologies like Accounting, MRP, CRM, CADCAM, and Digital Marketing may increase insight and collaboration.
- Modeling: Modeling can help with demand forecasts, manufacturing layout planning, and supplier risk assessments. COVID questions the validity of existing demand forecasting methods since past data is no longer reliable.
- Real-time monitoring and action: Real time monitoring using advanced tools is imperative for buiding resilience as it helps in better prediction and timely action.

According to the recent forecasts, digital technology will be at the forefront of many firms' minds as they consider how to restore operations and create the strength needed to deal with future crises. According to a recent McKinsey poll of industrial and supply-chain executives, 93 percent intend to focus on supply-chain resilience, and 90 percent plan to invest in skills for digitalization.

MANUFACTURING RESILIENCE IN POST-COVID ERA WITH COUNTRY COMPARISONS

The Covid-19 breakout challenges all spaces of financial matters including, however not just, wellbeing, mechanical association, macroeconomics, account, history, improvement, imbalance, political economy and public money, and concerns hypothesis just as exact proof.

India's economy could end up being the "strongest" in the subregion of South and South-West Asia over the long haul, as indicated by a report by the UN, which says a positive yet lower financial development post COVID-19 pandemic and the nation's huge market will keep on pulling in speculations.

The report named 'Unfamiliar Direct Investment Trends And Outlook In Asia And The Pacific 2020/2021', and arranged by United Nations Economic and Social Commission for Asia and the Pacific (UNESCAP), expressed that internal FDI streams to South and South-West Asia somewhat diminished by 2% in 2019, from USD 67 billion out of 2018 to USD 66 billion in 2019. The development, in any case, was mostly determined by India, which represented 77% of the complete inflows to the subregion and got USD 51 billion out of 2019, up 20 percent from the earlier year. The report said most of these streams were bound for the Information and Communications Technology (ICT) and the development of sub-area. As to the ICT area, the report said the speculation to India has advanced from data innovation administrations for Multinational ventures (MNEs) to the flourishing nearby computerized environment where numerous homegrown players, particularly in internet business, have pulled in extensive global speculation.

The report added that FDI outpourings from South and South-West Asia expanded for the fourth sequential year, humbly developing from USD 14.8 billion in every 2018 to USD 15.1 billion out of 2019. The geological spread of FDI outpourings from the subregion stayed lopsided, with only two nations (India and Turkey) representing by far most of the surges in 2019, it said.

Accordingly, the slight expansion in outward FDI was transcendent because of an increment in outpourings from India, which represented 80% of complete outward speculation from the subregion, the report said, adding that in 2019, India contributed USD 12.1 billion abroad, a 10 percent increment contrasted and the earlier year.

The report noticed that temporarily, the two inflows and outpourings from and to the subregion are relied upon to decay. In the initial 3/4 of 2020, the worth of Greenfield FDI inflows declined by 43% contrasted with a similar period a year ago, flagging an inversion of the development pattern in the subregion. A large portion of the Greenfield streams (87%) were bound for India, albeit the, generally speaking, greenfield inflows to the nation declined by 29%. Similarly, FDI from India is projected to decrease in 2020, with the biggest MNEs changing their income somewhere around 25% in mid-2020 because of the effects of the pandemic.

Be that as it may, India's economy could demonstrate the strongest in the subregion over the long haul. FDI inflows have been consistently expanding and positive, yet lower, monetary development after the pandemic and India's huge market will keep on drawing in market-chasing speculation, the report said.

India's quickly developing telecom and advanced space, specifically, could consider a to be bounce back as worldwide funding firms and innovation organizations keep on showing revenue in the nation's market through acquisitions. It was noticed that Facebook and Google's interest in Jio Platforms in 2020 worth USD 5.7 billion and USD 4.5 billion separately were demonstrations of this pattern.

Evaluations recommend that by 2025, center advanced areas, for example, IT and business measure the board, computerized correspondence administrations, and gadgets manufacturing could twofold in size.

Moreover, the pandemic has just additionally expanded the propensity of numerous areas like horticulture, instruction, energy, monetary administrations, coordination to digitalise, as COVID-19 has pushed numerous individuals and organizations to receive advanced arrangements and cycles.India has executed various essential venture arrangements and measures since 2019. Some of them remember the unwinding of cutoff points to FDI for the protection area, advancement of FDI rules which finished value covers in a few areas including coal and lignite mining, contract manufacturing and single-brand retail exchanging and expansion in the roof for FDI into the guard area to 74 percent through programmed endorsement course.

Notwithstanding these actions, and in direct reaction to the COVID-19 pandemic, the public authority likewise presented strengthened FDI screening techniques from adjoining nations, including Afghanistan, Bangladesh, China and Nepal. Looking forward, the transient interest in drug manufacturing is a gauge to diminish as numerous European and the United States drug organizations may switch halfway to more confined sourcing attributable to store network disturbances in the drugs area during the COVID-19 pandemic. This will be significant for drug manufacturing centre points around there, especially in India.

Looking at the USA, after the COVID-19 pandemic, US authorities are asking for essential commodities supply chains to be reshored to the United States, particularly medical supplies and high-tech items. However, reshoring such supply chains entirely is not the solution. It is also possible that domestic providers may be harmed. And such a shift would make American firms less competitive, putting them at odds with enterprises in other (often antagonistic) countries that continue to support globalization and promote key industries with strong policy initiatives like subsidies and currency controls.

UK too faced similar situation. The Covid-19 epidemic has wreaked havoc on the UK manufacturing industry. The Purchasing Managers' Index (PMI) for manufacturing in the United Kingdom fell to 32.6, the lowest level since records began over 30 years ago. 70 percent of firms have experienced a drop in orders and revenues, and a quarter of them anticipate to lay off workers in the next six months. This is supported by the latest UK GDP statistics, which showed a 20.4 percent drop in April alone. Most UK manufacturers began to place a greater emphasis on long-term recovery than on short-term survival, and with the proper assistance, the sector may lead the way to a global, green, and digital economic resurgence. Any economic rebound in the United Kingdom, however, will be contingent on how our international clients react. (Make UK: COVID 19 Manufacturing Monitor, May 2020).

As per preliminary statistics from Germany's Federal Statistical Office (Destatis), the Covid-19 epidemic caused a substantial drop in industrial production in March 2020. In March, industrial production decreased -9.2 percent month over month and -11.6 percent year over year. This is the most significant drop after recorded history in 1991. As a result of sluggish external demand, export sales continued to fall faster than overall new orders in May. However, compared to April, the rate of reduction in both categories has reduced. Looking ahead, manufacturers' production forecasts for the remainder of 2020 improved somewhat from April, although stayed in the negative area. The majority of businesses remained gloomy about the future, with considerable concerns about the pandemic's long-term impact on demand and supply (IHS Markit/ BME 2020).

China, on the other hand, is in a different stage of the Covid-19 cycle, with the actions taken to reopen sectors of the economy beginning to show up in official statistics. China's economy was rebounding in April, according to the National Bureau of Statistics (NBS), despite severe obstacles in the operational environment, as its domestic economy recovered from months of inactivity and the virus continued to spread in other global markets. According to NBS data, Chinese industrial production increased 3.9 percent year over year in April 2020, marking the nation's first recovery in the year.

CONCLUSION

In this chapter, key issues concerning the role of technological innovations in improving manufacturing resilience in the post-Covid era: a cross country comparison are discussed. The chapter highlights the critical importance of technological innovation, the significance of advancement in manufacturing, technological advancement, the role of technology in innovation manufacturing resilience for sustainable development.

In the aftermath of the new coronavirus epidemic, tough truths have been learnt. Manufacturing has been affected very severely. Companies who were able to respond fast, retool their facilities, reroute their supply networks, and use digital technologies to satisfy critical requirements and generate new possibilities swiftly switched gears.

After the COVID-19, lockdowns disturbed global supply chains and put the ideas of production network resilience and reshoring on each policy maker's lips. To adapt to the emergency, most organizations depended on supporting through protection, amassing and the quest for elective stock answers for initiate when required. Organizations additionally connected effectively in a superior observing and comprehension of supply chains.

Using smart manufacturing technologies and automation solutions offered by Industry 4.0, organizations can better satisfy their customers' demands in every situation while also expanding business. Despite the fact that the manufacturing business does not always operate in crisis mode, the pandemic has taught us a lot about resiliency. Any manufacturer may apply these principles to their production and turn it into a smart, agile, and responsive environment that can withstand whatever changes come their way.

The scenario seems to make organization think will COVID-19 imprint the start of the finish of globalization. Majority of organizations starts favouring nearshoring for example carrying creation to a close-by country (especially if it's essential for similar traditions association or Free Trade Agreement). Organizations are partitioned on the purposes behind this decision, from discovering better quality providers, expanding turnover and edges to diminishing postponements and better-overseeing inventories.

Governments have a task to carry out in boosting homegrown production network resilience. However, there is no wonder medication and organizations' reactions are parted across various strategy measures, which underlines the complex eventual fate of global creation. The attention is on work market adaptability and R&D venture to declare the nation's place in global value chains, while organizations are worried about homegrown assessment motivators to improve engaging quality.

REFERENCES

Ahsan, K. M., Islam, M. S., Litan, M. M., & Huang, X. (2020). Cash Conversion Cycle Connection with Industrial Productivity and Volume. *Globus An International Journal of Management & IT*, *12*(1), 66–70.

Dev, U. (2020). Re-Engineering Expert System Powered by Machine Learning. *Cosmos Journal of Engineering & Technology*, *10*(1), 1–5.

Gupta, D. A. (2019). Making India Digital: Transforming Towards Sustainable Development. *Cosmos Journal of Engineering & Technology*, *9*(2), 1–6.

Kenge & Khan. (2020). A Conceptual Study of The Supply Chain Management 4.0 Implementation Process. *Cosmos Journal of Engineering & Technology*, *10*(2), 1–5.

Khari, D., Sharma, V., & Agarwal, D. N. (2020). Effect of Pandemic COVID-19 on Economic Crisis and Health Issues Globally. *Cosmos Journal of Engineering & Technology*, *10*(1), 1–7.

Kusiak, A. (2020). Resilient manufacturing. *Journal of Intelligent Manufacturing*, *31*(2), 269. doi:10.100710845-019-01523-7

Make UK: COVID 19 Manufacturing Monitor. (2020, May). Author.

Ranjan, S., Gupta, D. R., & Gupta, D. A. (2020). Artificial Intelligence in Financial Acumen: Challenges and Opportunities. *Cosmos Journal of Engineering & Technology*, *10*(1), 1–5.

United Nations. (2018). *World Economic Situation and Prospects 2018* (Sales No. E.18.II.C.2). Author.

United Nations Global Pulse & WFP. (2016). *Using financial transaction data to measure economic resilience to natural disasters*. Project Series, No. 24.

World Health Organization (WHO). (2018). World Health Statistics 2018: Monitoring Health for the Sustainable Development Goal. Author.

Chapter 8
Role of Information Technology and Its Perspectives in Research and Development of Economy

Bhawna Yadav
Globus Education and Research Association, India

Anna Liza R. Alfonso
Far Eastern University, Philippines

ABSTRACT

Technology is widely acknowledged in economics as the primary source of economic development. Technological advancement enables more efficient production with more and superior products and services, which is essential for development. Technology encompasses a vast body of knowledge and instruments that make it easier to make efficient and creative use of economic resources to generate goods and services. Technological advancement is necessary for economic growth and development, and the more sophisticated the technology, the faster the local and global economies may improve. Globalization further fueled and results in increased importance of social and economic analysis and also necessitates coordinated development efforts using technology.

INTRODUCTION

Because of the factual features that apply at this moment, IT may have a unique function to play in growth and development. The fast innovation in IT, in particular, has made it a vibrant segment which is an appealing prospect as a driver to growth with that purpose solely, much like the auto industry being sought by the Japanese after WWII. On the other hand, there may be aspects of IT that make it appealing from the standpoint of economic growth theory.

IT mileages with respect to business world and it allows associations by working related with more productively and to amplify efficiency, etc (Gupta, Kumar 2013). Information Technology structures come looking as various innovatively good gadgets that assist with conveying valuable information to

DOI: 10.4018/978-1-7998-8705-8.ch008

heads of various organizations and consequently, they make use of this information to solve urgent requisite regarding tasks of organization. IT make enable with PC applications, and after this, practically workplace becomes reliant (Goel 2008).

Capacity frameworks, like virtual vaults, guard information by just permitting certain clients inside our organization to get to, pull out, add or change the records. IT security designing frameworks shield our electronic information from being hacked, or cleared out during a mechanical catastrophe (T, Basar 2012). Electronic security designing means our significant records will stay distant. Information technology works on our organization's productivity by creating robotized cycles to take trouble off our staff. Thus, our representatives are allowed to deal with numerous objects as PC functions with reports, creates questions, locates ventures and screens financials aspects (Kumar, Kapri 2010 ; Kumar 2008).

IT structures provides us distant admittance at our organization's as electronic organization, so we may telecommute or out as well as about. This is noted that availability allows us for expanding our efficiency as we may complete our task, in any event, when we aren't truly at workplace. This is also seen that correspondence is fundamental for business scenario, and information technology provides our organization as an asset, requisites to impart rapidly with successfully (Ghai, Tyagi & Gupta 2020).

IT may have a one-of-a-kind influence on growth. In this perspective, IT plays a unique role in the innovation process because it influences the rate at which prospective new ideas are transformed into contributions to the useable pool of knowledge in ways that no other factor can. The paradigm of recombinant growth was used to formalize this unique role. (Weitzman, 1998).

OBJECTIVES

1. To study the Research and development of IT.
2. To study the role of IT in economic growth.
3. To study the role of IT in Research and Development with reference to economic growth.

LITERATURE REVIEW TO SHOW THE ROLE OF IT IN ECONOMIC GROWTH

Information Technology and the Japanese Economy by Dale W. Jorgenson and Kazuyuki Motohashi, 2005, In this paper they compare sources of economic growth in Japan and the United States from 1975 through 2003, focusing on the role of information technology (IT). they adjusted Japanese data to conform to U.S. definitions in order to provide a rigorous comparison between the two economies. The adjusted data show that the share of the Japanese gross domestic product devoted to investment in computers, telecommunications equipment, and software rose sharply after 1995. The contribution of total factor productivity growth from the IT sector in Japan also increased, while the contributions of labor input and productivity growth from the Non-IT sector lagged far behind the United States.

Innovation and economic growth in China at WU business school the university of Western Australia, 2010, explained that How China has enjoyed high economic growth for three decades since the initiative of economic reform in 1978. This growth has however been driven mainly by labour-intensive, export-oriented manufacturing activities. Has innovation played a role in China's economic growth? What are the determinants of innovation in the Chinese economy? These are some of the questions which are to be explored in this study. Answers to these questions have important policy implications for China's economic development in the future as innovation is vital for the transformation of the country's growth model.

ROLE OF INFORMATION TECHNOLOGY

The **information technology** consists merit to go by assuming about all inescapable part related to human asset. In present situation, we are related with **information technology (IT)** period. Each and every group will be very much affected by it. Various groups have effectively started utilization with this technology (Agarwal & Shiju 2018). Information technology works with putting away and recovering colossal information rapidly along with assistance related apparatus as well as programming organizations with workstations with respect to lesser expenses. Information technology creates us powerful by mixing and setup regarding information to create unmistakably the new one information that supports in settling our speedy choices.

The worldwide development of exchange and trade has used to work within organizations by considering globally need to conveying organization by satisfying their needs. IT network starts empower us to provide information for people at all part of world. In continuation, this technology supports by consisting admittance about any information by settling at fast options along with choices. HR can be used in the most ideal way with the assistance of information technology to have the strategic advantage by expanding functional proficiency of HR and expediently expanding the efficiency.

The following century will be overwhelmed by the utilization of information technology. The high level information is made open today itself. IT will be a help for human asset the executives. A lot of information identifying with work investigation, work configuration, work determination and depiction, execution assessment, work assessment, pay design, pay and recompenses of every representative and chief, their augmentations with date, season of retirements leave records, the skill, information acquired by representatives and what not can be put away, joined and recon-figurate and make it accessible at the fingertips of the administrator in practically no time, along these lines saving time and cost and expanding significantly the usefulness and effectiveness of the representatives.

It can likewise decide the requirement for preparing in future for the workers and chiefs. The whole information can be configured to get new information in huge amount. The information technology outfitted human asset division with huge information to help different branches of the association to have admittance to human asset information to take choices identifying with representatives of their specialties. It will along these lines diminish the authoritative weight and cost. It works with cooperation between the representatives of various divisions and interdepartmental aiding in to fabricate collaboration.

Authoritative information bases make accessible a storage facility of information that can be used for compelling administration. The additional benefit is that the heuristic strategy can likewise be utilized to extricate information for use. The persevering chief and workers can utilize the information for their profession arranging.

The utilization of information technology requires more specialized and expert information which is to be obtained by the current staff and recently procured work force's should have it. They should know the ability of getting sorted out the information into steady and clear bundles that can be utilized by others. This requirements thorough instructive preparing to be given to the staff and leaders too. It will make them proficient to acknowledge testing and complex errand driving them to procure critical thinking abilities. To embrace information technology the association is to reengineer the human asset interaction to receive the change.

The prepared staff's are needed to enter, store and alter information in regard of HR. The representatives can be permitted to check the information with respect to themselves and get fulfilled. In this manner the framework is made on line open. The advantages of information reach to everybody in the association and every division assisting them with taking care of their issues identified with HR. Web has made open the preparation, learning and instructive materials accessible universally. This is accessible in practically no time, hence saving gigantic expense and time.

The utilization of information technology will change the work style of customary nature in light of the fact that the choice emotionally supportive network will help in settling on speedy choices by the forefront bosses which were taken by higher ups in the administrative order. This will diminish the administrative propensities. IT will start client arranged methodology. The staff's working in the field will actually want to make more contacts with the clients and customers. PCs them massively in this regard.

SIGNIFICANCE OF INFORMATION TECHNOLOGY IN ECONOMIC GROWTH

The significance of information technology regarding the view of general scenario in context of economic growth is as per the following:

1. **Business**: We know that business plays the vital role in the economic growth of any nation in the world. Using of technology, business scenario has been changed overall. Utilizing of technologies, organizations provide the best services to their clients with areas of expertise as planned. In business, all the departments may coordinate easily by the use of technologies (K Praveen, 2014).
2. **Training**: In any training part, the technology, plays the key role and supporters of instructors through various instruments like tablets, PCs, mobile and so on. In COVID-19 period, the full education system of the world is dependent on this technology and each educational institutions could easily carry their training through these latest aspects of technology.
3. **Easy Use of Money**: With the use of technology, everything is now digitized in the new name of e-commerce. At his platform, the supplier and the customers are available and they may use their money as well as talent in better, quicker and simpler way.
4. **Medical Care**: Technological aspects is a key supporters related to diagnosis in medical care. After new technological innovation, the working scenario related to medical experts become easier in working.
5. **Security:** Security is an important aspect in all the fields. Information plays the key role in creating the healthy environment in the globe. Latest technologies are doing drastic work in consideration of defence areas, scientific fields and so on. Utilizing authentication, passwords as well as encryption, the technologies conceals the safety in advanced manner.

PERSPECTIVES OF INFORMATION TECHNOLOGY

While information technology improves plan of frameworks and existing associations, it likewise empowers the plan of on a very basic level new associations and frameworks. Hence, endeavors in this space remember proactivity for the feeling of monitoring future innovative, hierarchical, and human concerns in order to help smooth advancement over the long haul to new information technology-based administrations. Among these future further developed admittance to information on numerous kinds.

The underlying endeavors at arrangement of information technology-based frameworks concerned help through further developed information technology-based equipment and programming. Some time back it was perceived that help could be given not exclusively to people in achieving such errands as report arrangement yet that the pervasive PC could offer help for bunches in noting questions of an imagine a scenario where nature with an assuming, reaction. This drove, a few decades prior, to the advancement of help through administration information frameworks (MIS) (Kumar, Gupta 2008 ; Agarwal. Kumar 2009). These frameworks have become very incredible today and are utilized for an assortment of purposes, for example, planning plane flights and booking front seats on them, and enrolling college understudies in classes.

An extra trouble is that it has gotten basically difficult to adapt to the plenty of new information technology-based emotionally supportive networks. The significant justification this is the absence of frameworks reconciliation across the huge assortment of such items and administrations. This has prompted the recognizable proof of an extra job for information technology experts, one including support through information frameworks coordination designing. An information frameworks reconciliation engineer is answerable for in general frameworks the board, including design the executives, to safeguard that assorted items and administrations are distinguished and collected into complete and coordinated answers for information frameworks issues of enormous scope and degree. There are numerous contemporary mechanical issues here.

There is a requirement for what are frequently called "open frameworks designs," or open frameworks conditions, that accommodate such necessities as between operability of uses programming across an assortment of heterogeneous equipment and programming stages. The critical thought here is the idea of open, or public, an idea that is expected to deliver agreement based advancements that will improve hardships related with absence of norms and the presence of exclusive interfaces, administrations, and conventions.

When brought to fulfillment, these information frameworks reconciliation improvements, and the related open frameworks conditions, will empower more productive and powerful setup administrations. This will bring about the advancement of information technology arrangements in empowering existing associations to work "better." However, there is likewise a requirement for "better" hierarchical plans. These necessities exist in an assortment of regions that reach from more productive and viable endeavor the board, to more proficient and compelling schooling of understudies in colleges, to more productive and powerful assembling measures. It is in this space that contemporary proactive information technology advancements guarantee the best result.

The initial three of the recommendations manage the consequences for subunit design and cycles. Huber states that the utilization of information technology will prompt: a bigger number and assortment of individuals partaking as information sources in the creation of choices; diminishes in the number and assortment of individuals containing the conventional up close and personal choice unit; and less authoritative time being consumed by choice related gatherings. Six recommendations manage the association in general. He shows that the utilization of information technology in a given association will prompt: a more uniform appropriation, across authoritative levels, of the likelihood that a particular hierarchical level will settle on a specific choice; a more noteworthy variety across associations in the levels at which a specific kind of choice is made; a decrease in the quantity of authoritative levels engaged with approving proposed authoritative activities; less halfway hubs inside authoritative information preparing networks; more regular turn of events and utilization of modernized data sets as segments of authoritative memory; and more incessant turn of events and utilization of in-house master frameworks as segments of hierarchical recollections.

Huber presents two recommendations that arrangement with circumstance appraisal. He expresses that the utilization of information technology will prompt more quick and more exact ID of issues and openings and to hierarchical circumstance evaluation that is more precise, complete, opportune, and accessible. At long last, he presents three suggestions that arrangement with information technology impacts on dynamic. It is hypothesized that the utilization of information technology will prompt greater choices, to a decrease in the time needed to approve proposed authoritative activities, and that the time needed to settle on choices will be diminished.

ROLE OF INFORMATION TECHNOLOGY IN RESEARCH AND DEVELOPMENT OF ECONOMY

There are various uses of IT in the development of economy as follows:

1. Technology's Role with Respect to Economic Development

Technology collaborates the colossal collection of data and devices that support in utilization related to monetary assets as way to develop the labor and various items effectively and inventively. Innovative advancement has the vital impact upon financial development with advancement, and use for further development in the aspect of technology accessible and globally economy may improve. Technology's part in monetary improvement is additionally covered also the following areas:-

- Time is Money
- Effectiveness
- Specialization
- Regular Sources
- Mechanical Expansion
- Examination
- Internet and International Trade

There are numerous features related to IT; recorded beneath:

1. **IT Administration**: Powerful blend related approaches and cycles to run of IT frameworks easily as well as inseparably with require association.
2. **IT Tasks:** Operation related to IT may be found regarding day-by-day work with respect to IT office. This gives technical support, network upkeep and process gadget the board.
3. **Equipment and Foundation**: The actual parts of Information Technology goes under its equipment. It incorporates setting up and keeping up with the gear like telephone frameworks, switches, workers, and PCs.

2. Business Related Information Technology

Significance of IT regarding business is tremendous. It supports each single trade area by computerizing process cycles and frameworks to aim destinations, produce income along with lessen shortcoming regarding work. Worth of BIT is expanding step by step with respect to regions, for example, business exchanges, by satisfying requests related with clients and administrative necessities.

Reason behind BIT is to satisfy ordinary developing necessities with respect to enterprises and satisfying about developing assumptions for clients of each field. To keep up with the harmony between complex PC situation with right acts regarding trade, managers related with solid BIT. Trade technology moves an organizations along with equipment framework, programming, framework and every one of the progressions in strategies. With the appropriate technology the executives, serving clients more will turn out to be truly simple as it helps in expanding representative commitment, offers admittance to data and gives adaptability as reacting to trade issues.

To find accomplishment in trade regions, this shows two non-material things consisting pertinent information as well as influential information. This adequately consolidates the executives abilities, correspondence technical aspects with skill of data. This is noted that sound correspondence framework and information, organization may limit about dangers, fortify with its framework and offer help to trade methodologies. Experts related with BIT propose displaying, skill regarding information security, the board as well as framework updates.

3. Significance Regarding IT

To direct about work, this requires applications which is based upon PC. PCs interface IT at numerous associations. It assists workers with keeping up with records of their various customers of different organizations. It assists patients with reaching doctors on the web and accept counsel in regards to their medical conditions. Additionally, records related with patients might be overseen appropriately through this framework.

By gathering information, knowledge, information transformation, information correspondences recovery and capacity, framework investigation are utilized. Indeed, even the instruction area has now been drastically modified about appearance of IT. To run trade in correct manner and produce anticipated results, PCs, programming, and web supports in ton.

Organizations are being currently consisting about virtual vaults as another type related with capacity framework; used to permit clients by keeping or pull-out the records. IT office provides the solid correspondence framework by conveying adequately. The utilization of PCs and the web expands the nature of training. The academic technique for instructing with learning are going to improve and IT adds further develop educational process system, understudies exercises as well as educating rehearses.

Understudies are more open to learn with current advances and zeroing in on web based educating more. Techniques relies upon communication related to educators and extraordinary sections regarding uncommon youngsters. Understudies not will undoubtedly utilize the normal, worn out conventional strategy for learning. This is noted that this create conceivable through presentation in consideration of technology related to training are and significance regarding technology may be viewed.

So here is a rundown of the advantages of information technology in our lives and furthermore there is a need of the Information Technology in each field.

1. With the headway in IT, one can get to the arrangement of the organization from any spot. It isn't required for the position to be in the workplace as it were. They can present their work from home too. Simple admittance to the framework has definitely expanded one's efficiency with no actual presence of the individual in the workplace.
2. There is a gigantic interest for IT experts in different fields. The interest opens an enormous chance for IT experts to investigate the field and show their ability. The IT field offers individuals to work for PC programming, framework investigation, testing, programming and equipment advancement, web application plan and so on
3. With the progression of information technology, the training field has changed its standpoint and has received an advanced method of instructing and learning. Educating on the writing board is currently something old. Instructors and establishments are utilizing current contraptions to show their understudies. A PC with a web association assists understudies with learning new things and comprehend the points effectively and profoundly.
4. Information technology assists patients with welling. They would now be able to interface with doctors and accept exhortation on the web. Likewise, there are numerous virtual medical services applications accessible to give direction. Electronic wellbeing records and tele-prescriptions are conveying effective and quality wellbeing to patients.
5. In the technology world, with information technology, the disadvantage of time and distance in business exercises has been eliminated. Presently, purchasing and selling are excessively simple. Clients can purchase online from their local people and worldwide sellers also.
6. With remote correspondence mediums, news communicates have gotten so simpler. A couple of moments are had to know the report from any side of the world.
7. Use of the web on cell phones, tablets, PCs, iPods, and different devices has been offering us limitless admittance to diversion mediums. Individuals can watch films or new melodies on OTT stages.
8. With the Information technology, correspondence between individuals has gotten less expensive, simpler and quicker than any time in recent memory. Messaging, video calling, sending messages are so natural these days. There are so numerous applications accessible online to offer these types of assistance.

CONCLUSION

Information technology advancements amplify the economic and social shifts that are reshaping business and society. A new type of economy is emerging: the information economy, in which businesses compete globally for knowledge, networking, and agility. Information technology has changed our lives definitely. These shifts necessitate a substantial adjustment for all countries in order to harness data for economic and social growth. New policies, regulatory and institutional reforms, and investments are all urgently needed to make this shift. In the midst of global information flows, competition, commerce, and investment, governments must achieve macroeconomic balance, political stability, and growth through this adjustment.

REFERENCES

Agarwal, & Shiju. (2018). A Study on Content Generation for Internet Usage. *International Journal of Advanced Research and Development.*, *3*(2), 1380–1382.

Agarwal, N., & Kumar, P. (2009). Role of Information Technology in Education. In *AICT Sponsored National Conference on Information Integrity & Supply Chain Management Abstracts Proceeding*. Book World Publisher.

Basar, T. (2012). A Game Theoretic Approach to Decision and Analysis in Network Intrusion Detection. *Proceedings of the 42nd IEEE Conference on Decision and Control*, 90(5), 3-12.

Devi & Yadav. (2017). Artificial Intelligence Through Machine Learning. *Globus An International Journal of Management & IT, 9*(1), 1-3.

Ghai, Tyagi, & Gupta. (2020). Leveraging Technology for Robust Financial Facilities: A Comparative Assessment of BRICS Nations. In *ICCAKM 2020*. IEEE Xplore.

Goel. (2008). A Global Change in Education through Information Technology and Communication. In Enterprises Information Systems & Technology. MacMillan Advanced Research Series.

Gupta, R., & Kumar, P. (2013). Information Technology Business Value Assessment: A Case of State Bank of India. *Globus: An International Journal of Management & IT, 4*(2), 30-34.

Kumar, P., & Gupta, R. (2008). Information System's Security by using Matrices and Graphs. *Conference Proceedings on Information Security and Mobile Computing*, 62-66.

Kumar, P., & Kapri, T. (2010). Web Content Management System. In Information and Communication Technology: Challenges and Business Opportunities. Excel Publishers.

Pandey & Kumar. (2017). A Study on Crash Attacks with Functions Related to Hash. *Globus An International Journal of Management & IT, 9*(1), 1-3.

Praveen Kumar, K. (2014). A Study On Cloud Computing. *Cosmos Journal of Engineering & Technology*, *4*(2), 1–3.

Puneet, K. (2008). *A Comparative Study of Information System's Security by using Graphs*. In *Enterprise Information Systems & Technology*. MacMillan India Ltd.

Weitzman, M. (1998). Recombinant Growth. *The Quarterly Journal of Economics*, *113*(2), 331–360. doi:10.1162/003355398555595

KEY TERMS AND DEFINITIONS

Economic Growth: Increase in the production of economic goods and services, compared from one period of time to another.

IT: Use of any computers, storage, networking and other physical devices, infrastructure, and processes to create, process, store, secure and exchange all forms of electronic data. The commercial use of IT encompasses both computer technology and telecommunications.

Research and Development: Activities that companies undertake to innovate and introduce new products and services. It is often the first stage in the development process. The goal is typically to take new products and services to market and add to the company's bottom line.

Chapter 9
Evaluation of Hospital Supply Chain Performance During the COVID-19 Pandemic:
Balanced Score Card Approach

Doni Maryono
Universitas Muhammadiyah Sidoarjo, Indonesia

Rita Ambarwati
Universitas Muhammadiyah Sidoarjo, Indonesia

ABSTRACT

The pandemic has an impact on almost all sectors of people's lives, in the economic, political, and socio-cultural sectors. The government has implemented large-scale social restrictions (PSBB) as an effort to stop the spread of the COVID-19 virus. With the PSBB, it causes disruption to the hospital supply chain management. As a step to anticipate the hospital's impact on the PSBB, the hospital needs to evaluate the performance of supply chain management. The purpose of this chapter is to describe the performance evaluation of hospital supply chain management using a balanced scorecard approach. A new finding from this study is to measure the performance of hospitals experiencing various disruptions in their supply chain management caused by the COVID-19 pandemic with a balanced scorecard. The author concludes that measurements with the balanced scorecard approach can provide information about the performance of hospital supply chain management broadly in areas experiencing disruption due to the COVID-19 pandemic.

INTRODUCTION

In the operational implementation of the company's organization, for the control function, information is needed about how it is performing. (Solihin, 2009) says managers will not be able to plan, organize, lead, and control effectively if they do not have adequate information. Information is a source of knowledge

DOI: 10.4018/978-1-7998-8705-8.ch009

and understanding of a person on a problem that is needed to make a correct decision. The leaders or managers who will perform the control function. As explained that in their informational role, managers continue to look for information that contains the performance of their units, managers' senses scan the unit's internal activities and their environment, Mintzberg in (Raymond & Schell, 2011). From the information obtained, it is known that the performance has been effective and efficient or not. (Solihin, 2014) said the goal to be achieved through controlling is the availability of tools for managers to direct and motivate their subordinates so that they can work towards organizational goals and provide feedback to managers on how well their subordinates are performing. Managers need to make corrections if their performance is low but if it is according to the planned standards then the company's operations are good and maintained to achieve the company's goals that have been set.

The company is a business organization which is an open system. Barnard in (Solihin, 2009) said that the organization as an open system like any other open system that will get influence from the environment. The company's environment will provide various inputs to the organization, so the company must always adapt itself to the development of the company's environment in order to maintain its sustainability. Grant in (Solihin, 2009) said that the general environment of the company consists of various factors such as social values, education level, politics, economy, law, demography, natural resource environment, technology. On the legal side, in 2020 the government issued a large-scale social restriction (PSBB) regulation to control the ongoing pandemic so that it does not spread further. The existence of this government policy has an impact on the nets of almost all companies. Disturbances that occur in the supply chain in the form of demand fluctuations and changes in the length of the order (lead time) are operational disturbances that commonly occur in the supply chain. Supply Chain Management is the management of the activities of procuring goods and services, converting them into semi-finished goods and final products, as well as delivery through the distribution system (Haizer & Render, 2010).

Strategic planning allows companies to anticipate conditions that are always changing, and provide a road map and direction to go and how to achieve it (Jauch & Glueck, 2004). Strategic planning is an important management tool that can help organizations perform their duties better, facilitate strategy development and implementation, and make organizations more sensitive to customer and market needs (Obeng & Ugboro, 2008). Strategic planning (strategic planning) is vital for the organization in maintaining its survival (Wheelen & Hunger, 2004).

Hospital is an entity that is engaged in the treatment and care of people who need health services. As a General Hospital company, it also implements a strategy related to the supply chain. With the PSBB imposed by the government, the supply chain of General Hospitals is also likely to experience disruptions like other companies. As an anticipatory step, General Hospitals against the impact of this PSBB, General Hospitals need to evaluate their supply chain performance, so as to get an overview of the company's supply chain performance during this PSBB. (Fahmi, 2016) said to avoid problems arising in uncertain situations, managers should conduct research first, to seek as much information as possible and use several decision-making methods that are most appropriate for each problem condition. To evaluate the supply chain performance of General Hospitals, several approaches can be used, including the Balanced Scorecard. Luis and Biromo (Gultom, 2009) say that the definition of the Balanced Scorecard is a performance management tool that can help organizations translate their vision and strategy into action by utilizing a set of financial and non-financial indicators, all of which are intertwined in a causal relationship. result. The Balanced Scorecard is a suitable tool for evaluating and designing operations strategy (Dodangh, Majid, & Nasehifar, 2010). Thus, to evaluate supply chain performance at a General Hospital, it can be done with the Balanced Scorecard approach.

From this urgency, it is necessary to analyze the performance of the supply chain at the General Hospital using the Balanced Scorecard approach. From the results of this evaluation, company leaders will get information on whether the company has a good performance in the current situation of the PSBB. Based on this information, the RSU can make corrections if its supply chain management performance shows that it does not meet the established standards.

LITERATURE REVIEW

Supply Chain Management

The supply chain is all stages involved directly or indirectly in meeting the demands of producers, suppliers, transporters, warehouses, retailers and end consumers (Chopra & Peter, 2007). Supply Chain Management (SCM) is a method, tool or approach to supply chain management (Pujawan, 2005). Supply Chain Management (SCM) is the integration of material and service procurement activities, conversion into semi-finished goods and final products, and delivery to customers (Haizer & Render, 2010). According to (Mulyadi, 2001) performance is the success of team personnel, or organizational units in realizing the strategic goals that have been set previously with the expected behavior.

There is a flow that occurs in supply chain activities, namely the flow of materials, information, and money (Chopra & Peter, 2007). The material in question is goods that can be in the form of raw goods, semi-finished goods or finished products, or services for companies engaged in services. Information is data that has been processed, and money is a medium of exchange that is issued to ensure the smooth flow of materials and information. The goal of SCM is to manage and improve the flow of materials from point of origin to point of delivery as well as information feedback from end consumers at the minimum possible cost. The flow of information is well integrated and transparent from the supplier to the end consumer.

According to Tjiptono (2014), "The distribution channel is a set of organizational participants who perform all the functions needed to deliver the product/service from the seller to the final buyer." Meanwhile, according to (Studies et al., 2018) Distribution or place is the process of distributing goods and services from producers to target consumers. From distribution channels to consumer product markets, intermediaries who directly deal with consumers are retailers or retailers.

The government as the regulator must be able to ensure that the entire food supply chain continues to run smoothly and without interruption. The food supply chain must continue to run with a new supply chain strategy in the conditions of covid 19. The continuity of the smooth distribution process without obstacles can avoid a shortage of goods so that there are no price spikes due to insufficient or even non-existent stock of goods. Besides these factors can also avoid the hoarding of goods by some speculators who want to take advantage.

Pandemic Corona Virus Disease 2019 (Covid 19)

Corona Virus Disease 2019 or COVID-19 is an infectious disease caused by a new type of coronavirus. Coronaviruses (CoV) are a large family of viruses that can cause a variety of mild to severe symptoms. In terms of symptoms, family viruses often attack the human respiratory system. At least, there are two types of coronavirus that have also attacked the people of Indonesia and their spread is quite high, namely

East Respiratory Syndrome Coronavirus (SARS-CoV) and Severe Acute Respiratory Syndrome Coronavirus (SARS-CoV). And recently, there has been a new coronavirus caused by the disease COVID-19. According to WHO (2020) based on Global Surveillance guidelines, the definition of COVID-19 can be classified into three parts, namely:

1. Suspected case
2. Probable case or probable case
3. Confirmed cases or patients who have been proven positive through laboratory tests.

Meanwhile in Indonesia Based on the Ministry of Health of the Republic of Indonesia (2020) the definition of the classification of COVID-19 cases is divided into:

1. Patients under surveillance or PdP
2. People in monitoring or OdP
3. People without symptoms or OTG

To stop the spread of the virus, the government has made various efforts. Among them are carrying out large-scale social restrictions (PSBB), instructions to always wear masks, always wash hands, keep a distance from one person to another.

Government Policy during the Pandemic Period According to the 1945 Constitution of the Republic of Indonesia

The policy regarding Large-Scale Social Restrictions (PSBB) in Indonesia was first implemented on April 10, 2020 in Jakarta, followed by several other regions in Indonesia. There are several regulations related to the implementation of the PSBB. These include Government Regulation (PP) Number 21 of 2020 concerning Large-Scale Social Restrictions in the Context of Accelerating the Handling of Corona Virus Disease 2019 (COVID-19), Minister of Health Regulation (Permenkes) Number 9 of 2020 concerning Guidelines for Large-Scale Social Restrictions in the Context of Accelerating Handling Corona Virus Disease 2019 (COVID-19), as well as Government Regulation in Lieu of Law (Perpu) Number 1 of 2020 concerning State Financial Policy and Financial System Stability for Handling the 2019 Corona Virus Disease Pandemic and/or in Facing Dangerous Threats National Economy and/or Financial System Stability.

In terms of the mechanism for the application of PSBB, it is stated in Government Regulation Number 21 of 2020 in Article 2, namely::

1. With the approval of the minister who administers government affairs in the health sector, the Regional Government may impose Large-Scale Social Restrictions or restrictions on the movement of people and goods for a particular province or regency/city.
2. Large-Scale Social Restrictions as referred to in paragraph (1) must be based on epidemiological considerations, magnitude of threat, effectiveness, resource support, operational technical, political, economic, social, cultural, defense and security considerations.

Minister of health regulation Number 9 of 2020 contained in Article 2, namely to be able to establish Large-Scale Social Restrictions, a province/district/city area must meet the following criteria: the number of cases and/or number of deaths due to disease increases and spreads significantly and rapidly to several regions; and There is an epidemiological link with similar events in other regions or countries.

Article 4 paragraph (1) Government Regulation Number 21 of 2020:

1. Large-Scale Social Restrictions at least include:
    a. school holidays and workplace
    b. restrictions on religious activities and/or
    c. restrictions on activities in public places or facilities.

Law Number 6 of 2018 concerning Health Quarantine in Article 59 paragraph (3), namely: yaitu:

1. Large-Scale Social Restrictions as referred to in paragraph (1) shall at least include:
    a. school and workplace holidays
    b. restrictions on religious activities

Impact of Large-Scale Social Restrictions on Supply Chain Management Activities

The results of Hadiwardoyo's research (2020) show that what is needed is the right policy, both in terms of location, time and procedure. If the PSBB can guarantee a break in the chain of transmission of Covid-19, then do it properly, and in the shortest possible time. Prolonged restrictions, or changing locations because they are not in sync, risk exceeding the survival capabilities of individuals and business entities. If that happens, then the rescue cannot be carried out, and the losses will be even greater both economically and socially.

We can see this in the various steps taken by the government both at the central and regional levels by recommending or urging the public to limit activities in certain sectors, including pressing the public to postpone activities that invite a lot of people. person. On the other hand, this condition almost stops aspects of daily life, trade and other economic activities (Thorik, 2020)

These impacts also revolve in several sectors of people's lives. Both in the economic, political, and socio-cultural sectors.

Since the pandemic that occurred in the international region, the economy of every affected country has experienced a slump.

Dito (2020) stated that the economic and trade sectors that had the biggest impact due to COVID-19 were the economic and trade sectors. Where the implementation of the PSBB causes the state and regional economies to weaken. Even Indonesia's export sector also experienced a weakening. Likewise, investors who seem reluctant to invest because they are in a difficult economic phase. The prospects for world and Indonesian economic growth in 2020 are potentially lower if the Covid-19 outbreak continues to spread, triggering the implementation of stricter restrictions or social distancing policies by various countries, and global financial market pressures continue due to high uncertainty (Michael, 2020).

The determination of the PSBB policy creates supply disruptions and distribution delays which can have an impact on scarcity and price increases (Ariani et al., 2012).

Balanced Scorecard

Definition of Balanced Scorecard

The Balanced Scorecard is a business performance measurement concept that balances the measurement of the performance of a business organization which has been considered too inclined to financial performance. Before the emergence of the balanced scorecard concept, what is commonly used in companies so far is the traditional performance measurement that only focuses on the financial sector.

It is quite realized today that the measurement of financial performance used by many companies to measure executive performance is no longer adequate, so the concept of the "Balanced Scorecard" was born. The balanced scorecard is a business performance measurement concept introduced by Robert S. Kaplan and David P Norton. The Balanced Scorecard consists of two words, namely the scorecard and balanced. A score card is a card used to record a person's performance score. The word balanced is intended to show that personnel performance is measured in a balanced way from two aspects: financial and non-financial, short-term and long-term, internal and external. From this definition, Mulyadi (2001) argues that in a simple sense the Balanced Scorecard is a scorecard used to measure performance by taking into account the balance of financial and non-financial, long-term and short-term, internal and external.

Luis and Biromo (Gultom, 2009) say that the definition of the Balanced Scorecard is a performance management tool that can help organizations translate their vision and strategy into action by utilizing a set of financial and non-financial indicators, all of which are intertwined in a cause and effect relationship result.

Advantages of Balanced Scorecard

In its development, BSC has helped many companies to successfully achieve their goals. BSC has several advantages that traditional strategic management systems do not have. Traditional management strategies only measure organizational performance from the financial side and focus more on measuring things that are tangible, but business development demands to change the view that intangible things also play a role in organizational progress. BSC answers these needs through a contemporary strategic management system, which consists of four perspectives, namely: finance, customers, internal business processes and learning and growth.

The advantage of the BSC approach in the strategic planning system (Mulyadi, 2001) is that it is able to produce strategic plans, which have the following characteristics:

1. Comprehensive
2. Coherent
3. Balanced
4. measurable

The benefits of the Balanced Scorecard for companies according to Kaplan and Norton (2000) are as follows:

1. The Balanced Scorecard integrates the company's strategy and vision to achieve short-term and long-term goals.

2. The Balanced Scorecard allows managers to see the business in financial and non-financial perspectives (customers, internal business processes, and learn and grow)
3. The Balanced Scorecard allows managers to assess what they have invested in the development of human resources, systems and procedures for improving the company's performance in the future.

Perspectives in the Balanced Scorecard

The perspectives in the BSC are as follows:

1. Financial Perspective

BSC uses financial performance benchmarks such as net income and ROI, because these benchmarks are generally used in companies to determine profit. Financial benchmarks alone cannot describe the causes that make changes in wealth created by companies or organizations (Mulyadi and Setyawan, 2000).

The Balanced Scorecard is a performance measurement method in which there is a balance between financial and non-financial to direct the company's performance towards success. BSC can explain further about the achievement of the vision that plays a role in realizing the increase in wealth (Mulyadi and Setyawan, 2000) as follows:

a. Increased satisfied customers thereby increasing profits (through increased revenue).
b. Increased productivity and commitment of employees so as to increase profits (through increased cost effectiveness).
c. Increasing the company's ability to generate financial returns by reducing the capital used or investing in projects that generate high returns.

In the Balanced Scorecard, financial measurement has two important roles, where the first is that all perspectives depend on the financial measurement that shows the implementation of the planned strategy and the second is that it will give impetus to the other 3 perspectives about the targets to be achieved in achieving the goals. organization goals.

According to Kaplan and Norton (2004), the business cycle is divided into 3 stages, namely:

a. Growth

   The growth stage is the initial stage in the business life cycle. At this stage the company tries to use its resources to increase its business growth. In addition, the company will invest as much as possible, increase new products, build production facilities, increase operating capabilities, seize market share, and create distribution networks. In this stage, the company will most likely always be in a state of loss, because at this stage the company focuses on investing in investments that will be enjoyed in the long term.

b. Sustain

   Is the second stage where the company is still investing and reinvesting by signaling the best rate of return. At this stage the company still has a good attraction for investors to invest their capital. At this stage, the company must be able to maintain its market share and must pay attention to better product quality and service so that it will gradually experience growth from year to year.

Financial goals at this stage are usually more profit-oriented. Objectives related to profitability can be expressed using measures related to operating profit. To get good profitability, of course, managers must work hard to maximize the income generated from capital investment, while for business units that already have autonomy, they are asked not only to manage the income stream, but also the level of capital investment that has been invested in the business unit concerned. Other benchmarks that are often used at this stage, such as ROI, profit margin, and operating ratio.

c. Harvest

This stage is the stage of maturity for a company, because at this stage the company is just reaping from the investments made in the previous stages, what must be done at this stage is that the company no longer invests, but only keeps the company running well.

2. Customer Perspective

In the customer perspective, the company needs to first determine the market segments and customers that are the targets for the organization or business entity. Furthermore, managers must determine the best measuring tool to measure the performance of each operating unit in an effort to achieve its financial targets. Furthermore, if a business unit wants to achieve superior financial performance in the long term, they must create and present a new product/service of better value to their customers (Kaplan, and Norton, 1996).

The product is said to be of value if the benefits received by the product are higher than the cost (if the product performance is closer to or even exceeding what is expected and perceived by the customer). The company is limited to satisfying potential customers so it is necessary to segment the market to serve in the best way based on existing capabilities and resources.

There are 2 groups of measurements in the customer perspective, namely:

a. Icore measurement group

This measurement group is used to measure how the company meets customer needs in achieving satisfaction, maintaining, obtaining, and seizing the targeted market share.

Within the core measurement group, we recognize five benchmarks, namely:

i. Market Share: This measurement reflects the company's share of the overall market, which includes: the number of customers, the number of sales, and the volume of sales units.
ii. Customer Retention: Measures the level at which a company can maintain a relationship with consumers.
iii. Customer Acquisition (customer acquisition); measures the degree to which a business unit is able to attract new customers or win new business.
iv. Customer Satisfaction: Assessing the level of customer satisfaction related to specific performance criteria in the value proposition.
v. Customer Profitability: measuring the profits obtained by the company from selling products or services to consumers.

b. Customer value proposition

This measurement group is used to find out how companies measure the value of the market they control and the potential market they might be able to enter. This measurement group can also describe performance drivers regarding what the company must provide to achieve high levels of satisfaction, loyalty, retention, and customer acquisition. Value proposition describes the attributes presented by the company in the products/services that are sold to create customer loyalty and satisfaction.

The customer value measurement group consists of:

i. Product/service attributes, which include: function, price, and product quality.
ii. Relationships with customers, which include: distribution of products to customers, including responses from the company, delivery times, and how customers feel after buying products/services from the company concerned.
iii. Image and reputation, which describe the intangible factors for the company to attract customers to relate to the company, or buy the product.

3. Internal Business Process Perspective

The internal business process perspective presents critical processes that enable business units to provide a value proposition that is able to attract and retain customers in the desired market segment and satisfy the expectations of shareholders through financial returns (Simon, 1999).

Each company has a unique set of value creation processes for its customers. In general, Kaplan and Norton (1996) divide it into 3 basic principles, namely:

a. Innovation Process

The innovation process is the most important part in the whole production process. But there are also companies that put innovation beyond the production process. The innovation process itself consists of two components, namely: identifying customer desires, and carrying out a product design process that is in accordance with customer desires. If the innovation results from the company are not in accordance with the wishes of the customer, the product will not receive a positive response from the customer, so it does not provide additional income for the company and even the company has to incur investment costs in the research and development process.

b. Operation Process

The operating process is an activity carried out by the company, starting from the time the order is received from the customer until the product is sent to the customer. The operation process emphasizes the delivery of products to customers in an efficient and timely manner. This process has, in fact, become the main focus of the performance measurement systems of most organizations.

c. Post-Sales Service

As for the after-sales service referred to here, it can be in the form of a warranty, replacement for damaged products, etc. The company can measure whether its efforts in after-sales service have met customer expectations, using benchmarks that are quality, cost, and time as carried out in the operating process. For cycle time, companies can use the measurement of the time from when a customer complaint is received until the complaint is resolved.

The following is a picture of the internal business process perspective:

Figure 1. The internal business process value chain perspective
(Source: Kaplan and Norton (1996)

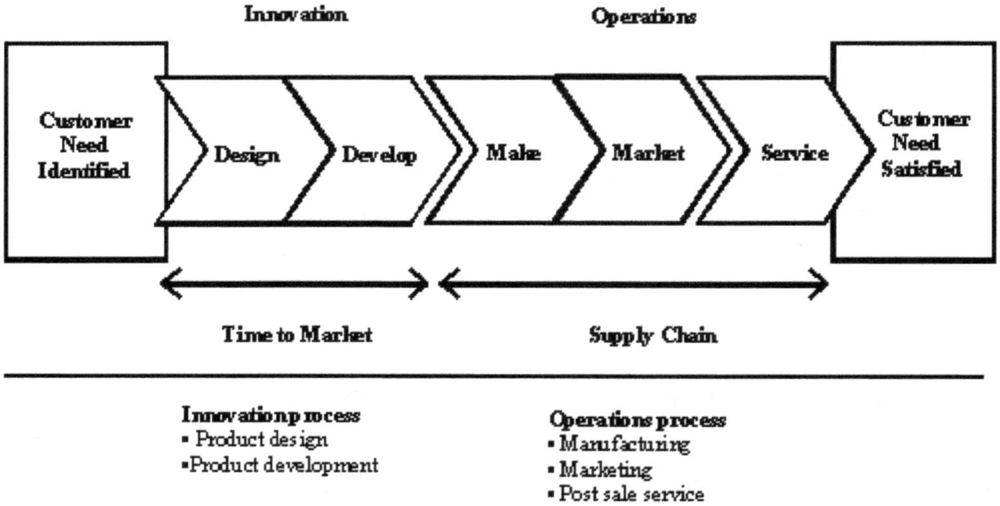

4. Learning and Growth Perspective

This perspective provides the infrastructure for achieving the previous three perspectives, and for generating long-term growth and improvement.

It is important for a business entity when investing not only in equipment to produce products/services, but also investing in infrastructure, namely: human resources, systems and procedures. Benchmarks of financial performance, customers, and internal business processes can reveal large gaps between existing capabilities of people, systems and procedures. To minimize this gap, a business entity must invest in the form of reskilling employees, namely: improving the ability of systems and information technology, as well as rearranging existing procedures.

The learning and growth perspective includes 3 principles of capability related to the company's internal conditions, namely:

a. Worker Capability

The ability of workers is part of the contribution of workers to the company. In relation to the capabilities of workers, there are 3 things that must be considered by management:

i. Worker satisfaction

Worker satisfaction is a precondition for increasing productivity, responsibility, quality, and service to consumers. Elements that can be measured in employee satisfaction are employee involvement in making decisions, recognition, access to information, encouragement to work creatively, and to use initiative, as well as support from superiors.

ii. Worker Retention

Employee retention is the ability to retain the best workers in the company. Where we know workers are a long term investment for the company. So, the absence of a worker who is not due to the company's wishes is a loss in the intellectual capital of the company. Employee retention is measured by the percentage of turnover in the company.

iii. Worker Productivity

Worker productivity is the result of the overall effect of improving skills and morale, innovation, internal processes, and customer satisfaction. The goal is to relate the output produced by workers to the number of workers who are supposed to produce that output.

b. Information System Capability
The benchmarks for information system capabilities are the level of availability of information, the level of accuracy of the information available, and the time period for obtaining the required information.

c. Organizational Climate
What drives the emergence of motivation, and empowerment is important to create workers who take the initiative. The benchmark for this is the number of suggestions given by workers.

The following is a picture of a learning and growth perspective:

Figure 2. Growth and learning perspective
(Source: Kaplan and Norton 1996)

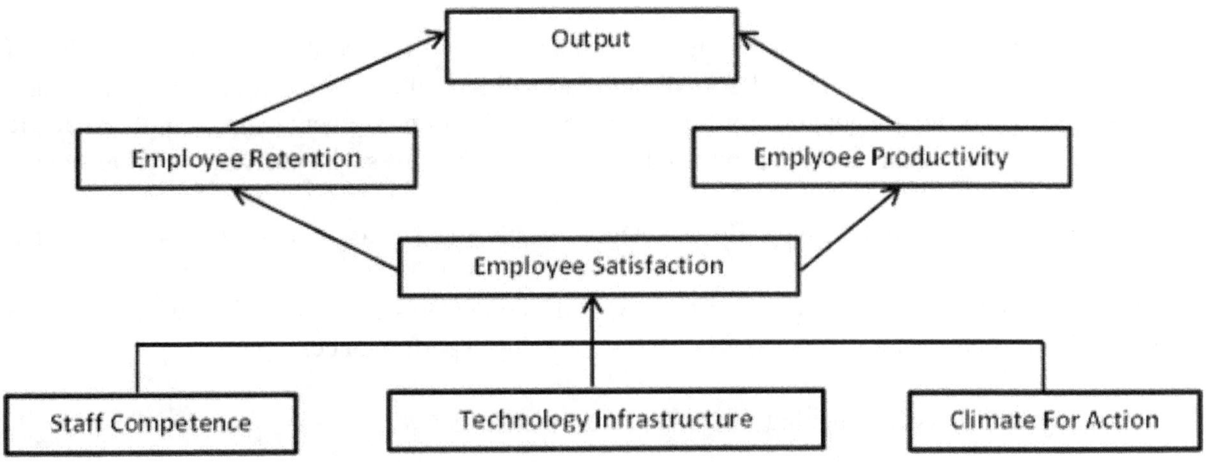

From the four perspectives, there is a causal relationship which is a description of the objectives and measurements of each perspective. The relationship between various strategic objectives that are generated in strategic planning with the Balanced Scorecard framework promises to increase the company's ability to produce financial performance. This capability is indispensable for companies entering a competitive business environment.

Here is an image that explains the causal relationship of the four perspectives in the Balanced Scorecard:

Balanced Scorecard Steps

The Balanced Scorecard steps include four new management processes. This approach combines long-term strategic goals with short-term events. The four processes according to (Kaplan and Norton, 1996) include::

1. Translating the company's vision, mission and strategy

Figure 3. Causal relationship of the four perspectives BSC
(Source: Kaplan and Norton 1996)

To determine performance measures, the organization's vision is described in terms of goals and objectives. Vision is a description of the conditions that will be realized by the company in the future. Goals are also one of the foundations for formulating strategies to make them happen. In the strategic planning process, these goals are then elaborated into strategic objectives with measures of achievement.

2. Communicating and linking the various strategic objectives and measures of the balanced scorecard

This can be done by showing each employee what the company is doing to achieve what the shareholders and consumers want. It aims to achieve good employee performance.

3. Planning, setting goals, aligning various business plan initiatives

Allows organizations to integrate their business plans and financial plans. The balanced scorecard as a basis for allocating resources and managing which ones are more important to prioritize, will move towards the long-term goals of the company as a whole.

4. Improve Feedback and strategic learning

This fourth process will provide strategic learning to the company. With the balanced scorecard as the center of the company's system, the company monitors what the company has produced in the short term.

Implementation of the Balanced Scorecard

Organisasi Organizations really need to implement the Balanced Sorecard as a set of multi-dimensional performance measures. This reflects the need to measure all areas of performance that are critical to organizational success.

(Tunggal, 2011) Four perspectives are considered in the BSC, namely::

1. Financial perspective, related to how to serve the shareholders. Measurements of cash flow, return on capital, sales and income growth are usually used for a particular financial perspective.
2. Customer perspective, related to the level of customer satisfaction. In general, the measurement of this perspective includes matters relating to the level of damage, timeliness of delivery, warranty support, product development and other things that come from direct input from customers and are associated with specific company activities.
3. The perspective of internal business processes, namely the perspective related to the main competencies and operational areas. Internal business processes are generally measured through productivity, cycle time, quality, various cost measurements and other related indicators.
4. Learning and growth perspective, which is a perspective related to continuous improvement and value creation. Measurement is usually emphasized on aspects related to organizational innovation and learning, such as: technology leadership, product development cycle times, operational process improvement, and others.

DISCUSSION

Linking Hospital Supply Chain Management Performance with Performance Measurement using the Balanced Scorecard

In the context of COVID-19, a skilled organization is an organization that is skilled in acquiring, creating, transferring knowledge about COVID-19, and modifying hospital behavior that reflects new knowledge and insights to maintain business continuity and prepare for the new normal.

Such rapid changes during the COVID-19 pandemic demand a quick response from top managers regarding the direction of the hospital's business continuity so that it does not collapse in the midst of the pandemic. To produce a fast and appropriate response requires the existence of a comprehensive database and accurate evaluation of the field conditions related to supply chain management and those affecting it.

The supply chain has been disrupted due to the ongoing COVID-19 pandemic. Actors in the supply chain have limited activities to avoid contracting COVID-19, distribution of drugs and medical devices has been hampered due to the PSBB, patients as end consumers of hospital services are also afraid to come to the hospital. Patients who suffer from pain that can still be endured will not go to the hospital to seek help, but will endure the pain first. Patients with only emergency cases speculated that they had ruled out the risk of contracting COVID-19, and finally they came to the hospital to seek help.

From a business point of view, the conditions due to the COVID-19 pandemic have changed everything. Hospital income will decrease because hospital service users as the main source of hospital income decline. Service to patients has also decreased because the implementation of procedures related to handling patients during the pandemic disrupts services, causing patient dissatisfaction with the services provided. In addition, the public's perception of the hospital as a place of service for COVID-19 sufferers has resulted in patients being afraid to visit the hospital. As a result of decreased patient visits, the level of hospital bed occupancy will also decrease. Disrupted hospital services will increase patient care time in the hospital.

The changes that occur require hospital entities to learn about what is happening, so that they can survive or even continue to benefit when the COVID-19 pandemic is running.

Changes in the internal and external environment of hospital entities, which in the perspective of hospital supply chain management are disruptions to supply chain activities, namely on the side of actors, products or information. The disruption that occurs disrupts the performance of the hospital's supply chain management. Disruption to supply chain performance requires hospital entities to evaluate, one of which is done with a balanced score card approach.

Using the Balanced scorecard to measure the performance of hospital supply chain management will result in measurements in 4 perspectives, namely:

1. Financial perspective provides information on measurement results regarding Net Profit Margin (NPM), ROI (Return on Investment), Economic Ratios, Efficiency Ratios, Effectiveness Ratios
2. Customer Perspective (Customer Perspective) provides information on measurement results regarding Customer Satisfaction Level, Consumer Profitability Level, Customer Retention/Retention Ability, Customer Acquisition Ability
3. The Internal Business Process Perspective provides information on measurement results from BOR (Bed Occupancy Rate or Bed Use), BTO (Bed Turn Over Rate or Bed Turnover), GDR (Gross Death Rate), NDR (Net Death Rate), ALOS (Average Legth of Stay), TOI (Turn Over Internal)
4. Learning and Growth Perspective (Learn and Growth / Infrastructure Perspective) provides information on the measurement results of Employee Productivity, Employee Turnover, Employee Satisfaction.

FUTURE RESEARCH DIRECTIONS

Research on evaluating the performance of hospital supply chain management during a pandemic needs to be done a lot because supply chain changes will continue to adapt to changes caused by the ongoing pandemic. As a follow-up to the evaluation of supply chain performance, there is a need for research on changes in hospital supply chain management strategies so as to get the right strategy regarding supply chain management during the COVID-19.

CONCLUSION

The COVID-19 pandemic has resulted in disruptions to hospital supply chain management activities. Evaluation must be carried out to obtain information on the level of effectiveness and efficiency of hospital supply chain management performance, which becomes a benchmark in determining the hospital's strategy so that it can continue to survive and even make a profit. Evaluation of hospital supply chain management performance using a balanced scorecard approach can provide balanced performance information between financial and non-financial, between internal and external hospital entities.

REFERENCES

Chopra, S., & Peter, M. (2007). *Supply chain management, strategy planning & operation* (3rd ed.). Pearson Prentice Hall. doi:10.1007/978-3-8349-9320-5_22

Dito. (2020). *Dampak pandemi Covid-19 terhadap perekonomian Indonesia*. Jurnal Benefita. Universitas Sumatera Utara.

Dodangh, J., Majid, M., & Nasehifar, V. (2010). Ranking of strategic plans in balanced scorecard by using electric method. *International Journal of Innovation, Management and Technology*.

Fahmi, I. (2016). *Teori dan paraktik pengambilan keputusan kualitatif dan kuantitatif.* Rajawali Pers.

Gultom, D. R. (2009). *Pengukuran kinerja perusahaan dengan balanced scorecard: studi kasus pada perusahaan perkebunan negara III (Persero) Medan*. Universitas Sumatra Utara.

Hadiwardoyo, W. (2020). Kerugian ekonomi nasional akibat PSBB. *Jurnal of Business and Entrepreneurship, 2*.

Haizer, J., & Render, B. (2010). *Manajemen operasi*. Salemba Empat.

Jauch, L. R., & Glueck, W. F. (2004). *Strategic management and business policy* (9th ed.). McGraw-Hill.

Kaplan, R. S., & dan Norton, D. P. (2000). Balance scorecard, menerapkan strategi menjadi aksi. Terjemahan. Penerbit Erlangga.

Kaplan, R. S., & Norton, D. P. (2004). *Strategy maps: Convert intangible assets into tangible outcomes*. Harvard Business School Press.

Kementrian Kesehatan Republik Indonesia. (2020). *Peraturan menteri kesehatan republik indonesia nomor 9 tahun 2020 tentang pedoman pembatasan sosial berskala besar dalam rangka percepatan penanganan corona virus disease 2019 (covid-19)*. Kemenkes RI.

McLeod, J. R., & Schell, G. P. (2011). *Sistem informasi manajemen*. Salemba Empat.

Michael, H. (2020). *Dampak coronavirus terhadap ekonomi global.* Bank Indonesia. https://www.bi.go.id/id/publikasi/ekonomi-keuangan-kerjasama-

Mulyadi & Setyawan, J. (2000). *Sistem perencanaan dan pengenalian manajemen* (2nd ed.). Jakarta: Salemba Empat.

Mulyadi. (2001). *Balanced scorecard alat manajemen kontemporer untuk memperlipatgandakan kinerja keuangan perusahaan*. Jakarta: Salemba Empat.

Obeng, K., & Ugboro, I. (2008). Effective strategic planning in public transit systems. *Transportation Research*, *44*(3), 420–439. doi:10.1016/j.tre.2006.10.008

Pujawan, I. N. (2005). *Supply chain management*. Surabaya: Gundawidya.

Solihin, I. (2009). *Pengantar manajemen*. Erlangga.

Solihin, I. (2014). *Pengantar bisnis*. Erlangga.

Studies, C., Cv, O., & Abadi, K. (2018). Analisis saluran distribusi kayu (studi kasus di cv. Karya abadi, Manado). *Jurnal EMBA: Jurnal Riset Ekonomi, Manajemen. Bisnis Dan Akuntansi*, *6*. Advance online publication. doi:10.35794/emba.v6i3.20444

Thorik, S. H. (2020). Efektivitas pembatasan sosial berskala besar di indonesia dalam penanggulangan pandemi covid-19. *Jurnal: Hukum dan Keadilan, 4*(1).

Tjiptono, F. (2014). *Pemasaran jasa – prinsip, penerapan, dan penelitian*. Andi Offset.

Tunggal, A. W. (2011). *Pokok-pokok performance measurement dan balanced scorecard*. Harvindo.

Wheelen, T. L., & Hunger, D. J. (2004). *Concepts in strategic management and business policy*. Prentice Hall.

Yulianti, A. (2020). *Knowledge management: learning organization di rs seri VIII*. http://mutupelayanankesehatan.net/sample-levels/19-headline/3437-keberlangsungan-usaha-rs-di-masa-covid-19-apakah-akan-menuju-new- normal-perspektif-learning-organization

Chapter 10
Improving Resiliency in Healthcare Service by Minimizing Unsatisfied Demand

MD. B. Sarder
Bowling Green State University, USA

Sarah R. Sarder
St. Vincent Medical Center, Ohio, USA

ABSTRACT

Natural or manmade disasters can bring havoc to the healthcare industry in terms of poor services, out of stocks, cost overruns, and loss of lives. Specifically, the aftermath of disasters can be brutal if not managed properly. The quicker the healthcare providers recover, the lesser the impact would be. A resilient system has the potential to reduce the recovery time significantly. Healthcare providers under emergency scenarios may realize out-of-stock situations for their critical medical supplies. The out-of-stock supplies potentially cause poor patient care including death. COVID 19 is an unfortunate example where critical medical supplies were completely out for many medical providers and that had a serious negative impact on healthcare service deliveries. Healthcare providers needed to replenish their supplies from the overseas manufacturing plants, or central distribution centers, or unaffected regional distribution centers. Most of the times healthcare authorities struggle to secure critical medical supplies from other distribution centers due to operational and transportation issues. Depending on the disaster condition, sometimes many health care providers are beyond reach due to damaged transportation networks. This is the perfect time to share critical medical supplies from unaffected regions. Proven techniques like operation research can alleviate this situation. There are very few works that have been done in the field of healthcare service deliveries in case of a disaster. This chapter discusses the modeling techniques using operations research to improve the service levels while minimizing unsatisfied demand in the natural disaster-affected zones.

DOI: 10.4018/978-1-7998-8705-8.ch010

INTRODUCTION

Emergency scenarios can be characterized as natural disasters and man-made disasters. In both cases, the impact could be severe depending on the population density and transportation network complexity. These disasters can make the transportation network unavailable or unusable for a longer period. In the recent times, the occurrence and severity of natural disasters has increased significantly (Sergio et al, 2012). A disaster is an interruption that physically affects a part or the whole system and threatens its normal operations (Van Wassenhove, 2006). A disaster can take variety of forms. However, the occurrence of a disaster does not necessarily mean that quick response is required to minimize unsatisfied demand of health care systems. If the disaster can be dealt with using existing routines then the situation is an emergency rather than a crisis (Tomasini and Van Wassenhove, 2004). When a disaster occurs, right emergency medical items must be sent to the right place, right time and right quantity.

Achieving efficiency in logistics is a key successful factor in a complex supply chain and efficient logistics ensures proper flow of goods and services. Logistics play an important role for quick response after a disaster. It is crucial factor for effectiveness and responsiveness of disasters recovery program (Sarder & Iqbal, 2013). Logistics create a bridge between disaster preparedness and responsiveness, and between different members of supply chain. Quick response for the critical medical supplies should be planned to allow a rapid response so that the impact of disaster is minimized. The supply of critical medical supplies during disaster period presents many unique challenges. The problems arise from disasters are coordination multiple members of supply chain, transportation infrastructure, and confined communication. Successful and rapid response relies on the logistical operations of supply delivery.

Uncertainty is dominant in the supply of emergency medical items. Supply delay is a major obstruction to medical items distribution. Sometimes quick delivery of medical items may not delay by lack of resources but by using resources to deliver the unnecessary medical items to the local health care organizations. Because of disorganized central warehouse significant time and efficiency loss occurs and as a result there exist a probability of unsatisfied demand. Unexpected fluctuation of demands can also result uncertainty.

Disasters that require quick response are particularly difficult to manage. During disaster period the health care organizations actively involved in several activities such as preparation, planning, ordering for medical items from central warehouse (if necessary), transportation, storage, service level tracking etc. During emergency conditions the health care organizations mainly focus on service level rather than profitability. In that case the supply chain needs to be flexible. Due to poor infrastructure of the road during and/after the disaster, sometimes it is quite difficult to deliver emergency items to the disaster affected regions. This is one of the issues among the difficulties to obtain the best service level in health care system. Geographical dispersion and insufficient or inaccurate information between different members of supply chain in health care system is another issue for service level. This information includes how many types and what quantities of emergency items needed, distance between the central warehouse and local health care organizations, transportation capacity of vehicles available on a particular period etc.

Health care organizations are started with the intent to provide emergency medical items immediately after the happening of any natural disaster. If a significant delay occurs for supplying emergency medical items, it can cost lives. So, health care organizations should be able to respond effectively and efficiently in case of irregular disasters. The main challenge faced by health care organizations during disaster period is continuous and timely flow of emergency items from central warehouse and deliver it to the needy people whose immediate or long-term existence depends on that emergency medical items.

The low quality of service levels and excess supply of unnecessary medical items to a certain health care organization may cause operational problems. The consequences are saturation of storage facilities with unnecessary medical items and shortage of required emergency medical items in other health care organizations as well as demand uncertainty. A critical challenge of health care organizations in response to a disaster is the immediate need to supplying simultaneously different type of emergency medical items. The capacity of vehicles to transport prevented the carry out of emergency items to occur quickly and efficiently to the mostly disaster effected regions. Generally, several problems associated with co-ordination, planning, storage, distribution and transportation of emergency medical items during and / after a disaster period. Central warehouse is selected as one of the major sources to deliver emergency items to the local health care organizations. Central warehouse has inexhaustible amount of emergency items to serve those local health care organizations.

Operations research model has the potential to help health care service providers to utilize the limited resources and maintain standards so that the unsatisfied demand is minimized. Accurate need assessment is essential for developing the accurate models as well as maximizing the benefits of distributing health care items to the disaster affected people. Need assessment is a challenging task at the beginning of planning period. It varies from organization to organization and changes as the disaster situation undergo development. Monitoring a disaster affected region to identify its needs and coordinating with local health care organizations to secure delivery of exact number of medical items takes significant effort.

By developing mathematical models, operations research has contributed to the health care systems to help plans logistics and transportation systems. This chapter develops a model to minimize unsatisfied demand and to maximize service level in health care system. This model may help health care system planners to design an efficient supply chain so that emergency medical items reach those in need.

LITERATURE REVIEW

Generally, there are two major research topics involved in achieving high service level in a disaster affected region. The first one is preparedness of resources in advance of disasters. Rawls and Turnquist (2010) developed an optimization model for pre-positioning of emergency supplies for disaster response. Their model provides pre-positioning strategy and emergency items storage under uncertain condition. They solved the model by decompose it into smaller sub-problems. Tzeng et al. (2007) works on designing of multi - objective optimal planning for relief delivery system. Most of these works are on disaster preparation or the immediate response phase. Görmez N et al (2010) developed a model to minimize the average distance traveled to serve disaster affected peoples and to minimize the number of new response points to establish. They consider the problem of locating disaster response in the city of Istanbul. Their model is mainly based on assumption that a major disaster is expected to occur in the near future. They conclude that small number of facilities will be sufficient, and the locations of those facility locations are robust with respect to modeling changes.

The second one is operational logistics planning after a disaster happens. Ozdamar et al. (2004) developed an emergency logistics model where they included dynamic and time dependent transportation problem. Sheu (2007) developed a model on emergency logistics distribution approach for quick response to urgent relief demand in case of disasters. In his model he includes fuzzy clustering and the model is based on multi objective dynamic programing model. In a disaster response setting after an earthquake, resource allocation was studied by Fiedrich et al. (2000). They developed a model on optimized resource allocation for emergency response after earthquake disasters. Lodree and Taskin (2008) discussed about quantitative approaches to disaster recovery planning in supply chain management based on Operations Research and Management Science methods.

Salmeron and Apte (2010) works on two-stage stochastic models for emergency item pre-locating and also take account penalty costs to avoid unsatisfied cost. Minimizing cost, maximizing of demand that has been satisfied and minimizing transportation time are considered in multi-objective model. They assume that demand is uncertain, not supply of items. Barbarosoglu and Arda (2004) developed a model based on two stage stochastic programming framework for transportation planning in disaster response. In their model, the first stage is about to move items between existed supply nodes to preposition them. The second stage is about uncertain, and demand and supply of emergency items are exposed and transported to final disaster affected peoples.

Healthcare service level depends on various factors including proximity and access to healthcare organizations. Wang et all (2021) modeled service areas by evaluating geographic variations of health care markets (Wang et all, 2021). They used two optimization algorithms that maximize flows within delineated communities while minimizing inter-community flows. In this particular models, existing unsatisfied demand was not considered. Other authors including Adamson K worked on developing optimization models for social care in emergency departments (Adamson K. et all, 2020). Their research didn't consider service level maximization. While Srivastava S. and Singh R. did consider improving healthcare services considering various factors such as supply chain, but the scope was limited to a particular case and not considering resiliency aspect (Srivastava S. and Singh R., 2021).

MODEL DEVELOPMENT AND UNDERLYING ASSUMPTIONS

To develop the mathematical model of the healthcare service level for minimizing the unsatisfied demand, the notation adopted in this chapter includes as follows:

$P = \{1,2,3\ldots p,\ldots, \overline{p}\}$ = the set of item types where $\overline{p}$ is the total number of item types.

$Q = \{1,2,3\ldots q,\ldots, \overline{q}\}$ = the set of local health care organizations where $\overline{q}$ is the total number of health care organizations.

$T = \{1,2,3\ldots t,\ldots, \overline{t}\}$ = the set of periods where $\overline{t}$ is the total number of planning time

W = large amount

i= the index of severe level of delay

j= the index of time period when the backorder amount of demand is delivered.

C_{vol}= maximum volume capacity of a vehicle

C_{wt}= maximum load weight capacity of a vehicle

t_{op} = allowable delivered time periods of item p without penalty

D_{pqt} = demand of item p in local health care organization q in time period t

$R = \{1,2,3..r,\ldots, \overline{r}\}$ = the set of route where $\overline{r}$ is the total number of route

$Z= \{1,2,3\ldots z\}$ = the set of vehicle

F_{pqrzt} = flow of amount of item p from central health care organization to local health care organization q in tour r by vehicle z in time period t

Figure 1. Supply of emergency medical items from central warehouse to local health care organizations during disaster period

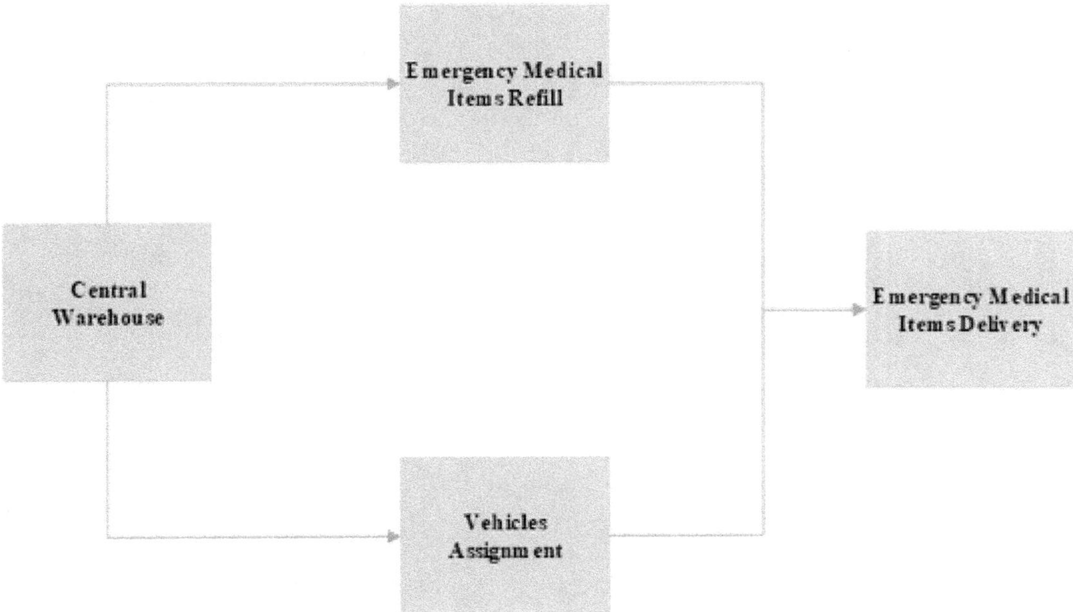

F_{pqrzmn} = flow of backorder amount of item p to local health care organization q in tour r by vehicle z in period m to satisfy demand in period n; m,n Î T
w_p = unit weight of item p
v_p = unit volume of item p
P_{pi} = penalty cost for item p if the severity level of delay is i
PUd_p = penalty cost of item p after the disaster period if there is remaining unsatisfied demand
S= maximum difference of satisfaction rate between any two local health care organizations
s_j = satisfaction rate of local health care organizations j

$$y_{rzt} = \begin{cases} 1 & \textit{when tour r is assigned to vehicle z in period t} \\ 0 & \textit{otherwise} \end{cases}$$

There are multiple numbers of health care organizations which are affected by disasters. They are served by a central warehouse to deliver emergency health care items. We assumed that central warehouse has unlimited supplies of medical items to serve local health care organizations. The distribution framework is shown in Figure 1.

The demand for different local health care organizations is known before the beginning of the planning. Based on the importance of medical items, the urgency level has been identified. To identify the local health care organizations expected waiting time to receive an emergency item, the allowable delivered time periods for that emergency item are predefined. A penalty cost is applied if an item cannot be delivered within the allowable time limit. The severity of the penalty cost depends on how long the delay in delivering an emergency item. The longer the delay in delivering an item, the more severe the penalty cost. We assumed that vehicles have limited volume and weight capacities. Tours are assigned to each vehicle in each period to deliver emergency items to one or multiple local health care organiza-

Figure 2. Distribution Network to respond quickly after a disaster

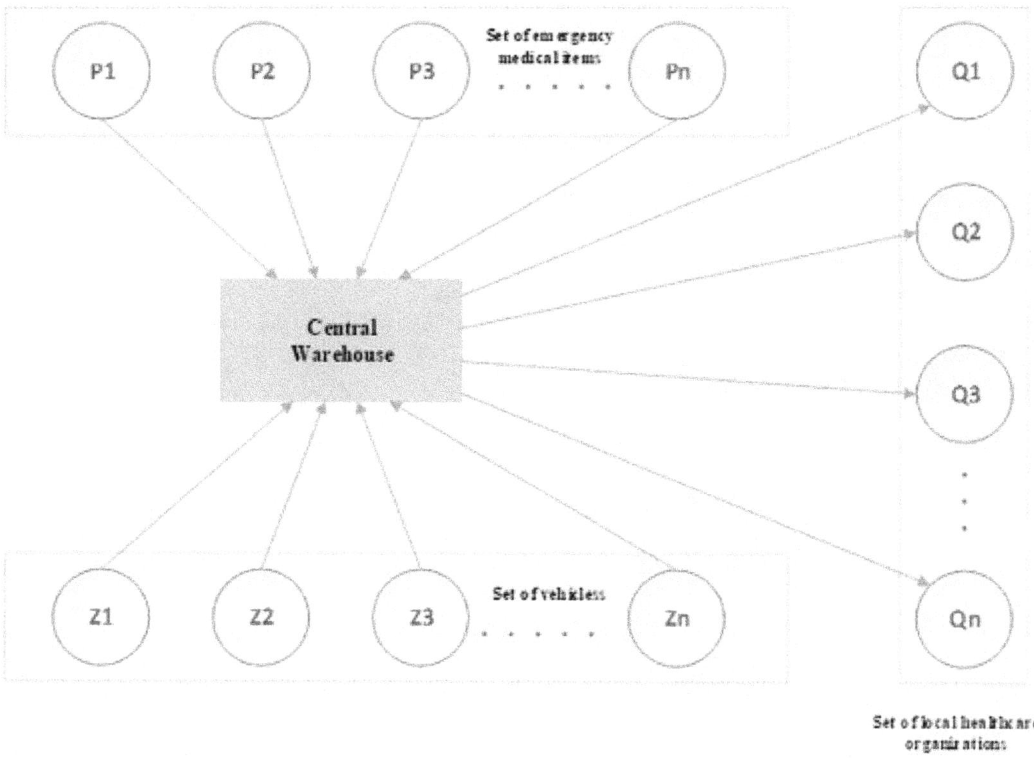

tions. Tours started at the central warehouse and continue to one or more local health care organizations and return to central warehouse. Any local health care organizations can be served several times by a single vehicle or multiple vehicles to meet its demand. This demand can satisfy fully or partially by a single time delivery.

MODEL FORMULATION

The model is developed based on the following distribution network described in Figure 2. This distribution network consists of a set of local healthcare organizations, a set of delivery vehicles, and a set of emergency items, all connected via central warehouse.

Unsatisfied demand (minimize) equation:

$$\sum_{p}\sum_{q}\sum_{i=1}^{\bar{t}-t_{op}}\sum_{t=1}^{\bar{t}-t_{op}-i+1}(D_{pqt}-\sum_{r}\sum_{z}(F_{pqrzt}+\sum_{j=t+1}^{t+i}F_{pqrzjt})).P_{pi}$$
$$+\sum_{p}((\sum_{q}\sum_{t}D_{pqt}-\sum_{q}\sum_{r}\sum_{z}\sum_{t}(F_{pqrzt}+\sum_{m>t,m\in T}F_{pqrzmt})).PUd_{p}) \quad \text{(i)}$$

Service level (maximize) equation:

$$S_q = \frac{\sum_p \sum_r \sum_z \sum_t \left(F_{pqrzt} + \sum_{m>t,m\in T} F_{pqrzmt}\right)}{\sum_p \sum_t D_{pqt}} \quad \text{(ii)}$$

Here S_q is the satisfaction rate. The satisfaction rate is defined as the ratio of requested demand by the local health care organizations and actual delivered items by the central warehouse.

CONSTRAINT EQUATIONS

$F_{pqrztn} \leq W\, y_{rzt}\ \forall p, \forall q \in Q_r, \forall r, \forall z, \forall t, \forall n < t$ (iii)

The above constraint equation says that, if tour r is assigned to vehicle z in period t then the total amount transferred in every tour should be greater than or equal to backorder amount of item p to local health care organizations q in period t to satisfy demand in period n.

$F_{pqrzt} \leq W\, y_{rzt}\ \forall p, \forall q \in Q_r, \forall r, \forall z, \forall t$ (iv)

At the same time, flow of amount of item p from central health care organization to local health care q should be less than or equal to total amount transferred in tour r assigned to vehicle z in period t.

The summation of flow of items p (both regular items and backorder items) from central healthcare organizations to local health care organizations in tour r assigned to vehicle z in period t must be less than or equal to demand of item p in local health care organization j in time period t. The following constraint equation enforces consistency of the amount p in local health care organizations.

$$\sum_r \sum_z \sum_t F_{pqrzt} + \sum_r \sum_z \sum_{m>t,m\in T} \sum_t F_{pqrzmt} \leq \sum_t D_{pqt} \qquad \forall p, \forall q \text{ (v)}$$

The maximum load weight capacity of q truck should be equal or greater than multiplication result of total item flow and unit weight of item p.

$$\sum_p \sum_q w_p (F_{pqrzt} + \sum_{n<t,n,t\in T} F_{pqrztn}) \leq C_{wt} \qquad \forall r, \forall z, \forall t \text{ (vi)}$$

If we multiply the total amount of items flow by unit volume of item p, then the multiplication result should be less than or equal to maximum volume capacity of a vehicle.

$$\sum_p \sum_q v_p (F_{pqrzt} + \sum_{n<t,n,t\in T} F_{pqrztn}) \leq C_{vol} \qquad \forall r, \forall z, \forall t \text{ (vii)}$$

$F_{pqrzt} \geq 0\ \forall p, \forall q \in Qr, \forall r, \forall z, \forall t$ (viii)

Figure 3. Transportation of two emergency items using two vehicles and each vehicle has two routes. The items transported to two local health care organizations.

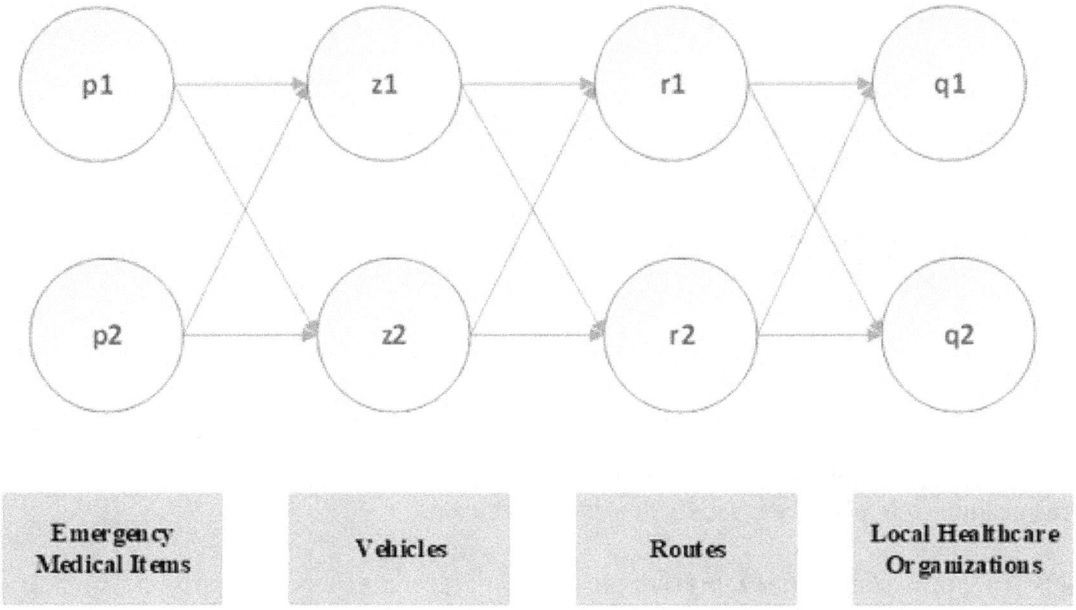

$F_{pqrzmn} \geq 0 \; \forall p, \forall q \in Qr, \forall r, \forall z, \forall t, \forall m \in T, \forall n \in T$ (ix)

$F_{pqrzt} = 0 \quad \forall p, \forall q \notin Qr, \forall r, \forall z, \forall t$ (x)

$F_{pqrzmn} = 0 \quad \forall p, \forall q \notin Qr, \forall r, \forall z, \forall t, \forall m \in T, \forall n \in T$ (xi)

$y_{rzt} \in \{0,1\} \; \forall r, \forall z, \forall t$.. (xii)

MODEL VERIFICATION WITH HYPOTHETICAL CASE ANALYSIS

In a disaster operation it is very common to transport medical items first from a central warehouse to local health care organization by trucks and then medical items are distributed to individuals from local health care organizations. To see how the developed model works we solved a hypothetical case study. It was assumed that when a disaster happens, local health care organizations order boxes of medical items to the central warehouse. We assumed that during disaster time there are demands for two medical items for two local health care organizations. These demands are fulfilled using two trucks (as shown in Figure 3).

Usually full truck load of single type of medical item give more efficient transportation. But generally during disaster period it is required to supply more than one medical item. For each truck there are two routes. For minimizing the penalty cost which occurs because of unsatisfied demand and for maximizing the service rate of different local health care organizations, it is necessary to send required number of medical items from central warehouse to local health care organizations using a vehicle and exact route. We know that, for each vehicle there are certain weight and volume limits for transportation of goods. Generally, the medical items are light in weight. So, it may come in mind that a truck can carry huge amount of medical item. But in reality, the volume is another fact. Usually every medical item is transferred using a box and each box captures some spaces in the truck. So, volume is another important factor. It has been assumed that two 18-wheeler trucks carry emergency medical items during disaster. The trucks are identical, and each truck can carry 10000kg of goods. The volume of each truck is 50 m^3. We assume that there are two emergency medical items need to be transport from central warehouse to local health care organization. Each medical item is transported in boxes. The weight of first medical item is 6 kg and weight of second medical item is 8 kg per boxes. Apparently, it seems that trucks can transport hundreds of medical boxes. But volume of medical item boxes put limit on how many boxes can be transported by truck. The volume of first medical item box is 0.1 m^3 and volume of second medical item box is 0.2 m^3. The weight and volume of these two boxes is one of the major factors of fulfilling unsatisfied demand. The disaster period is assumed for two days. During this disaster period, each of the local health care organization has demand for two medical items. These medical items are emergency item. The central warehouse needs to response quickly when local health care organizations ask for these medical items. But because of some constraints it is not always possible to fulfill all of the demand on time. It is very important to minimize the unsatisfied demand and maximize the service level. The demand was assumed. The model for minimizing unsatisfied demand cost and maximizing satisfaction rate for two local health care organizations was solved based on the following demand data which are assumed. (Table 1)

Table 1. Model assumption parameters

Time period= 1	Time period = 2
Demand of medical item p_1 at local health care organization q_1 = 500 boxes	Demand of medical item p_1 at local health care organization q_1 = 600 boxes
Demand of medical item p_2 at local health care organization q_1 = 700 boxes	Demand of medical item p_2 at local health care organization q_1 = 600 boxes
Demand of medical item p_1 at local health care organization q_2 = 300 boxes	Demand of medical item p_1 at local health care organization q_2 = 700 boxes
Demand of medical item p_2 at local health care organization q_2 = 400 boxes	Demand of medical item p_2 at local health care organization q_2 = 500 boxes

As the items need to be supplied to the affected people urgently, allowable delivered time for both emergency items without penalty was assumed 1 day. That means the demand must be fulfilled at the day when it is requested. If the demand cannot fulfill at the same day, then we penalized that delay in our model with certain penalty cost. The penalty cost increases with the severity of delay. We used penalty cost \$8 for medical item 1 if severe level of delay is 1 day, \$10 if severe level of delay is 2 day. For medical item 2, the penalty cost is \$10 if the severe level of delay is 1 day and for 2 day it is \$15. Penalty cost for unsatisfied demand was assumed \$20 for both 1st day and 2nd day.

Table 2. Solver solution

i=1, t=1, j=2 $F_{p1q1r1z1t1}$ 9 boxes $F_{p1q1r2z2t1}$ 12 boxes $F_{p1q1r1z1j2t1}$ 15 boxes $F_{p1q1r2z2j2t1}$ 17 boxes $F_{p1q2r1z1t1}$ 19 boxes $F_{p1q2r2z2t1}$ 20 boxes $F_{p1q2r1z1j2t1}$ 20 boxes $F_{p1q2r2z2j2t1}$ 20 boxes $F_{p2q1r1z1t1}$ 19 boxes $F_{p2q1r2z2t1}$ 18 boxes $F_{p2q1r1z1j2t1}$ 16 boxes $F_{p2q1r2z2j2t1}$ 13 boxes $F_{p2q2r1z1t1}$ 10 boxes $F_{p2q2r2z2t1}$ 6 boxes $F_{p2q2r1z1j2t1}$ 1 boxes $F_{p2q2r2z2j2t1}$ 0 boxes	i=1, t=2, j=3 $F_{p1q1r1z1t2}$ 34 boxes $F_{p1q1r2z2t2}$ 33 boxes $F_{p1q1r1z1j3t2}$ 31 boxes $F_{p1q1r2z2j3t2}$ 29 boxes $F_{p1q2r1z1t2}$ 27 boxes $F_{p1q2r2z2t2}$ 24 boxes $F_{p1q2r1z1j3t2}$ 21 boxes $F_{p1q2r2z2j3t2}$ 17 boxes $F_{p2q1r1z1t2}$ 13 boxes $F_{p2q1r2z2t2}$ 9 boxes $F_{p2q1r1z1j3t2}$ 5 boxes $F_{p2q1r2z2j3t2}$ 0 boxes $F_{p2q2r1z1t2}$ 9 boxes $F_{p1q2r2z2t2}$ 17 boxes $F_{p1q2r1z1j3t2}$ 0 boxes $F_{p2q2r2z2j3t2}$ 0 boxes	i=2, t=1, j=2 $F_{p1q1r1z1j2t1}$ 19 boxes $F_{p1q1r2z2j2t1}$ 12 boxes $F_{p1q2r1z1j2t1}$ 0 boxes $F_{p1q2r2z2j2t1}$ 20 boxes $F_{p2q1r1z1j2t1}$ 19 boxes $F_{p2q1r2z2j2t1}$ 16 boxes $F_{p2q2r1z1j2t1}$ 20 boxes $F_{p2q2r2z2j2t1}$ 20 boxes
i=2,t=1, j=3 $F_{p1q1r1z1j3t1}$ 15 boxes $F_{p1q1r2z2j3t1}$ 9 boxes $F_{p1q2r1z1j3t1}$ 9 boxes $F_{p1q2r2z2j3t1}$ 9 boxes $F_{p2q1r1z1j3t1}$ 17 boxes $F_{p2q1r2z2j3t1}$ 9 boxes $F_{p2q2r1z1j3t1}$ 12 boxes $F_{p2q2r2z2j3t1}$ 12 boxes	t=1, m=3 $F_{p1q1r1z1m3t1}$ 10 boxes $F_{p1q1r2z2m3t1}$ 10 boxes $F_{p1q2r1z1m3t1}$ 10 boxes $F_{p1q2r2z2m3t1}$ 10 boxes $F_{p2q1r1z1m3t1}$ 20 boxes $F_{p2q1r2z2m3t1}$ 10 boxes $F_{p2q2r1z1m3t1}$ 10 boxes $F_{p2q2r2z2m3t1}$ 15 boxes	t=2, m=3 $F_{p1q1r1z1m3t2}$ 10 boxes $F_{p1q1r2z2m3t2}$ 30 boxes $F_{p1q2r1z1m3t2}$ 25 boxes $F_{p1q2r2z2m3t2}$ 10 boxes $F_{p2q1r1z1m3t2}$ 15 boxes $F_{p2q1r2z2m3t2}$ 20 boxes $F_{p2q2r1z1m3t2}$ 10 boxes $F_{p2q2r2z2m3t2}$ 20 boxes

COMPUTATIONAL RESULT

By using excel solver, the solutions based on the above objective functions and constraints are shown in Table 2:

Now based on this result, the satisfaction rate for local health care organizations can be calculated. From equation (ii) it is clear that, satisfaction rate is the ratio of fulfill demand and requested demand.

$$\text{Satisfaction rate for } q_1 = \frac{148+242+125}{2400} = 0.2146 = 21.46\%$$

$$\text{Satisfaction rate for } q_2 = \frac{131+182+110}{1900} = 0.223 = 22.3\%$$

DISCUSSION

Based on the constraint equations, solver gives a solution to minimize the overall unsatisfied cost. Due to the mismatch of actual demand and on hand inventory, there is some demand which remains unsatisfied and a penalty cost should be incurred for that. In case of sustained disruptions, the shortage of medical supplies is very likely. The penalty cost used to solve the model was hypothetical value. It may vary medical items to medical items. Based on those penalty cost, the minimum total cost for unsatisfied demand $ 130,719. For simplicity, we assume that vehicle 1 follows route 1 and vehicle 2 follows route 2. There is also uncertainty of route during transportation. There are many possible sources of uncertainty, such as damage to transportation infrastructure. Even if vehicles are known with certainty, unexpected event may occur when in route. These issues may cause delay of supply of medical items which reduce the satisfaction rate. The satisfaction rate for local health care organization 1 is 21.46% while it is 22.3% for local health care organization. Actually, this satisfaction rate is subject to time and resource constraint in the case study. There is a difference of satisfaction rate between two local health care organizations. Generally, every local health care organization is responsible for fulfilling the requirements of disaster affected people. Central warehouse is responsible for managing its own vehicle to transport the medical items during disaster period. From results it is clear that, satisfaction rate is lower for local health care organization 2 than local health care organization 1. But the demand in local health care organization 1 is higher than local health care organization 2. So, the top management can take decision based on this satisfaction rate to improve their service level. The best scenario corresponds to the highest satisfaction level can achieve if all vehicle capacities can fulfill by only a specific item. The satisfaction rate gives lower value because of soft time window characteristics in the objective function which allowed delayed satisfaction of demand. Penalty cost setting affect the percentage of demand being delivered for different medical items. Which type of medical items should be delivered on which vehicle is depends on shipping size and weight, travel distance etc. As it's not possible to forecast unsatisfied demand accurately, appropriate value for penalty cost is necessary to identify the optimum cost. The model is sensitive to the choice of penalty cost value and demand.

CONCLUSION AND SCOPE OF FUTURE WORK

In this chapter, a model for minimizing cost of unsatisfied demand and maximizing satisfaction rate of different local health care organizations has been developed. The model is for supply of emergency medical items after a disaster. The model considers multi item, multi vehicle, multi route, and multi destination point. The model can also take over in any supply chain system which has similar characteristics i.e. where emergency parts are required to respond quickly. To assess the model, a case study was brought in to assess the effects of model parameters on the optimal solutions. Health care system can minimize unsatisfied demand and maximize service level by assigning dedicated personnel that make continuous monitoring of the total supply chain to conduct need assessment. The proposed model can be extended in several ways. The productiveness of the drivers and other persons can be added as an additional restriction with respect to the number of local health care organizations which can be served. The transshipment of medical items between local health care organizations can also be incorporated in the model. We considered only one local health care organization. The model can be extended by considering more than one central warehouse. The relocation of temporary depot between central warehouse and local health care organizations can also be added into the mode.

REFERENCES

Adamson, K., Bliss, R., Shahab, R., Sengsavang, S., Craig, S., Rankin, V., & Sur, D. (2020, November). The SCOPE Intervention: Impact of a Social Care Optimization Pilot Initiative in the Emergency Department. *Health & Social Work*, *45*(4), 284–288. doi:10.1093/hsw/hlaa021 PMID:33313754

Barbarosoglu, G., & Arda, Y. (2004). A two-stage stochastic programming framework for transportation planning in disaster response. *The Journal of the Operational Research Society*, *55*(1), 43–53. doi:10.1057/palgrave.jors.2601652

Fiedrich, F., Gehbauer, F., & Rickers, U. (2000). Optimized resource allocation for emergency response after earthquake disasters. *Safety Science*, *35*(1-3), 41–57. doi:10.1016/S0925-7535(00)00021-7

Görmez, N., Köksalan, M., & Salman, F. (2010). Locating disaster response facilities in Istanbul. *The Journal of the Operational Research Society*, *62*(7), 1239–1252. doi:10.1057/jors.2010.67

Lodree, E. J. Jr, & Taskin, S. (2008). An insurance risk management framework for disaster relief and supply chain disruption inventory planning. *The Journal of the Operational Research Society*, *59*(5), 674–684. doi:10.1057/palgrave.jors.2602377

Ozdamar, L., Ekinci, E., & Kucukyazici, B. (2004). Emergency logistics planning in natural disasters. *Annals of Operations Research*, *129*(1-4), 217–245. doi:10.1023/B:ANOR.0000030690.27939.39

Rawls, C., & Turnquist, M. (2010). Pre-positioning of emergency supplies for disaster response. *Transportation Research Part B: Methodological*, *44*(4), 521–534. doi:10.1016/j.trb.2009.08.003

Salmeron, J., & Apte, A. (2010). Stochastic optimization for natural disaster asset prepositioning. *Production and Operations Management*, *19*(5), 561–574. doi:10.1111/j.1937-5956.2009.01119.x

Sarder, M. D., & Iqbal, G. (2013). Healthcare Service Modeling to Minimize Disruptions due to Natural Disasters. *Proceeding of the Annual Industrial & Systems Engineering Research Conference (ISERC)*.

Sergio, R., Argollo, C., Gouvêa, C., Vânia, B., Mello, B., & Renata, A. (2012). Supply Chains in Humanitarian Operations: Cases and Analysis. *Procedia: Social and Behavioral Sciences*, *54*, 598–607. doi:10.1016/j.sbspro.2012.09.777

Sheu, J.-B. (2007). An emergency logistics distribution approach for quick response to urgent relief demand in disasters. *Transportation Research Part E, Logistics and Transportation Review*, *43*(6), 687–709. doi:10.1016/j.tre.2006.04.004

Srivastava, S., & Singh, R. (2021). Exploring integrated supply chain performance in healthcare: A service provider perspective. *Benchmarking*, *28*(1), 106–130. doi:10.1108/BIJ-03-2020-0125

Tomasini, R., & Van Wassenhove, L. N. (2004). *A framework to unravel, prioritize and coordinate vulnerability and complexity factors affecting a humanitarian operation*. Academic Press.

Tzeng, G., Cheng, H., & Huang, T. (2007). Multi-objective optimal planning for designing relief delivery systems. *Transp Res E*, *43*(6), 673–686. doi:10.1016/j.tre.2006.10.012

Van Wassenhove, L. N. (2006). Humanitarian aid logistics: Supply chain management in high gear journal of the operational research society. *The Journal of the Operational Research Society*, *57*(5), 475–489. doi:10.1057/palgrave.jors.2602125

Wang, C., Wang, F., & Onega, T. (2021, April). Network optimization approach to delineating health care service areas: Spatially constrained Louvain and Leiden algorithms. *Transactions in GIS*, *25*(2), 1065–1081. doi:10.1111/tgis.12722 PMID:34456609

Chapter 11

Skill Proficiency and Managerial Role in Different Sectors From Globalised to Localised

Surinder Sangwan
Pandit Neki Ram Sharma Government College, India

Wilfredo Daradar Quijencio Jr.
Far Eastern University, Philippines

ABSTRACT

Skills and information are the driving powers of financial development and social improvement of any country. They have become more significant given the increasing speed of globalization along with innovative modification. Nations related to higher as well as better degrees regarding skills change consist successfully with difficulties and option regarding globalization. The roles and duties of governments have been redefined by the winds of progress achieved by globalization. Notwithstanding, administration of globalization itself arose as a daunting assignment, given its mind-boggling interplay in different domains. The three main domains have been monetary, political, and social, with war and strategy included within the political trades. Notwithstanding various different difficulties emerging from globalization, dangers likewise changed in structure, setting, and degree.

INTRODUCTION

Synchronous pressures among fracture and integration, just as among restriction and internationalization turned out to be more clear in the course of the last decade, and over the most recent couple of years, powers of patriotism and protectionism came in direct clash with powers of globalization, blurring the distinction between worldwide to nearby and neighborhood to worldwide. For enormous organizations, decisions for setting-up and/or running manufacturing and R&D offices at assorted areas across the globe as opposed to doing so locally in their particular nations today have gotten more earnestly (Gupta, 2008).

DOI: 10.4018/978-1-7998-8705-8.ch011

The possible effect of COVID19 on globalization itself has been a subject of intense discussion over the most recent two months. New constraints, other than those identified with exchange wars/obstructions, have been worried. Public and nearby independence have been a critical facilitator in driving food and financial action in certain spaces in these challenging occasions. Decentralization of industrial and business exercises has been noted as an early exercise. Relocation because of absence of chances in local regions, especially from rustic to metropolitan, has exacerbated reaction challenges while making a critical commitment to new and extra joblessness.

The confinement methodology of the public authority would basically include ventures for bigger portion of the public demand being met by neighborhood organizations, and improving India's situation in the worldwide store network through center around cost intensity, quality, infrastructure, and framework efficiencies. Somehow or another, it has some likeness to US President Donald Trump's call for 'Making America Great Again', by seeking to move significant piece of American manufacturing back to the continental United States.

A push for increasing nearby substance has been endeavored in India previously, with appropriate arrangements in FDI approaches, incentives, balances (mainly in guard), Make in India and so on, however with restricted achievement. It is assumed that the new approach proclamation would look to make an extreme takeoff from incrementalism (business as usual), and that we would see execution of an unmistakable system, which has evaluated and set down proportions of viability.

Literature Studied

Independence in basic sectors like atomic, space and protection has been an expressed target in India for quite a while. Accentuation on this goal started to be anxious from mid 1960s, with clear articulation after the 1965 Indo-China battle, as unfavorable circumstance and exercises learnt required this methodology. It was initially wanted to be sought after through designated import replacement (Pradhan, 2018). In the mid 1980s, a steady shift to trade direction of public industries was looked to be stretched out to the guard sector. Nonetheless, considerable industrial capacity remained saved for the public sector (in light of the primary industrial approach goal of 1948, which was restored in progressive five-year plans).

Additionally, R&D exertion in the guard sector was initiated in 1949, heavily influenced by the public authority. Guiding considered retaining sovereign control and opportunity of activity, without outside interference and pressing factors, as likewise capital and industrial base inadequacies restricted the advancement on confidence, however continuous and incremental advancement was made in reducing the import content and increasing the indigenous substance. Afterward, private sector cooperation was permitted in chosen regions, Procurement and Production arrangements spelt out (with center around confidence), and the general framework streamlined (Sudhakar, 2014). Endeavors were sustained to make innovation moves meaningful, to empower leapfrogging, and to move from innovation impersonation to innovation. FDI permitted in protection has been continuously increased somewhat recently however the genuine inflow has been little. Confidence in some basic innovations continues to remain subtle. Space section has fared far superior, for an assortment of reasons.

After the Cold War, numerous western nations moved to the idea of 'Significant worth for Money', as against total confidence. Joint and community oriented projects were viewed as more reasonable, with benefits of avoiding duplication and accessing a more extensive mechanical base. In India too, an integrated methodology of indigenization and an incentive for cash was received.

Sectors other than atomic, space and safeguard, were likewise taken up in India, and numerous different nations, for enhancing confidence. The level of accomplishment accomplished shifted generously, from one finish of the range to other. In the new years, India's reliance on imports from China increased generously, leading to store network worries during the pandemic. High input costs, problematic seriousness, and restricted market access have been the critical explanations behind numerous Indian manufacturing organizations, especially drugs, hardware, automotive, synthetic substances and so on, seeking less expensive crude materials from China.

Furthermore, numerous organizations rely upon advances from different nations. These difficulties have been known for quite a while, however the current difficulty makes them more articulated and noticeable. Turning this affliction into a chance is a decent optimistic goal, yet needs to consider India's involvement with driving independence, sector explicit plans, increase systems, CAPEX (both public and private) during this emergency (there has been no particular declaration in the bundle identified with spurring CAPEX) and smothered demand, and boosting R&D consumption (Kumar, 2009). The affliction is additionally a chance to take note of that about portion of the segment profit opportunity period is finished and has not been ideally used, and that similar should be concurred need, with speed and exhaustiveness of execution.

OBJECTIVES

1. To study the Skill Proficiency in different sectors.
2. To study the Managerial role of administrators in different sectors.
3. To study the Skill Proficiency and managerial role globally.

SKILL PROFICIENCY

Skills can have a proficiency setting empowered, and specialists with that skill have their proficiency levels allotted. The proficiency level indicates the specialist's experience or qualities with a skill and can be utilized for routing interactions to suitable assets. For instance, a standard Support solicitation may just need the Help skill task, yet a raised solicitation may require a proficiency of at any rate.

The proficiency range accessible in Engage is somewhere in the range of 1 and 100, notwithstanding that can change by skill dependent on customer needs. For instance, a typing skill can have a rating of 1 to 100, where 25 could indicate fledgling or beginner level for a client and 95 indicate high proficiency and master levels. A similar client can have a Spanish speaking skill doled out with a rating of 1 to 5, where 3 could indicate useful utilization of the language and 5 indicate that they are a local speaker.

Skill Proficiency is Empowered at the Skill Level yet Doled out at the Client Level

The Proficiency Levels are portrayals of how individuals can manage language as far as speaking and listening as well as writing and reading at certifiable circumstances under an unconstrained and non-practiced setting. Considering every skill, the following conditions recognize following significant degrees regarding proficiency:

1. Superior
2. Intermediate
3. Distinguished,
4. Advanced
5. Novice.

Significant stages like Advanced, Intermediate along with Novice become partitioned into Large, Mid and Low substages. Stages regarding conditions portray a continuum with respect to proficiency related with exceptionally expressive, knowledgeable language client to a degree of practically no useful capacity.

Ordinary practices are related with every proficiency level. The average practices for every one of the abilities (widespread and specialized) outline how a specific skill is applied at different degrees of proficiency. A portrayal of the minimum proficiency level expected for that work characterization is additionally recognized.

SKILL DEVELOPMENT AND SELF-EMPLOYMENT

NSSO 61st Round information additionally uncovers that the extent of people (15–29 years) who got formal professional training was around 3% for the utilized, 11% for the jobless and 2% for people not in the workforce. In request to link skills formed into real useful use thereof including independent work, steps will be required in the Eleventh Five Year Plan by providing sufficient incentives, not really money related but rather as far as skill and business advancement and forward and in reverse linkages to finance, marketing and human asset the executives, to the individuals who are or look to act naturally utilized to upgrade their usefulness and worth expansion, making it an alluring choice, instead of be a choice faute de mieux as of now.

Worldwide uber patterns like the rising role of innovation, environmental change, segment movements, urbanization, and the globalization of significant worth chains are changing the idea of work and skills demands. To prevail in the 21st century work market, one necessities an extensive skill set made out of:

1. Cognitive skills, which envelop the capacity to understand complex thoughts, adjust successfully to the climate, gain from experience, and reason. Essential education and numeracy just as imagination, basic thinking, and critical thinking are intellectual skills.
2. Socio-enthusiastic skills, which portray the capacity to explore interpersonal and social circumstances viably, and include administration, cooperation, discretion, and coarseness.
3. Technical skills, which allude to the obtained information, aptitude, and interactions expected to play out a particular assignment, including the dominance of required materials, tools, or advancements.
4. Digital skills, which are cross-cutting and draw on the entirety of the above skills, and depict the capacity to get to, oversee, understand, integrate, convey, assess, and make information securely and suitably.

The advancement of skills can add to primary change and monetary development by enhancing employability and work usefulness and helping nations to turn out to be more cutthroat. Investment in an excellent labor force can make a righteous cycle, where applicable and quality skills empower usefulness development and unfamiliar direct investment, which bring about more and better positions for the current labor force and more open and private investment in the instruction and training framework. This, in turn, increases the employability and efficiency for both the current and future labor force.

However, most nations continue to battle in delivering on the guarantee of skills advancement. There are tremendous holes in essential proficiency and numeracy of working-age populaces, as 750 million individuals matured 15+ (or 18% of the worldwide populace) report being not able to peruse and compose, with gauges being almost twice as huge in case education is estimated through direct appraisals. An increasing number of people in India are turning to the services sector for employment due to the relative low compensation offered by the traditional agriculture and manufacturing sectors. The organized retail market is growing at 3.5 percent annually while growth of unorganized retail sector is pegged at 6 percent. The Retail Business in India is currently at the point of inflection. Rapid change with investments to the tune of US $ 25 billion is being planned by several Indian and multinational companies in the next 5 years[1]. Huge scope international evaluations of grown-up skills for the most part point to skills confounds just as enormous variety in the profits to schooling across fields of study, institutions, and populace gatherings. Managers in many developing nations report that an absence of skilled laborers is a significant and increasing bottleneck for their activities, affecting their ability to innovate.

The COVID-19 pandemic has brought the pre-emergency vision of fair, important, and quality skills advancement into more keen help, adding unanticipated earnestness to the calls for change and highlighting the colossal expenses of inaction.

The Major Questions Nation Need to Handle for Skills Advancement are:

- Access and finish: Across the world, investments in instruction and skills advancement-from preschool through present auxiliary schooling on professional training-have significant yields. All things considered, arrangement of evenhanded access is a test in some low-income and center income nations. Moreover, numerous understudies who figure out how to select instruction or training programs don't finish their investigations and pass up obtaining formal capabilities, which can significantly diminish the profit from the instructive investments as far as lifetime earning potential.
- Quality: Numerous youngsters go to schools without acquiring essential proficiency skills, leaving them incapable to contend in the work market. Specifically, specialized and professional training (TVET) frameworks in numerous nations face difficulties identified with quality confirmation, resulting in impression of the professional track being a second-most ideal alternative contrasted with general optional or tertiary schooling.
- Relevance: Specialized and professional instruction and training - which can last somewhere in the range of a half year to three years-can give youngsters, particularly ladies, the skills to go after better paying positions. In any case, more should be done as far as engaging neighborhood businesses to guarantee that the educational plan and conveyance of these projects reacts to work market needs.
- Efficiency: Difficulties identified with administration, financing, and quality affirmation likewise sway the effectiveness of skills advancement programs. The resulting pointlessly significant expenses can restrict openings for distraught youth and grown-ups to get to these projects.

Fortunately the proof on what works and what doesn't in skills advancement, and for whom, is growing. At the World Bank Group (WBG), we support governments all throughout the planet in designing, implementing, and learning from changes and projects pointed toward addressing the most central difficulties of skills improvement.

MANAGERIAL ROLE IN DIFFERENT SECTORS

Administrators work in various roles including leading, sharing information, and making choices.

Informational Roles

This includes about receiving as well as sending regarding information-regardless of whether the representative as the mentor or trainer or administrator. This is noted that top administrator consists the voice related to association and must having the knowledge that even genuine beliefs will imagine (regardless) about trade. Due to availability regarding information available at Internet, this is truly challenging for top supervisors as isolate themselves regarding their ranks. Like, this was the customer feedback in the period of 2017 when Uber CEO Travis Kalanick used to acknowledge the seat of President Hon'ble Trump's financial related warning committee. This is noted that Kalanick initially conveyed that he used to "go to utilize [his] position on the chamber to stand up for what's right." He surrendered in some days with this fact because of this dissent.

Center directors should skillfully determine what information related to top administration as ought to be granted with another person, how this ought to be evaluated, and how this ought to be considered for introduction. Also, they should relate with gauging about worth of information they receive at first-line supervisors and workers in request to opt what to provide the advance regarding top administration. However, communicated information will consider in general be consider as false or inconsequential, then, at this vertex the administrator will be viewed as the non-reliable resource and their opinions limited.

Informational role regarding first-line directors is fundamentally as one of disseminating what they use to provide and supporting workers to perceive how they're at own commitments related with hierarchical aims. They have an obligation by viewing that workers understand as they should be consider at effective with their positions.

Dynamic Roles

All administrators are needed by deciding, yet supervisors at various stages settle on numerous types of choices. As per Mintzberg, there are the four main types related to board select roles. These include following:

- Entrepreneur: Trade visionaries about firm are complexity top-stage chiefs. They use to recognize monetary freedoms, lead initiative for modification and settle as item options.
- Disturbance handler: Top as well as center supervisors will consider for responding regarding aggravations (surprising circumstances) with association-regardless whether inner or outer.
- Resource allocator: All type of degrees related with executives will use to settle down regarding asset portion preferences, depending upon whether preferences impressions related with whole association, a single office, or for the specific assignment or specific action.

- Negotiator: Based on effect upon association, with most exchange is used to finish by top as well as center stage supervisors. Top administrators will handle arrangements regarding association agreements as well as economic accords.

SKILL PROFICIENCY AND MANAGERIAL ROLE IN DIFFERENT SECTORS FROM GLOBALIZED TO LOCALIZED

It is hard today to utilize "globalization" without a certain feeling of incongruity, remorseful or something else. Riven by philosophy, religion, and question, the world appears to be more divided, more in conflict, than whenever since, seemingly, World War II. Be that as it may, nonetheless profound the political divisions, business aims continue to traverse about globe, and chiefs actually require by sorting out some path by running them proficiently and well.

"There is nothing of the sort," as they use to express, "as an all-inclusive worldwide chief." Multinational enterprises instead need of three kinds regarding trained professionals-trade directors, country supervisors, as well as utilitarian administrators along with the bunch related to senior leaders by supporting subject matter analysis and coordinate their endeavors.

In the beginning phases of its drive abroad, Corning Glass employed an American ex-envoy to head up its international division. He had magnificent contacts in the legislatures of numerous countries and could talk in a few dialects, yet he was less acquainted with Corning and its businesses. Interestingly, ITT chose to set up a gigantic instructive program to "globalize" all chiefs liable for its overall telecom business-basically, to supplant the organization's public experts with worldwide generalists. Security experts have been discussing the problems with password security for years. If you control authentication using passwords only, it is at greater risk for intrusion and hacking attacks than those that use some form of multifactor authentication. The problem lies with the ever-increasing abilities of computers to process larger amounts of data in a smaller amount of time. If you control authentication using passwords only, it is at greater risk for intrusion and hacking attacks than those that use some form of multifactor authentication. The problem lies with the ever-increasing abilities of computers to process larger amounts of data in a smaller amount of time (Chaudhary, 2015).

Corning and ITT in the end acknowledged they had taken wrong turns. In the same way as other different organizations organizing for overall activities as of late, they tracked down that a tip top of joyriders was regularly hard to integrate into the corporate mainstream; nor did they need an international group of higher perspective regulators to the prohibition of centered specialists.

Accomplishment in today's international environment-a long ways from just 10 years prior-demands profoundly specific yet firmly linked gatherings of worldwide business chiefs, country or territorial supervisors, and overall utilitarian directors. This kind of association portrays a transnational as opposed to an old-line multinational, international, or worldwide organization[3]. Transnational integrate resources, assets, and different individuals in operating units all throughout the planet. Yet, an emerging gathering of transnational organizations has started to change the exemplary order of central command auxiliary connections into an integrated organization of specific yet interdependent units. For some, the best constraint in creating such an association is a serious deficiency of leaders with the skills, information, and complexity to work in an all the more firmly linked and less traditionally progressive organization (Anu Radha, 2015).

Truth be told, in the unstable universe of transnational enterprises, there is nothing of the sort as a widespread worldwide supervisor. Maybe, there are three gatherings of subject matter experts: business supervisors, country chiefs, and useful administrators. And there are the top chiefs at corporate central command, the pioneers who deal with the unpredictable interactions between the three-and can recognize and foster the gifted leaders an effective transnational requires.

One of the difficulties that associations have been continually facing is the shortfall of good administration skills in the labor force. As globalization assumes control over the functioning of associations, the requirement for amazing managerial skills among all workers has gotten pressing. Viable administration skills are not just instrumental in driving organizations to statures of achievement, yet similarly add to the vocation movement of workers. Possessing these skills gets ready experts to take on more elevated level roles across industries.

DISCUSSION

A contributing factor to vocation movement is to flourish for continued proficient and self-improvement. On the off chance that you set your heart to it, enhancing your managerial skills is anything but a troublesome errand to achieve. This blog will zero in on what the significant managerial skills are and how you can create and further develop them (Goel, 2008).

Different Kinds of the Board Skills

Specialized Skills: specialized skills empower experts to foster wide information over an assortment of tools and strategies which can be utilized to accomplish business destinations. These skills are not restricted to the information on the best way to work machines and utilize the product, yet additionally includes skills pertaining to boosting deals, plan different items and benefits and implementing marketing endeavors to advance them.

Theoretical Skills: unique thinking and thought definition are the absolute most grounded suits of the executives experts. Reasonable skills help experts in a managerial situation to picture an idea, investigate the difficulties and foster inventive arrangements. This gives administrators an advantage as it permits them to anticipate possible dangers in the business and plan accordingly.

Interpersonal Skills: while this probably won't appear to be a significant managerial skill, it holds equivalent importance contrasted with specialized and calculated skills. Interpersonal or human skills permit administrators to interact viably and work productively with their associates and subordinates. Moreover, it helps the board experts to utilize human potential to the upside of the association and upgrade worker efficiency.

CONCLUSION

Relational Abilities: powerful relational abilities are a resource for experts, regardless of if they are in a managerial role. Experts who are going to take up the role of a director or try to do as such should have amazing relational abilities. This will guarantee that information is shared viably with all the colleagues.[4] This information could include system outlines, task designation and hierarchical objectives. Possessing compelling relational abilities will likewise guarantee that clashes are settled skillfully, ensuring the smooth functioning of business activities. In any case, relational abilities are not confined to an individual at a managerial position, yet in addition expects supervisors to make proficient correspondence channels within the association to guarantee compelling cooperation with colleagues, decrease in struggle rates and straightforwardness in measures.

Authoritative Skills: in case you are working as an administrator, the shots at dipping your toes in an assortment of capacities with a tremendous heap of errands are high. To guarantee that each errand is cultivated effectively and within the set time period, have great hierarchical skills. As a chief, you need to guarantee that business activities are completed in line with the set guidelines. Moreover, it would likewise expect you to recognize and set attainable targets, foster business techniques, delegate errands and guide the colleagues to accomplish the put forward objectives[5].

Dynamic Skills: supervisors assume an essential part in dynamic cycles which hence directs the business towards progress. Great dynamic skills are significant to the accomplishment of an association just as the vocation movement of an expert. While thoroughly examined and painstakingly settled on choices can support an individual's profession, rushed and helpless choices can have the contrary impact. Directors should take responsibility for their choices and own up to mistakes in judgment.

Appointment Skills: since directors are answerable for driving the group to accomplish business objectives, it is significant that they have a distinctive thought regarding the skills, qualities and short-comings of the labor force under them. They should designate work in the wake of considering these factors about the colleagues. Experts in a managerial position ought to likewise be ready to redistribute the undertaking, on the off chance that the initial designation doesn't work out as arranged. At the same time, they should think about the points that they missed initially and work around them. Compelling assignment guarantees that the undertakings are finished rapidly and without any problem.

Motivating Skills: in request to expand the usefulness of representatives, it is fundamental that chiefs set up their motivating skills as a regular occurrence. In a worldwide business setting, it is normal for the labor force to be assorted. This additionally indicates that different individuals will be driven by different persuasive factors. It is the duty of directors to distinguish what inspires their colleagues and execute a comparable methodology. Valuable criticism goes about as an extraordinary motivator and can upgrade group efficiency. Then again, administrators need to guarantee that criticism doesn't influence workers antagonistically[8].

RECOMMENDATIONS TO FURTHER DEVELOP THE SKILLS

Compassion: an incredible method of developing administration skills is by introducing your compassionate side to your work life. To oversee individuals, you should initially zero in on genuinely caring for them. You can work on this quality of being a chief by having one-in one conversations with your colleagues, understand the issues that they are going through grinding away, get some information about their own life and in case they are open to sharing about it and attempt to make a human association with them[7].

Don't Miniature Oversee: while it is prudent to know about what is happening in the group, refrain from imposing force. In the event that you resort to micromanaging, odds are that you will be under a ton of stress and it will move to your colleagues too. Trust your colleagues to accomplish the work distributed and give them space. Understand that every individual has a different speed and a different interpretation of undertakings. Intervene in their work cycle just in case it is totally essential.

Fitting Articulation: as a chief, you will be needed to interact with ranking directors and the administration group. Nonetheless, when dealing with experts at a higher position, realize how to communicate your thoughts.

REFERENCES

Chaudhary. (2015). Globalization and Education. *Globus Journal of Progressive Education*, *6*(1), 1–6.

Ghai, R., Tyagi, M., & Gupta, R. (2020). *Leveraging Technology for Robust Financial Facilities: A Comparative Assessment of BRICS Nations. In ICCAKM 2020. IEEE Xplore.*

Goel, A. N. (2008). A Global Change in Education through Information Technology and Communication. In Enterprises Information Systems & Technology. MacMillan Advanced Research Series.

Gupta, R. (2008). Information Security: An Economic Perspective. In Business and Competitive Dynamics. Macmillan India Limited.

Kumar, P. (2009). Convergence of Rural Marketing Strategies and Trends in Developing Economics. *Globus - An International Journal of Management and IT, 1*(1), 61-66.

Malik. (2015). Impact of Emotional Intelligence on Job Satisfaction. *Globus Journal of Progressive Education*, *5*(2), 1–5.

Mishra, S., & Soni, D. (2016). A Study on Technology, Thinking Styles, and Content of Education. *Cosmos An International Journal of Art & Higher Education*, *5*(2), 1–4.

Modi, P. K. (2015). A Study on Life Insurance Companies Related to Service Quality. *Cosmos An International Journal of Management*, *4*(2), 7–9.

Nautiyal, A. (2015). Role of Life Insurance in India. *Cosmos An International Journal of Management*, *5*(1), 1–3.

Pradhan, D. (2018). Problems Facing Indian Economy. *Cosmos An International Journal of Art & Higher Education*, *7*(1), 12–15.

Radha, A. (2015). Retailing: Emerging Challenges and Future Prospects In India. International Journal of Scientific Research and Management, 89(76), 6-13.

Rajashekar, S. (2015). Agricultural Marketing of Products A Case Study of Haveri District. *Globus Journal of Progressive Education*, *5*(1), 1–2.

Sengupta, A. (2013). Emergence of modern Indian retail: An historical perspective. *International Journal of Retail & Distribution Management*, *36*(9), 689–700. doi:10.1108/09590550810890939

Sudhakar, S. (2014). Growth of Retail Industry in India. *Globus An International Journal of Management & IT*, *6*(1), 1–4.

KEY TERMS AND DEFINITIONS

Managerial Role: Managerial roles are specific behaviors associated with the task of management. Managers adopt these roles to accomplish the basic functions of management just discussed: planning and strategizing, organizing, controlling, and leading and developing employees.

Skill Proficiency: Proficiency in a skill means an individual can add his or her proficiency bonus to ability checks that involve that skill. Without proficiency in the skill, the individual makes a normal ability check.

Chapter 12
Digitalization and Urbanization

Anish Gupta
Chandigarh University, India

Hayri Uygun
Recep Tayyip Erdogan University, Rize, Turkey

Rashmi Gujrati
CT University, India

Dhiraj Gupta
GNIOT Group of Institutions, India

ABSTRACT

The business world is transforming into digitalization. To stay modest and appropriate, it has become necessary to adopt digitalization. The construction industry is entirely ready for the opportunity that will come through digitalization. Currently, we are in the finishing days of the industrial age. With this advanced revolution, the future will be reshaped in two trends: digitalization and urbanization. At the starting of the 19th century when the industrial revolution was in full bloom, a small amount of the population was living in the cities. As it has been for thousands of years, the world is still rural and agricultural.

INTRODUCTION

For cities and towns, urbanisation is the process of relocating people from rural to urban regions. It's also been dubbed a reformist increase in the number of people living in cities and towns. The fact that metropolitan areas and towns have made more monetary, political, and social strides than rural areas has a significant impact.

Also, in constructing and produced worlds, urbanisation is very common since an ever-increasing number of people have a preference for moving closer to cities and towns in order to benefit from "unique" social and monetary services. Benefits such as higher education, medical care, sterilisation, and housing, as well as business opportunities and transportation are all part of this package of services.

DOI: 10.4018/978-1-7998-8705-8.ch012

Rural to urban population shifts, population declines, and society's responses to these changes are referred to as urbanisation (or urbanisation). It is primarily the process through which towns and cities are created and grow in size as more people move into urban cores."

The majority of people choose to live in cities and towns rather than rural areas because they perceive rural areas to be difficult and/or characterised by primitive ways of living. As people migrate to newly developed locations (such as cities and suburbs), the consequence is rapid urbanisation.

Land for commercial buildings, social and financial institutions, transportation, and private constructions is constantly being advanced as a result of this practise Finally, these activities bring up a few problems related to urbanisation.

VARIOUS CAUSES / FACTORS THAT LEAD TO URBANIZATION

Industrialization

Produce is a pattern that addresses the shift from traditional rural financial concerns to the emerging non-horticultural economy, creating a forward-thinking connection. Because of more established economic opportunities in urban areas as a result of the contemporary insurgency, more people have relocated from rural areas.

The industrialization has expanded business openings by allowing individuals the opportunity to work in current areas in work classifications that guides to mix financial turns of events.

Commercialization

Business and exchange assume a significant part in urbanization. The dispersion of labour and products and business exchanges in the advanced period has created current promoting organizations and trade techniques that have hugely led to the development of towns and urban areas.

Exploitation and dealing accompany the overall insight that the urban communities and the towns offer better business openings and returns contrasted with the rustic regions.

Social Benefits and Services

There are different ethical advantages ascribed to life in urban areas and towns. Models incorporate improved instructive offices, better expectations for everyday comforts, better sterilization and lodging, better medical services, better entertainment offices, and better public activity when all is said in done.

On this record, an ever-increasing number of individuals are provoked to relocate into urban communities and towns to get a wide assortment of social advantages and administrations which are inaccessible in country regions.

Occupation Possibility

In urban communities and towns, there are plentiful open positions that consistently draw individuals from rustic regions to look for a superior job.

Subsequently, to get to well-paying positions most individuals often move into metropolitan regions in information area Innumerable work open doors in metropolitan reason instruction, transport, sports and entertainment, ventures, and business are like general well being, endeavour. After adding the occupation and prompts the biggest business

Adding the occupations, and opening the greater business opening the administrations and ventures has produced and increment higher worth.

Adaptation and Modification in the Manner of Realistic

With the modern agreement, base, medical institution offices, dressing code, condition, promotion, and other social comforts approach ability, metropolitan regions have become more innovative and individuals accept they can have a glad existence in urban areas. In the methods of living individuals additionally embrace changes, specifically private tendency, attitude, stuffing, food, and belief in metropolitan regions. Hence, the urban communities are developed by engrossing to the developing number of individuals for a long time and individually relocating to urban areas.

Transformation of Rural-Urban

More productive and prosperous territories become due to the revelation of minerals, asset misapply, or farming exercises, urban areas begin arising as the rustic regions change into urbanism. business openings added The monetary development and higher worth and the expansion in efficiency prompts for the betterment of lodging, administration, transportation, schooling organization, foundation, wellbeing offices, and the foundation of banking establishments,

To looking for a superior life. Metropolitan focuses to keep on developing as more individuals that move to such areas to rustic networks begin to embrace the metropolitan culture and eventually.

IMPACTS OF URBANIZATION ON OUR URBAN COMMUNITIES

Living Accommodations Problems

Urbanization draws in individuals to urban areas and towns which prompts a high populace increment. With the expansion in the quantity of individuals living in metropolitan habitats, there is a proceeded with shortage of houses.

This is because of inadequate extension space for lodging and public utilities, destitution, joblessness, and exorbitant structure materials which must be managed by a couple of people.

Overcrowding

Congestion is a circumstance whereby countless individuals live in a little space. This type of clog in metropolitan regions is steady a result of overpopulation and it's anything but a viewpoint that builds step by step as more individuals and migrants move into urban areas and towns looking for a superior life.

The vast majority from country or lacking regions consistently have the desire of relocating into the city that regularly prompts blockage of individuals inside a little region.

Jobless

The issue of underemployment is most noteworthy in metropolitan regions, and it is significantly upper among instructed individuals. It is assessed that the greater part of jobless adolescents throughout the satellite resident lives in the urban areas.

Moreover, in the metropolitan region pay is much high and the livelihoods and living expenses are low. The main source of metropolitan joblessness is the s expanding migration of individuals from rustic or creating regions to metropolitan regions

Slums Growth

In metropolitan regions the average cost for basic items is high. Addressed by ghettos and vagrant's unlawful occupant settlement to joined just as joblessness. In metropolitan regions the development of ghettos and vagrants is too much to boot change by fast-moving industrial enterprise, absence of created land for lodging, a huge flood of provincial migrants to the urban areas looking for a superior life, and the raised costs of land past the compass of the metropolitan poor.

Water Supply and Cleaning Problems

The average cost for basic items in metropolitan regions is high. At the point when this is joined with irregular and surprising development just as joblessness, there is the spread of unlawful occupant settlements addressed by ghettos and vagrants.

The development of ghettos and vagrants in metropolitan regions is much additionally exacerbated by quick moving industrialization, absence of created land for lodging, a huge flood of provincial migrants to the urban areas looking for a superior life, and the raised costs of land past the compass of the metropolitan poor.

Spread of Diseases of Pitiful Health

The social, financial and everyday environments in blocked metropolitan regions influences access and usage of general medical care administrations. Ghetto regions specifically experience helpless disinfection and lacking water supply which for the most part make ghetto populaces powerless to transferable sicknesses.

Ecological issues, for example, metropolitan contamination likewise cause numerous medical conditions in particular sensitivities, asthma, barrenness, food contamination, malignant growth, and unannounced astonishingly financial loss.

Traffic Congestion

One of the important troubles given is in the matter structure. At the point when the more single move to towns and urban areas. More number of individual vehicles which quick traffic jam and conveyance pollution.

A lot of people individually moving to the metropolis, and it is increasing traffic issues in the office time morning and evening same when people move for shopping in complex shops or social palaces there also, we can see a lot of crowd and traffic blockage.

Urban Crime

Many social problems like as cruelty, drug abuse, and wrongdoing are caused by the fact that crime is growing as a result of individuals being unemployed, having no assets, being mixed up, or having a lack of social management and direction.

Crimes such as murder and assault are more common in urban areas, as are riots, attacks, burglaries, theft, and commandeering, according to statistics. Additionally, in rapidly growing urban regions, neediness-related offences are the most notable. These urban wrongdoing protests often disturbed the peace and tranquilly of cities and towns.

SOLUTIONS TO URBANIZATION

Provision of Essential Services

Metropolitan partners should guarantee all populaces inside the metropolitan regions approach sufficient fundamental social administrations to be specific instruction, wellbeing, disinfection and clean water, innovation, power, and food.

The target here is to give and carry out business openings and abundance creation exercises so that individuals can make money to pay for the support of the administrations.

Endowments can likewise be benefited by the public authority to bring down the expenses of essential medical care, fundamental schooling, energy, training, public transportation, correspondence frameworks and innovation.

Creation of More Jobs

To decrease the adverse consequences of fast urbanization while simultaneously rationing regular environments, private ventures ought to be urged in order to use normal assets and set out more occupation open doors.

The travel industry advancement and the feasible misuse of normal assets can make more positions for metropolitan populaces. Endowments and awards should be given to unfamiliar and private interest in harmless to the ecosystem advancement projects that empower work creation.

Population Control

Key partners in metropolitan regions should give missions and advising to successful clinical wellbeing centres and family intending to assist with diminishing the high paces of populace development.

Clinical wellbeing facilities arranged towards family arranging choices should be made available across the whole metropolitan region with the goal of controlling illnesses and populace development.

DIGITIZATION AND URBANIZATION: THREE MAJOR CHALLENGES

Challenges and Opportunities of Digitalization

At the point when individuals envision the urban communities of things to come, they ordinarily imagine the metropolitan scenes of sci-fi: sparkling cities with flying vehicles and innovation driving everything. Truth be told, in any case, the city of things to come will depend undeniably more on essential arranging and administration than it will on innovation (Winden et al, 2017).

Honestly, innovation can be sure assist with settling a portion of the enormous and developing difficulties of urbanization. By 2030, more than 5 billion individuals—60% of the 2010 worldwide populace—will live in urban communities (UN DESA, 2018). Addressing the necessities of these metropolitan occupants will put a gigantic strain on civil governments, and many are hurrying to put resources into innovation, trusting that it's anything but a quick and simple arrangement. The motivation is reasonable: innovation is progressing quickly and has changed numerous ventures. In any case, under the current way to deal with execution—a progression of momentary choices—innovation is probably not going to accomplish its maximum capacity.

To take care of the issues of urbanization and to plan bearable, economical urban areas of things to come, governments need to receive an undeniably more essential methodology, of which innovation is just a single part. They need clear forthright examination to distinguish the greatest issues that their urban communities and constituents face, and they need to plan shared and resident driven arrangements that utilization innovation to address different useful groups: energy, versatility, natural maintainability, public administrations, and structures. This is possibly harder and additional tedious than essentially purchasing programming from a seller. Yet, it is the best way to create reasonable outcomes.

Urbanization Brings New Challenges

Urbanization will introduce difficulties for a huge scope. About 55% of the total populace as of now lives in urban communities, as indicated by the UN, and projections require this number to increment as provincial populaces contract. Not all urban areas are developing at a similar speed, in any case. By 2030, about one-6th of the total populace will live in only 41 huge urban communities—each with a populace of more than 10 million individuals ((UN DESA, 2018). That sort of focus among populaces can make clashes—and more prominent criticalness for regional authorities—in three explicit regions:

- Economic Contest Among Urban areas. Huge urban communities regularly siphon capital and business movement away from more modest urban communities close by. Also, in light of the fact that concentrated populaces lead to expanded monetary freedoms—an impact that becomes self-building up—huge urban communities win and more modest urban communities close by lose. New turn of events and foundation can in some cases strengthen the issue.

China, for example, built a high-speed rail link between Wuhan and Guangzhou in 2008, reducing travel time between the two cities (about 600 miles) from 11 to around 3 hours. The slower trains used to make more stops in such metropolitan areas, but the faster trains didn't stop there either. As a result, the populations of many smaller urban towns fell between 2008 and 2016, whereas the populations of metropolitan regions grew substantially at various resting points, creating financial benefits.

- Concentrated Openings: Five percent of the world's cities, according to one estimate, would produce more than a fifth of global GDP by 2030. This concentration of monetary activity may lead to greater wage disparities between the populations of large and small metropolitan areas. Even within the confines of a single city, wealth accumulates at the top, leading to an increasing divide between the wealthy and the poor, as well as social flimsiness at times. In the United States, four of the five cities with the highest per-capita GDP—Boston, New York, San Francisco, and Washington, DC—also exhibit the largest wages gap. Only the city of Seattle has found out how to keep the uniqueness of its compensation to a minimum.
- Environmental Difficulties. A concentrated populace takes into consideration the conveyance of more proficient public administrations, yet as urban communities develop greater, governments regularly battle to address the issues of bigger populaces. At present, about 35% of the world's metropolitan populace faces either lacking or excessively expensive lodging. Occupants in the 25 biggest urban communities lose an expected 66 hours of the year sitting in gridlocks—and expanded traffic prompts expanded contamination. Just 10% of the worldwide metropolitan populace lives in regions that at present satisfy World Wellbeing Association guidelines. The ecological difficulties develop as urban communities extend in size, and the impact is generally articulated in creating economies, where most of megacities are found.

In the total, critical intricacies for city governments are emerging in each of the three regions and making expanded direness to tackle them.

Technology Offers Possible Solutions

To address these difficulties, numerous urban communities are putting resources into advanced innovation, which holds extensive potential to assist pioneers with working on metropolitan arranging, cultivate even handed financial development, convey benefits all the more productively, and utilize more reasonable assets.

To further develop arranging, for instance, governments can utilize information framework and insightful devices. An administration organization entrusted with planning and building a downtown area can't do so viably except if it has exact data about the extended uses for the site, the quantity of individuals who will utilize it, the kinds of administrations those residents will require, and other basic data.

Urban regions may also benefit from innovation by cultivating more equitable development. The "smart city" innovation industry is growing at a rate of 21% per year and is expected to reach $1.5 trillion in value by 2022. In all, China spent up to $250 billion in 2017, although the United States and Western Europe developed faster. Busan, South Korea's cloud server facility will create 30,000 jobs (Bokolo, 2021).

Furthermore, innovation may assist cities in making better use of their resources and creating more hospitable urban environments. Urban areas may reduce CO_2 emissions, energy and water use, gridlock, and misbehaviour by 15 to 30 percent with the use of computerised arrangements. They also help urban towns provide administrative significantly more effectively by means of the internet and mobile devices. Around 80% of the population in Australia, for example, must reach taxpayer-driven organisations by 2020 through computerised means.

As a result, local governments are increasing their expenditure on research and development. The Indian government plans to invest more than $1.5 billion in 100 metropolitan areas via innovation initiatives.

Over 500 metropolitan districts in China received pilot projects in 2017 alone. By 2020, Canada wants to build 100 smart buildings and reduce the energy consumption of existing ones by 17% (Louis, 2019).

Limitations on Technology

Many metropolitan areas are investing resources to deal with these issues. However, innovation is often accompanied by its own set of problems, making it difficult to control its full benefits. There are many partners involved in digitization initiatives, such as government efforts to make e-administrations available to its citizens. Organizers are forced to work together to fulfil the demands of the vast number of participants. Furthermore, project initiators sometimes have a poor understanding of the centre clients of another arrangement — or the problems these customers are trying to address — and they don't care about an ordered method to deal with the action plan of plan. As a result, selection rates are capped when projects are finally made available on the internet.

Furthermore, a few urban communities put resources into a progression of individual arrangements and applications that are not viable with each other. Frameworks and data sets are not incorporated, frequently because of rivalry among merchants, however the expense of supplanting those things is high to such an extent that urban communities can't stand to transform them.

Indeed, even ventures that are effective at the pilot stage can run into issues when they are carried out across the more extensive regional government. Basic obstacles regularly incorporate adjusting the hierarchical construction and building the right interior abilities to meet the necessities of the new framework.

Monetary requirements are intensifying this load of issues. The expense of metropolitan development in numerous urban areas is becoming quicker than Gross domestic product and taking up a bigger portion of city incomes. Government obligation is becoming around the world. In the long haul, innovation ventures that are insightfully planned and carried out can create an alluring profit from speculation—for instance, by prodding monetary development and permitting governments to convey benefits all the more productively. In any case, that is little assistance for governments that just don't have the money to make the necessary forthright venture (Khanna et al, 2018).

Making the Future City from Scratch: A Systematic Approach

As a result of these difficulties, governments can't go to innovation for a prompt fix. All things being equal, they need to see how innovation can address human necessities. At the end of the day, they need a far-reaching way to deal with metropolitan arranging—one that joins innovation to work with more extensive arrangements.

This Methodology has a Few Perspectives.

To begin with, every city needs to foster an essential vision for the future that mulls over a few factors: its extraordinary conditions; the greatest issues it is probably going to look as far as administrations, assets, populace development, and different components; and how it intends to address those issues—not as far as months or years but rather many years.

Makes an Essential Vision to Foster Two Metropolitan Locale

It's critical to have a clear picture of two fundamental principles that will determine how events turn out: local centrality and collaboration. The first step is for government officials to think about their constituents, asking themselves who these new groups are and what their needs are. If governments follow the second central guideline, they should work together openly with their citizens, including people in designing and testing arrangements that will result in higher appropriation rates when such arrangements are finally implemented Residents and organisations.

The third layer of a far-reaching arrangement comprises of useful bunches—the real gatherings of administrations and arrangements that legislatures offer: energy, versatility, ecological supportability, public administrations, and structures. Metropolitan governments need to distinguish and focus on enhancements in these bunches based on the most direct requirements.

At last, city organizers can go to innovation to construct the real computerized framework—the organization, applications, sensors, investigation bundles, and different instruments—that can assist with empowering the arrangements distinguished in past advances. Basically, any innovation should be very much planned and dissected as far as its expenses and likely advantages. The plan and testing of new administrations is additionally significant preceding execution, especially for those with a wellbeing perspective, like transportation. Also, sometimes, innovation itself can be utilized to test possible contributions, through reproductions and different apparatuses.

In whole, innovation holds huge guarantee to assist city governments with making the keen city of things to come, yet just in the event that they get brilliant about the execution interaction. Maybe than just purchasing singular arrangements, governments need to foster a more complete system that puts residents first and depends on coordinated effort. Thusly, governments can create the most noteworthy conceivable profit from their speculations and assemble a drawn-out arrangement that will serve their necessities paying little heed to which innovations are in or out of vogue.

Urbanization Brings New Challenges

- Economic Competition among Cities. Concentrated Opportunities.
- Environmental Challenges.

Urbanization in a Digital World: Theory of Change

- Urban economic changes
- Opportunities for a more efficient urban management
- Social dimensions

URBACT cities are grasping the possibility and Digitization is ubiquitous in today's social and urban life.

URBACT Thematic Programme Expert Marcelline Bonneau claims that URBACT cities have seized their potential to create local economics and governance models.

Tech Revolution The Network's Lead Expert, Alison Partridge, has long said that cities must 'adapt or perish,' because "cities of all sizes need to better grasp the possibilities provided by digital and tech and seize on them to create higher-value employment and start-ups for local people. All degrees of social group and organisation are meta-analysed on all levels of digital availability and digital instrumentation for growth, aggregation and use of data to continue to change employment and good.

In European cities, a digital revolution is taking place, which means that computer science skills and algorithms are being used more and more in our everyday lives. –"The use of new technologies to transmit and way information is dynamic in the way society functions", the path to society is built on "virtual", intangible, vectors and computer methods and algorithms.

The Action Plan was announced by the Partnership for a Digital Transition Urban Agenda. Citizens' digital lives are becoming increasingly absolute in both the public and private sectors.

New patterns of consumption and production are emerging, as is social interaction. On the other side of the digital divide, people are more relaxed about personal data privacy and have more freedom of choice.

A city's ability to stimulate other cities at the city level processing more merged administration movement and benefit from the digital transition's possibility is an asset for cities, not only in terms of business development and job creation, but also in terms of city governance and bringing the local level closer to the national level.

Aim of Digital Transformation is to Transform Local Economic Growth in Cities.

Cities are attempting to change themselves digitally as a means to an end. Aside from that, digital industries have seen advancements. More and more towns are implementing smart city initiatives only to get an advantage in the marketplace. As a new approach to dealing with pressing social problems such as the current situation and social ones requiring a strong stance, dedication, and expenditure of resources focused on improving local economies,

URBACT networks such as Tech Town, GENERATION Y CITY and Synergistic Cities are helping to stimulate the development of employment and skills in metro areas by digitising them. The metropolis's support system for tech and integer efficiency, Tech Place's show case for instances of a current economic situation As for social media, digital strategy and other technologies cities are using such as online education and digital wellness, co-working spaces and other types of co-working facilities It's a content-sharing platform for things like pieces, recordings, podcasts, and talks.

The DI4C system's first component, developing digital strategies for one of the 23 new Activity Preparation Systems, integrating digital innovation into both the hard and soft substructure. It aspires to have an impact on global imagery's infancy, as well as to improve technical and professional competence in general. The main goal of the Tech Modification programme is to promote digital development and knowledgeable economies by encouraging knowledge-based occupations and businesses across all sectors and commercial enterprises, all of which are supported by a business assistance system that helps create a "ecosystem." Barnsley (UK) and its Digital Media Centre are being moved.

As a result of the Urban Agenda Relationship on Occupation and Ability, URBACT has also supported existing local digitization ability in business, education, and preparation at the level of Digital Acquisition Mapping. When it comes to the acquisitions required to make the transition to a more digital city,

A Method Digital transformation: A Governing Body Direction

On the second side, Digitization can be seen as a epistemology. Everyday life is managed to make the city work as well as. The process, encouraging social and urban transformation, has a strong effect on the

Figure 1. NeleLeosk, 2019, DIGITAL TRANSITION ABC

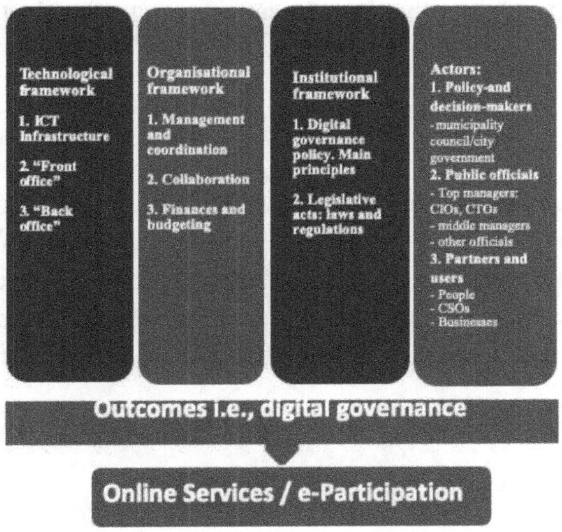

organization, in individualize the use of services technology can lead to "*Transformation the obstruction between the citizenry and the employment which their revenue enhancement money*" (Desilava, 2020)

URBACT City Lab 3 by Eddy Adams following, is as pointed out it is key to use capable communication which does not estrange people. To understandable both sides. And to know each other and to select a communication so, administrations and citizens need to get that. Can be controlled to change cities into level of open creation and produce digital urbanization by the Digitization and new technologies.

The ESPON working paper on the "In urban environment Digital creation: sustainable and fluently working cities is for solutions" the benefit is back for straight and crosswise co-creation of cities.

To make organization more comprehensive, democratic, and much capable. Digital transformation can be helped by particular instruments like the rest of European cities. Bigger metropolis and Northern European metropolis are much progressive which has been known by ESPON.

Urban schedule Partnership on Digital Transformation can be supported by 4 frameworks: Scientific, organizational, organization, and by neutral (see Figure 1). Such a process, according to that, what is a critical significance in metropolis, that is not due to technology used but how it is used.

In the Card 4 URBACT system, the message sits in the middle. This system will serve as a one-stop shop for all things nationality related and ensure that all people with different nationalities are treated equally. By utilising this card, you'll be able to access cutting-edge services and technology. To change their job and utilise it as a component of construction involvement. As a result, cities may collect data. This card could be used for the use of citizen's time period (for public services), local transportation, assemblage, Water Park, local bathroom, sharing cars, and so on. Creating a Smart City with Smart Citizens can be a practical way to encourage ethical situations as well as domestic business, municipal movement, and sustainable lifestyles. To enhance the quality of life in European cities of all sizes. The Internet of Things (IoT) exchange system also makes an effort to improve performance as a consequence of the IoT. Using a computer-based device. Engagement and citizen get-together are also growing at the same time and depending on Great Exercise, an online activity that combines offline and online promotion. New synergistic platforms, such as Agen's Tell My City, are being processed by the participatory budget of Paris URBACT. Small and medium-sized communities, like Agen (FR), are implementing a new system called Progressive Citizen that puts the interests of the residents first.

CONCLUSION

Looking after the today's scenario maximum peoples are moving towards urbanization. There are many challenges which every individual needs to face. At the same time there are various actions which is taken to ensure the appropriate compliance of every challenge in order to accommodate every individual. Digitalization is playing vital role in the improving urbanization. As per the current study it will take another 5-10 years to improve environment and condition of the urban are for the newcomers.

REFERENCES

Anthony, B. Jr. (2021). Managing digital transformation of smart cities through enterprise architecture – a review and research agenda. *Enterprise Information Systems*, *15*(3), 299–331. doi:10.1080/17517575.2020.1812006

Bettencourt, L. M. A. (2019). *The digital transformation of metropolises*. Metropolis Observatory.

Botseva. (2020). Digital Transformation of Cities and Digital Transformation of Citizens. In *Economic Science, education and the real economy: Development and interactions in the digital age*. Publishing House Science and Economics Varna.

Khanna, LaBresh, Kengelbach, Selikowitz, Argent, & Burke. (2018). *The $75 Trillion Opportunity in Public Assets*. Boston Consulting Group Report.

UN DESA. (2018). *The 2018 Revision of the World Urbanization Prospects*. Population Division of the United Nations Department of Economic and Social Affairs.

van Winden, W., & de Carvalho, L. (2017). *Cities and digitalization*. Amsterdam University of Applied Sciences.

Chapter 13
Protection and Promotion of Intellectual Property Rights (IPR) for Economic Competitiveness and Growth

Puneet Kumar
Kalinga University, India

Abdul Sattar A. Al-Ausi
American University in the Emirates, UAE

ABSTRACT

The intellectual property they possess of an innovative technological invention that they have created is the only thing that matters to certain small businesses. IPR has genuinely grown as an "intellectual currency," aiding in the advancement of global economic development, corporate prosperity, and creativity. In many fields of technology, intelligence, and culture, governments around the world are searching for ways to develop their economies, assist their people, and create national capabilities. This chapter discusses and describes the importance of intellectual property (IP) rights in achieving these vital objectives. This chapter will also offer an empirical summary of how a successful intellectual property rights regime can support or impede economic growth (IPRS).

INTRODUCTION

IP is linked to human psyche creation as well as insight. This has resulted in intellectual property being extremely valuable and significant. In India, there are well-established regulatory, legislative, and judicial institutions in place to protect intellectual property. This is noted that India needs to conform to the Agreement related with Trade-Related IPR at sanctioning vital rules. IPRs manage Trademark, Copyrights, Patents and Geographical Indications of merchandise. Law securing regarding uncommon types related to IPRs are as follows:

DOI: 10.4018/978-1-7998-8705-8.ch013

- The Geographical Indications of Goods (Registration and Protection) Act, 1999;
- Trade Marks Act, 1999;
- The Semiconductor Integrated Circuits Layout Design Act, 2000;
- The Protection of Plants and Varieties and Farmers Rights Act, 2001;
- The Biological Diversity Act, 2002;
- The Copyright Act, 1957; and
- The Patent Act, 1970

IPRs consists incredible significance in development of the nation. This law is distinctive in every nation of the world. In consideration of developed nations, severe enforcement related to IPR job consists gigantic commitment with respect to economic growth and its developments (Sangwan, 2019). IPR elevates advancement that prompts economic development and growth. These days each trade on planet have formation related to development and Innovation. The present time has very well understood importance and significance of these laws.

Connection Amid Intellectual Property and Growth Related to Economy

The basic purpose is:

- To give elite rights as well as securing premium of maker and energize interest through examination and knowledge creation;
- To forbid about contenders as well as anyone by abusing / abuse property without consent by maker;
- To make the business opportunity through development so this very well may provide to acceptable use and will persuade another to advancement along with creation.

Presently IPR gives selective rights to the proprietor or maker of the property. The proprietor can choose the reasonable esteem and can offer them to anybody. A sound re-visitation of designers will urge him and another by creating new advancements and moreover, we may advance development. However, this type of privilege may likewise abuse through proprietor, individual and organization may charge far more than negligible expense. Various studies have noted that this elite right may make the syndication on lookout (Pradhan, 2018; Rajesh et al 2018). Syndication prompts imbalance and divergence in the market in both utilization and creation. The general set of laws has IPR just as antitrust areas.

Rivalry has its vital job on the lookout, this consists checks related to lookout, and this influences purchaser fulfillment. It is also noted that some huge monsters in market consists outright force on related lookout. They consist force assets through control and control this. Market uses to produce using shopper maker and engineers and IPR provides rights as well as assurance to designers and more prominent that consists rivalry alive. In continuation, there should be the harmony amid on lookout. IPR may utilize like an apparatus for keeping up proper balance on lookout. IPR provides elite rights for proprietor as well as gives power to move his entitlement to use to others so the individual can approve anybody to utilize it in return for cash.

Review of Literature

Fatima Mard (2017), Stronger IPRs are said to benefit both developed and developing countries. On the one hand, Northern firms will have adequate incentives to invest in R&D and innovation. They may, on the other hand, be in favor of licensing the information and working on joint ventures with firms in the South. Greater inflows of technology transfer will help developing nations. On the other hand, critics of IPR protection have contended that increasing IPR protection might lead to higher costs, distorting consumer choice and lowering welfare. They claim that a strong IPRs system can hinder knowledge transfer by restricting the scope of imitation, making it more difficult to close the North-South technical divide. When developing nations align their IP rules to meet those of rich countries, they will bear short-term costs associated with rent transfers, administration, and enforcement, diverting precious resources away from other important sectors.

IPR protection and competitiveness have been connected in the literature since the 1970s, although more prevalently during the late 1970s and 1980s, when IPR protection started to be framed as a competitiveness issue (Muzaka, 2013) .

Currently, IPR protection, more than being used by companies as a tool to attract investment (Glass and Saggi, 2002, Smarzynska, 2004) and create wealth (Schneider, 2005), has been recognized as a source of competitive advantage (Singh, 2015). IPR protection prevents firm innovations from being exposed without any kind of protection and explored by competitors, giving the companies a portion of market power and, sometimes, monopoly power, materialized in the exclusive use and commercialization of their innovations, since they are legally protected from potential violations (Sey et.al., 2010).

The type of IPR protection used seems to help companies to create and sustain competitive advantage in several ways: it can provide a temporary technological lead (incumbency advantages), protect strong brands, help to establish a standard in the market, and to protect key components, thus increasing switching costs.

BACKGROUND

This concept is certainly not the other idea. This concept is first introduced at North Italy during period about 1474. Venice gave this law managing the procedures say licenses assurance; allowed the select ideal in consideration of proprietor. Copyright traces all the way back in the period of 1440 A.D. when Johannes Gutenberg imagined about print machine that replaceable as well as moveable type of wooden as well as metal letters. At the period of nineteenth century, numerous nations felt about requirement of setting down legal aspects directing IPR. Universally, shows establishing reason related with IPR framework globally had been marked; at Paris Convention for the Protection of Industrial Property in the period of 1883 and Berne Convention for the Protection of Literary and Artistic Works in the period of 1886.

Security related to IPR permits about trailblazer, brand proprietor along with patent holder and copyright holder at profit by his/her related work, work and speculation, that doesn't regard syndication related with astuteness. Such types of rights are being set out through International Declaration with respect to Human Rights, that accommodates option with profit by insurance in consideration of good and actual well-being coming about because of the correct holder's work; strict or imaginative item. This consists the following as under:-

Patent

This is utilized by considering an innovation from being create, sold, as well as utilized by other gathering without consent. Licenses are being considered as most well-known sort with intellectual property rights that uses to go for individuals' psyches when they support IPRs insurance. The patent holder has each privilege in market about the patent, consisting purchasing and selling about patent or conceding the permit at development to other outsider into commonly concurred conditions.

Brand Name

This is other type of recognizable sort related to IPRs security. This is considered as unmistakable symbol that allows purchasers effortlessly distinguish particularly merchandise by which organization provides.

Copyright

Copyright doesn't secure thoughts. Maybe, it just covers "unmistakable" forms of manifestations and unique work–for instance, craftsmanship, music, structural drawings, or even programming codes. The copyright proprietor has the elite option to sell, distribute, and/or replicate any scholarly, melodic, sensational, imaginative, or design work made by the creator.

Proprietary Advantage

This is privileged insights related to business. This includes restrictive structures, formulas, modules, etc another information mean secret and isn't intentional considering unapproved trade using through another. This is the fundamental form at assurance that may support organizations by acquiring with upper hand.

Intellectual property reflects result related with human keenness and rights conceded at permit the proprietor at profit related to products with intellectual undertaking through making restraining infrastructure considering this. Such advantage isn't generally a characteristic right however requires acknowledgment by a resolution.

Intellectual property rights (IPRs) assume a critical part in each area and have become the reason for urgent venture choices. IPRs are selective rights and therefore there is consistently a test to find interests of the general public on the loose. Another significant factor is having a sufficient lawful structure to ensure the interests of pioneers and motivate certainty that their intellectual property will be secured, thus setting off additional advancement. IPR case in India is very different attributable with huge procedure of courts, changing level with involvement of legal officials related to IPR cases and fluctuating habits with respect to training. The vast majority related to cases for encroachment are recorded in urban cities.

Purpose

There are fundamental primary economic destinations with arrangement at intellectual property assurance. Firstly is related with advance interests by information creation and business development through setting up select rights with utilization and sell presently developed innovations, labor and products. Not giving such rights would prompt economically significant information could be appropriated without remuneration by aggressive opponents; henceforth establishments and people would be hesitant to put cash and effort into exploration and commercialisation exercises.

Brand names secure the rights to showcase labor and products under recognized names and images. Brand names and brand names should be adequately extraordinary to abstain from confounding shoppers, in this manner assuming the significant part of decreasing customer search costs. These rights urge firms to put resources into name acknowledgment and item quality. They likewise initiate licensees to ensure the worth of resources by selling merchandise of ensured quality levels. On the off chance that brand names were not secured, rival firms could make their lower-quality merchandise look like genuine renditions of those delivered by perceived organizations. The present circumstance would reduce motivations for keeping up quality and would raise shopper search costs. Business analysts for the most part accept that the risk of market predominance through maltreatment of brand names is slight in aggressive economies yet such stamps could be joined by critical market power in nations with different hindrances to passage.

The factors of an intellectual property module are about its enforcement. Such enforcement consists two restricting assignments: rebuffing encroachment through free riders as well as training undertakings that consider to attempt with broaden their rights past proposed levels by acting in an enemy of serious way. These goals require the advancement of broad legitimate and logical aptitude.

Kinds of Competitiveness

Value Competitiveness

Value competitiveness alludes to how well UK sends out look at as far as cost. This is influenced by various elements, including:

Non-Value Competitiveness

Non-value competitiveness alludes to how well UK fares of branded labor and products do in abroad business sectors in parts of rivalry not related with cost, for example,

1. Product quality and plan.
2. Business Research and Development (R&D), particularly new item improvement
3. Product unwavering quality
4. The strength or shortcoming of 'nearby' brands
5. The adequacy of advertising in abroad business sectors

The World Economic Forum Global Competitiveness Report

1. Effective foundations – which establish an economic climate wherein organizations can create, and purchasers have certainty. These ought to be 'sound, genuine and reasonable'.
2. Effective framework – which gives viable vehicle and energy supplies.
3. A sound large scale economic climate, including sound public funds, and low and stable swelling.

The Economic Jump - Significant Reforms of the '90s

The reform cycle in India has been dispatched to speed up the speed of economic growth and to annihilate neediness. Albeit economic advancement in India can be traced all the way back to the 1970s, the economic reforms began in July 1991. The equilibrium of installments emergency around then prepared for a program of the International Monetary Fund (IMF), program that prompted the reception of a significant reform bundle. Despite the fact that stores were immediately recuperated and the proficient impermanent impact of the IMF and the World Bank finished, the reforms proceeded.

Economic growth in India has begun toward the start of the 1980s, while economic reforms didn't happen before 1991. All things considered, the underlying increment has been gone before by huge public interest in foundation during the 1970s and mid 1980s, and the continuous change to a more open political business climate.

ECONOMIC COMPETITIVENESS

The term of "**competitiveness**" is perhaps the most ordinarily utilized ideas in economics yet it isn't sufficiently exact, what implies that there is no commonly acknowledged meaning of competitiveness. This is related to capacity with economy considering contend decently and measure effectively with respect to business sectors by globally exchanged labor as well as products that takes into consideration rising standards of living over the long run.

The term began from the Classical Latin word "petere" which means to look for, assault, focus on, want, and the Latin prefix "con-" which means together. As of now, it is frequently utilized in various settings, which means disparate things to various scientists. The expression was instituted during the 70s of the 20th century. It was then that American financial experts, under the proof of serious exchange fight among American and Japanese organizations, embraced the fi rst endeavors to decide the level of competitiveness between the opponent economies.

Financial specialists contend that economic globalization has the capability of expanding economic government assistance for all. In old style economics, the competitiveness of nations is resolved through creation inputs. Information sources like work, land, capital, and regular assets were the proportions of competitiveness- - generally quantifiable components that added to the GDP of a country. In the cutting edge time of globalization and the subsequent interlink among nations and their economic reliance, the traditional hypothesis of competitiveness isn't relevant because of some unique changes in perceiving competitiveness. It creates the impression that, other than quantifiable variables, subjective impacts or 'delicate' factors like political soundness, government arrangements, nature of instruction ecological conditions, institutional elements, social, and social issues are for the most part similarly significant in deciding competiveness (Kumar., 2017; Yadav et al., 2020)

ANALYSIS AND INTERPRETATION

Presently different hypotheses propose IPR that generate adversely affects on economy. This is noted about China that in the period of 1980s, the name related to brand encroachment contrarily influenced Chinese inventive endeavors. Neighborhood organizations began abusing about grounded organization through creating duplicated items and dispatching this on the lookout. In consideration of India that is possible about most creating economies at planet bringing efficiency on the lookout. India consistently now knows as outstanding administrations in world. The study discusses that one may build profitability through continuously improvement in innovation and strategy (Sangwan, 2019). Development requires ventures, this needed the lot of speculation. We may view and gain considering created nations as USA and Japan with pace related to advancement expanded through multiple times by execution IPLs.

Copyright infringement have a comparative effect. In nations where intellectual property laws are powerless privateer firms begin misusing the law and the market. In spite of the fact that inferior quality duplicates or pilfered duplicates accessible with respect to market the innovative development would be considered hampered that will straightforwardly influence upon economy. IPR related legal laws ought to provide motivators considering both makers and buyers by putting resources into market.

Worldwide Competitiveness, Financial Turn of Events and Growth in India

As per the World Economic Forum, India is an economy in the principal phase of improvement, one dependent on creation factors (GDP/capita underneath $ 2000). In the World Economic Forum report on worldwide competitiveness file in 2012-2013, India was positioned 59, down three spots from a year ago. India is as yet an arising nation, buried in neediness and ignorance issues, in spite of the fact that it has an atomic arms stockpile and the second number of qualified people on the planet in the product area, after the United States. India's accomplishments in science and innovation and the creating information based ventures have caused world to notice this arising country with a billion occupants, country that has confronted troubles in staying up with the growth paces of 'tigers' and "mythical serpents" in the ASEAN locale, or with that of China, its monster northern neighbor (Pradhan, 2018).

India keeps on encountering frustrating performance in regions viewed as the principle factors supporting competitiveness. Transport framework, ICT and energy remain generally lacking and not well adjusted to the requirements of the economy. Without a doubt, Indian business local area over and again refers to foundation as the single biggest impediment for working together, well before the debasement and administration. It ought to be noted, nonetheless, that the circumstance has improved somewhat since 2006. The image is much more distressing in wellbeing and instruction. In spite of enhancements lately, helpless standards of wellbeing and state funded schooling stay the primary driver of low efficiency in India (Mishra & Soni, 2016).

Getting back to the nation's foundations, the business local area disappointment stays high because of absence of reforms and the public authority's inability to apply them. In reality, public trust in government officials has dropped over the most recent three years. In the mean time, the macroeconomic climate keeps on being described by huge and tireless government shortfalls and a high portion of obligation in GDP between BRICS nations. As a more sure note, swelling got back to single digits in 2011 (Rajesha & Gupta, 2018). In spite of these difficulties, India has various qualities among the most progressive and complex mainstays of competitiveness. This model of improvement "turned around" is normal for India. It very well might be founded on a monetary market all around created and refined that can channel monetary assets to great utilize and can uphold very complex and imaginative business.

Realizing that components of worldwide competitiveness likewise act inside the human improvement region, way to deal with human advancement in India is of indispensable significance on the grounds that a huge piece of the populace lives underneath the neediness line and pay disparity is developing continuously. It is assessed that in excess of 800 million Indians live on under 20 rupees each day. There are contrasts between states, among provincial and metropolitan regions and between gatherings. Over 60% among ladies are constantly poor. Neediness rates among the Tribes and Castes stays high. Numerous occupants don't approach fundamental administrations. In excess of 296 million are uneducated and 233 million experience the ill effects of hunger. Workforce support of ladies is a large portion of that of men, and almost 96% of ladies work in the informal area.

As of late delivered interval Statistical assessment of the Millennium Development Goals shows that India is having issues in gathering a few targets identified with craving, kid and maternal mortality and avoidance of intestinal sickness and different illnesses. Despite the fact that growth rates were high, an excessive number of Indians actually come up short on the essential conditions for fair expectations for everyday comforts as far as sustenance, wellbeing, admittance to training and other public administrations, for example, water supply and disinfection. Burdened gatherings, especially standings and clans and minorities have profited less from these conditions. Provincial abberations have arisen between and even inside states.

Intellectual property (IP) rights are lawful and institutional gadgets to ensure manifestations of the brain like creations, show-stoppers and writing, and plans. They likewise remember marks for items to demonstrate their distinction from comparable ones sold by contenders. Throughout the long term, the fairly versatile IP idea has been extended to incorporate licenses, copyrights, brand names, and modern plans yet additionally proprietary innovations, plant reproducers' rights, geological signs, and rights to spread out plans of coordinated circuits, in addition to other things.

IP rights have never been more economically and politically significant than they are in the present alleged 'information based society.' Neither have they at any point been so disputable. IP rights are oftentimes referenced in conversations and discussions on such assorted subjects as basic freedoms, agribusiness, wellbeing, training, exchange, modern arrangement, general wellbeing, biotechnology, biodiversity, natural insurance, information innovation, the amusement and media enterprises, and the augmenting hole between the pay levels of the created nations and the non-industrial nations.

The greatest downside of IPR is it in some cases it confines the innovation to be utilized in the best reasonable manner. The individual who is holding rights in some cases abuses their rights. They can charge as per their will and on account of assurance under IPR that advancement can't be utilized by the contenders. Rivalry is the main factor for the improvement of an economy. The soul of rivalry keeps check and equilibrium on cost and just as on the nature of the item. However, IPR laws are contrary to the standard of rivalry.

The law is made for society, not the other way around. Every one of the laws are made for the advantage and improvement of society. Each law has its positive just as adverse consequences on society. Article 31 of the TRIPS Agreement accommodates the award of mandatory licenses, under the accompanying circumstance:

In light of a legitimate concern for general wellbeing if there should arise an occurrence of public crisis Anti-serious practice. Thus, in India, the Intellectual Property Right law doesn't make the market unbending simultaneously powerful in nature.

Economic examination of Intellectual Property Rights is utilitarian, addressing whether the advantages of any framework exceed its expenses, both in static and dynamic terms. The expected advantages and expenses rely upon attributes of business sectors, items and social establishments (Yadav et al, 2020; Mishra et al, 2016)

CONCLUSION

Think about now the other way of causation. Market analysts perceive a few channels through which IPRS could invigorate economic turn of events and growth. These cycles are related and it is suitable to receive an extensive perspective on the motivations related with intellectual property insurance.

Intellectual property rights could assume a critical part in empowering advancement, item improvement, and specialized change. Non-industrial nations will in general have IPRS frameworks that blessing information dispersion through minimal expense impersonation of foreign items and innovations. To get cutthroat, undertakings in non-industrial nations normally should embrace new administration and hierarchical frameworks and procedures for quality control, which can especially raise profitability.

Such ventures are exorbitant however will in general have high friendly returns since they are critical for raising efficiency toward worldwide standards. They are bound to be attempted in a climate where dangers of uncalled for rivalry and brand name encroachment are little. Besides, IPRS could help reward innovativeness and hazard taking among new endeavors and business visionaries. Nations that hold frail standards could stay subject to powerfully wasteful firms that depend on duplicating and impersonation.

Intellectual property rights additionally could invigorate obtaining and dispersal of new information. Patent cases are distributed, permitting rival firms to utilize the information in them to foster further creations. This learning interaction happens in 10 to a year in the United States. Information formation is total and as new innovations expand on past rehearses the cycle of specialized change could speed up. Licenses, brand names, and proprietary advantages additionally afford firms more prominent conviction that they face restricted dangers of uncompensated allotment. This conviction could instigate them to exchange and permit their innovations and items all the more promptly, improving their dissemination into the economy.

It is conceivable that the new patent systems presented by TRIPS could change the present circumstance. The all out market size for drugs of the nations that should overhaul their patent assurance over the medium term is adequately huge that, even at current portions of medications protected somewhere else, the ascent in demand could be just about as much as 25% of worldwide spending. Hence, the motivations created for R&D zeroed in on infections of helpless nations could be huge. While this is an unrefined computation, it proposes that drug firms could expect higher benefits in non-industrial countries, some bit of which could be committed to investigate on their endemic illnesses.

REFERENCES

Glass, A. J., & Saggi, K. (2002). Intellectual Property Rights and Foreign Direct Investment. *Journal of International Economics*, *56*(2), 387–410. doi:10.1016/S0022-1996(01)00117-9

Kumar. (2017). Demonetization in India: Impact on the Economy. *Globus An International Journal of Management & IT, 9*(1), 1-4.

Mard, F. (2017). The effects of intellectual property rights protection in the technology transfer context on economic growth: The case of developing countries. *Journal of Innovation Economics & Management*, *23*(2), 33–57. doi:10.3917/jie.023.0033

Mishra, & Soni. (2016). A Study on Technology, Thinking Styles, and Content of Education. *Cosmos An International Journal of Art & Higher Education*, *5*(2), 1–4.

Muzaka, V. (2013). Intellectual Property Protection and European 'Competitiveness'. *Review of International Political Economy*, *20*(4), 819–847. doi:10.1080/09692290.2012.724436

Pradhan. (2018). Problems Facing Indian Economy. *Cosmos An International Journal of Art & Higher Education*, *7*(1), 12–15.

Rajesha & Gupta. (2018). Microfinance and Poverty Reduction in India. *Globus An International Journal of Management & IT, 9*(2), 1-6.

Sangwan. (2019). Innovation In Instructional Strategies & Design. *Globus Journal of Progressive Education, 9*(2), 1-3.

Schneider, P. H. (2005). International Trade, Economic Growth and Intellectual Property Rights: A Panel Data Study of Developed and Developing Countries. *Journal of Development Economics*, *78*(2), 529–547. doi:10.1016/j.jdeveco.2004.09.001

Sey, A., Lowe, B., & Poole, N. (2010). The Use of Intellectual Property Protection by Micro, Small, and Medium-Scale Enterprises: A Case Study of Ghana. *Enterprise Development & Microfinance*, *21*(1), 67–83. doi:10.3362/1755-1986.2010.006

Singh, S. (2015). Innovation, Intellectual Property Rights and Competition Policy. *Innovation and Development*, *5*(1), 147–164. doi:10.1080/2157930X.2014.1003450

Smarzynska, B. K. (2004). Composition of Foreign Direct Investment and Protection of Intellectual Property Rights: Evidence from transition Economies. *European Economic Review*, *48*(1), 39–62. doi:10.1016/S0014-2921(02)00257-X

Yadav, L., Devi, S., Vaidh, N., & Sharma, S. (2020). Psychological, Social and Economic Effects Of COVID-19 Pandemic. *Cosmos Journal of Engineering & Technology*, *10*(1), 1–2.

Chapter 14
Sustainable Gig Economy Finance Towards GDP Growth of India Through "Aatmanirbhar Bharat"

Durga Madhab Mahapatra
FM Autonomous College, India

Shiv Ranjan
Amity University, India

Sukanta Kumar Baral
https://orcid.org/0000-0003-2061-714X
Indira Gandhi National Tribal University, India

ABSTRACT

In recent years, India has become the world's fastest-growing major economy. Its development has been fuelled mostly by the services sector, which accounts for over 55% of GDP, as contrasting to the industrial sector, which has remained stable at roughly 16%. To facilitate 'Aatmanirbhar Bharat', the government has brought in the product-linked incentive (PLI) scheme to encourage several sectors to increase their local manufacturing and supply chain base, among other things, to help India become self-reliant for high end products. These efforts will aid in the creation of jobs, the alleviation of stressed sectors, the assurance of liquidity, the boost of manufacturing, the energization of the real estate industry, and the assistance of farmers. The chapter aims to evaluate the Balance of Payment of India as structural growth country wise and sector wise growth of FDI in India as well as the 'Aaatmanirbhar Bharat' status and stimulus packages, which have been announced for sustainable growth of GDP during this pandemic situation.

DOI: 10.4018/978-1-7998-8705-8.ch014

INTRODUCTION

Covid-19 disrupted employment for millions of people and forced them to go into the gig economy practically immediately. Despite the turmoil created by the government's suspension of operations, there is still a lack of knowledge about the extent of India's gig economy and how it impacts the labor market. Thus, largest online gig work aggregators and job-tech start-ups in India point to several interesting trends that could potentially shape the future on India's employment landscape. During the pandemic, the maximum demand for gig workers was for jobs such as last mile delivery of essential goods, creation, moderation and cataloguing of digital content, telesales and operations management. In the past eight months since the Covid-19 epidemic broke out, 78 percent of micro-small and medium-sized enterprises (MSMEs) and start-ups in India have decreased staff. According to the results of a study conducted by Local Circles, just 22 percent of start-ups and micro-enterprises have an expanded staff or a match with pre-Covid levels. Due to the Covid-19 epidemic and the ensuing shutdown, India's start up and MSME environment has had a very difficult period, although India's outstanding performance in the worldwide fight against COVID-19 has been extensively acknowledged and praised. Most companies reduced expenses to weather the storm, leading to others to go out of business temporarily or permanently. CMIE estimates that 6 million white-collar jobs have been lost in India over the March-August timeframe. A study was performed on start-ups and small and medium-sized enterprises (SMEs) to identify any effect that Covid may have on their workers. The study got over 7,000 answers from start-ups, micro and small- and medium-sized enterprises, and entrepreneurs that are based in 104 different high-traffic commercial areas in the nation. Throughout the Covid-19 epidemic, start up and micro business firms were questioned about the changes to their personnel that had occurred during the pandemic. Of those surveyed, 15 percent said that they had a 50 percent or more staff reduction, while 25 percent stated that their company had shut down and all personnel had been let go. Additionally, about 19 of percent respondents said that their staff has been cut by as much as 25 percent to 50 percent. Further, around six percent claimed their staff has grown, while another sixteen percent indicated their employment is the same as prior to the period before to Covid-19. Moreover, 78 percent of the MSMEs and start-ups in India have decreased employment as a result of the Covid-19 epidemic, whereas 22 percent of start-ups and MSMEs have an expanded headcount. The government launched a program to assist small companies, the Aatmanirbhar Bharat programme, but businesses' responses in July this year indicate that the benefits of the program have been modest. Indian Prime Minister Narendra Modi approved a bill increasing the amount of paid maternity leave to six months in 2017, putting India at the third highest in the world. Kapoor, Mohit (2020)

Indians are one of the three biggest startup ecosystems in the world. The NASSCOM figures indicate that till 2016, India has gained a total of 1,400 new companies, bringing the number to over 4,750. Inefficiencies in logistics, healthcare, education, and financial services start-ups in India are being solved using machine learning and artificial intelligence. Start-up technology companies are considered crucial in regards to invention, production, growth, and employment, with their introduction aiding in a Country's Competition. The emergence of a unique entrepreneur's ecosystem, which suppers and promotes technology start-ups is an essential factor for a city to harbor-technology start-ups. Microsoft has introduced "Microsoft's startup engagement was driven by a "Catch them Young Approach". Further, Microsoft's "Cloud platform Azure" will come for B2B startups. India's Unicorn Club or list of start-ups valued more than $1 billion i.e., Byju's (March 2018 Rs. 5.4 billion), Swiggy (June 2018) Rs. 3.3 billion), Big Basket (March 2019 Rs. 2.3 billion), Paytm Mall (April 2018 Rs. 2.0 billion), Bill Desk

(November 2018, Rs. 1.8 billion), Delhivery (March 2019, Rs. 1.6 billion), Dream11 (April 2019, Rs. 1.5 billion), Uddan (September, 2018, Rs. 1.2 billion), Policy Bazzar (June, 2018, Rs. 1.2 billion). Malik, Yuvraj (2019). A company's success depends on the integration of people, processes, and technology. The startup must adopt a process that can be continually deconstructed, re-designed, and deployed in response to disruptions. As a result of the epidemic, new standards have been set. Many companies that have been in existence for some time now need to find ways to test and verify their current processes against basic principles. It is necessary for them to reflect on how a 1.3-billion-person economy can continue to create products and services, have secure incomes, and be celebrated for their contributions to society, all while going through hard times. The kind of start-ups that concentrate on innovation may help older companies to innovate by opening up new process avenues.

One of the crucial components of the economy, the micro and small-medium-sized businesses have suffered greatly because of the Covid Pandemic and the lockdown. However, the government's efforts to increase liquidity, together with slower payback periods, are improving the situation. MSMEs and Small Business are the backbone of a resilient national economy. Further, innovation drives to ensure inclusive growth as "Aatmanirbhar Bharat" will depend on their sustainability. The "Aatmanirbhar Bharat" package comprises tax breaks on some property sales, a small company credit guarantee scheme, and job development incentives. "Aatmanirbhar Bharat Rozgar Yojana", active from October 1, 2020 to June 20, 2021 to encourage new job creation during COVID recovery. The "Aatmanirbhar Bharat" program helps all sectors of society. Solicitors and accountants are among those who will benefit from the efforts. In the global bribery risk matrix, India placed 78 in 2019 with a score of 48, and 77 in 2020 with a score of 45. Civil society, including the media, has a role in this equation, which also includes transparency in government and service to the public. Aatmanirbhar Bharat" aiming to create scale and capacity for Indian companies' reforms are a must to make India's enterprises globally competitive. The SME sector serves as a backbone for the entire Indian Economy. It providing employment to more than 11 Crore individuals and contributing 6% to the manufacturing GDP. Besides contributing over 24 percent to the service GDP of the country. The MSMEs suffered as production and sales came to a halt because to the onset of the covid-19 epidemic, which occurred shortly after. The Government of India and RBI are concerned and supporting the MSMEs. Schemes like Guaranteed Emergency Credit Line (GECL) and Emergency Credit Guarantees (ECG) offer funds to the MSMEs with nominal rates. The Government also taking new initiative like (a) Make in India, (b) Vocal for Local and (c) "Aatmanirbhar Bharat". The "Vocal for local" campaign will lead to structural strengthening of MSME units and help them to enhance their brand identity and create a long-term sustainability for the engineering of MSMEs of India. Today, as the world is shifting towards sustainable, handmade and organic products, digital e-commerce has become the main sourcing and consumption platform globally. It is now imperative that steps are taken to upskill India's handicraft artisans and connect them with both domestic and international e-marketplaces.

The TRACE organization's list shows which countries, territories, and semi-autonomous regions have an above-average risk of corporate bribery. While Denmark, Norway, Finland, Sweden, and New Zealand have a low commercial bribery risk, North Korea, Turkmenistan, South Sudan, Venezuela, and Eritrea provide the highest danger. Also, bribery in public services persists in India. Bureaucratic red tape, confusing regulatory frameworks, and slow and complex bureaucratic processes compel people to seek alternative solutions via familiar networks and petty corruption. On average, almost half of those who paid bribes were requested to do so, whereas 32% of those who utilized personal connections claimed they would not have received the service otherwise. The study is based on a 2,000-person poll

Table 1. Projected growth rate of GDP of leading countries

Country	2017	2018	2019	2020f	2021f	2020f	2021f
United States	3.3	3.0	2.4	-5.2	4.2	-7.7	-1.6
Euro Area	2.5	2.1	1.6	-7.0	3.9	-8.4	2.4
Japan	2.2	0.3	0.7	-6.1	2.5	-6.8	1.9
China	6.8	6.6	6.1	1.0	6.9	-4.9	1.1
Brazil	1.3	1.3	1.1	-8.0	2.2	-10.0	-0.3
India	7.0	6.1	4.2	-3.2	3.1	-9.0	-3.0
Pakistan	5.2	5.5	1.9	-2.6	-0.2	-5.0	-3.2
Bangladesh	7.3	7.9	8.9	1.6	1.0	-5.6	-6.3

Source: Compiled by Authors

performed between June 17 and July 17 2020 in India. India has the greatest bribery rate (39%), as well as the largest use of personal ties to obtain governmental services (46 per cent).

India had a public debt of Rs.24.62 lakh crore in tin the year 1951. Rs.94.62265 lakh crores were the total liability of the Government of India in March 2020. There has been a slight increase. The total liabilities of the central government increased to Rs.101.35600 lakh crore by June 2020.India had external debt of $85 billion in 1991, which increased to $317 billion in 2011. India had a foreign debt of about $558 billion in March 2020. External debt on the country declined by $3.9 billion to $554 billion in June 2020.The good thing for India is that India relies more on internal debt and less on external debt. Due to this policy of India, about 20% of the total debt is external debt and the remaining 80% is internal debt. This is the reason why India's financial position is strong despite the Corona pandemic. Debt pressure is mounting on all the states in the country. By March 2020, there was a total debt of about Rs.40 lakh crore on all the states of the country. By the March 2021, there could be a debt of up to Rs.60 lakh crore on all states. Recent care rating data shows that almost all states of the country have debt of millions of crores of rupees. There is total debt of Rs.6.02 lakh crore on Uttar Pradesh, Maharashtra Rs.5.02 lakh crore, West Bengal Rs.4.37 lakh crore, Tamil Nadu Rs.4.04 lakh crore, Rajasthan Rs.3.43 lakh crore, Andhra Pradesh Rs.3.41 lakh crore, Gujarat Rs.3.26 lakh crore, Karnataka Rs.3.17 lakh crore There is a debt of Rs Rs.2.66 lakh crore on Kerala, Madhya Pradesh Rs.2.34 lakh crore, Punjab Rs.2.30 lakh crore, Telangana Rs.1.68 lakh crore and Orissa 1.33 lakh crore. In this context, per capita debt varies as per total debt in states. Per capita debt for the residents of Punjab is Rs.82771, Haryana Rs.81287, Kerala Rs.79771, Tamil Nadu Rs.56134, Gujarat Rs.53931, Karnataka Rs.51981, West Bengal Rs.47881, Maharashtra Rs.44734, Madhya Pradesh Rs.32354 and of Uttar Pradesh is Rs. 30136.There has been a slight increase in debt on the country and all the states (Table 1).

OBJECTIVES OF THE STUDY

The purpose of this paper is to look at India's long-term economic potential;

1. To evaluate the Balance of Payment of India as a structural growth,
2. To investigate the growth of FDI in India by nation and sector, and

3. To discuss the "Aatmanirbhar Bharat" status and stimulus packages which is announced for sustainable growth of GDP during this pandemic situation.

METHODOLOGY

The current research is descriptive and covers from secondary data sources. The material in this study was gathered from publications, news articles, and websites of research institutions and ministries.

ANALYSIS AND DISCUSSION

India has always been more dependent on internal debt. India's dependence on external debt has been low. The concern is only when the public debt of any country exceeds 77 percent of GDP. At present, the situation in India is much better because the total public debt of India is equal to about 71 percent of the GDP. However, under such scenario pandemic like COVID19 in the country; The public debt in the country was equal to 84.2 percent of GDP in 2003. However, despite of odd situation like Covid19 pandemic, the country's public debt of 2020 is only 71 percent of GDP. This is the better position as compared to all other countries of the world. The public debt of industrialised countries such as Japan is 240 percent of GDP, whereas the public debt of the United States is 107 percent of GDP. Furthermore, India is in a very favourable situation in terms of external debt now. India's external debt is equal to 21% of its GDP. The external debt of France is 277 percent of GDP, Germany's is 153 percent, and Japan's is 94 percent of GDP.

India has always been more dependent on internal debt. India's dependence on external debt has been low. The concern is only when the public debt of any country exceeds 77% of GDP. At present, the situation in India is much better because the total public debt of India is equal to about 71% of the GDP. That too when there is a terrible pandemic like COVID19 in the country. There would like to remind that in the year 2003, the public debt in the country was equal to 84.2% of GDP. Despite the Covid19 epidemic, the country's national debt currently stands at just 71% of GDP. We're in a better place now. When compared to other countries in the globe, Japan's public debt is equal to 240 percent of GDP. The national debt in the United States is 107 percent of GDP. In terms of external debt, India is now in a pretty strong situation. India's external debt is equal to 21% of its GDP. The external debt of France is 277 percent of GDP, that of Germany is 153 percent, and that of Japan is 94 percent of GDP. There is no need to worry about the financial situation and debt. The country's economic situation is constantly improving. After having COVID19 vaccine in the coming few months, the country's economic condition will continue to improve further. India is on the verge of becoming an economic superpower (Table 2).

To qualify, a business must contain the following (chemical, pharmaceutical, electronic manufacturing, steel, and automotive manufacturing have all contributed to India's industrial development.) An expansion of these sectors, which may employ millions in the future, can be achieved with the right government support. India's automobile industry now accounts for 7.1 percent of the country's GDP and 49 percent of manufacturing GDP. It sold 3.81 million automobiles in 2019, making it the world's sixth-largest market. The car sector employs close to 29 million people and is one of the biggest employers in the nation. The automobile industry is a major economic multiplier and one of the most vital. The car sector in the US has one of the greatest "employment multipliers" of any business, meaning it helps

Table 2. Country wise FDI inflows during 2015-16 to 2019-20(U$ $ million)

Country/ Year	2015-16	2016-17	2017-18	2018-19	2019-20 P
Singapore	12,479	6,529	9,273	14,632	12,612
Mauritius	7,452	13,383	13,415	6,570	7,498
Netherlands	2,330	3,234	2,677	2,519	5,295
Cayman Islands	440	49	1,140	863	3,496
U.S.A.	4,124	2,138	1,973	2,823	3,401
Japan	1,818	4,237	1,313	2,745	2,308
France	392	487	403	375	1,167
United Kingdom	842	1,301	716	1,211	1,125
South Korea	241	466	293	982	777
Hongkong	344	134	1,044	598	678
Cyprus	488	282	290	161	657
Germany	927	845	1,095	817	443
Belgium	57	172	213	56	388
U.A.E.	961	645	408	853	323
Luxembourg	784	99	243	251	252
UK Virgin Islands	203	212	21	290	250
China	461	198	350	229	162
Others	1,725	1,905	2,498	2,768	1,796
Total FDI	**36,068**	**36,317**	**37,366**	**38,744**	**42,629**

Note: Includes FDI through SIA/FIPB and RBI routes only. P: Provisional
Source: Reserve Bank of India Annual Reports
https://m.rbi.org.in/Scripts/AnnualReportPublications.aspx?Id=1307

generate jobs outside of manufacturing. Every automotive job supports seven additional employments in the U.S. economy, creating a multiplier impact of 8. Much like in the United States, a lot of commodities like steel, aluminum, plastics, and other products are imported to the Indian automobile sector from elsewhere. The success of these international businesses also helps strengthen the country's image as an attractive investment location, echoing the government's demand for "manufacturing in India for the world". Nearly 13 million people are employed by the electronics sector and indirectly by the steel industry. The chemicals industry contributes more than 2% to the country's GDP, while direct and indirect employment in the medicines industry stands at nearly 5 million. With respect to the sectors listed above, there is significant export potential. Poor innovation, high taxation, and limited R&D investment have created a situation where Indian products have failed in the global market, and the Indian market has been flooded with foreign imports. More comprehensive and sector-specific strategies are required to promote exports in accordance with "Aatmanirbhar Bharat". One of the newly unveiled packages of the BJP is a "Aatmanirbhar Bharat" that provides tax relief on house sale transactions, a credit guarantee scheme for small companies, and financial incentives for new job development. "Aatmanirbhar Bharat Rozgar Yojana", an operational job creation program running from October 1, 2020, to June 2021 to create new employment possibilities as the economy is going through a time of COVID recovery. Extended through March 31, 2021, the emergency credit line guarantee program. the "Aatmanirbhar Bharat" package will benefit all sectors of society as it continues the Government's ongoing efforts. By saying these measures would help generate employment, help relieve the strained sectors, guarantee liquidity, promote manufacturing, energize the real estate industry, and assist farmers, he's predicting that this economic package will be both widely popular and very beneficial.

With a median age of 27 years, India is one of the youngest nations in the ageing globe. Based on work by sociologists Alfred G. Strauss and Neil Howe, a generational theory was developed in 1991 called the Strauss and Howe generational theory. This theory classifies generations as follows: Silent Generation (born between 1915 and 1945): Traditionalists; Baby Boomers (born between 1946 and 1964): Generation X; Millennials (born between 1977 and 1995): Generation Y; Generation Z (born after 1996): Centennials Going by the United Nation's population statistics at medium variant, today, Gen Z population constitute 42.5 percent of the total population in India, followed by Millennials (29.4 percent). Population in the age group of 15-40, who is believed to be tech-savvy constitute nearly 42 percent of the total population. Mass digital adoption and availability of digital infrastructure in the country would further widen the digital-savvy customer base to a new height.

The beginning of the next decade and a new normal mean that 2021 will be a major turning point in our history. The new normal will offer new difficulties to current procedures and methods, which will need the creation of new opportunities. The increasing success of new enterprises and start-ups will serve as the basis for an independent, digital India. This class represents a paradigm shift: Start-ups with new processes and new technology are redefining the new normal. In 2021, start-ups' focus will be on creating business models that are both efficient and nimble. In order to overcome difficulties in the 21st century, start-ups will have to look for novel procedures, technology, and people to put in place. As Covid-19 defines the new normal with the increasing adoption of virtual banking, it has pushed banking, financial services and insurance (BFSI) players to revisit existing business models. Technology services providers, which traditionally focused on application / infrastructure services, are now offering platform-based solutions.

In order to encourage companies to produce pharmaceutical ingredients domestically, the government has implemented policies such as the production linked incentive (PLI) scheme, which offers electronics manufacturers 4–6% production-linked incentives, and nearly Rs 1 lakh crore to fund the manufacturing of pharmaceutical ingredients by 2023. While the government should be commended for its efforts, it must continue to assist and support these industries. With appropriate government backing, these industries may help India become a global manufacturing centre and contribute to the bulk of manufacturing GDP. As a result of the COVID-19 epidemic, the manufacturing, services, and commercial sectors have been hard affected as well as India's much-publicized agricultural growth plan, which seeks to quadruple farmers' income by 2022. Major changes to the food supply chain, shortage of labor, and lower overall demand have all negatively impacted small- and large-scale farmers alike. More than half of India's population is under 25, and that demographic will be seeking employment over the next decade. More people are projected to live in rural India by 2050, and therefore there is a critical need to improve rural youth's access to high-quality vocational training (Table 3).

Demonetisation and the inability to manage the non-performing assets problem in India sent the economy spiraling. From 2005 to 2012, the government sector added 1.3 million jobs each year, but from 2012 to 2018, it added just 0.4 million. It also attempted to promote the illusion that self-employed people can generate enough employment. Despite government efforts (such as MUDRA), the number of self-employed teenagers decreased from 81 million in 2005 to 63 million in 2012, and from 49 mil-

Table 3. Sector wise FDI inflows during 2015-16 to 2019-20(U$ $ million)

Industry/ Year	2015-16	2016-17	2017-18	2018-19	2019-20 P
Manufacturing	8,439	11,972	7,066	7,919	8,153
Communication Services	2,638	5,876	8,809	5,365	6,838
Retail & Wholesale Trade	3,998	2,771	4,478	4,311	4,914
Financial Services	3,547	3,732	4,070	6,372	4,326
Computer Services	4,319	1,937	3,173	3,453	4,104
Business services	3,031	2,684	3,005	2,597	3,684
Restaurants and Hotels	889	430	452	749	2,546
Transport	1,363	891	1,267	1,019	2,333
Construction	4,141	1,564	1,281	2,009	1,937
Electricity and other energy Generation, Distribution & Transmission	1,364	1,722	1,870	2,427	1,906
Real Estate Activities	112	105	405	213	564
Education, Research & Development	394	205	347	736	528
Miscellaneous Services	1,022	1,816	835	1,226	443
Mining	596	141	82	247	217
Trading	0	0	0	0	0
Others	215	470	226	102	137

Note: Includes FDI through SIA/FIPB and RBI routes only. P: Provisional
Source: Reserve Bank of India Annual Reports
https://m.rbi.org.in/Scripts/AnnualReportPublications.aspx?Id=1307

lion in 2012 to 2018. Despite the fact that 95% of MUDRA loans are in the "Shishu" category. The gig economy is temporary work aided by technologically enabled media. Workplace culture and personality are rapidly shifting to accommodate the new-normal of the gig economy. In a gig economy, companies may save money on HR perks, office space, and training. The necessity to employ full-time specialists who are required just for a limited period is also reduced. A gig economy may enhance freelancers' quality of life and work-life balance. Last year, the worldwide digital gig economy produced over $200 billion. The gig economy is expected to expand by 17% annually to $450 billion by 2023. After the US, China, Brazil, and Japan, India now ranks 5th in flexi staffing. Gig workers in India have no social security and their contracts with gig platforms are opaque. The Rescue Packages as a global stimulus package for coronaviruses compared the financial reaction as a percentage of the GDP to the COVID-19 pandemic according to the statistical data on 10 May 2020. The following nations are the USA (13.0), Japan (21.1), Sweden (12.0), France (9.3), Spain (7.3), Italy (5.7), Great Britain (5.0), China (3.8) and South Korea (2.2)

India had a public debt of Rs.24.62 lakh crore in tin the year 1951. Rs. 94.62265 lakh crores were the total liability of the Government of India in March 2020. There has been a slight increase. The total liabilities of the central government increased to Rs.101.35600 lakh crore by June 2020.India had external debt of $85 billion in 1991, which increased to $317 billion in 2011. India had a foreign debt of about $558 billion in March 2020. External debt on the country declined by $3.9 billion to $554 billion in June 2020 (Table 4). The good thing for India is that India relies more on internal debt and less on external debt. Due to this policy of India, about 20 percent of the total debt is external debt and the remaining 80 percent is internal debt. This is the reason why India's financial position is strong despite the Corona pandemic. Moreover, the Debt pressure is mounting on all the states in the country. By March 2020, there was a total debt of about Rs. 40 lakh crores on all the states of the country.

The Care Rating data shows that almost all states of the country have debt of millions of crores of rupees. There is total debt of Rs.6.02 lakh crore on Uttar Pradesh, Maharashtra Rs. 5.02 lakh crore, West Bengal Rs. 4.37 lakh crore, Tamil Nadu Rs.4.04 lakh crore, Rajasthan Rs. 3.43 lakh crore, Andhra Pradesh Rs. 3.41 lakh crore, Gujarat Rs. 3.26 lakh crore, Karnataka Rs.3.17 lakh crore. Further, there is a debt of Rs 2.66 lakh crore on Kerala, Madhya Pradesh Rs.2.34 lakh crore, Punjab Rs.2.30 lakh crore, Telangana Rs.1.68 lakh crore and Orissa Rs.1.33 lakh crore. In this context, per capita debt varies as per total debt in states. Per capita debt for the residents of Punjab is Rs. 82771, Haryana Rs. 81287, Kerala Rs.79771, Tamil Nadu Rs.56134, Gujarat Rs.53931, Karnataka Rs.51981, West Bengal Rs. 47881, Maharashtra Rs. 44734, Madhya Pradesh Rs. 32354 and of Uttar Pradesh is Rs. 30136 (Table 5).

The Centre has also announced two stimulus packages "Aatmanirbhar Bharat Yojana" in May 2020 which is totalling 1.5 percent of GDP. The following such as (a) MGNREGS is Rs.0.48 lakh Cores for MGNREGS allocation, viability gap funding for social infrastructure. (b) Allocation of Rs.1.5 lakh Crores for agricultural infra financing and animal husbandry. (c) the GARIB Kalyan package is Rs.1.93 lakh Crores including allocations to the health sector. (d) MUDRA Shishu loans Rs.3.1 lakh crores apart from free food grain to migrants. Further, (e) STIMULUS for MSMEs is Rs.5.95 lakh Crores discoms, shadow banks and real estate. And other (f) various Rs.8.01 lakh Crores is related to Reserve Bank measures, including liquidity infusion. According to a Nasscom report, for calendar 2020, gig workers comprise more than 5 per cent of the total headcount in 48 per cent of tech firms, and more than 30 per cent in nine per cent of the firms. The 2020-21 Economic Survey says that India has become one of the biggest flexicurity marketplaces in the world due to the rapid increase in the e-commerce and retail industries. For the very first time, Finance Minister Nirmala Sitharaman in the Budget 202122 mentioned gig and platform workers and the need to provide them with social security. She also mentioned that a portal will be created to collect information on gig, building and construction workers. This is also the first time that the FM has proposed to incorporate the Social Insurance Code, which provides for the universalization of social security for all workers, including gig and platform employees. A key proposal of the code is the creation of a social security fund, which is to be 1 per cent of the total turnover of the aggregator. So far, only preliminary discussions have been held on the subject. Currently, there are no minimum wages or health benefit packages or pension in case the person has been regularly contributing to a company's growth. Add to this the fact that there are no internal grievance redressal mechanisms if a conflict arises. According to a poll by the Associated Chambers of Commerce and Industry of India, India's gig-economic development will reach $4 billion in three years at a CAGR of 17%. (Assocham). India has 15 million freelancers in the IT and programming, finance, HR, and design white collar industries, according to Assocham. The Covid-19 epidemic also pushed companies to operate remotely and showed the possibility of gig workers in testing the virtual working paradigm (Table 6).

The CSR agenda is currently being extended to encompass new vaccines, medicines, and medical devices research and development (R&D) businesses by extending the scope of CSR expenditures. Those changes to the CSR regulations allow businesses to classify COVID-related R&D activities as CSR activities, even if they are carried out in their regular course of business. Two further policy adjustments have been made; the first has been to enable all COVID contributions to qualify for a 100% tax deduction. The second enables companies, who give more than the minimum specified amount, to subsequently

Table 4. **India's overall balance of payment during 2015-16 to 2019-20***(US$ million)*

Year/ Particulars	2015-16	2016-17	2017-18	2018-19	2019-20 (P)
A. CURRENT ACCOUNT					
1. Exports, f.o.b.	2,66,365	2,80,138	3,08,970	3,37,237	3,20,431
2. Imports, c.i.f.	3,96,444	3,92,580	4,69,006	5,17,519	4,77,937
3. Trade Balance	-1,30,079	-1,12,442	-1,60,036	-1,80,283	-1,57,506
4. Invisibles, Net	1,07,928	98,026	1,11,319	1,23,026	1,32,850
a) 'Non-Factor' Services of which	69,676	68,345	77,562	81,941	84,922
Software Services	71,454	70,763	72,186	77,654	84,643
b) Income	-24,375	-26,302	-28,681	-28,861	-27,281
c) Private Transfers	63,139	56,573	62,949	70,601	76,217
5. Current Account Balance	-22,151	-14,417	-48,717	-57,256	-24,656
B. CAPITAL ACCOUNT					
1. Foreign Investment, Net (a+b)	31,891	43,224	52,401	30,094	44,417
a) Direct Investment	36,021	35,612	30,286	30,712	43,013
b) Portfolio Investment	-4,130	7,612	22,115	-618	1,403
2. External Assistance, Net	1,505	2,013	2,944	3,413	3,751
3. Commercial Borrowings, Net	-4,529	-6,102	-183	10,416	22,960
4. Short Term Credit, Net	-1,610	6,467	13,900	2,021	-1,026
5. Banking Capital of which	10,630	-16,616	16,190	7,433	-5,315
NRI Deposits, Net	16,052	-12,367	9,676	10,387	8,627
6. Rupee Debt Service	-73	-99	-75	-31	-69
7. Other Capital, Net[$]	3,315	7,559	6,213	1,057	18,462
8. Total Capital Account	41,128	36,447	91,390	54,403	83,180
C. Errors & Omissions	-1,073	-480	902	-486	974
D. Overall Balance [A (5) +B (8) +C]	17,905	21,550	43,574	-3,339	59,498
E. Monetary Movements (F+G)	-17,905	-21,550	-43,574	3,339	-59,498
F. IMF, Net	0	0	0	0	0
G. Reserves and Monetary Gold (Increase -, Decrease +)	**-17,905**	**-21,550**	**-43,574**	**3,339**	**-59,498**
of which: SDR allocation	0	0	0	0	0
Memo: As a ratio to GDP					
1. Trade Balance	-6.2	-4.9	-6.0	-6.6	-5.5
2. Net Services	3.3	3.0	2.9	3.0	3.0
3. Net Income	-1.2	-1.1	-1.1	-1.1	-1.0
4. Current Account Balance	-1.1	-0.6	-1.8	-2.1	-0.9
5. Capital Net (Excluding changes in reserves)	2.0	1.6	3.4	2.0	2.9
6. Foreign Investment, Net	1.5	1.9	2.0	1.1	1.5

P: Temporary, Amounts received awaiting issuance of shares under FDI and delayed export revenues, 1. Returning Indians' gold and silver have been listed as imports, with a counter entry in private transfer receipts, 2. DGCI&S data on exports and imports vary from DGCI&S data on coverage, value, and time. RBI

Source: Reserve Bank of India Annual Reports

https://rbidocs.rbi.org.in/rdocs/AnnualReport/PDFs/8TEA15E224703342F48AAFC08340E95FE2.PDF

Table 5. Stimulus measures by the government of India

Sl.No.	Name of the Scheme	Amount
1.	Pradhan Mantri Garib Kalyan Package (PMGKP) +	1,92,800
2.	Armanirbhar Bharat Abhiyaan 1.0	11,02,650
3.	PMGKP Anna Yojana – extension of 5 mo4nths from July-Nov 2020	82,911
4.	Aatmanirbhar Bharat Abhiyaan 2.0	73,000
5.	Armanirbhar Bharat Abhiyaan 3.0	2,65,080
6.	RBI measures announced till October 31, 2020	12,71,200
	Total	**29,87,641**

Source: Compiled by Authors

compensate, if they so choose, the excess of the CSR duty accruing in future years. Company India has previously proposed that the Indian government allow the vaccination of its workers using CSR money. The suggestion was made in a report titled 'Protecting India: a Public Private Partnership for Vaccination against COVID' by the Indian Chambers (FICCI) and Ernst & Young (EY). The study states that approximately 60 percent of India's current public health infrastructure would have to be transformed into vaccination centers in order to have 1.3-1.4 lakh centers for inoculation. The study also notes how the public sector may possibly offer only 60,000-70,000 inoculators in healthcare, as opposed to a minimum of one lakh. CSR is the key word for how an enterprise connects to its wider cultural, economic and political environment. It is one of the greatest buzzes in a firm, which indicates that an enterprise is concerned and it combines profit with principle. Corporate governance, human rights, health and security, the environment, working conditions, and economic growth contributions are among the themes covered. According to a Credit Suisse report from 2019, 4,460 Indians have a net worth of more than $50 million apiece (over 350 crore). India has around 750,000 millionaires as of mid-2019. However, according to the 2019 report, significant contributions from ultra-high net value people, over 10 pounds (defined as net worth of above 25 pounds) account for 55% of the individual philanthropist's financing, and about 80% is donations from Azim Premji. Global wealth studies show out that Covid did not truly affect the real rich, even if the revenues of huge parts were damaged. When the health and education sectors are under stress, the social expenditure purse has to grow.

Though the CSR Act of 2014 was met with initial resistance, it is now being followed by companies. Thanks to CSR, terms such as purpose, inclusion, and sustainability entered the corporate lexicon. Funding for social causes has steadily grown. More philanthropists are setting up operating foundations. Indeed, there are some complex unresolved issues: almost no unrestricted funding especially for organization costs, unrealistic measurement expectations, a short-term orientation, and a band aid approach to solutions (Table 7). The wild pandemic was repurposed by the corporate honchos to combat COVID infections, with Tata Sons with a pledge of Rs 1.500, followed by Premji at Rs. 1.125, and Ambani's Rs. 510 Crore. The PM-CARES Fund, with Rs 500 crore pledges from Reliance Industries and the Aditya Birla Group donation Rs 400 crore, seemed to have a majority of company commitments (Table 8).

Table 6. The "Aatmanirbhar Bharat" overall stimulus package

Part-1	**5,94,550**
Emergency W/C Facility for businesses, including MSMEs	3,00,000
Subordinate debt for stressed MSMEs	20,000
Fund of funds for MSME	50,000
EPF support for business & workers	2,800
Reduction in EPF rates	6,750
Special liquidity scheme for NBFC/HFC/MFIs	30,000
Partial credits guarantee scheme 2.0 for liabilities of NBFCs/MFIs	45,000
Liquidity injection for DISCOMs	90,000
Reduction in TDS/TCS rates	50,000
Part-2	**3,10,000**
Free food grain supply to migrant workers for 2 months	3,500
Interest subvention for MUDRA shishu loans	1,500
Special credit facility to street vendors	5,000
Housing CLSS-MIG	70,000
Additional emergency working capital through NABARD	30,000
Additional credit through KCC	2,00,000
Part-3	**1,50,000**
Food micro enterprises	10,000
Pradhan Mantri Matsya Sampada Yojana	20,000
TOP to TOTAL: operation greens	500
Agri infrastructure fund	1,00,000
Animal husbandry infrastructure development fund	15,000
Promotion of herbal cultivation	4,000
Beekeeping initiative	500
Part-4 & 5	**48,100**
Viability gap funding	8,100
Additional MGNREGS allocation	40,000
Total (parts 1+2+3+4+5)	**11,02,650**
Earlier Measures (Including PMGKP)	1,92,800
RBI Measures (Actual)	8,01,603
Grand total	**20,97,053**

Source: Compiled by the Authors

CONCLUSION

The "Make in India" and "Atamnirbhar Bharat" initiatives were launched in 2014-15 to promote India as a worldwide manufacturing centre. This scheme's success will need broad-based governmental measures to improve human capital, input and financing availability, and connectivity. Also, India's Global

Table 7. Foreign investment inflows in India during 2010-11 to 2019-20

	Gross inflows/ Gross Investments		Repatriation/ Disinvestment		Direct Investment to India		FDI by India		Net Foreign Direct Investment		Net Portfolio Investment		Total	
Year	₹ Crore	US $ Million	₹ Crore	US $ Million	₹ Crore	US $ Million	₹ Crore	US $ Million	₹ Crore	US $ Million	₹ Crore	US $ Million	₹ Crore	US $ Million
2010-11	164255	36047	31898	7018	132358	29029	78257	17195	54101	11834	139381	30293	193482	42127
2011-12	220000	46552	65039	13599	154961	32952	51794	10892	103167	22061	85571	17170	188738	39231
2012-13	186869	34298	39915	7345	146954	26953	38768	7134	108186	19819	146467	26891	254653	46711
2013-14	218595	36047	31765	5284	186830	30763	56860	9199	129969	21564	29680	4822	159650	26386
2014-15	276400	45147	60506	9864	215893	35283	24675	4031	191219	31251	257853	42205	449072	73456
2015-16	364146	55559	69888	10652	294258	44907	58476	8886	235782	36021	-27203	-4130	208579	31891
2016-17	404057	60220	120765	18005	283292	42215	44379	6603	238913	35612	50482	7612	289394	43224
2017-18	392944	60974	138968	21544	253977	39431	58925	9144	195052	30286	142632	22115	337684	52401
2018-19	433069	62001	131136	18699	301932	43302	87896	12590	214036	30712	-1857	-618	212179	30094
2019-20	527347	74390	130392	18384	396955	56006	92135	12993	304820	43013	7395	1403	312215	44417

Source: Reserve Bank of India Annual Reports
https://www.rbi.org.in/scripts/bs_viewcontent.aspx?Id=2513

Table 8. Foreign exchange reserves in India during 2010-11 to 2019-20

	SDRs		Gold		Foreign Currency Assets		Reserve Tranche Position		Total	
Year	₹ Crore	US $ Million	₹ Crore	US $ Million	₹ Crore	US $ Million	₹ Crore	US $ Million	₹ Crore	US $ Million
2010-11	20401	4569	102572	22972	1224883	274330	13158	2947	1361013	304818
2011-12	22860	4469	138250	27023	1330511	260069	14511	2836	1506130	294398
2012-13	23540	4328	139740	25692	1412630	259726	12510	2301	1588420	292046
2013-14	26830	4464	129620	21567	1660910	276359	11020	1834	1828380	304223
2014-15	24940	3985	119160	19038	1985460	317324	8080	1292	2137640	341638
2015-16	9960	1502	133430	20115	2219060	336104	16290	2456	2378740	360176
2016-17	9380	1447	128830	19869	2244940	346319	15050	2321	2398200	369955
2017-18	10020	1540	139740	21484	2597570	399442	13520	2079	2760850	424545
2018-19	10076	1457	159585	23071	2665564	385357	20657	2986	2855882	412871
2019-20	10800	1433	230527	30578	3333815	442213	27013	3583	3602155	477807

Source: Reserve Bank of India Annual Reports

Innovation Index rating (2016) rose 15 places to 66 out of 128 nations. Further, The Make in India concept stated that (a) Ease of entry and exit of firms, (b) A vibrant financial sector that allocates capital to new profit potential, (c) A culture of entrepreneurship and requirement of political empowerment of the common man. The Insolvency and Bankruptcy Board of India was set up to create a new insolvency law to ease business in India. It has set high standards from the start and must keep raising them. Global norms require insolvency regulators to be independent of governments. Over the Indian economy, the Insolvency & Bankruptcy Code, 2016 ("Code") has been a game changer for the past twenty-five years. The CSR movement started as a reaction to the prevalent belief that companies should play a part in alleviating societal challenges because of their large economic resources and overall impact on people's everyday lives. Steel industrialist and one of its leading philanthropists, Andrew Carnegie, one of the first proponents of the idea of CSR whose corporate credo was "to do well in order to do good." Businesses are strong social institutions, and the most respected among them believe that they have to do much more than make money. They trust in the ability of a company to solve harsh issues that afflict society. They take part in a broad range of issues, including education, health care, skills training, entrepreneurship, women's empowerment, food safety, livelihoods and support services. India has a unique legislation – the Companies Act, 2013 and the CSR regulations — which came into force on 1 April 2014. It is the first nation to provide for businesses to spend their resources on successful CSR programs. The eradication of extreme hunger, poverty, and education, gender equality and women's empowerment, and reduced child mortality, better maternal health, and disease prevention are all allowed activities under Schedule VII of CSR. Other actions allowed under the CSR are to ensure environmental sustainability and encourage employment to improve professional skills.

REFERENCES

Ali, C. (2020). *The case of missing data on migrant workers deaths: The Free Press, 22nd September2020*. Indore Edition.

Bhargav, R., & Bhargav, R. (2020). A dignified period in an unprecedented era. *The Guardian*, p. 4.

Bhatia, G. (2020, Sept. 23). Devise a new labour law regime for gig economy workers. *The Hindustan Times*, p. 8.

Bidyadhar, P. (2020, Sept. 22). Child Labour in India. Around Odisha, p. 4.

Chandra, A. (2020). Working towards a single license, registration, and return regime. Academic Press.

Chandra, S. (2004). Small Industries Development Organization (SIDO) in Global perspective. *Laghu Udyog Samachar: Journal of Small-Scale Industries, 28-29*(12-2), 249-253.

Demand for work under MGNRGEA up by 40 percent. (2020). *The Pioneer*, p. 7. Available at https://www.dailypioneer.com/2020/india/demand-for-work-under-mgnrega-up-by-40---parl-told

Jha, S. (2020, Oct. 29). Gig workers to contribute for social security cover. Business Standard, p. 15.

Lakshmi, P. (2020, Sept. 22). The future of work. The Indian Express, p. 7.

Lalit, G. (2020, Nov. 9). Evaluation is key for good governance. The Avenue, p. 6.

Magazine, A. (2020). In labour codes, what changes for workers, hirers. *The New Indian Express*. Available at https://indianexpress.com/article/explained/govts-new-versions-of-labour-codes-key-proposals-and-concerns-6603354/

Meheta, B. S., & Kumr, A. (2020, Oct. 1). *White collar Blues*. The Pioneer, p. 9.

Nanda, K. (2021, Apr. 24). Growth-Oriented Plan needs nurture in current scenario. Free Press Journal, p. 6.

Nitin, M. (2021, June 22). *Rethinking Fenestration*. The Pioneer, p. 11.

Ranks, I. (2015, Aug. 26). 9th in Brookings Financial Inclusion Report Card Business. Standard, p. 4

Ravi Kumar, V. V. (2020, Oct. 28). *It's a matter of skills*. The Pioneer, p. 12.

Report, A. (2016-17). *Ministry of Micro, Small & Medium Enterprises, Government of India*. Available at https://www.msmedithrissur.gov.in/assets/uploads/downloadfile/Annual%20Report%202016%20-17%20of%20MSME-DI,%20Thrissur.pdf

Report of Prime Minister's Task Force. (2010). *Micro Small and Medium Enterprises*. Government of India. Available at http://dcmsme.gov.in/final_report.pdf

Rituraj, T. (2020, June 6). States told to pace up distribution of free grains to migrants. *The Economic Times*, p. 7.

Sanju, V. (2020, Sept. 29). PM Modi's game-changing labour reforms to boost growth. *The Guardian*, p. 5.

Shishir, S. (2020, Sept. 17). Govt clueless on number of jobs lost during pandemic. The Business Line, p. 1.

Somesh, J. (2020, Sept. 28). Six months on Migrants caught between hope and despair. Business Standard, p. 1.

Subhadra, C. (2020, Sept. 28). Unused rural funds hint migrant s may be back at work in cities. *The Hindustan Times*, p. 1.

The Insolvency and Bankruptcy Code. (2017, September). *Chartered Secretary*, *47*(9), 6.

Chapter 15
Sustaining India's Gig Economy in Industry 4.0:
Regulatory Framework and the Proposed Model

Vidushi Vatsa
Amity University, Noida, India

Ruchika Gupta
Amity University, Greater Noida Campus, India

Priyank Srivastava
ASET, Amity University, Noida, India

ABSTRACT

Today's corporate landscape is undergoing a transformation process, and India is not untouched by these phases of transition as humans are replaced by computers and brick-and-mortar firms are substituted by e-commerce companies. In the midst of these shifts, issues such as labour dynamics have changed dramatically. One such consequence is the Gig Economy. With the gradual improvement in the labour market and the focus of government on localisation, it remains important to analyse the widespread influence of growing gig culture in making India a self-reliant economy. This chapter of the book therefore seeks to review the different components of the gig economy along with the advantages and disadvantages and how gig can contribute towards a localised and self-reliant Indian economy. The chapter also evaluates the regulatory framework of the gig economy in India. The chapter also proposes a conceptual model incorporating various pillars that could serve as an analytical framework for the rapidly increasing number of concepts and policy proposals.

INTRODUCTION

In the early 2000, Nokia, the largest phone manufacturing company was a household name for most

DOI: 10.4018/978-1-7998-8705-8.ch015

Indians. They were pioneers in the market due to their affordable mobile phones for the masses. At one point in time, Nokia had the market share which was supposed to be unbeatable by their competitors, but with time this was all lost. Nokia failed to innovate, change and move forward with the new technology.

Kodak, who was the leader in digital photography also failed to retain its market share due to technology disruption. The disruption was so huge that Kodak had to file for bankruptcy in 2012. The main reason for their failure was that they failed to innovate with the fast-moving technology. (Minds Brand, 2018)

The above examples bring light to the fact that, if we don't upgrade ourselves and move ahead with time, we won't be able to survive in this fast-changing technological era. The last few decades have seen a paradigm shift in the business environment. The way business processes are changing due to technological advancements and the world converging to a single marketplace, all must be ahead of the disruptors.

As per the report of the Bureau of Labour Statistics (U.S.) 2020, the median number of years a salaried employee worked with his employer is 4.1 years. Workers in the manufacturing sector have the highest median tenure of 5.1 years whereas, workers in leisure and hospitality have the lowest median tenure of 2.3 years. (*Employee tenure in 2020*, 2020)

The fourth industrial revolution, popularly known as Industry 4.0 is driven by low-cost automation, smart machines, artificial intelligence, machine learning, etc. Industry 4.0 is characterized by better connectivity, data sharing on real-time basis, and accessibility through cloud computing.(Amity University. Dubai Campus et al., n.d.; *What Is Industry 4.0? | The Industrial Internet of Things | Epicor India*, n.d.)

Businesses today have no option but to re-engineer/rethink every process to face the market challenges. The business practices which were considered viable and effective a few decades earlier make no sense today and this holds good even about manpower employed by the entities. A new concept popularly known as the *gig economy* has emerged over the last few years which companies cannot afford to overlook due to the potential advantages it offers.

GIG ECONOMY

Rohit (name changed) aged 32 works with Uber application-based cab service. He gets paid for the trips he makes in a day. He sometimes gets ten to fifteen trips a day and someday barely five. He on some days works for Swiggy or Zomato, a food delivery platform. Rohit is his own boss, he decides at what time he needs to start his day and there are some days when he wants a break from his routine life as a cab driver. Just like Rohit, there are three million gig workers in India. (Banik Nilanjan, 2020) . Three million, though is a very small number if we compare it with our 1.3 billion population, there is a tremendous opportunity for exponential growth in this segment. The gig economy is all set to take off and the recent regulatory changes in form of four labour codes are a great enabler for the same.

The Code on Social Security had defined a gig worker as "a person who performs work or participates in a work arrangement and earns from such activities outside of a traditional employer-employee relationship". (The Code on Social Security, 2020)

The term "gig" was first used in the year 1915 for live musical performances. It gained popularity due to jazz performances by musicians.(*Gig (Music) - Wikipedia*, n.d.; Whitehead Gabrielle Pickard, 2019)

The gig economy is a collection of short duration, project-based, freelance, and other temporary work, wherein the gig worker (gigger) and the service user enter into a contract for a specific gig (activity) on the mutually agreed terms and conditions. (Gillis S. Alexander, 2020; The Associated Chamber of Commerce and Industry of India, 2020)

Technology plays a major role in boosting the gig economy. In the 21st century connecting with gig workers has become easier because of improvements in communication technology. Many such platforms are available, wherein a gigger from India can offer services across the globe. Those who do not take advantage of this technology/platforms will surely lack behind and cannot command a premium for their services. (*(5) What Is GIG Economy? Pros and Cons of GIG Economy Explained, Is Indian Economy Becoming GIG Economy? - YouTube*, 2019)

The concept of the gig is not a new phenomenon, rather it's an old concept, especially amongst those employed in the informal sector of the economy. The hiring of workers in factories or at the construction site on a day-to-day basis and giving them each day's task is a common feature prevalent even today, which is very similar to the way gig workers perform.(Augustinraj Rajah & Bajaj Samar, 2021)

Over the years, thanks to the advent of gig platforms, we can access the gig worker's services very conveniently. The tremendous advancements in communication technology have further fuelled its growth. The gig is an emerging concept which is widely being accepted by the millennium's hence it is important to understand the key aspects as listed below:(Augustinraj Rajah & Bajaj Samar, 2021)

- Demographic profile
- Work and earning pattern,
- Motivation for gig jobs,
- Key growth drivers.

Demographic Profile: Workers of the gig economy are relatively younger population as compared to the traditional sector and they generally are in the age group of 18 to 23 years. Since gig workers enjoy the advantage of flexi hours therefore even students take up the gig roles along with their studies. As compared to the traditional jobs where there is a widespread gender gap, we find gender inclusiveness in gig jobs due to freedom in work timings.(Augustinraj Rajah & Bajaj Samar, 2021)

Women can easily take up the jobs as per their skill and time availability, even they have the freedom to choose whom to work for. It is generally seen that in terms of educational qualification, gig workers lack a bit as compared to their counterparts in the traditional sector, however, there is a huge difference in the skills that traditional and gig workers possess. Due to the repetitive nature of work, generally, gig workers are more skilled for the work they undertake.(Augustinraj Rajah & Bajaj Samar, 2021)

Work and Earning Pattern: Gig workers have the choice of working for flexi hours; they choose according to their time preference as compared with the traditional job where 9 to 5 working is mandatory. Gig workers have the option to work for lessor time as there are no mandatory working hours in a day and their pay-outs vary based on hours they spend on gigs. On an average, gig worker earns INR 20,000 a month in India, as per high-level estimates. (Augustinraj Rajah & Bajaj Samar, 2021)

Motivation for Taking up the Gig Work: The primary motivation for any kind of work is to earn, to afford the basic needs of life. Both the traditional employees and the gig workers need money to meet their monthly household expenditure, but gig workers take up a particular job because of factors other than just earning their livelihood. Some take up gig work because to fund some one-time expenses like medical, marriage, and education. Students take up gig work because they want to be financially independent, hence generally gig workers take up the work to support their family and they are generally not the primary earning member in the family. (Augustinraj Rajah & Bajaj Samar, 2021)

Growth Drivers: Traditional jobs are characterised by stable monthly income, whereas gig workers do not have this advantage. Social security and post-employment benefits such as employer's provident fund, ESI benefits, gratuity, leave encashment and non-monetary benefits like motivation and personality development training are only available in the traditional job environment. (Augustinraj Rajah & Bajaj Samar, 2021)

Gig labour and platform services have a significant influence on the economy of Western countries. Platform companies like Uber, Uber Eats, Airbnb, and many others have attracted millions of workers from around the world to serve customers in almost every major service sector of the global economy. Around 11% of the European Union workforce has worked on a platform at least once according to the European Commission. Platform services have gained popularity because of their low costs and ease of use for both workers and consumers. Issues like unstable employment with little protection in the event of illness etc. remain unanswered despite the rapid expansion of these flexible kinds of work. The Supreme Court of UK ruled in February 2021 that British Uber drivers were not freelancers, but actual firm employees. The global legal perspective of gig workers is examined below.

Platform workers in Belgium do not have a distinct legal standing under Belgian labour laws. These workers can be either classified as employees or self-employed. Their status would eventually depend on the contractual agreement between the platform company and the gig workers. Belgian courts have not yet given a decisive judgment about platform workers' status. In Belgium, no significant legislative changes are presently being considered. However, it might not be the case in the long run as representatives of the Belgian government have asked for clarifications from platform companies on the status of gig workers. Furthermore, several legal cases have been filed about the status of independent employees of platform firms, therefore, Belgian courts are likely to rule in near future on the legal status of gig workers.

Platform drivers in Chile are not considered full-time employees, instead, they are classified as freelancers since they have the freedom to choose when, where, and for how long they perform their services. As these individuals are classified as freelancers rather than regular employees, they are not subject to labour laws, and as a result, platform firms do not deduct taxes or social security contributions. This arrangement is unlikely to persist in the long run, since many Chilean labour authorities have already established the existence of an employment tie between transportation platform firms and their drivers. Additionally, numerous measures in Chile's Parliament are being considered that would designate platform "drivers" as regular employees. It is anticipated that Chile will follow the United Kingdom's case laws in protecting the rights of gig workers.

Colombian laws currently do not recognize platform workers as employees. To be defined as a regular employee under the current Colombian laws the following requirements should be met:

- The employee must adhere to agreed working hours
- The employer must provide the worker with the tools needed to complete operations
- The worker must be paid the same monthly wage for work completed.

Platform employees do not satisfy these requirements since they regulate their time, own their tools, and are paid based on the quantity of work completed. In Colombia, a new law has been introduced that provides social security contributions for platform employees based on the number of hours they work. A dynamic system is proposed in this statute, where payments can be paid by the day or by the hour. This gives gig workers the freedom to choose working hours and also the benefits of social security schemes. This legislation is a great step in protecting the rights of workers in the evolving gig economy in our new age society.

In France, employee status is granted to platform workers. There are two types of status under French labour laws: either there is an employment contract between the parties or the individual operates as an independent worker. An employment contract is based on the existence of a "subordination relationship," which is marked by the employer's authority to give commands and instructions, to oversee the performance of workers. However, the Supreme Court of France has reclassified ties between platforms and individuals as work contracts on multiple instances, providing employee status to some platform delivery employees and drivers. According to the report on "regulation of digital working platforms", platform employees should be employed by a third-party intermediary, which would be treated as their employer. This status would be obligatory only when workers perform minimum gigs and are subject to a threshold revenue.

As per the German Civil Code, an employee is anyone who, based on a contract, is employed in the service to perform work subject to instructions by another person. The German Federal Employment Court ruled that platform workers will have employee status, based on the following factors:

- The platform worker was obligated by stringent guidelines regarding the time and content of their tasks.
- And there was a reward system in place to motivate constant work, in which the platform worker obtained "experience points" for regular work, which allowed them to apply for multiple and better jobs.

Who All Are a Part of the Gig Economy?

Any individual, company, platform, and aggregator who are not part of the traditional employer-employee relationship will come under the preview of the gig economy. Presently giggers can be found in almost all sectors of the economy particularly in the following areas.

- Information technology
- Creative fields such as art and craft
- Entertainment fields like dance, singing, role plays
- Application-based services like Uber, Swiggy, Zomato
- Designing
- Construction
- Education

  (Gillis S. Alexander, 2020; The Associated Chamber of Commerce and Industry of India, 2020)

The relative advantages and disadvantages of the gig economy have been one of the most debated topics amongst academicians and labour economists across the globe and have been summarized below.

ADVANTAGES OF THE GIG ECONOMY

- **Autonomy:** Gig workers enjoy full autonomy. They have the right to choose assignments or projects to work for. They also have the liberty to select which time of the day to work for. The autonomy that gig workers have, cannot be enjoyed by the traditional workers where an employer-employee relationship exists. Gig workers are their boss and manager.(Gillis S. Alexander, 2020; The Associated Chamber of Commerce and Industry of India, 2020)

- **Specialized skills:** Gig workers are specialists in their field. They possess the skill sets necessary for performing a particular task. They are experts in their fields and keep them updated on communication technology which generally is the backbone of gig assignments. In the present scenario, everyone wants to get the work done by experts, who are innovative, talented, and have the necessary skillset, so giggers are a perfect choice. (*Ways Your Business Can Benefit from the Gig Economy | Moonlyte*, 2021)
- **Flexibility –** Gig workers enjoy flexibility in terms of the time and days they want to work. They have the flexibility to choose at which hour of the day they want to work and also have the option to work from home. (*The Pros and Cons of the Gig Economy*, 2018).
- **Client base –** Gig workers are independent workers; they have the freedom to choose their clients and have an option to choose the projects on which they wish to work. As giggers have the option to work with different clients hence gig economy is known for its huge customer base. (*The Pros and Cons of the Gig Economy*, 2018)
- **Immediate payments-** Gig workers get immediate payment for the projects or tasks they complete; they do not get a fixed salary unlike traditional employees in 9 to 5 jobs. Their payouts are based on the completion of gig they do for their clients(*The Pros and Cons of the Gig Economy*, 2018)
- **Job security –** Gig workers have much more job security in their work as compared to a traditional job. In a traditional employer-employee relationship, the employee can be fired from the job anytime depending upon the fancies of the reporting manager, however, there is the comparative job security of workers in the gig. (*How Does the Gig Economy Benefit Employees & Businesses? TSheets*, n.d.)
- **Work-life balance -** In a traditional 9 to 5 job, workers are stressed about completing their assignments, reports, etc, as for every assignment there is a deadline defined by the employer. Usually, because of all these hassles and work pressure, they tend to mix their professional and personal life, which is not the case with the gig workers as there are no defined targets, deadlines, and work pressure as such. Gig workers comparatively can maintain a good work-life balance. (Gillis S. Alexander, 2020)
- **Cost-saving -** In the gig economy, the company saves a lot of money for work done on a gig basis, as there are no pay-outs related to social security schemes like provident fund, gratuity, medical benefits, house rent allowances, paid leaves, maternity benefits, etc. The company will just have to pay for the particular job once it is complete.(*(5) What Is GIG Economy? Pros and Cons of GIG Economy Explained, Is Indian Economy Becoming GIG Economy? - YouTube*, 2019)
- **Profitability –** Gig workers can help protect the profitability of the company as payments are done only for the work assigned to gig workers and there are no monthly fixed pay-outs. Gig workers get paid only for the work assigned to them which protects the bottom line of the company especially in case of downside in the business. Businesses impacted due to seasonal variation in demand for their products also favor getting work done on a gig basis for maintaining their bottom lines in the off-season. This concept is relevant, particularly with start-ups as the revenue flows are not predictable in the initial years for them hence getting work done on an assignment basis is becoming very popular in such organizations. It is generally believed that our labour laws were hindering the growth of the economy as involuntarily removing the workers in the formal employer-employee

relationship required a lot of approvals and financial payout to workers, hence this was a great disincentive for the units to employ manpower beyond a threshold limit to avoid getting into the legal hassle of taking various approvals at the time of involuntary layoffs. However, with the growing gig economy more and more workers are moving towards it and the recent regulatory changes brought in by the government would go a long way to promote the gig economy and protect the rights of gig workers. (*The Top Five Advantages and Disadvantages of Gig Economy Workers Revealed – Engage Employee*, 2018)

- **Saving of resources –** Working in a gig economy saves a lot for the companies in terms of resources, as they do not require a workspace for the gig workers who generally operate from the field or their homes. The communication technology advancements and very minimum cost of data sharing through the internet have fuelled the growth of the gig economy. The gig workers are generally considered to be experts in their domain; hence, companies save a lot on induction and training costs also. (*(5) What Is GIG Economy? Pros and Cons of GIG Economy Explained, Is Indian Economy Becoming GIG Economy? - YouTube*, 2019)

DISADVANTAGES OF THE GIG ECONOMY

- **Unstable income-** Unlike the traditional workers, gig workers do not have a fixed monthly income. They rely on the project/task for which they get paid once their task is completed. There might be few days when they might earn huge money whereas, on some days, they might have no income.
- **Strategic positions resource crunch** – Over time, as the gig economy grows and matures, there will be more individuals particularly millenniums who would more than be willing to work in a flexible environment. It is a known fact that strategic jobs cannot be outsourced or done on an assignment basis, hence there can be a severe resource crunch, maybe a few decades from now when most of the workers would like to be freelancers.
- **Insecurity amongst traditional workers** – The growing practice amongst companies to hire gig workers for a particular project/task is breeding insecurity amongst other employees in the company. This also leads to a lack of motivation in job and trust in their companies.
- **Lack of personal touch or trust** – Gig workers perform jobs on a contractual basis; they are not permanent employees in the company, hence, the trust level that an employer can have and the bond the employer share with their employee is missing in the gig economy.
- **Lack of social security-** Gig workers are not entitled to any social security schemes unlike workers in a formal employer-employee relationship. They are not entitled to provident funds, paid leaves, medical benefits, maternity benefits, or other post-employment benefits like gratuity, etc.

GIG ECONOMY - GLOBAL PERSPECTIVE

During the ongoing pandemic, gig jobs are on the rise, and it holds good both for blue-collar and white-collar jobs. The pandemic has forced companies to reengineer their business strategies and also the way the work is carried out. As the platform-based companies continue to grow like Swiggy, Zomato, Ola, Uber, etc., other sectors of the economy would also try to gradually adopt the gig concept for the non-core activities considering the uncertainties due to the ongoing pandemic. As per the report jointly published by Boston Consulting Group (BCG) and Michael & Susan Dell Foundation gig economy has seen tremendous growth between 5 to 12% in developing countries like India, Canada, Brazil, etc, as compared to developed countries like the United States, Germany, Australia, etc. where gig economy grew by a modest rate of 1 to 4%. The type of jobs that the gig workers mostly do in developing countries is low-income and low-skill jobs like deliveries, cab services, micro-tasks, etc. India is witnessing a rise in gig workers and the four major sectors which will contribute to this trend in the future are manufacturing, construction, retail, and transportation. The basic reason which can contribute toward the growth of this sector is that the organisations during the ongoing pandemic are more inclined towards paying workers on a job (gig) basis rather than committing for fixed monthly pay-outs.(Augustinraj Rajah & Bajaj Samar, 2021)

In the United States, the gig economy accounted for 35% of their workforce as of 2020, it has seen a considerable rise from 20% in 2014. U.S. gig economy is one of the largest in the world which contributes nearly $ 1 trillion annually and approx. 57 million people are engaged in some sort of gig work. This trend is further expected to continue and it is expected that nearly half of the American's would be a part of the gig economy by 2023. (Henderson Rebecca, 2020)

The United Kingdom has also accelerated its journey towards the growth of the gig economy. In 2018, UK saw an increase of gig workers by 31%. The year-on-year growth in the UK is 59% and there are approx. 5 million gig workers. [18]. Ukraine, which is the second-largest country in Europe has a huge pool of students pursuing IT courses, hence it boasts of having the highest gig workers in the IT sector making up to 54% of its workforce. (ca buxozypk, 2020)

MAKING INDIA A LOCALISED AND SELF-RELIANT ECONOMY

India is on the road towards becoming a self-reliant economy. The Indian government has given a call to its citizens for being "vocal *for local* "to bring focus on products and services that are available locally and hence can be a giant step towards promoting the concept of "*make in India*". The gig economy can be a major enabler towards this well-timed move of making India a self-reliant economy. Globally, the gig economy generates a gross value of approx. $204 billion and is expected to double to nearly $455 billion by the year 2024.(Monga Pooja, 2020)

India holds 5th place after the US, China, Brazil, and Japan in terms of flexi staffing. Haryana, Madhya Pradesh, Andhra Pradesh, Gujarat, and Telangana are amongst the few states in India that have the maximum growth potential. (Monga Pooja, 2020)

Rapid advancements in communication technology have helped in fuelling the growth of gig and reduction in transaction cost for non-core activities, thereby facilitating a substantial increase in the number of tasks that can be performed by gig / flexi workers.(Monga Pooja, 2020)

Gig culture is growing and is very popular amongst the millenniums because of certain factors like the freedom to perform the job as per choice, advancement in communication technology, and enhanced skills, etc. (Monga Pooja, 2020)

As internet penetration is growing in India and smartphone usage is on the rise, hence it opens up various avenues for gig workers on the digital platform to explore different services as per their choice and skillsets. Few popular use cases in India are Uber/Ola which offers cab-based services, BookMyChotu which provides domestic help for homes, Urban Company which provides different services at doorsteps.(Monga Pooja, 2020)

To make India a self-reliant and localised economy, it is important to encourage the growth of the gig economy. The idea is fast catching up with the corporate world also as it offers many advantages to either side. The gig economy in long term is expected to generate appx. 90 million jobs in India (excluding the agricultural sector). The gig economy can generate an aggregate value of USD 250 billion and can contribute to 1.25% of India's GDP. (Augustinraj Rajah & Bajaj Samar, 2021)

The profile of 90 million jobs expected to be generated in the gig economy is as follows:(Augustinraj Rajah & Bajaj Samar, 2021)

- Skilled and semi-skilled ~ 35 million
- Service sectors ~ 5 million
- Household service demand ~ 12 million
- Unskilled jobs in other sectors ~ 38 million

In the next few years, the perceived advantages of the gig economy will bring transformational changes in the nature of existing and future jobs. Considering the interest of millennium's, existing non -core jobs to the extent possible will be shifted to gig platforms and the new jobs would preferably be handled under the flexi staffing concept. Around 24 million jobs are in the planning stage for migration to the technology-based gig economy in the short to medium term.(Augustinraj Rajah & Bajaj Samar, 2021)

Gig workers can play a crucial role in economic growth, particularly in the wake of the COVID-19 pandemic. In the current scenario, because of uncertainties, new hiring across the board is on hold. A gig can be a cost-effective solution as companies can hire workers on-demand basis and hence gig economy can be a catalyst in economic growth and for employing millions of Indians. (Augustinraj Rajah & Bajaj Samar, 2021)

Despite the ongoing pandemic, the gig is amongst the very few segments that have seen U-shaped recovery and have reached the pre-Covid levels in terms of employment and income levels. The gig sector was severely hit during the first lockdown in April 2020 with employment levels at 53% and income levels at 38% as compared to pre -Covid period, however as the economy opened up in unlock phase, the gig segment saw a speedy recovery as people preferred services at doorsteps. (Augustinraj Rajah & Bajaj Samar, 2021)

The gig economy in India is presently predominated by workers engaged in offline jobs, but the future lies in *online mode*, if focussed actions on bringing down the digital divide supported by growth in internet and communication technology are taken by all stakeholders.

POTENTIAL OF GIG-BASED TECHNOLOGICAL PLATFORMS IN INDIA

Over the past decade, the gig economy has seen considerable growth all over the world. The perceived advantages that the gig economy offers have escalated the adoption level across both developed and developing countries. The gig economy has been so disruptive that its impact is felt even in other sectors and the average job span of employees has considerably reduced even in the traditional employer-employee relationship. The gig economy in the medium to long term can be one of the few sectors offering employment to millions of Indians and can hence contribute towards the economic growth of the country. Currently, the gig economy is based on traditional low-skill job-based services but the future lies in technology-based gig services.(Augustinraj Rajah & Bajaj Samar, 2021)

Technology-based gig platforms offer services on demand for the public at large, hence can be a tool that can be used not only by the general public but also by corporates. These technology platforms popularly known as aggregators will help resolve two main issues, first India is a country that has an abundant labour force but still when the need arises employers find it difficult to get the workforce to meet their urgent or seasonal requirements. The technology-based gig platforms can fill the gap when a sudden need arises. Secondly, these technology platforms can also have a pool of skilled gig workers who can offer specialised services, hence, employers can have the flexibility of hiring from the pool of qualified gig workers only for the required time and can thus save a lot of money on account of fixed monthly payouts. (Augustinraj Rajah & Bajaj Samar, 2021)

The Gig concept and its advantages can be understood by the following example from a construction site where the workers are being hired on monthly basis alternatively the employer also has an option to hire gig workers at the construction site. The workers who are hired on monthly basis have to be paid for 7 to 8 hours irrespective of the downtime for reasons like shortage of material, whereas the gig workers would be called only on days when all material and other resources are available, hence gig workers gets paid only for the productive work. Also, there can be cases where specialised services are required only for some days in a month at the construction site, hence gig economy offers a unique solution wherein specialised gig workers can be hired only for the days when he is required, which can be a win-win situation for both the employer and the gig worker as it improves employer's profitability and the gig worker can take up any other work for rest of the days.(Augustinraj Rajah & Bajaj Samar, 2021)

The gig economy can be a catalyst in formalizing the labor market as there is a widespread unorganised sector in India. The unorganised sector works by personal whims and fancies of employers however the aggregators like Ola, Uber, Zomato, Urban company, Swiggy, etc have set some standards of pay-outs and working conditions, hence these aggregators can thus act as a change catalyst for improving the working conditions in other unorganised sectors. (Augustinraj Rajah & Bajaj Samar, 2021)

Uber an app-based cab service provider, has an option to rate their driver's basis user experience, hence those who are rated high can command a premium and can pocket certain extra incentives like higher earnings per ride, discounts, etc. which in turn motivates them towards improving productivity and performance towards their work. The gig economy has huge employment potential in India and thus helps improve economic growth in the long term, provided a conducive environment and regulatory framework is put in place. (Augustinraj Rajah & Bajaj Samar, 2021)

REGULATORY FRAMEWORK

India accounts for 93% of the workforce in the unorganised segment. (Rana Riya, 2020)

As per the report of Periodic Labour Force Survey (PLFS) 2018-2019, the following data points need to be considered. [20]

- 51.9% of the salaried workforce were not eligible for any social security benefits.
- 53.8% of the workforce who were salaried employees were not entitled to any paid leaves.
- 69.5% of the salaried workforce had no written job contracts.

These figures are quite alarming, hence there was a pressing need for some stringent laws and regulations in our country. So, to take care of various issues faced by our labour force, more so in the unorganized sector, the four labour codes were recently passed by the Indian parliament. All the earlier 29 labour laws were subsumed into these four labour codes. (*Overview of Labour Law Reforms | PRSIndia*, n.d.)

The four labour codes are as follows (*Labour Law Reforms | Ministry of Labour & Employment*, n.d.)

- The Code on Wages
- The Occupation, Safety, Health, and Working Condition Code
- The Code on Social Security
- The Industrial Relations Code

For the first time in India, the Code on Social Security clearly defined gig workers. The Code on Social Security also proposes to form a National Social Security Board for unorganised workers. The board has been authorised to perform various functions such as(The Code On Social Security, 2020, 2020)

- To give recommendations to the central government for framing schemes for the welfare of the gig workers.
- To advise to the central government on matters related to the administration of the Code on Social Security.
- To monitor social welfare schemes for gig workers which are run by the central government.
- To review the records at the state level
- To review the expenditure from the funds and accounts
- And, to perform any other functions as given by the central government.

The Code on Social Security, authorizes the central government to launch various social security schemes for the welfare of the gig workers on the following matters relating to:(The Code On Social Security, 2020, 2020)

- Life and disability cover
- Accidental insurance
- Health and maternity benefits
- Old age protection
- Crèche

The Code on Social Security requires mandatory registration for the gig workers and the following two conditions are to be fulfilled (The Code On Social Security, 2020, 2020)

- An individual should have completed sixteen years of age.
- The individual has to submit a self-declaration electronically

The unique feature under the provisions of the Code on Social Security is that the aggregators have to contribute for the welfare of the gig workers, which shall not exceed two percent, but not less than one percent, as may be notified by the central Government, of the annual turnover. The code further provides that the contribution by an aggregator shall not exceed five percent of the amount paid or payable by an aggregator to gig workers and platform workers. The amount contributed by the aggregators will be deposited in a social security fund for social security and welfare of the gig workers which will be set up by the central government (The Code On Social Security, 2020, 2020).

These provisions under the code on social security shall go a long way in taking care of the social security needs of the gig /platform and other workers in the unorganized sector.

WAY FORWARD

The workers in the organized sector have been under the protection of various social security laws in India, but those in the unorganized sector did not have the benefit of any social security schemes. This has changed with Code on Social Security, where the focus has not only been on consolidation of the existing social security laws but also on providing social security cover to gig/platform and other workers in the unorganized sector.(*Overview of Labour Law Reforms | PRSIndia*, n.d.)

Time would be the best judge to see the effective implementation of various schemes to be rolled by the government on the advice of The National Social Security Board formed under the Code on Social Security and its qualitative impact on the life of gig/platform workers, however, in my opinion, we must work *on a self-sustaining gig model, based on market forces, powered by technology and supplemented by data empowerment.*

It is the need of the hour to promote the gig economy so that the aspirations of 1.3 billion Indians can be met. Getting jobs in the formal sector is becoming difficult day by the day, hence all efforts must be made to promote /formalize the gig economy which has huge potential of providing livelihood to millions of workers and making India a localised and self-reliant economy. The millenniums who do not want to do stereotyped jobs and want flexibility are more than willing to participate in the growing gig economy, hence the focus of the government should be to provide a level playing field to gig economy which not helps in its growth but also takes care of social security requirements.

The Code on Social Security has mandated for electronic registration of workers in the unorganized sector which is a good start, however, we have to plan and work for a paradigm shift in the gig economy, to see the real change in the life of workers in unorganized sector. The following vision of "Gig economy" based on the concept of data empowerment can be a game-changer and can bring qualitative change in the life of gig workers.

GIG ECONOMY MODEL

A new model for the gig economy is conceptualised based on the powerful idea of the account aggregator ecosystem popularly known as SAHAMATI. (*Sahamati - Collective of the Account Aggregator Ecosystem*, n.d.) The proposed model of the gig economy would have the following key pillars /stakeholders.

- Gig portal
- Giggers
- Information providers **(IP)** like platforms and aggregators
- Information users **(IU)** like banks, platforms, regulators, insurance companies, general public
- Government of India

Figure 1. Gig model
Source: (Sahamati - Collective of the Account Aggregator Ecosystem, n.d.)

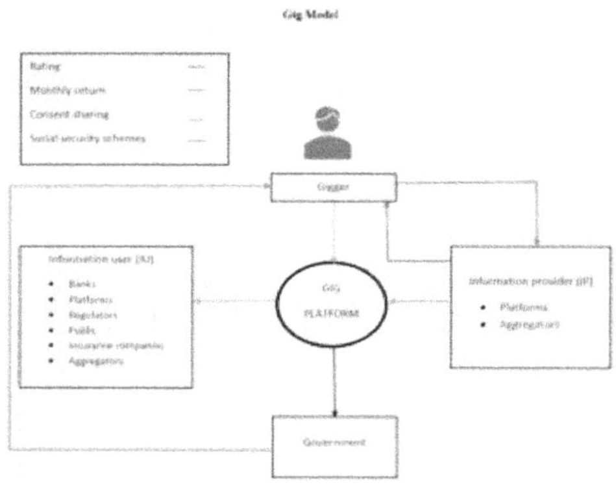

Government should focus on building a portal to be nick-named as "Gig portal" which would be administered by the National Social Security Board. The portal would be an open API (application programming interface) wherein other players can conveniently build interconnected layers on top of it for providing various services.

The giggers would be encouraged to register themselves on the portal either voluntarily or through the platforms and aggregators. The registration would be linked to Aadhaar; hence it takes care of a monumental problem of KYC. The registration process on the gig portal has to be kept simple to the extent possible. A printable identity card with a photograph can be self-generated after a successful registration. The following details will be captured in the registration process on the gig portal.

- Name
- Address (to take care of migrant workers issue, it is important to capture the present address of the gigger)
- Skill sets (drop-down options would be available in the registration form)
- Experience (number of years in the trade)
- Specific training (if any undertaken under skill India mission or similar program run by state governments)
- Qualification details
- Awards and recognition if any

The gig portal, administered by the National Social Security Board would eventually promote innovativeness and would encourage entrepreneurs to come forward for building interconnected layers on it, which eventually will lead to the growth of the gig economy (Figure 1).

The other important pillar of the gig portal would be the information providers (IP) who would be mandated under the law to provide structured data on monthly basis in electronic form. This information would be around the number of hours the gigger has worked in the month and the amount paid for his services. The Code on Social Security will have to be amended so that for availing gig services the platforms and aggregators will have to ensure that the gig worker is registered with the portal within 30 days of the first gig. This registration process on the portal draws it parallel to provident fund, employees state insurance, and gratuity registration in the organized sector.

The platforms and other aggregators would be both information providers (IP) and information users (IU) as they would have access to the data of millions of workers in the gig economy who have either registered directly on the portal or by the platforms/aggregators. There would be no scope of duplicity as the registration would be linked to Aadhaar. Thus, the gig portal would promote healthy completion amongst the aggregator's / platforms and giggers would prefer working with the one which offers the best rates and good working conditions. This would also be a win-win situation for aggregators as the on-boarding of giggers becomes extremely easy, fast, and paperless.

The gig portal, to support the gig economy would have a unique feature of 360-degree feedback, unlike in the traditional employer-employee relationships wherein the employers rate their employees only as part of the appraisal process. However, under the proposed gig economy model, the giggers' would be rating platforms and aggregators, vice versa platforms and aggregators would also have the opportunity to rate the giggers', basis the services provided by them. The rating scale would be between one to five. This unique rating feature would help improve the visibility of efficient gig workers who then can command better rates /premiums in the open market. Rating of the platforms/aggregator's would help potential giggers to take a judicious call on selecting one amongst the many.

The open rating system will help reduce the exploitation of gig workers as no aggregator or platform would like a bad name on a gig platform which can eventually impact their business. Fear of action by regulators will be a great deterrent to avoid exploitation of gig workers and a bad reputation on gig platforms can have serious implications for platforms/aggregators.

Other important players on gig platforms can be banks and fintech, who can offer microcredit to giggers which can eventually help fulfill their entrepreneurial ambitions. The *flow-based credit* can be a virtual reality as the gig portal has digital footprints of the transaction of giggers, courtesy of the monthly filling by aggregators and platforms.

Insurance companies can be other big players on gig platforms, as they can offer life /accidental cover to millions on gig portals, thus bringing a big chunk of the gig economy on the social protection network.

Other important information users (IU) can be regulators who can keep a close vigil on the various developments/concerns raised by giggers on the gig platform. The proactive approach of regulators in ensuring that the aggregators/platforms are spending on the social security of gig workers as mandated under the law will help promote the growth of the gig economy in a big way.

Lastly, the most important information user (IU) can be the general public who can avail the services of gig workers, registered on the portal. The general public will have confidence in availing services from the giggers registered on the gig portal due to KYC norms. The unique rating feature on the gig portal can help the general public in identifying good giggers and thus those with consistently good ratings can also command a premium for their services.

It is generally believed that India would become data-rich even before it becomes economically rich. [24] Concepts like gig *portal* would further this belief and would be a great milestone in the digital India mission. The gig portal would then be a great repository of data; however, it is very important to explicitly define issues related to ownership of data.

It is generally believed that data belongs to the entity that is the custodian of it like banks, insurance companies, income tax departments, and telecom companies. However, this perception needs to be changed, as in our opinion the data belongs to the giggers and they should have the liberty to share the same with his consent and for his benefit. Hence, data on the gig portal can be publicly viewed only if the gigger has at the time of registration given consent for the same. Sharing of data with information users (IU) like banks, insurance companies would also require specific approval from the gigger.

The other important aspect which would guide the growth of the gig economy is the social security needs of gig workers. The concept of gig portal, registration of gig workers, and the monthly filling by aggregators/platforms are the important enablers towards solving the issue of social security schemes in the unorganized sector. To date, we do not have any structured data of the unorganized workers in our country who constitute 93% of our workforce, however, a gig platform can go a long way in solving this problem.(Rana Riya, 2020)

As has been the case of DBT (direct benefit transfer), the data on the gig portal can conveniently be used by the government (both central and state) towards administering various schemes for the welfare of gig workers. The Aadhaar based registration on the gig platform would ensure no leakages and will result in targeted delivery of benefits to gig workers. The social security schemes for the gig workers would go a long way in promoting the growth of the gig economy.

India would very soon be amongst the very few countries in the world, who would have a forward-looking law on *data protection* which would be a great milestone in promoting the growth of the gig economy, by providing regulatory protection of data on the gig portal.

The proposed law would have the following rights (*The Personal Data Protection Bill, 2018 Chapter I Preliminary*, n.d.)

- Right to confirmation and access
- Right to correction
- Right to data portability
- Right to be forgotten

CONCLUSION

We are living in a disruptive world, wherein technology-enabled changes occur very often and at a pace beyond our imagination. Communication technology has brought down the geographical boundaries, hence services can be offered across the globe by giggers from any part of the world and can command a premium for specialized services. Few examples of gig services that can be remotely offered across the globe are e- coding, designing, solving complex engineering issues, advisory services, etc.

However, unfortunately, this is not true for all the services, and a majority of gigs can be offered only within the limited geographical area like the case of cab services, food delivery, home services, construction services, etc. Most of the giggers, especially in developing countries are those who do not have the option of getting full-time employment, hence just for their livelihood, they opt for being a gigger with some aggregator /platform.

Hence, there is a clear divide in the gig economy between those offering specialized services without any geographical limitation and others offering generalized services. Giggers doing specialized services command premium to take care of financial and other social security needs, unlike the majority offering generalized services.

The gig culture is an inevitable reality and is here to stay and grow. Despite all the challenges in the gig economy, the disruptions are visible and will be more apparent in times to come. We are seeing *outsourcing / short-duration work assignments* in one form or the other not only in the private sector but also in the government, educational intuitions, and other local bodies. Artificial intelligence, machine learning combined with gig culture are a real threat to the traditional employer-employee relationship-based jobs due to its perceived benefits, however, we must take this as a challenge and prepare ourselves to face this massive disruption.

Brazil, United States and United Kingdom are the ones having highest share of gig workers with Art & Design, Construction and Entertainment sectors taking the lead. Globally it is estimated that one third of the working population is part of the gig economy and this trend would continue to rise. The ongoing pandemic has further given push to the gig culture worldwide as traditional 9 to 5 job are treated as unsafe.

Over the years, India has witnessed tremendous growth in the gig economy which has been there in some form or the other for ages, however with digital divide barriers falling apart, growth of the internet and communication technology, it has the potential to penetrate all sectors be it manufacturing, education, healthcare, construction, etc. thereby improving India's GDP and a great move toward localised and self-reliant Indian economy. (Augustinraj Rajah & Bajaj Samar, 2021)

The unique feature of *flexibility* in the gig economy is willingly driving the millenniums towards the same, however, the real challenge is for the other millions of workers who are part of the gig economy without any social security cover. The *gig model* envisaged in this chapter, backed by necessary regulatory changes can go a long way in protecting the minimum pay rights and other social security needs of giggers.

REFERENCES

Alexander, G. S. (2020). *What is the gig economy? Definition from WhatIs.com*. https://whatis.techtarget.com/definition/gig-economy

Amity University, Dubai Campus, Institute of Electrical and Electronics Engineers, UAE Section, & Institute of Electrical and Electronics Engineers. (n.d.). *Abstract proceedings of International Conference on Computation, Automation and Knowledge Management (ICCAKM-2020) : 9th-10th January 2020*. Author.

Brand, M. (2018). *Why Did Kodak Fail and What Can You Learn from its Demise? | by BRAND MINDS | Medium*. https://brand-minds.medium.com/why-did-kodak-fail-and-what-can-you-learn-from-its-failure-70b92793493c

ca buxozypk. (2020). *Top Countries in the Gig Economy | Gigonomy*. https://gigonomy.info/top-countries-in-the-gig-economy/

Employee Tenure in 2020. (2020). www.bls.gov/cps

Gig (music) - Wikipedia. (n.d.). Retrieved February 9, 2021, from https://en.wikipedia.org/wiki/Gig_(music)

How Does the Gig Economy Benefit Employees & Businesses? TSheets. (n.d.). Retrieved February 9, 2021, from https://www.tsheets.com/resources/gig-economy-employees

Labour Law Reforms | Ministry of Labour & Employment. (n.d.). Retrieved February 11, 2021, from https://labour.gov.in/labour-law-reforms

Nilanjan, B. (2020). *Gig economy: Opinion: India's gig economy needs affirmative policy push, Government News, ET Government.* https://government.economictimes.indiatimes.com/news/economy/opinion-indias-gig-economy-needs-affirmative-policy-push/73121847

Overview of Labour Law Reforms I PRSIndia. (n.d.). Retrieved February 11, 2021, from https://www.prsindia.org/billtrack/overview-labour-law-reforms

Periodic Labour Force Survey (PLFS) Ministry of Statistics and Programme Implementation Annual Report Periodic Labour Force Survey (PLFS) Government of India Ministry of Statistics and Programme Implementationin GoIStats GoIStats Periodic Labour Force Survey (PLFS) Ministry of Statistics and Programme Implementation goistats. (2020). www.mospi.gov.inwww.mospi.gov

Pickard, W. G. (2019). *The History and Future of the Gig Economy - Small Business Trends.* https://smallbiztrends.com/2019/11/the-history-and-future-of-the-gig-economy.html

Pooja, M. (2020, January). *Gig Economy – Shaping the Future of Work.* https://www.investindia.gov.in/team-india-blogs/gig-economy-shaping-future-work

Rajah & Samar. (2021). *In India Economy Unlocking the Potential of the Gig Economy in India.* Academic Press.

Rebecca, H. (2020, December 10). *How COVID-19 Has Transformed The Gig Economy.* https://www.forbes.com/sites/rebeccahenderson/2020/12/10/how-covid-19-has-transformed-the-gig-economy/?sh=313143416c99

Riya, R. (2020). *India Lockdown: Most Affected Is Unorganized Sector; It Is 93% Of The Total Workforce, 41 Crore People Lack Economic Security - Inventiva.* https://www.inventiva.co.in/stories/riyarana/india-lockdown-most-affected-is-unorganized-sector-it-is-93-of-the-total-workforce-41-crore-people-lack-economic-security/

Sahamati - Collective of the Account Aggregator Ecosystem. (n.d.). Retrieved January 22, 2021, from https://sahamati.org.in/#

The Associated Chamber of Commerce and Industry of India. (2020). *Gig economy national conference aligning consumer preferences: the way forward background note.* www.assocham.org

The Code on Social Security. (2020).

The Controller of Publications. (2020).

The Personal Data Protection Bill, 2018 Chapter I Preliminary. (n.d.).

The Pros and Cons of the Gig Economy. (2018). https://www.wgu.edu/blog/pros-and-cons-gig-economy1808.html

The top five advantages and disadvantages of gig economy workers revealed – Engage Employee. (2018). https://engageemployee.com/top-five-advantages-disadvantages-gig-economy-workers-revealed/

Ways your business can benefit from the gig economy I Moonlyte. (2021). https://www.moonlyte.com/blog/56/Ways-your-business-can-benefit-from-the-gig-economy

What is Gig Economy? Pros and Cons of GIG Economy explained, Is Indian Economy becoming GIG Economy? - YouTube. (2019). https://www.youtube.com/watch?v=qECRrrQu8y8&t=75s

What is Industry 4.0? | The Industrial Internet of Things | Epicor India. (n.d.). Retrieved February 7, 2021, from https://www.epicor.com/en-in/resource-center/articles/what-is-industry-4-0/

Chapter 16
Implementing Atma Nirbhar Bharat:
A Project Management Approach

Siddharth Varma
International Management Institute, New Delhi, India

ABSTRACT

From small companies to major enterprises, the COVID-19 pandemic put us all to test. While it has left us facing an unpredictable future, it also offers us the chance to create a self-sufficient and self-reliant India, or "Atma Nirbhar Bharat." The motivation towards a self-reliant India became stronger after the border conflict with China. Being dependent on China for both finished products and raw material, it is imperative for India to reduce this dependence. The "Atma Nirbhar Bharat" needs to be planned and executed as a nationwide program comprising several projects. Successful execution of this program needs to follow a systematic project management approach. This chapter tries to develop a blueprint for planning and execution of this program which is aimed at a self-reliant India.

INTRODUCTION

Globalization is defined as the increase in the flow of goods, services, capital, people, and ideas across international boundaries. Globalization is necessary for progress of the economy. At the same time this may cause disproportionate growth between and within nations. Localization is the process of adapting content, products, and services to specific local markets. Localization keeps in mind the requirements of the local population. Globalization versus localization can be an unending debate. Perhaps both globalization and localization are required for growth of the economy. A balance between these two may be required. This has led to the coining of a new term: Glocalization. This means globalizing but keeping local requirements and preferences in mind and modifying products and services accordingly.

The recent pandemic has shifted the focus to localization and the importance of being self-reliance came to the forefront. India has also adopted a policy to enhance self-reliance. This has been announced under the Atma Nirbhar Bharat program. The word Atma Nirbhar means self- reliant. On 12 May 2020,

DOI: 10.4018/978-1-7998-8705-8.ch016

the Indian Prime Minister raised a clarion call for **Atma Nirbhar Bharat** meaning a **self-reliant India**. Union Finance Minister Nirmala Sitharaman announced Rs 2.65 lakh crore worth economic stimulus package, termed as Atma Nirbhar Bharat 3.0 (Sharma, 2020). The Atmanirbhar Bharat initiative is supposed to be based on the following five pillars (Atmanirbhar Bharat Abhiyan, 2021).

- Economy: quantum jumps, not incremental changes
- Infrastructure: representing modern India
- Systems: technology driven systems
- Demography: vibrant demography of the largest democracy
- Demand: full utilization of the power of demand and supply
  A stimulus package was also announced in order to implement the Atma Nirbhar Bharat (ANB) mission. The stimulus package was meant for five broad areas (Atmanirbhar Bharat Abhiyan, 2021):
- Relief measures for business including MSMEs, NBFCs, HFCs, contractors, real estate and salaried workers
- Poor including farmers, migrant workers, street vendors
- Agriculture and allied sectors such as dairy, animal husbandry and fisheries
- New horizons of growth like defense, airspace production, atomic energy, space sector.
- Government reforms enabler

Broadly, the concept of ANB would help in achieving the following objectives.

1. Reduce dependence on other countries in several sectors of the economy particularly critical sectors like pharmaceuticals and defense. This would make the economy robust which becomes especially important in view of the geo-political developments in the country. The recent confrontation with China is a case on point.
2. Reduce unemployment by provide work to the teeming millions of the country.
3. Develop the economy of India contributing to making it a 5 trillion dollar economy.
4. Make Indian industry globally competitive not only for catering to local demand but be able to export to other countries.
5. Develop supply chain and logistics in the country

LITERATURE REVIEW

The past decade has witnessed the popularization of two intertwined trends in geographic competitiveness: globalization and localization. As firms globalize, the significance of local relationships reduces and they develop new capabilities (De Martino et. al., 2006). Neither globalization nor localization can be considered as mystic forces. Local advocacy is a necessity from the region's point of view (Cabus, 2001). Wilhelmina et. al. (2010) have examined the effect of global-local interactions on food production and consumption in Ghana. They recommend that production practices be improved using technologies which reflect changing consumption dynamics and thus exploit the opportunities due to global-local interaction. Hines (2003) feel that globalization is occurring increasingly at the cost of social, environmental and labor improvements. This is increasing inequality in the world. Localization can reduce poverty and inequality and improve livelihoods, social infrastructure and environment. Ramarapu and Timmerman (1999) present a study which examines the factors suggesting a fit between strategic thrust and target cultural dynamics. They offer a model to facilitate this selection. The role of globalization and localization in bringing in Foreign Direct Investment has been studied and it was found that FDI cannot be explained by a single factor. Also, different types of FDI are influenced by different motives (Seyf, 2001). Since the 9/11 terrorist attack in USA it is being recognized that unequal world is also deeply insecure. Globalization has a major role to play in worsening the gap between the rich and poor. This can be countered with localization (Lucas, 2003). A study of the glocalization patterns in the international construction industry has found companies adopt glocalisation to strike a balance between globalization and localization to enhance the consistency and efficiency of their CSR strategies (Ye, 2020). Electrolux which is a worldwide household appliances company has tried to balance between globalization and localization which is based on its dedication to local consumer insight (Hollensen, 2018). McDonald's is another company which is globalized and yet keeps in mind the preferences of the local population. The company has glocalized successfully. This has been revealed in a research study which examined McDonald's strategy across dimensions including menu, promotion, restaurants and employees (Crawford et. al., 2015).

MANAGERIAL SIGNIFICANCE OF THIS PAPER

This paper is not a research paper but rather a document meant for officials or professionals linked with implementation of ANB. It tries to provide a high level plan for carrying out the ANB program. The government needs to carry out the ANB initiative in a well thought out manner if India has to be made self-reliant. This paper can provide a rough blueprint to take the ANB initiative forward and can be useful for government officials and top management involved in planning and execution of ANB.

An ad hoc approach to carrying out projects can result in substantial cost over runs, time over runs and compromised scope fulfillment. Consequently, the higher goal of making India self- reliant may not be achieved. A standardized methodology needs to be adopted in order complete the projects related to ANB successfully. This paper is an attempt to provide such a standardized methodology which can be used for the ANB program and each of the projects under ANB initiative. By using this methodology, the chances of success of ANB initiative can be substantially enhanced. The paper also provides the project management tools which can be used for implementing the Atma Nirbhar Abhiyan as a program. For managers, this paper can server as a guide at the macro level for taking the Atma Nirbhar Bharat Program forward. It may also be used as an input for policy making by the Indian government for implementing this program.

OBJECTIVES OF THIS PAPER

The objectives of this paper are

- To provide a rough blueprint for implementing Atma Nirbhar Bharat as a program
- To provide an overview of the activities to be carried out in each phase of projects under the Atma Nirbhar Bharat program

- To identify the project management tools which can be utilized across the project life cycle of each project

IMPLEMENTATION CHALLENGES FOR ANB

While the concept of ANB is excellent for India it is the implementation of this initiative which is the real challenge. The objectives of ANB are defined, the money has been made available but this is not adequate to make it a success. The ANB concept has the potential to redefine the Indian economy and has to be a massive country wide initiative. If the government shifts the responsibility of making India self-reliant to private entrepreneurs by merely budgeting an amount for the ANB initiative it is unlikely that India will become self- reliant in the near future. Government of India has to be take responsibility of implementing the ANB initiative beyond the economic stimulus package it has announced for this. Unless ANB initiative is backed with a clear plan for managing it, it may not yield the sort of benefits which are envisaged from this initiative. It may be delayed so much that the objectives may not be achieved. For example, if the rate at which it generates jobs is less than the rate of growth of unemployment in the country, it will fail to achieve the objective of reducing unemployment. Specifically, the following challenges can be identified in implementing ANB.

- Timely execution
- Cost management
- Resource management
- Scope management

Many of the projects identified under ANB mission may belong to the small and medium industry (SME) category. Dasari et. al. (2015) have studied the reasons behind delays and cost escalations in SME projects and identified the following reasons.

1. Market Fluctuations: Price fluctuations in market affect the raw material procurements by escalating the project estimated budget.
2. Mistakes During Agreement: Misunderstandings and misinterpretation of requirements that happen during signing of agreement with the customer lead to scope creep, thereby leading to erroneous time and cost estimations.
3. Change Requests: Some users may come up with requests for adding some more specialized features in the product. Similarly, to enhance quality in the performance of project, the SME may undertake some modifications at its end.
4. Expansion Programs: Some progressing projects may be targeted by the requests of customers to have some options

Henry (1973) has discussed problems in the management of government and industry programs in the U.S. He identified the following problems.

1. Challenge of achieving incompatible objectives
2. Problem of ill-defined and overlapping work assignments;

3. Problems due to the division of a particular type of work between agency and contractor personnel
4. Improper contractor supervision
5. Cost overruns and ineffective control
6. Incomplete and inconsistent cost accounting
7. Bureaucratic structures
8. Inflexible manpower utilization

Even though this study may seem outdated, some of the findings may still be relevant to our country and it may be worth looking at our own systems for implementing government programs keeping in mind the problems identified for government programs in the US.

RELEVANCE OF PROJECT MANAGEMENT APPROACH

Projects can be defined as a set of activities which have a specific start and a specific end. These are often one time activities which are highly customized. Though each project may be unique in its own way managing these projects need not be done in an ad-hoc manner. The Project Management approach is a systematic approach to handling projects. The approach has several benefits. It helps in generating credible schedules for execution of work. It proactively identifies risks and tries to mitigate them. It identifies resource requirements in a time phased manner and thus helps in managing resources effectively. It clearly spells out responsibility and authority of each team member. All this helps in fulfilling the scope of the project within the constraints of time and cost.

A set of similar projects make up a program. Program Management may be defined as the centralized coordinated management of a program to achieve the program's strategic objectives and benefits. A program is a group of related projects managed in a coordinated manner to obtain benefits and control which may not be available from managing them individually (Program Management, 2021). Program management is often closely related to systems engineering. Programs bring together related projects, which help the program manager manage interdependencies between these projects, facilitate control of resources, manage risks and identify opportunities to drive efficiencies.

Nel (2001) investigated the application of a project management approach to the implementation of development programmes in the local government sphere. According to him local authorities can apply project management as a particular technique to ensure that the objectives of development policies and programmes are attained with an optimal utilization of scarce public resources.

ANB is not a single project but a set of related projects. It is in fact, a strategic level program for the government of India supposed to deliver benefits in the medium to long term. Hence, ANB initiative has to be executed like a program: a set of large number of projects executed with the over-arching goal of making India self-reliant. It is not enough to achieve objectives of individual projects but important to achieve the overall goal of self-reliance for the country. A systematic approach for executing the program and a standardized approach for executing each project has to be developed. This will help in maximizing the benefits of ANB program.

IMPLEMENTING ATMA NIRBHAR BHARAT

At the Program Level

Identification and Prioritization of Industry Sectors and Projects

While the ANB initiative is supposed to cover a gamut of industry sectors which can be critical to the economy of the country, it is still important to not only to identify the specific sectors of the economy to be covered but also prioritize these sectors. The government has identified 12 sectors, including auto components, textiles, industrial machinery and furniture; where focus would be given with a view to make India a self-reliant country and a global supplier (Goyal, 2021). However, it is still important to prioritize these sectors. The criteria for this prioritization have to be laid out. Some of these criteria could be the following.

- -Criticality of the sector, e.g., pharmaceuticals is critical for the health of the people. Its importance has been felt in the Covid-19 pandemic. Defense can be important for the sovereignty of the country. The recent Chinese conflict drove home this point.
- -Extent of imports in the sector- sectors in which we are losing huge foreign exchange in imports can be a priority sector as these can save precious foreign exchange.
- -Possibility of employment generation-sectors which can employ people in large numbers can help substantially in employment generation
- -Availability of expertise-sectors in which we already have local expertise can be more easily developed.

The identification and prioritization of sectors has to be carried out at ministerial level. Once the sectors have been identified, the exact products or intermediate raw materials which need to be produced in each sector have to be ascertained. This may result in a list of projects for each sector. Within each list, prioritization needs to be done. This prioritization may be done on the basis of the same criteria which were used for prioritization of industry sectors. Prioritization is an important activity because

- It will help in phased requirement of resources rather than making resources for all the projects being made available at one time.
- Project management including monitoring and control may also be easier with a limited number of projects in progress at a certain point of time.
- It can also help to maximize returns with the available resources.

Integration of Projects

The individual projects are part of a larger program called ANB. Integration is an important part of program execution. Integration will help in saving costs, timely execution of projects and more efficient utilization of resources. The following aspects for integration may be worth considering.

- In the initial stages while the projects are being identified for ANB it is possible that certain interfacing projects were not considered due to oversight. Such projects need to be identified. The best way to identify such projects would be study the whole supply chain of the finished product and identify if any missing links exist. The finished product may be an assembly of components or may require intermediate raw material. Merely setting up a factory for the final product may be of little use unless sourcing of all the components and raw material is also made indigenous. A self-reliant India cannot be producing the finished product only while remaining dependent for the inputs on other countries. Unless these missing links are taken care of, the purpose of carrying out the project would be lost.

- An integration team needs to be set up for each sector identified for the ANB mission. Resources for such a team have to be identified. This could be a virtual team which can be made up of senior project professionals and an industry expert. Additionally, presence of a government official can be helpful in getting over administrative problems and also facilitate decision making.
- Frequency of integration meetings and their schedule needs to be decided. The participants for such meetings also need to be identified in order to make such meetings productive. Apart from the integration team other participants could be the project managers handling various projects, and sometimes vendors and major contractors too.
- A very important aspect of integration is the identification of information required for integration by the integration team. Such information could include designs of plants, requirement of plant and machinery and requirement of construction materials. Integration of designs may be relevant for engineering projects.
- Looking for joint efficiencies while executing multiple projects can be an important part of program management. Aggregated procurement which means combining the requirement of many projects under ANB into a single purchase order can bring in substantial economies due to quantity discounts which vendors will offer. It will also reduce the work involved in follow up with vendors saving a lot of man hours which can be utilized for other more productive work.
- Efficiencies can also be enhanced by sharing of resources. Such opportunities need to be identified by the integration team. For example, one project manager could look after more than one ANB project. Alternately, a Program Manager could be assigned for the projects being carried out for one industry sector. Similarly, phased usage of construction equipment could mean the same equipment is used for more than one project reducing the requirement for purchasing or leasing multiple units of the same equipment.
- Risk reviews can be done jointly for multiple projects. This will require inputs from project teams involved in project execution also. Apart from the project team, contractors could also provide useful inputs for this. Similar risks identified in multiple projects can help in formulating a standardized plan for mitigating the risk.
- Managing project interdependencies: Project interdependency can happen when two or more projects are related to each other in certain ways. Project interdependency can enhance the risk level for a project because if one of the project fails to deliver expected results then other projects which are dependent on this project are also likely to fail, especially if the interdependency is of critical nature. Some examples of interdependencies in projects are as follows.
    1. *The same resource is shared by several projects*: This means that the resource cannot be used by both projects at the same time. Resource sharing is important to bring in efficiencies in program execution. At the same time it needs to be ensured that this sharing of resource does not delay the execution of one or more projects. Resource conflicts need to be identified to avoid non-availability of a resource when it is required.

2. *Two or more projects have a finish to start precedence relationship*: This means that one project cannot be started until the other is finished. Alternatively, some deliverable from one project may be an input for another project.
3. *The funds available are limited*: This is usually the case. This may cause a resource crunch for one project while the other project takes up a large share of the funds due to cost overruns or incorrect estimation of costs.

Monitoring and Control

Control of the implementation of projects and programs is one of the most important elements in connection with the project management. This allows one to clearly identify the problem and its reasons in real time. Program monitoring and control can be carried out by the "Development Monitoring And Evaluation Office" of the Government of India. The Development Monitoring and Evaluation Office (DMEO) has been formed by merging the erstwhile Program Evaluation Office (PEO) and the Independent Evaluation Office (IEO). It is attached to the NITI Aayog and is aimed at fulfilling the organization's monitoring and evaluation mandate and building the monitoring and evaluation ecosystem in India (Developing, (Monitoring and Evaluation Office, 2021).

The DMEO has the following functions

1. To monitor progress and efficacy of strategic and long term policy and programme frameworks and initiatives to help innovative improvements, including necessary mid-course corrections
2. To actively monitor and evaluate the implementation of programmes and initiatives, including the identification of the needed resources so as to strengthen the probability of success and scope of delivery.
3. DMEO also has advisory powers across the Ministries and Departments of the Union Government. It provides a cross- and inter-ministerial perspective. DMEO can share reports and reviews directly with key decision makers in the government to initiate action ((Monitoring and Evaluation Office, 2021).

The DMEO will be useful in monitoring and control of ANB projects in the following ways.

- It can identify the factors which prevent the successful implementation of projects and programs by causing cost and time overruns. Such factors can be identified for all stages of project and program implementation.
- It can study the compliance of the planned project parameters and reveal deviations from estimated figures. It can also identify the reasons for such deviation. This can be helpful not only in ensuring the current projects are successfully completed but can be useful in managing future projects also.
- It can provide a plan for corrective action to the relevant state and central bodies for keeping the program on track.

At Project Level

The ANB program will involve setting up of production units for finished products or for intermediate raw materials required for the finished product. A project management approach needs to be adopted and setting up of each production unit needs to be handled as a project. Each project can be divided into the following phases.

Conceptualization or Initiation

The conceptualization phase should commence with analyzing the need to carry out the project. The project is justified only if it helps in enhancing self- reliance for the country. The higher level goal of self-reliance needs to be kept in mind while conceptualizing any ANB project. Identification of critical sectors and prioritizing these would be done at the program level. This has been discussed in an earlier section of this paper.

Feasibility Analysis- Once a project has been identified under the ANB initiative a feasibility analysis would still need to be done. While the project would make India self- reliant in some way it is necessary that it should be economically feasible. The feasibility need not be limited to economic feasibility only. It should cover various aspects: political, economic, social, technological, legal and environmental. In other words, a PESTLE analysis can be used as a comprehensive feasibility analysis. Since ANB is a government initiative it is unlikely that political feasibility would be problem. Even legal issues may not become a serious constraint with the government supporting the project. However, following aspects still remain important from feasibility point of view.

1. Economic aspect: These related to the financial feasibility of the project. While the major objective of the project is to achieve self-reliance in a particular sector of the economy, the project needs to be financially feasible also. Financial feasibility can be measured in terms of well-known metrics like Net Present Value, Internal Rate of Return or Payback Period. Since the project would be replacing a product which is currently imported the cost of indigenous product needs to be compared with that of the imported product .This is important because the output of this project could be an input for another product and any change in price would have a cascading effect on the products for which this product serves as an input material or component.
2. Social aspect: The impact of the project on the society needs to be analyzed. A project offers certain services, products and activities. These are outputs. As a consequence of these outputs, results are produced within the target groups. These are outcomes. These outcomes can be of various kinds. The outcomes in turn can have results at the level of society as a whole. This would be an impact. Impacts could be of various types. Examples of such impacts are: change in living standards or life styles, change in skill levels, changes in behavior.
3. Technological aspect: This is a crucial aspect of the feasibility analysis. This is also closely related to the economic aspect. Since the project is going to replace an item which is currently imported one needs to study whether the project is technologically feasible. Does the country have the technology to produce the item indigenously? In many cases, this technology may need to be imported. This will have a direct impact on the economic aspect as purchase of technology or technology transfer would incur costs. Technology transfer can also be time consuming. In case the technology has to be developed indigenously, it would require even longer period of time. Development of indigenous technology may itself become a project on its own. It is important to understand that the main project may require related projects to be executed.
4. Environmental aspect: This is an important aspect of any project these days. The impact of the project on the environment needs to be studied. With the increased focus of the Government of

India on sustainability an Environmental Impact Assessment for each project needs to be prepared. In case the environmental impact is adverse an alternate technology may be required to reduce this impact.

It is clear that the various aspects discussed above are not independent on each other. The environmental impact can affect the technology to be used which in turn can affect the economic aspect of the project.

Tool to be used: NPV, IRR, Payback Period, PESTLE Analysis, Environmental Impact Assessment

Once the feasibility report is complete, a Detailed Project Report (DPR) or a Business Case needs to be prepared. This would include among other things, the following:

- Goal of the project
- Objectives of the project
- Broad scope of project
- Organization structure required
- Constraints, if any
- Assumptions, if any
- Approximate budget
- Approximate timeline
- Resource requirement
- Stakeholder analysis

An external consultant may be hired in order to prepare the DPR. Assumptions made should be realistic while a plan needs to be formulated to manage the constraints. The Detailed Project Report should be put up to a high level committee comprising industry experts for the respective sector, ministry representatives and project management experts. Unless the DPR is approved by this committee the project should not be allowed to take off.

Stakeholder analysis- Stakeholders can make or break a project, depending on how they have been handled. It is important to do a stakeholder analysis in the Initiation phase itself. The well-known Power-Interest Matrix can be utilized to prioritize stakeholders based on the impact of the stakeholders on the outcome of the project. Stakeholders who can have profound effect on the outcome of the project need to be handled carefully. Keeping in mind the interest of each stakeholder and the influence exerted by the stakeholder on the outcome of the project, a stakeholder management plan needs to be prepared.

Approving and regulatory agencies are important stakeholders in a project. They have the potential to delay a project or even kill the project. Approvals from various agencies are a major bottleneck for project execution in India. Approvals required are often sequential in nature which makes things even worse. Delay in approvals is a major cause for delay in projects in India. Once the feasibility report has been accepted the applications for approvals need to be moved as soon as possible. This is a critical activity for any project. Handling approving and regulatory agencies must be given due importance. Projects under the ANB initiative should be given accelerated approvals. This can be a big help in expediting projects.

Funding agencies could be another category of important stakeholders. Such stakeholders belong to the high power, low interest category. This can include banks or NBFCs which may be providing loans for the project. Government should provide easy funding for projects which are being carried out under the ANB program.

Projects which are likely to have a substantial environmental impact can become controversial. A plan for handling the environmental impact needs to be put in place. Such projects may also be resisted by NGOs who may be fighting for the cause of environment. Such NGOs may not have much formal power but still have the capability to mold public opinion. Hence, they need to be taken seriously.

A formal stakeholder management plan has to be prepared in order to manage each stakeholder. The plan should include the following information for each of the important stakeholders: interest of the stakeholder, impact on the project and a brief action plan for managing the stakeholder. This plan may need to be revisited from time to time as new stakeholders may come into the picture and action plans may need to be modified. A stakeholder Engagement Matrix can be used to record the current and desired states of engagement of the stakeholders.

Tool to be used: Power Interest Matrix, Stakeholder Engagement Matrix, Stakeholder Management Plan

A project charter can be issued for communicating to internal stakeholders that the project has been approved for execution. This marks the end of the Initiation/ Conceptualization phase of the project.

Planning

Planning is an important phase of project management. The planning for any project begins with defining the scope of the project. A project well planned is half done! Substantial time may require to be spent on planning. Execution should not be started unless planning is completed. Hasty commencement of execution can be detrimental for the project.

For planning of ANB projects it may be useful to form a committee for each sector of the ANB program. This committee should have subject matter experts as well as project management professionals. The scope of the project needs to be defined carefully such that it satisfies the goal of making India self- reliant. The main production unit to be set up may require setting up of ancillary industries too. The whole supply chain related to the product needs to be kept in mind while planning is being done. A systems thinking is required to define the scope of the project. Also, scope has to be defined in sufficient detail. Inadequate scope definition can result in cost and time overruns later. Once the scope has been defined in detail, it needs to be put up to the government for approval of scope. This process is termed Scope Verification. Variations in scope are common during project implementation stage and a process of allowing such variations need to be set up. Without such Scope Control mechanism scope may go out of control.

Detailing of scope can be done through a Work Breakdown Structure (WBS). A WBS is the basis of planning in projects as it breaks down the project into smaller, manageable activities. It is considered a convenient method for dividing a project into small 'work packages' or tasks, thereby increasing the probability that each project activity will be accounted for (Kerzner, 1992)

The WBS may be required to be made at different levels. While a high level WBS is required for the top management a more detailed WBS would be required at the site level where the project is actually being executed. Once a WBS is made, the following plans can be prepared.

Tools to be used: Scope Definition, Scope Verification, Scope Control Mechanism, Work Breakdown Structure

Cost Plan or Budget

While an approximate budget may have been allocated in the initiation phase a more accurate working out of the cost of the project needs to be determined. This can be done only when the scope has been defined in sufficient detail. A bottom up budgeting can provide accurate cost estimates though this process may be slightly time consuming.

Apart from determining the total cost of the project which can help in deciding the overall budget, a Time Phased budget also needs to be prepared. This can help in managing cash flows effectively. Funding of the project either through bank loans or through internal resources can be more easily managed if the cash requirements for each period of the project is known.

A Value Engineering mindset needs to be incorporated while preparing a cost plan. Value Engineering is the systematic application of recognized techniques which can help in fulfilment of a function at reduced costs. According to a report by McKinsey, Value Engineering mindset is often missing in projects in our country (McKinsey, 2009).

Tools to be used: Bottom up Budgeting, Time phased Budgeting, Value Engineering

Time Plan or Schedule

A schedule for the project requires determining the start and end times for each activity of the project. This can be made by first identifying the activities required for project execution, their estimated durations and predecessor activities. This requires involvement of experts who have experience of executing similar projects.

The time plan can be prepared in the form of a network plan. Network plans can be useful for high level monitoring of the project preferably by a government appointed committee of experts. The network plan can be converted into a Gantt chart which is a more user friendly and easily understandable representation of the time plan.

Time plans will need to be prepared at multiple levels. A high level time plan based on a high level network diagram can be used for monitoring by a ministerial committee. Lower level plans can be used for site execution and monitoring. As already mentioned, the WBS has to be prepared at different levels and this can be used for preparing a time plan at different levels.

Tools to be used: Network Plans, Gantt Charts

Resource Plan

Any project requires resources of various types. The major resources required are: manpower, equipment and material. Finally, all these resources require money. The cost plan is therefore linked to the resource plan. A time phased cost plan is based on a time phased resource plan.

The resource planning process would commence with identifying the requirements for various types of resources in a time phased manner. This can be represented on a resource histogram. Histograms provide easy to understand time phased requirements of resources. Each type of resource would require a separate histogram. Time phased resource requirements obtained from the histograms can be converted into time phased cash requirements.

Once the resource requirements are identified the resources are to be arranged for. Instead of arranging resources for a particular project only, it may be better to look at resource requirements for a set of ongoing projects. Some resources could be shared and this could bring about more efficient utilization of resources. Some of the resources which could be shared are: Senior Project Managers, Project Management Experts/ Consultants and Subject Matter Experts.

Purchase orders have to be placed well in time for equipment and material to arrive in time for the project. Projects are often delayed due to late delivery of equipment. Under the ANB projects consolidated requirements for material and equipment should be determined and centralized procurement can be made. This can reduce purchase costs through bulk discounts offered by vendors. Also, follow up with vendors would become more efficient as this could be centralized instead of follow up done by personnel for each ANB project. Such cost savings can be substantial. Hence, a centralized procurement cell needs to be established for the ANB program.

Tools to be used: Resource Histogram, Requirement Consolidation, Centralized Procurement

Risk Management Plan

Risks are inherent part of projects since each project is unique by itself. Risk management needs to be carried out throughout the project life cycle. A risk management exercise needs to be done for each project under the ANB initiative. This will help in proactively managing risks before they become serious. Some of the likely risks for ANB projects could be: delay in land acquisition, delay in mandatory approvals, delays in funding and inability to acquire appropriate technology.

The first step in preparing a risk management plan would be identification of possible risks in the project. Various inputs can be used for doing this. A committee of experts who have experience in executing projects should be formed. The committee can do a brain storming exercise to identify risks. Also, the scope document prepared and the WBS can be used as inputs for identifying risks. The WBS provides details of the scope and hence can be very useful in risk identification. Any assumptions made during initiation phase can also prove to be a risk. Hence, assumptions which have been made need to be analyzed to determine whether they are realistic or not.

Once the risks are identified, they will need to be quantified or measured. Quantification can help in prioritizing the risks. Quantification can be done in the following ways.

- Considering that risk is the product of probability and impact, the value of Probability x Impact can be calculated for each risk. The larger this value, the bigger is the risk.
- Another way to quantify risks could be to determine the financial impact of the risk. Every risk has a financial impact. Larger this impact, more serious is the risk.
- A third way to measure the risk could be to use the concept of Decision Tree which determines the Expected Monetary Value of the risk.

This process of quantification of risk would require use of historical data; especially while using the Decision Tree which requires values of probability which can be based on historical data. Historical data on projects executed in India needs to be collected and analyzed. Such data may be available with Ministry of Statistics & Program Implementation (MoSPI).

Once the risks have been prioritized, a plan to mitigate the more serious risks needs to be formulated. The risks and the risk mitigation plans need to be documented. This document is known as a Risk Register. This documentation is necessary since risk management is an ongoing exercise and one needs to refer to this Register periodically. This Register will also serve as a document for knowledge management and can be utilized for executing other projects under ANB. Such a record of risks and their mitigation plans can be of immense use for future projects. The results of the mitigation exercises can also be documented so that the effectiveness of the mitigation measure is also known.

It needs to be emphasized that risk management is not a one-time exercise and the risks and risk mitigation plans have to be continuously monitored to pro-actively manage risks for ANB.

Tools to be used: Probability-Impact Matrix, Financial Impact Assessment of Risks, Decision Tree, Expected Monetary Value, Risk Register

Organizational Structure

Once plans have been prepared, an organization structure for managing the project needs to be made. A project structure with a dedicated project team for each ANB project would be ideal. However, as already mentioned, some of the resources could be shared which could save costs. A Responsibility Assignment Matrix (RAM) can help in allocating responsibilities to the team members. Each project team should regularly report to a Project Management Office (PMO). Each sector of the industry for which ANB projects are being carried out should have a PMO. The various PMOs should in turn report to the DMEO.

Tool to be used: Responsibility Assignment Matrix

Tendering

An RFQ or RFP needs to be floated to get the quotations or proposals respectively from bidders. In case, the technology and work to be done is understood well, only an RFQ is required. However, if the technical specifications and design are not well understood it is more appropriate to float an RFP which can have the bids in two parts: the technical bid and the price bid. Once the technical bid is acceptable, the price bid can be considered. Once bids are evaluated, negotiations may be carried out with the bidders and contract awarded.

It is worthwhile to note here that the lowest price bid is not necessarily the best bid. The government has to get out of the "lowest bid" syndrome. The complete impact on revenues and cash flows needs to be considered while evaluating a bid. A higher bid in which the vendor promises to complete the work faster may be better than a lower bid in which the vendor would take more time. It has to be remembered that time and cost can be substituted with each other to a large extent. A project which is completed faster will start earning revenues earlier and can be more profitable, even at a higher cost of execution.

Tools to be used: Request for Proposal, Request for Quotation.

Implementation and Monitoring

Implementation can commence only if the land has been acquired. As already mentioned, delay in land acquisition can be a major problem in projects carried out in India (McKinsey, 2009). Government has to ensure land acquisition is done in a timely manner. A separate department or cell needs to be created in order to monitor and assist land acquisition and allotment for all projects under the ANB initiative. This can be of great help in ensuring timely implementation of projects. No Letter of Intent (LOI) or contract should be awarded to any contractor unless land has been acquired for the project.

Contracts which are signed with the contractor for executing the ANB projects must be carefully drafted. Penalty clause for late delivery should be a mandatory part of contracts. A schedule in the form of a Gantt Chart should also be part of the contract. Milestones should be depicted in the chart and any deviation from achieving these milestones should ring alarm bells for both the contractor as well as the government. This time plan should be agreed by the contractor before commencing work at site.

Appropriate types of contracts should be used. If the scope of work is clearly understood by both the client and contractor, Lump Sum or Turnkey contracts can be signed. However, if there is any ambiguity or doubt regarding the scope of work such contracts should not be used. Unit rate contracts could be more ideal with approximate quantity of each item mentioned in the contract.

Based on a resource requirement plan prepared during the Planning phase, resources need to be arranged for well in time.

Monitoring and Control: This is a critical part of any project, especially during the implementation phase Monitoring needs to be done at three levels. These are

- Site level monitoring to be done by project staff posted at the site and getting work done on day to day basis
- Project level monitoring by the Project Management Office for that industry sector.
- Ministerial level monitoring by the Government of India to be done by DMEO.
    1. Site level monitoring is to be done on daily basis by the project personnel. Weekly meeting between client and contractor are essential to keep track of the work. Any problems are to be identified as early as possible before they become serious. Tools to be used are Gantt Charts for day to day monitoring. Weekly targets must be fixed and if these are not achieved it should set the alarm bells ringing. Gantt Charts must be updated on weekly basis before the weekly meeting with contractor.
    2. Project level monitoring by a Project Management Office and should be done on monthly basis. This committee would be monitoring a set of similar projects. The PMO may use the following tools.
- Earned Value Management concept can be used for monitoring. This will combine both time and cost metrics to evaluate how the project is progressing. Desirable metrics for EVM are as follows.
  Schedule Performance Index should be at least equal to 1 (for project to complete on time)
  Cost Performance Index should be at least equal to 1 (for project to be completed within budget)
- Network charts may be used to monitor critical path activities or activities which are likely to become critical. Adequate resources should be provided for activities on the critical path or activities feeding into a critical path. Immediate remedial action needs to be taken if any critical path activity is delayed. PMO should have the authority to provide extra resources or shift resources from one project to another.

3. c) Ministerial level monitoring by DMEO should be done on quarterly basis for each project. Likely cost and time overruns should be closely monitored. PMO must report to DMEO on monthly basis. Meeting between DMEO and PMO should be done on quarterly basis to sort out problems. Project Manager should be part of this meeting.

Any delay in a Critical Path Activity or a milestone should send the alarm bells ringing. Crashing of Critical Path Activities may need to be done to bring the project back on track. The PMO should be making recommendations for corrective action after reviewing the progress of the project. Crashing costs for activities need to be ascertained for this.

Tools to be used: Network Plans, Gantt Charts, Earned Value Management, Crashing

Project Evaluation

Post project evaluation is an important part of project management. Each project under ANB must be evaluated for adherence to the triple constraints of time, cost and scope of project. Beyond this it may be evaluated also for sustainability in terms of environmental impacts. Another aspect on which a project may be evaluated is in terms of the desired outcome of the project. Project evaluation is an essential component of control in that it involves double-checking, by means of comparison, whether the project has indeed met predetermined standards. Project evaluation, requires determining performance standards, measuring achievements against those standards, evaluating deviations and implementing corrective action, when required. Performance standards may be expressed in monetary terms such as revenue or profits but may also be stated in other terms, such as units produced or levels of quality or customer service. Post project evaluation can be done using quantitative tools or surveys, interviews and focus group discussions.

Tools to be used: Quantitative Tools, Surveys, Interviews, Focus Group Discussions.

Knowledge Management

Projects are unique in nature and executing each project provides a different experience. The experience gained in handling the problems arising in each project can be very useful in executing projects in future. The knowledge gained by this experience is often lost as employees retire or leave the organization to join another organization. Knowledge management should be included as an important part of project management. The government should standardize the process for collection of experiences gained in managing ANB projects and have these experiences documented. The documentation could be in electronic form or hard copy form but should be accessible to people handling projects in future. A knowledge management tool helps provide a central repository for all information, data, and knowledge, facilitating easy storage and retrieval.

Tools to be used: Software Tools for Knowledge Management: Document360, Ameyo

CONCLUSION

The ANB initiative of the Government of India is a well-intentioned one with the primary goal to make the country self-reliant. This becomes very relevant today with the swiftly changing geo political environment of India and too much dependence on China for important raw materials as well as finished products. Atma Nirbhar Bharat needs to be implemented as a program made up of several projects aimed at making India self-reliant. To maximize benefits from this initiative and to achieve the objectives of ANB it is important for the government to actively participate in this process instead of merely announcing an economic stimulus package for making India self- reliant and waiting for things to happen.

A timeline needs to be set to achieve the objectives of ANB program. Each project under this initiative has to be professionally carried out through the initiation, planning and implementation phases. Inputs from both industry professionals as well as project management professionals are needed for this. This paper provides a rough blueprint for taking forward the ANB initiative. It discusses the processes to be followed in each phase of the project and the tools to be used in each phase. While more detailing requires to be done before the ANB program is actually implemented, this paper provides specific inputs which can drive the ANB program in the right direction.

REFERENCES

Atmanirbhar Bharat Abhiyan. (n.d.). Retrieved on June 25, 2021. https://www.investindia.gov.in/atmanirbhar-bharat-abhiyaan

Cabus, P. (2001). The Meaning of Local in a Global Economy: The 'Region's Advocacy of Local Interests' as a Necessary Component of Current Global/Local Theories. *European Planning Studies*, *9*(8), 1011–1029. doi:10.1080/09654310120093322

Crawford, A., Humphries, S. A., & Geddy, M. M. (2015). McDonald's: A Case Study in Glocalization. *Journal of Global Business Issues*, *9*(1), 11–18.

Dasari, Sudhakar, Jigeesh, Nasina, & Prabhukumar. (2015). Analysis of Project Success Issues: The Case of a Manufacturing SME. *IUP Journal of Operations Management*, *14*(1), 32-38.

De Martino, R., Reid, M. H., & David, Z. (2006). Balancing localization and globalization: Exploring the impact of firm internationalization on a regional cluster. *Entrepreneurship and Regional Development*, *18*(1), 1–24. doi:10.1080/08985620500397648

Developing, Monitoring and Evaluation Office. (n.d.). Retrieved on June 24. 2021. https://niti.gov.in/development-monitoring-and-evaluation-office

Goyal. (2020). *Govt has identified 12 sectors in which India can become self-reliant, global supplier*. https://www.outlookindia.com/newsscroll/govt-has-identified-12-sectors-inwhich-india-can-become-selfreliant-global-supplier-goyal/1842028

Henry, H. M. (1973). Efficiency Is a Valid Goal: Improving the Management of Government/Industry Programs. *Management Review*, *62*(8), 4–18.

Hines, C. (2003). Time to Replace Globalization with Localization. *Global Environmental Politics*, *3*(3), 1–7. doi:10.1162/152638003322469240

Hollensen, S., & Møller, E. (2018). Is "glocalization" still the golden way for Electrolux? Is there more to be done? *Thunderbird International Business Review*, *60*(4), 463–476. doi:10.1002/tie.21923

Kerzner, H. (1992). *Project management: A systems approach to planning, scheduling and controlling* (4th ed.). Van Nostrand Reinholdt.

Lucas, C. (2003). Localization – an alternative to corporate-led globalization. *International Journal of Consumer Studies*, *27*(4), 261–265. doi:10.1046/j.1470-6431.2003.00317.x

McKinsey. (2009). *Building India: Accelerating Infrastructure Projects*. Author.

Nel, H. J. (2001). A project management approach to the implementation of development programmes within the local government sphere: An empirical analysis. *Development Southern Africa*, *18*(5), 605–624. doi:10.1080/03768350120097450

Program Management. (n.d.). Retrieved on June 20, 2021. https://www.pmi.org/learning/featured-topics/program

Ramarapu, S., Timmerman, J. E., & Ramarapu, N. (1999). Choosing Between Globalization and Localization As a Strategic Thrust for Your International Marketing Effort. *Journal of Marketing Theory and Practice*, *7*(2), 97–105. doi:10.1080/10696679.1999.11501832

Seyf, A. (2001). Can Globalization and Global Localization Explain Foreign Direct Investment? Japanese Firms in Europe. *International Journal of the Economics of Business*, *8*(1), 137–153. doi:10.1080/13571510151075350

Sharma, M. (2020, November 12). *Govt announces Atmanirbhar Bharat 3.0; claims COVID stimulus now worth Rs 29.8 lakh crore*. https://www.businesstoday.in/current/corporate/govt-announces-atmanirbhar-bharat-30-covid-stimulus-worth-rs-29-lakh-crore/story/421809.html

Wilhelmina, Q., Joost, J., George, E., & Guido, R. (2010). Globalization vs. localization: Global food challenges and local solutions. *International Journal of Consumer Studies*, *34*(3), 357–366. doi:10.1111/j.1470-6431.2010.00868.x

Ye, M., Lu, W., Flanagan, R., & Chau, K. W. (2020). Corporate social responsibility "glocalisation": Evidence from the international construction business. *Corporate Social Responsibility and Environmental Management*, *27*(2), 655–669. doi:10.1002/csr.1831

Chapter 17
Smart Monitoring IoT-Based System for Hydroponic Agriculture

Sunil Kumar Chowdhary
Amity University, Noida, India

Shailendra Kumar Jain
Amity University, Noida, India

Seema Rawat
Amity University, Noida, India

Shabana Urooj
Princess Nourah Bint Abdulrahman University, Riyadh, Saudi Arabia

ABSTRACT

In India, the land of farmers, where agriculture has always been the primary occupation of the people, more than 50% of the population is still engaged in agriculture and its allied sectors. However, over the years, a significant decline has been observed in the contribution by the agriculture sector towards India's GDP. This chapter aimed towards identifying the gap between the ratio of high inputs and low yields by portraying the various limitations in traditional Indian agriculture methods and how hydroponic agriculture is the need of the hour for the growth of Indian agriculture. Hydroponic agriculture or hydroponics, around the world, has proved to be an efficient and more productive method of agriculture than geoponics (i.e., the traditional agriculture practice carried out in the soil). Although bearing a large bouquet of advantages, there are some limitations associated with it as well. This chapter aimed at overcoming these limitations to enhance this novel approach of agriculture even further.

INTRODUCTION

Hydroponics, or hydroponic agriculture (Pal, 2016), is the practice of growing crops in a solution me-

DOI: 10.4018/978-1-7998-8705-8.ch017

dium. The solution generally consists of water-based solvent with minerals, nutrients, and other organic components dissolved in it to support plant growth. Unlike traditional farming culture, hydroponics does not involve the use of soil, sand, gravel, and other similar mediums. Since, the nutrients and minerals are readily available for absorption by plants, the crop growth and yield are much higher compared to soil-based farming. Also, this method does not promote the use of commercial chemical fertilizers and pesticides. Rather, organic household and farm waste are used to maintain the nutrient balance of the solution. This organic approach gives the crops higher nutrition values. Hydroponics is also referred to as controlled environment agriculture (CEA), as it involves a very close monitoring of the environment aspects like pH and nutrient-levels of the solution, temperature, light, etc.

In traditional agriculture methodology i.e., the geoponics, the soil is the binding agent, which is used to hold and support the roots of the plant, so that the plant remains stable and firm. It entraps the water along with the dissolved minerals and nutrients between its particles so that the plant can absorb them through the process of translocation. Though the soil is the primary factor in the traditional agriculture, there are various problems associated with it, some of which are: infertility of soil, soil erosion accelerated by various factors, the existence of harmful pests affecting the growth of the plant, unwanted weeds that grow in the soil, and so on. Hydroponics, on the other hand, is the solution of most of the problems associated with the ongoing approach of agriculture. In hydroponics, the soil is replaced by water, and the entire farm is shifted from agricultural land to indoor grow-rooms, designed strategically for the purpose. Normally the grow-rooms are designed using PVC pipes which provide a channel for the water-based solution to be circulated in the setup. These pipes have holes carved into them, to hold the plants at equal distances. This method is called nutrient-film technique (NFT). Although there are other approaches as well, like static solution culture which uses rectangular tanks, NFT is the most preferred implementation of hydroponic agriculture.

Researchers and innovators around the world are trying to technically enhance the hydroponics methodology to enhance the yields further. For this, smart and sophisticated "grow-rooms" have been proposed and designed by integrating IT domain to this agriculture sector. Further, specialized hardware modules, wireless sensor networks, IoT applications, etc. have been proposed and developed to remotely monitor and control the setup and its environment to optimize the crop-growth and reduce manual labour requirements.

BACKGROUND

India is still chiefly an agrarian-based economy. Agriculture has been the primary occupation of Indian people since ancient times. However, this sector has not seen significant advancements on a very large scale. The technological advancements that have taken place in this sector are fairly less and the number of farmers aware and using these technologies is even lesser. Despite huge demand, farmers in India are not able to generate enough income for themselves. The crops are regularly marred by climatic factors, inadequate or over-irrigation, pest infestations, overuse of chemical fertilizers, etc. Though agriculture forms the backbone of Indian economy, its contribution to the GDP has been on a steep decline in the post-independence period, being 45.48% in FY 1950-51 to just 15.87% in FY 2018-19 which is clearly depicted in fig. 2. Moreover, the crop yields do not show any evident increase and sometimes it fails to even maintain a consistent graph in spite of the hard work put in by the farmers and plans introduced by the government. This is clearly shown by fig. 3.

Figure 1. A schematic representation of a hydroponic setup
[Source: https://offgridgorilla.com/off-grid-systems/food/hydroculture-hydroponics/]

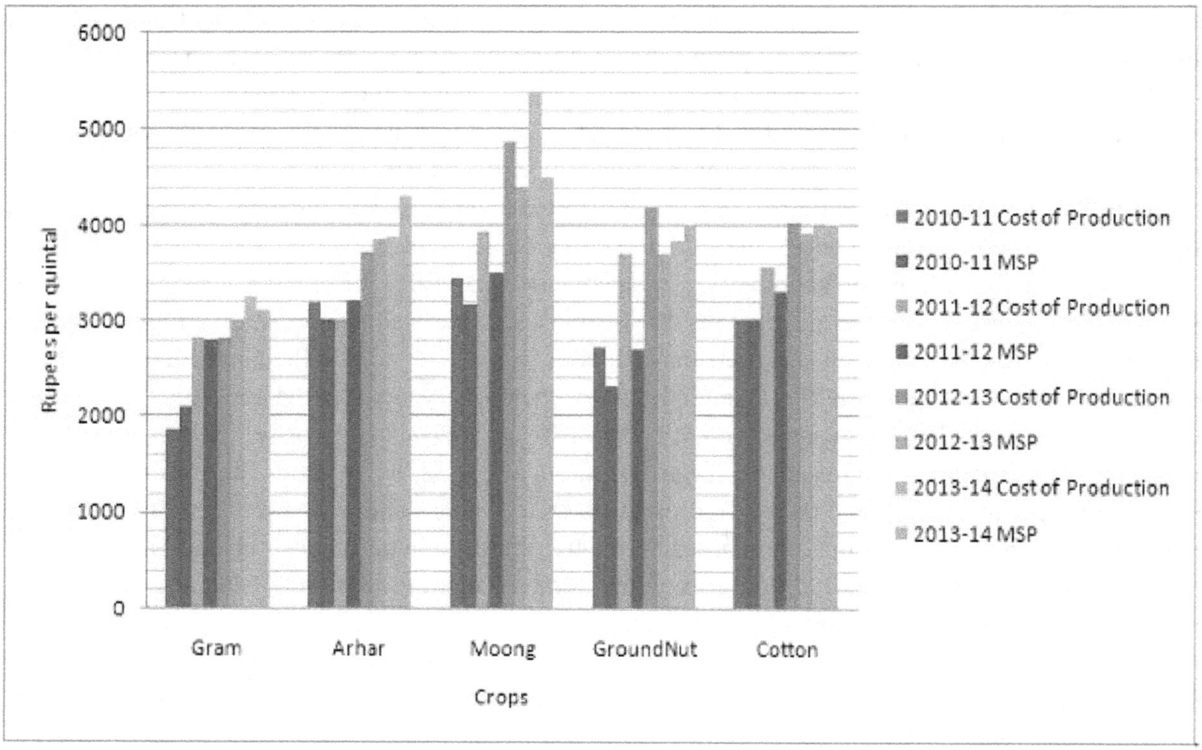

Further many farmers are forced to give up agriculture because of the low profits margin and very minimal and sometimes even negative difference in the minimum support price (MSP) and the cost of production of the crops as depicted by fig. 4. The urbanization process has further worsened the scenario by converting arable lands into concrete jungles.

Some of the factors that have restricted Indian farmers in meeting up with the market requirements and upgrading themselves with better technologies have been discussed below.

1. Uneducated Farmers: India's literacy rate is somewhat around 74%, which has seen a rise in recent years. Most of the farmers or laborers associated with agriculture are still uneducated and are dependent upon the techniques they acquired from their bloodline or adopted from neighbours, which in turn does not guarantee the appropriate or the most optimized agricultural techniques available. Lack of knowledge regarding the various techniques to replenish the fertility of soil, the types of fertilizers and pesticides, optimized amount of water that would be required to grow a particular crop, the plant which will be best suited for their soil are still some of the major challenges for them.
2. Green Revolution: Though it has been of great help to the agriculture industry, yet a large number of problems came with it, a large quantity of chemical fertilizers, inorganic manures, and irrigation facilities are required for higher yield. This is believed to be the reason for the development of hazardous weeds and insects around the fields.

Figure 2. Contribution of the agriculture sector to India's GDP over the years
[Source: statisticstimes.com]

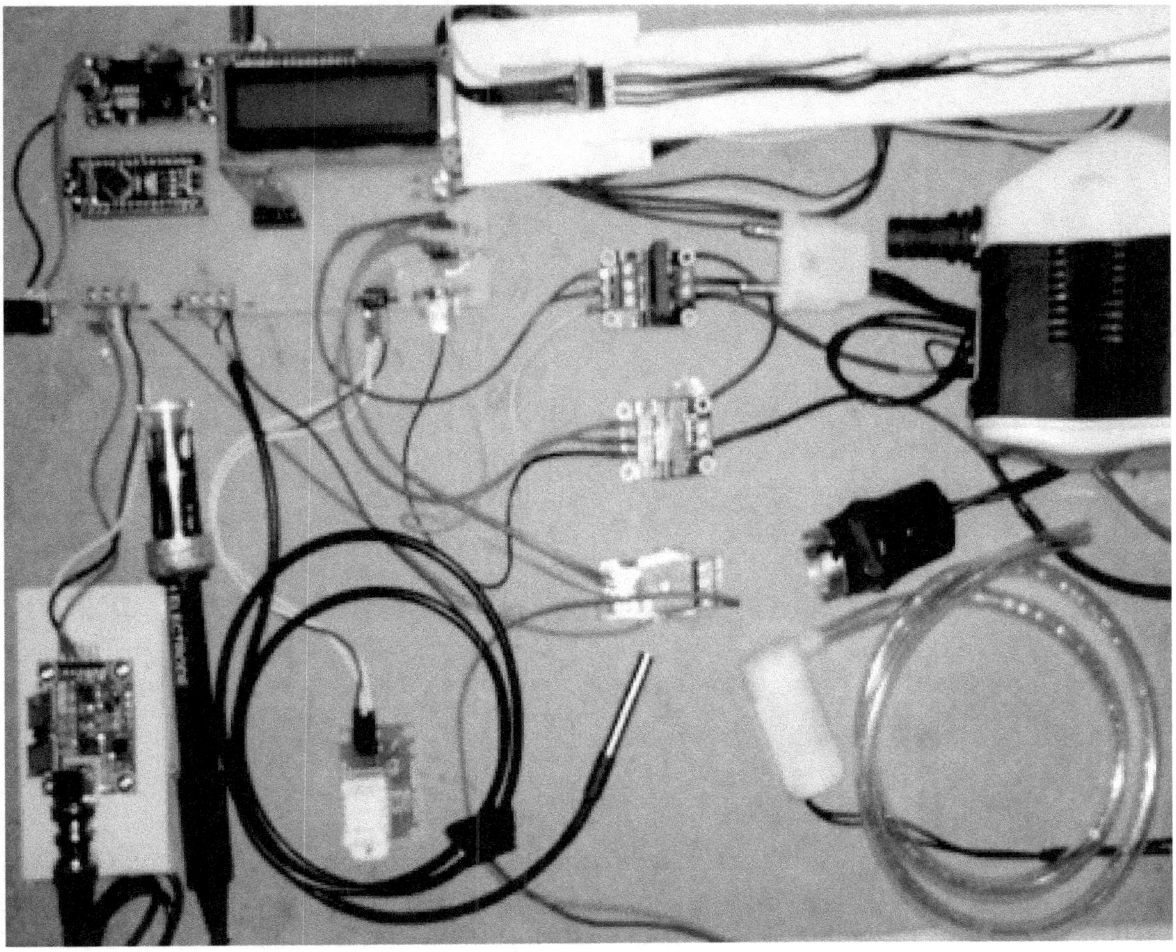

3. Dependency on monsoon: Since earlier times due to low irrigation supplies and facilities, a large population of farmers has always been dependent on monsoons which have never been steady. It varies season to season which has resulted in droughts in some areas while some areas saw a complete loss of cultivation for continuous years.
4. Outdated Technology: Though we are one of the tech-savvy giants, yet there are parts of India in the agriculture sector who haven't yet witnessed a combine in their tenure. This is because the machinery is really costly and poor farmers with little land find it useless to invest in such machinery, furthermore, no machinery is provided on a rental basis by the government to save time.
5. Limited Storage Facilities: If there are years where monsoon is favourable and there is a surplus in that year, the number of grains gets wasted due to the shortage of storage facilities. About 1.94 metric tons of grains were wasted from the year 2005-2013 as revealed by Food Corporation India against an RTI filed.

Figure 3. Crop yields during 2010 – 2014 [Source: Statistical yearbook India 2015 (MoSPI, GoI)]

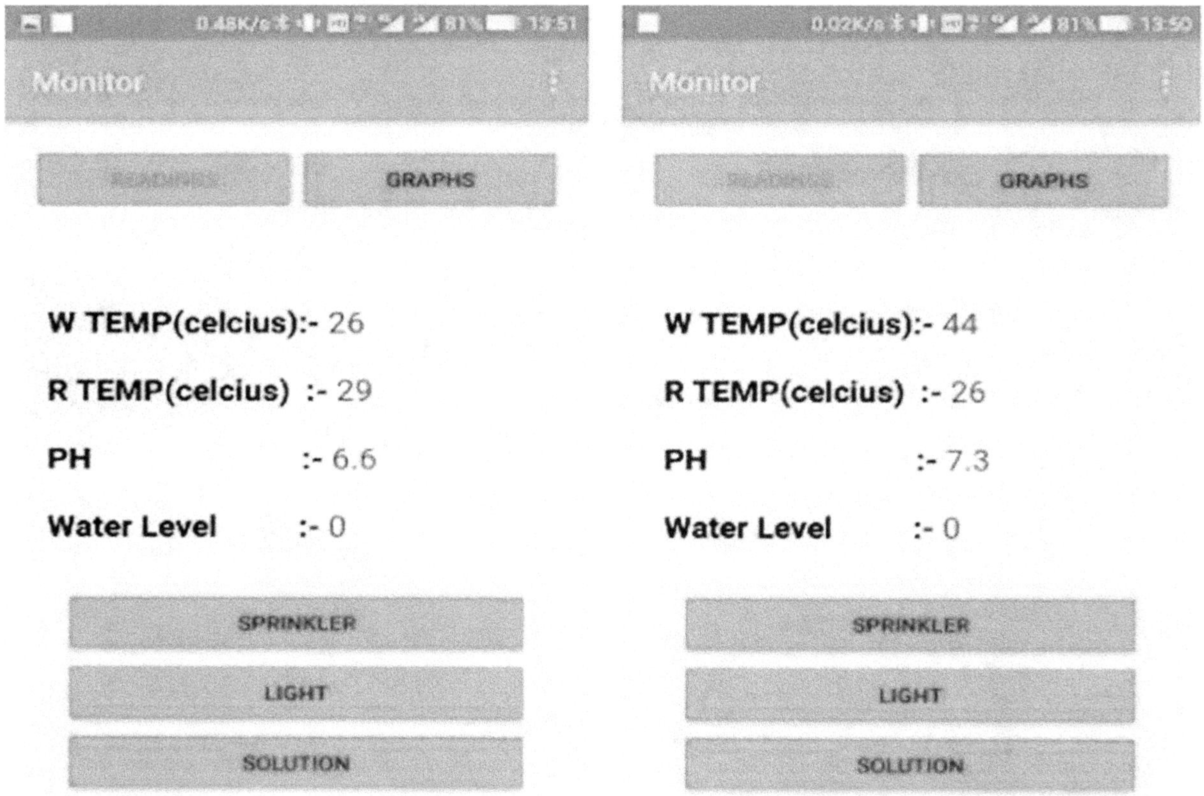

6. Unhealthy Government reforms: There are various reforms that the government introduces for the welfare of the farmers. On paper, they are definitely beneficial, but the ground reality is that farmers don't even get the promised MSP (minimum support price) which the government defines.

The rate at which the population and poverty in India are rising, soon we will be out of food to feed our population, and a large amount of population will be sleeping hungry or won't have adequate food to eat. Most of the crops and vegetables are grown in particular seasons only and then need to be stored in cold storage thus adding further to the costs.

Hydroponic agriculture provides an innovative approach in overcoming most of these limitations of traditional agriculture system. Being an approach of controlled environment agriculture (CEA), it offers an effective solution as its various parameters can be manually controlled or/and can be automated to various levels with latest innovations to obtain a higher yield. It is beneficial in the following ways:

1. It can be carried out even on barren and infertile land which gives India the biggest opportunity to use its wastelands in the states of Rajasthan and Gujarat for farming. More quantity of crops can be grown from the fixed area of land, as hydroponics can be practised in the multi-storey buildings and each floor acts as a separate piece of land.
2. The growth observed from the hydroponic agriculture is almost twice than that of normal agriculture thus the amount of produce obtained in a year will be far greater.

Figure 4. Comparison between cost of production and minimum support price for different crops during 2010 – 2014 [Source: Statistical year book India 2015 (MoSPI, GoI), farmer.gov.in]

3. In a country like India, agriculture is not learned in universities and colleges rather passed on in a hierarchical fashion, so the farmers have limited knowledge of growing plants and the cropping pattern depends upon particular seasons. Hydroponics gives the freedom to set up an artificial environment in which the particular crop can be grown throughout the year.
4. Since there is no soil, so there are no problems of soil-based diseases or growth of weed around the plant or breakout of pests and diseases which will affect the plant and being free from all these things there is no need spray pesticides on the plants.
5. Since there isn't any use of chemical fertilizers and pesticides, yields obtained from it are completely organic and rich in nutrients. Moreover, the crop health is also better comparatively.
6. Hydroponics being an indoor practice eliminates the risks of crop failures due to cattle and animal invasion into fields, pest infestations, natural calamities, etc.
7. India where there is a lot of scarcity of water and a large number of farmers still depend upon the rain and monsoon season for irrigating their crops, hydroponics can be a boon, as the amount of water required in the hydroponics is nearly 20 times lesser than the water required in the normal agriculture.
8. The cost of production is minimized by reducing the expenditure requirements on labour wages and chemical fertilizers. Since only scheduled monitoring and maintenance need to be done once in a while after the plants have been set up, thus it in turn, reduces the amount of labour required.

Figure 5. An implementation of NFT hydroponic setup

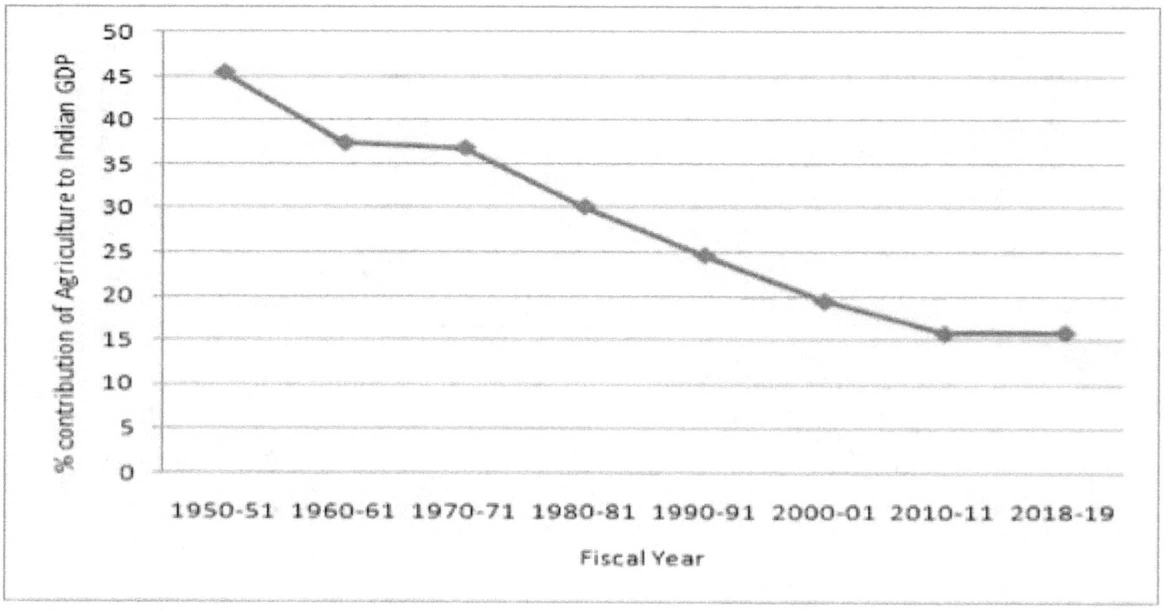

Despite having so many advantages, there are certain challenges associated with hydroponic agriculture as well, some of which are:

- Water-borne diseases can bring down the whole cultivation at once.
- There can be accelerating change in the nutrients' concentration present in the setup at any point in time.
- Need for an expert worker for looking after the surroundings.
- Initial setup costs.
- Selective absorption of the nutrients by plants.

Most of these challenges can be tackled by designing a dedicated monitoring system for the setup. The system will routinely monitor the setup's environment and adjust the parameters accordingly. The system will look after the whole environment and surroundings so that less skilled labour is needed, and the cost will come down by a certain factor. The environment can be adjusted according to the plant's needs based on the values defined in the system individually for each crop.

INTERNET OF THINGS (IOT)

We are talking about and aiming at developing an IoT based solution for the purpose of smart monitoring and control of a NFT hydroponic setup. Hence, we must first know the basic idea about the concept of Internet of Things i.e., IoT. This chapter will discuss about the IoT, its need, its benefits and limitations, and its application particularly in agriculture domain.

Internet of Things (IoT) may be regarded as the network of various interconnected physical objects which include - computing devices, digital devices, sensors, etc. which are connected via Internet, and are capable of collecting data and exchanging information within the network, without requiring much or any human interaction. The term IoT first came into existence in the year 1999. To connect various physical objects with each other, there is a need of network to exist. This could be any network either being a personal connection or a local area connection. But to utilize the collected data by one and all, the Internet is preferred as it is the largest and the fastest growing network. Over the last decade there is a sharp increase in the number of Internet users throughout the globe due to rapid increase in technology and rapidly decreasing prices of Internet usage. Hence the data can be shared really fast with any device lying anywhere across the globe. While the term 'object' can refer to any tangible and visible entity which can possibly cast its shadow, here the term specifically refers to any object around us having some kind of electronic circuit capable of generating or gathering data and transmitting it in form of signals.

Need for Internet of Things

In this world of fast-moving technologies and gadget development, with advancement in media technologies and easy access to internet, a large amount of population is wholly dependent on Internet as the source of information. This information may be used for making intelligent predictions, planning strategies, etc. and thus the reliability of this information becomes crucial. Due to human involvement in data capturing, the accuracy of data captured comes into question.

In the world where time means money, and where there is no room for the slightest of mistakes, there arises a need of usage of machines and intelligent sensors for capturing the data, thus increasing the accuracy, and decreasing the time required for data capturing and updating the pre-existing data available over the network. With the use of IoT devices data can be directly and effectively captured and can be directly uploaded in negligible time.

Benefits of Internet of Things

Implementing the concept of Internet of things has a multitude of advantages, some of which have been listed down below.

a. Saves time and resources: Due to the integration of devices over IoT, people don't need to manually operate each of the devices. Rather the devices based on their programming logics, function with partial or full automation, thus reducing the need for human efforts and other resources like time and money.
b. Quality of life: IoT helps us to create a better living lifestyle where we need not to be involved in much of the work manually.
c. Autonomous data processing: The process of collecting data results and formation of structured information which can be further utilized for the various purposes is done autonomously by the dedicated devices programmed specifically for the purpose.
d. Remote monitoring: With the presence of IoT, we need not to be present physically for the monitoring, analysis or control of a setup and its surroundings. It can be done remotely using sensors and mobile or web applications.

e. M2M communication: IoT enables communication amongst the devices across the globe due to its presence on the Internet. Since there is a machine-to-machine interaction there is not even the slightest chance of an error, and thus increases reliability and transparency in the information.

Limitations of Internet of Things

Despite being so advanced and beneficial, there are certain limitations associated with the concept of IoT.

f. Privacy concerns: The data has to be transmitted to the servers and has to be downloaded from the same when required, which increases the risk of losing privacy. It could lead to loss of personal data or its utilization by someone else without your permission.
g. Network dependency: IoT wholly depends upon the Internet or any other network and having no connectivity will dampen or collapse the entire system.
h. Complexity: IoT involves a complex network of devices, thus any sort of bugs found in the software or the hardware will have serious consequences on the entire system. Moreover, different manufacturers manufacturing various devices may have compatibility issues and may not be possible to connect with each other.
i. Less employment: With the devices doing all the work autonomously through communicating with each other, the requirement of human presence and manual efforts is reduced to a great extent, thus the employment opportunities get affected.

Applications of Internet of Things

IoT with its smart devices and reliable networking has found its application in diverse range of domains. From the development of smart cities, smart traffic management systems, and smart healthcare devices like Fitbits in urban sectors to the precise farming in rural areas, and weather monitoring systems for environmental purposes, IoT has integrated itself in almost every day-to-day area of our lives. However, our interest lies mainly in discussing its applications in agriculture sector to identify the positive outcomes that it can bring in agriculture sector.

Implementations of IoT in Traditional Soil-Based Agriculture

A number of small DIY IoT-based projects for soil-based agriculture i.e., geoponics can be found on the internet which helps in not only increasing the crop yields but also reduces the wastage of human efforts and resources in terms of time, money for fertilizers, etc., and also help in strategically planning the events during a crop cycle. This concept of implementing IoT into agriculture to make it more systematic and controlled is known as 'Precision Farming'. It involves the monitoring of soil, monitoring of crop growth, monitoring of livestock, identification of animal invasions into field, and monitoring of the weather conditions. Some of these systems have been briefly discussed below.

1. Smart irrigation system: In this system, soil humidity and moisture levels are kept in close check through dedicated sensors. Additionally, temperature sensors may also be integrated with the system. When the readings reach a critical value pre-specified in the system, the sensor sends signal to the microcontroller which in turn triggers pumps and sprinklers to balance out the water requirements.

The farmer is also notified through SMS or notifications as programmed. Excess irrigation is also avoided through such monitoring.

2. Smart crop protection system from animals: Animal invasion is one of the major causes for crop damage in India. This system uses motion sensors and cameras to identify animals approaching into the fields and sounds alarms to make the animals run away while sending alert notifications simultaneously to the farmer via a mobile application.
3. Plant disease detection robot (Farmaid): Developed by scientists at MIT, Farmaid is a self-driving robot equipped with cameras, sensors and microcontrollers that can identify the disease infestations in crops. It uses object detection and image processing techniques to identify the presence of disease in crops and generates SMS alerts for the users if the disease is found in number above threshold value.
4. Raspberry Pi based weather monitoring: This system monitors temperature, humidity, and rainfall, three of the important climatic factors having significant effect on the crops. The system constantly keeps analysing these parameters and notifying them to the farmer who can according plan the events in crop cycle and take necessary actions to enhance the crop yields.

LITERATURE REVIEW

As discussed in above, it is clear that Internet-of-Things has found positive usage in the traditional agriculture methods. IoT devices have been successfully integrated with geoponics i.e., soil-based agriculture to increase the crop yields. However, hydroponics, itself being a relatively new domain in agriculture, has been quite less explored in terms of innovations and integration of ICT applications with it. Further this chapter will discuss about some of the latest technologies and innovations that have been proposed or implemented to upgrade regular hydroponic farms to smart hydroponic farms.

Researchers and scientists have observed that although the yields of hydroponic setups are higher than that from traditional farming, clearly depicted in table 1, developing smart and sophisticated grow-rooms can enhance the productivity to even greater extent. These grow-rooms are equipped with IT enabled devices like IOT sensors, microcontrollers, wireless networks, and mobile applications that help to remotely monitor and control the environment parameters of the setup. Through this constant monitoring and control, favourable conditions are provided to the crops which results in their higher growth, better health, and higher nutrition values. This is clearly evident from the table 2 given below.

(Nishimura, Okuyama & Matsushita, 2016) developed a sensor module based on simple oscillator circuits. The module was designed to be compatible with Arduino microcontroller and had the ability to measure the nutrient concentration and electrical conductivity (EC) of the water-based solution used in hydroponic setup. (Andaluz, Tovar & Bedon, 2016) used vernier sensors to monitor pH, EC, moisture, and temperature, and developed a control mechanism for drip irrigation of Daniela tomato crop in a hydroponic environment.

(Ruengittinun, Phongsamsuan & Sureeratanakorn, 2017) designed a hydroponic farming ecosystem (HFE) for farmers with relatively less knowledge. The HFE is basically an integration of IOT sensors coupled with Arduino to remotely monitor and control the parameters like water flow, temperature, and pH of the setup. It has capabilities of generating alarm notifications and autonomously triggering control measures if any critical change is observed in the parameters. (Peuchpanngarm, Srinitiworawong, Samerjai & Sunetnanta, 2016) designed a mobile application integrated with sensors to achieve automa-

Table 1. Comparison of yields in soil-based agriculture and hydroponic agriculture, based on case study in Bengal [9]

Crop	Soil Average Per Acre	Hydroponic Equivalent Per Acre
Beetroot	9,500 lb.	20,000 lb.
Cabbage	13,000 lb.	18,000 lb.
Cauliflower	15,000-35,000 lb.	30,000 lb.
Cucumber	7,000 lb.	28,000 lb.
Lettuce	9,000 lb.	21,000 lb.
Maize	1,500 lb.	8,000 lb.
Okra	5,000- 10,000 lb.	19, 000 lb.
Potatoes	8 tons	70 tons
Peas	25,000 lb.	140,000 lb.
Rice	750-900 lb.	12,000 lb.
Soya beans	600 lb.	1,500 lb.
Tomatoes	5-10 tons	180 tons
Wheat	5,600 lb.	8,000 lb.

tion in control of hydroponics. The application included features to read data through sensors, manage them and plan the harvest accordingly. The system architecture is based on raspberry platform and data is maintained in the cloud. (Crisnapati, Wardana, Aryanto & Hermawan, 2017) developed Hommons, a web-based application to remotely monitor and manage a NFT hydroponic farm. The hardware components of Hommons are powered by solar energy. (Umamaheshwari, Preethi, Pravin & Dhanusha, 2016) discussed a system aimed at integrating IOT sensors to achieve scheduled working and monitoring of hydroponic setup through automation. The system used the concepts of embedded systems. (Helmy, Mahaidayu, Nursyahid, Setyawan & Hasan, 2017) designed a wireless sensor network to remotely monitor a hydroponic setup implementing nutrient film technique (NFT) approach. The system used 5 sensors that analyze the hydroponic setup with main focus on nutrient concentrations in terms of pH and EC and examines the growth of lettuce plant in the setup with the changes in the nutrient values. (Manju, Karthik, Hariharan & Sreekar, 2017) discussed a system with 5 sensors for measuring temperature, pH,

Table 2. Comparison of produces of lettuce in smart and regular hydroponic agriculture [16]

Feature	Regular Farm	Smart Farm	Change (%)
Plant height (cm.)	22.45	14.23	-36.60
Plant width (cm.)	15.40	14.23	-7.54
Stem diameter (mm.)	0.60	0.68	13.90
Number of leaf	23.00	26.96	17.20
Leaf area (cm.^{2})	67.89	65.11	-4.10
Total fresh weight (g.)	50.26	68.65	36.59
Nitrate content (mg./kg.)	3485.22	3198.18	-8.24

ammonia, water level and moisture in an aquaponic setup, which is a variation of hydroponic agriculture. Aquaponics utilizes wastewater from fish tanks as the solution for hydroponics setup as it already contains the necessary nutrients. The sensors were integrated with LumisenseIOT board to collect and save data over internet for future analysis. (Siregar, Efendi, Pranoto & Ginting, 2017) designed a web-based application for remote monitoring of hydroponic system based on Libelium's Open Garden hydroponics kit using integration of various sensors, Open Garden modules and Arduino Uno.

(Melvix & Sridevi, 2014) identified technical faults to be the most critical hurdles in large-scale implementation of hydroponic agriculture. They proposed an algorithm based on fuzzy inference system for the purpose of grading of solution in a hydroponic setup. The system parameters were optimized using genetic algorithms and the algorithm simulation was done through Matlab and LabView. The outcomes achieved were in form of higher resource utilization and better convergence efficiency. (Yolanda, Hindersah, Hadiatna & Triawan, 2016) proposed 12 inference rules of fuzzy logic to control the pH and EC of the solution in hydroponic setup. The fuzzy control method controlled a number of tanks containing different nutrient solutions to be discharged into the system as required, to maintain the chemical composition of the solution flowing in the setup.

SYSTEM DESIGN

The contrived monitoring system basically includes five components: sensors, actuators, microcontroller, Bluetooth, and mobile application. There are sensors to measure the pH, room temperature and temperature of the solution flowing in the setup. These parameters are very significant for plant health and growth and hence these need to be monitored constantly. Additionally, there is a water level sensor to identify the level of solution flowing in setup. All of the sensors are integrated with an Arduino microcontroller which coordinates with the Android application by sending the data to it through a Bluetooth module. The application allows users to access the data generated by sensors, visualize them in form of graph over a period of time, and generates alert notifications if the pH and room temperature rise above or fall below a certain limit. Additionally, the microcontroller is able to control the parameters through actuators triggered from the mobile application. There is a sprinkler system to control the rise in room temperature, a light bulb to control the drop in room temperature and also provide an alternative for daylight to extend the photosynthesis period of plants, and a pump to discharge buffer solution to maintain the pH of the solution flowing in the setup.

Tools and Technologies

In this section, authors discuss about the tools and technologies used to develop this system.

1. Arduino

Arduino is one of the most popular platforms for developing small circuit-based projects and prototypes. Its popularity lies in its versatile range of hardware compatible to each other and easy-to-program software. Arduino platform includes its family of microcontrollers that come in various sizes and processing capabilities. Arduino microcontroller boards can be understood as simple computers that have been reduced down to the size of small circuits on a single board with an embedded processor to perform

Figure 6. Schematic diagram of the developed monitoring system

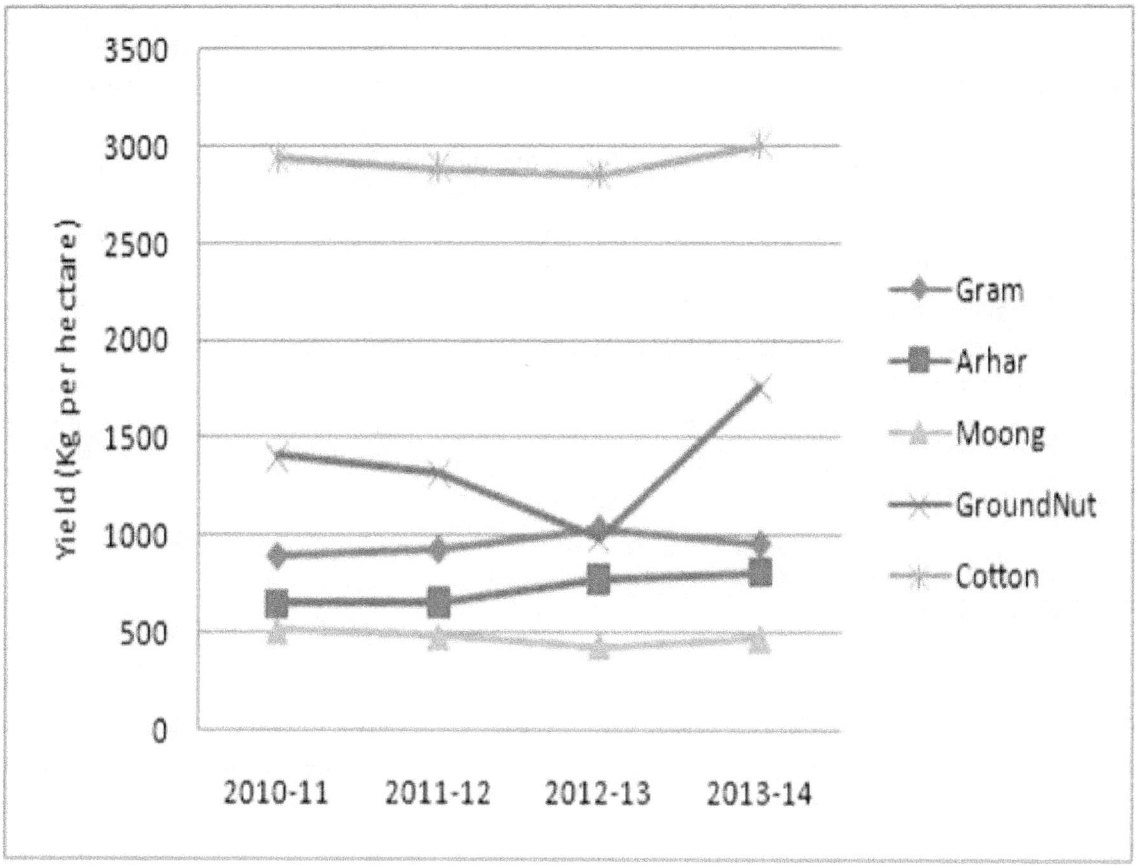

the operations. Its success lies in the fact that it is an open-source platform which implies that any help required with coding is easily available online. Further it is compatible with large number of electric and electronic components and hence can be used to develop entirely different circuits for a variety of purposes very easily. Most of the Arduino boards use Atmel AVR processors which are also used in ATmega microcontrollers. Arduino programming is done with embedded C language, which is an extension of tradition C programming language.

Arduino microcontrollers support analog as well as digital values due to dedicated pins available for the purpose. Arduino boards come with following onboard chip functions.

a. Power supply: Arduino boards are powered through USB jacks or specialized power supply called Barrel Jack. The same jack can be used to transfer code to the microcontroller. The preferred voltage range for input current supply is 5-12 volts.
b. Reset: Reset button is used to restart the Arduino microcontroller and thus restart the code execution in case of unexpected crash or error in code execution when the circuit development is in process.
c. Power indicator: An onboard LED is provided on the Arduino board that starts glowing when power is supplied to the Arduino board and its starts executing the resident code.

d. IC: The IC or the processor can be referred to as the brain of the Arduino where the code is stored, and the processing takes place.

2. Arduino IDE

Arduino IDE is an integrated platform for writing and uploading codes to the Arduino microcontrollers. It is a free to use software that can be downloaded from www.arduino.cc/main/ software. It has been developed in Java language and hence is platform independent implying that it is compatible with Windows, Mac, and Linux operating systems alike. It supports writing code in C, C++, and Embedded C programming languages. Although developed for Arduino platform, it also supports other microcontrollers developed by third-party. Developers can directly start coding once it installed. Two main segments that must be explicitly defined in the code are setup () and loop () methods for the Arduino board to function properly. For uploading the code to Arduino board, one needs to install CH340 driver files which is an USB to serial driver for transferring the code from PC / laptop to the Arduino via an USB channel. The Arduino IDE used for programming the hardware in this project is version 1.8.9.

3. Android

Android is Linux-based, free and open-source mobile operating system platform. Initially designed for smartphones, today Android finds its usage in many other devices like tablets, smart watches, smart TVs etc. It is one of the most popular and successful mobile OS owing to the fact that it offers a unified approach for application development. This implies that developer just needs to design applications for Android and the application can be readily installed and used in all Android compatible devices. First developed in 2005 by a start-up, Android platform is now owned by Google and has several versions, the latest one being Android 9.0 code named Pie, released in August 2018, with Android 10.0 development in progress. The Android OS architecture has been divided into four layers and five sections, namely:

a. Linux Kernel: It forms the core of the Android operating system.
b. Libraries: It includes the libraries that define the basic functionalities of Android like SQLite for database, Web Kit for web browsing, etc.
c. Android runtime: It includes the core libraries written in java for the purpose of application development. It also includes a dedicated virtual machine designed specifically for Android to give optimized performance in low-power devices.
d. Application framework: It includes the different capabilities of Android for the use of developers such as Layout manager, Resource manager, Activity manager, etc.
e. Applications: It includes the applications that come built-in with the device like Phone, Contacts, Browser, Play Store, etc.

Being an open-source platform, Android is open to various customizations in its configuration depending upon the need. Some of the features that make Android popular among its users are:

a. Storage: Integrated with SQLite, a lightweight SQL based database, Android provides optimized data storage and retrieval.

b. Connectivity: Android supports multiple mobile connectivity technologies including GSM, EDGE, CDMA, UMTS, Wi-Fi, LTE, Bluetooth and others.
c. Media support: Android has in-built support for multiple file formats for documents, videos, audios, pictures including PNG, GIF, JPEG, MP4, Ogg Vorbis, PDF, DOCX, AMR, MIDI, etc.
d. Hardware support: Android supports various types of hardware and sensors embedded into them like accelerometer, light sensor, touch sensor, proximity sensor, camera, GPS and much more.
e. Tethering: It supports sharing of Internet data among devices via wired/ wireless hotspot.

Developing an Android application is very easy. A basic program requires developing and modifying only three files, which are: java file for defining the functioning of the activity, layouts file for defining the appearance of the activity, and Android Manifest file which is an xml file that defines the app permissions, flow of control, intent-filters, etc.

Android Studio is the official development platform supported by Google for developing Android applications. Based on JetBrains' IntelliJ IDEA software, it is an integrated development environment implying that it contains all features required to develop an application in a single platform be it writing code, testing, and refactoring the code, emulating the code over different APIs, and building the APK file for application deployment. Android Studio is a dynamic and interactive platform in the sense it can detect errors in the code and also provide possible suggestions to rectify them. It is easy to use for even beginners as it doesn't require to code everything explicitly like the layout of activities can be designed in GUI approach rather than hard coding the individual layout files. It is compatible with Windows, Mac and Linux based operating systems and is free to use. It can be downloaded from developer.android.com / studio. Its popularity can be observed from the fact that it has completely replaced Eclipse ADT as the primary IDE for android application development.

4. Bluetooth

Bluetooth is a close-range, wireless signal transmission technology developed in 1989. The popularity of Bluetooth lies in its capability of creating small personal area networks (PAN) by pairing different types of electronic devices like laptops, phones, speakers, and other circuits having integrated Bluetooth transceiver device. Bluetooth operates through UHF radio waves in the frequency band of 2.400 – 2.485 GHz. Bluetooth implements packet-based protocol where data transmission takes place in master / slave architecture.

Bluetooth serial port profile / protocol (SPP) is a Bluetooth transmission standard that establishes a serial, transparent connection between the paired devices. It is one of the fundamental and initial standards implemented by Bluetooth technology to perform serial transmission. The transmission performed using serial port profile imitates the functioning of wired RS232 cable transmissions where the devices send and receive data as if physical Tx and Rx lines connect them. Serial Port Profile enables enhanced data rate (EDR) allowing transmission data rate to be 2-3 Mbit per second. Our project uses HC05 Bluetooth module with SPP to establish data connectivity between the hardware module and mobile application.

5. Firebase

Firebase is a cloud-hosted database platform developed by Google for mobile application platforms like Android, iOS, and others. It is a free to use, backend as a service technology that enables mobile application developers to create a database for their application in a secure and scalable manner. Firebase is a NoSQL based database that operates in real-time which implies any changes in data gets automatically synchronized to the server within moments. When the device in which the application resides is connected to the Internet, the data gets updated instantly, whereas in the offline state, the data is stored locally on the client device and gets updated as soon as connected to the Internet. Firebase is capable of generating messages, mails, and notifications for multiple platforms through its Firebase cloud messaging. Firebase Cloud Fire store, the next generation database platform to the original Firebase database system was released in January 2019. Since Firebase is a Google product, one just needs to login to his Google account to start using it. In our project, Firebase backend has been used for authenticating user login and to save alert notifications generated over time.

SYSTEM IMPLEMENTATION

The system has been implemented in two parts: hardware module and mobile application, both of which communicate over Bluetooth technology to realize a system with routine monitoring and partially automated control capabilities.

Hardware Module

The hardware module is an integration of four sensors and three actuators with an Arduino microcontroller. The hardware module resides physically with the NFT hydroponic setup and keeps monitoring the setup parameters through its sensors and transmitting the data to the mobile application. The actuators serve the purpose of controlling the parameters when they get triggered from the mobile application. The hardware components along with their use and description have been listed down below.

1. Power Supply: The entire hardware circuit is powered by 12 V - 2 Amp Direct Current (DC) through an AC-DC supply adaptor which converts the 220 V AC supply into DC for functioning of the Arduino circuit.
2. Step-down converter: The LM2596 series DC-DC step-down buck converter steps down the 12 V DC supply to 5 V DC supply as mentioned in the operational specifications of the Arduino board and sensors used. The LM2596 is an easy-to-use converter working with a switching frequency of 150 kHz and efficiency as high as 92%. It ensures that the input current supply doesn't damage the microcontroller and the sensors.
3. Arduino microcontroller: This is the main component of the hardware module as it controls and coordinates all other components. The microcontroller used in the project is Arduino Nano board. It has an embedded ATmega 328 P-AU processor with 16 MHz CPU speed. It has same processing capabilities as that of much popular version Arduino Uno but is much smaller in size making it preferable when complex circuits are to be implemented in smaller sizes. The Arduino Nano board holds the code which reads all the data through the sensors, transmits to the application, displays on the LCD and triggers the relays.
4. pH sensor: The E201 BnC general-purpose pH probe has been integrated with the Arduino Nano to monitor the pH level of the water-based solution flowing in the setup. The pH reading gives an overview about the nutrient concentrations in the solution. The probe is first calibrated using two

standard solutions of pH 4.1 and 9.2 respectively. The probe is connected with an Op-Amp circuit which converts its analog readings to digital readings and sends them to the Arduino. The probe is completely submersible in water and starts giving stable pH readings after 2-3 minutes when kept submerged in the solution.

5. Room temperature sensor: The DHT22 room temperature and humidity sensor is a small, easy to use and efficient sensor for measuring room temperature. This sensor has been installed to check the temperature from rising very high or falling very low and alert the user accordingly as the atmospheric temperature has a significant impact on the plant growth and health. The DHT22 gives digital outputs and requires no prior calibration i.e., can be used directly after connecting.
6. Water temperature sensor: The DS18B20 is a waterproof temperature sensor that has been used to monitor the temperature of solution flowing in the setup. It can be kept submerged in water completely. Similar to DHT22, it gives digital outputs and requires no prior calibration.
7. Water level sensor: The water level sensor is an analog sensor that operates on the conductivity of water. The sensor includes five wires: four level wires and a ground wire. The level of water is identified on the basis of the wire conducting current through it by completing the circuit with ground wire through the water. The sensor can identify 5 level of water through L0 (empty) to L4 (full). The sensor is used to monitor the water level available in the setup.
8. Bluetooth: The HC05 Bluetooth module has been integrated with the Arduino to enable data transmission between the hardware and the mobile application. HC05 Bluetooth module implements serial port protocol (SPP) which enables 3 Mbps modulation with complete 2.4 GHz radio transceiver and baseband. It establishes a transparent serial connection between the hardware and the mobile application for the exchange of sensor data and trigger commands for the relays.
9. LCD: A 16*2 LCD screen has also been connected to the Arduino to display the readings at the setup itself. The LCD can display two lines of text with 16 characters per line. It is a simple display module that finds its usage in a wide range of applications, particularly in IoT circuits due to its cheap pricing and easily programmable nature with ability to display even custom characters.
10. Relays: The relays are simply switching to on/off the actuators (electric components / loads) through programming logic. There are three relays in the hardware module: two solid state relays (SSRs) for AC loads and one simple relay for DC load. The SSRs have semiconductor-based circuits embedded in them which enable them to operate under AC current. The SSRs have a separate AC input supply of 220 V for operating the AC loads along with the DC input from the Arduino to receive trigger commands. The DC relay operates the load directly from the 12 V DC supply input to the circuit from the adaptor.
11. Submersible motors: Two water submersible motors have been connected in the hardware module, one 220 V AC motor connected to one of the SSRs and one 12 V DC water motor connected to the DC relay. The AC motor is used for a sprinkler system by connecting a pipe and a shower to it to sprinkle water over the plants in case the temperature rises very rapidly. The motor can pump water up to a height of 2 meters. The AC motor is switched on/off from the mobile application. The DC motor is connected to be submerged in a container filled with buffer solution to discharge in the setup in case the pH value drops significantly. The DC motor is switched on from the mobile application and it automatically switches off itself after operating for 1 second thus discharging about 10 mL of the buffer solution into the setup at a time.
12. Light bulb and holder: A light bulb holder have been connected to one of the SSRs to fix a halogen bulb which will act as a sunlight substitute. It can be switched on during night to extend the pho-

tosynthesis process and also if the temperature falls down rapidly it can be switched on to provide heat for the plants.

Figure 7. Circuit diagram of the hardware module

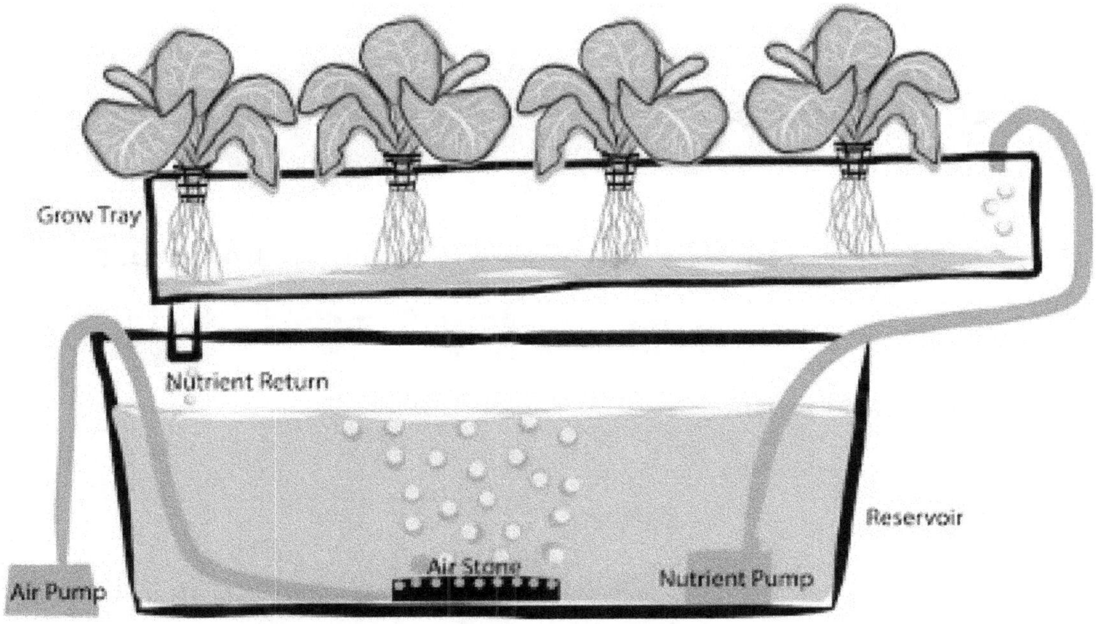

Mobile Application

The mobile application provides the users an interface to get the real-time readings from the setup as well as provides control to trigger the actuators. The primary idea behind the application is to create a user-friendly environment that makes it easy for users to receive and analyse the data in timely fashion and carry out required actions as the variables change in the setup's surroundings. The application consists of various different activities which are discussed as follows:

1. Login: The Login activity contains fields for entering username (email id) and password. It also has functionalities for signing up a new user and link for Forgot Password activity. The data entered is validated with the database existing online in Firebase and on successful authentication the user gets logged in otherwise the application displays 'authentication failed' message.
2. Forgot Password: The Forgot Password activity allows users to enter his email id. If the email id already exists in the database, an email is sent to the provided email id with a reset password link.
3. Home: The Home activity contains a welcome message and a navigation menu for the users to explore different activities. The navigation menu also contains a log out functionality. On clicking the 'Go' button available in the Home, the list of available Bluetooth devices is displayed where the user can choose the HC05 option to connect with the hardware.
4. Monitor: The Monitor activity display the data received from the sensors in a formatted manner. The readings get updated every 2 seconds via Bluetooth connection. Additionally, there are three

Figure 8. Assembled hardware module

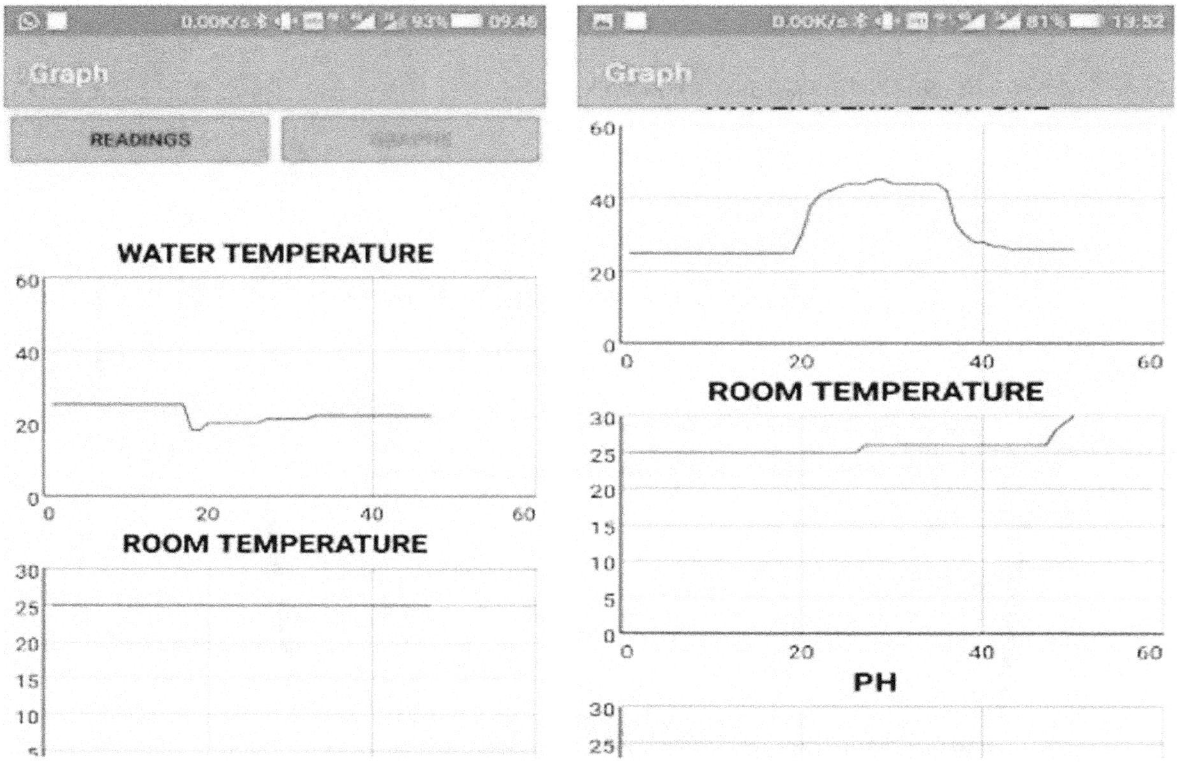

buttons for the three relays respectively, clicking on which generates the trigger commands that are transmitted to the Arduino via Bluetooth.

5. Graphs: The Graph activity shows graphical plots of the readings for pH, room temperature, water temperature and water level over a period of time. Due to the application's memory constraints, currently the plotting is done for readings obtained during last one minute.
6. Notifications: The Notifications activity shows the list of notifications that have been generated in the past. Notifications are generated when the pH values and the room temperature values rise above or fall below a critical limit. The notifications are stored in a file in the database created in Firebase. The notifications are saved with the date and time they were generated along with the notification message and the corresponding parameter's value at that time. The activity retrieves the file from the Firebase and displays the past notifications.
7. Plant Info: The Plant Info activity displays the pH and EC requirements of 15 different plants that can be grown in a hydroponics setup. The information is displayed in the form of a static table for the user to get an idea about the nutrient concentration levels that must be maintained in the solution flowing in the setup.

Figure 9. Screenshots of the mobile application showing positive testing for variations in the water temperature, room temperature and pH values

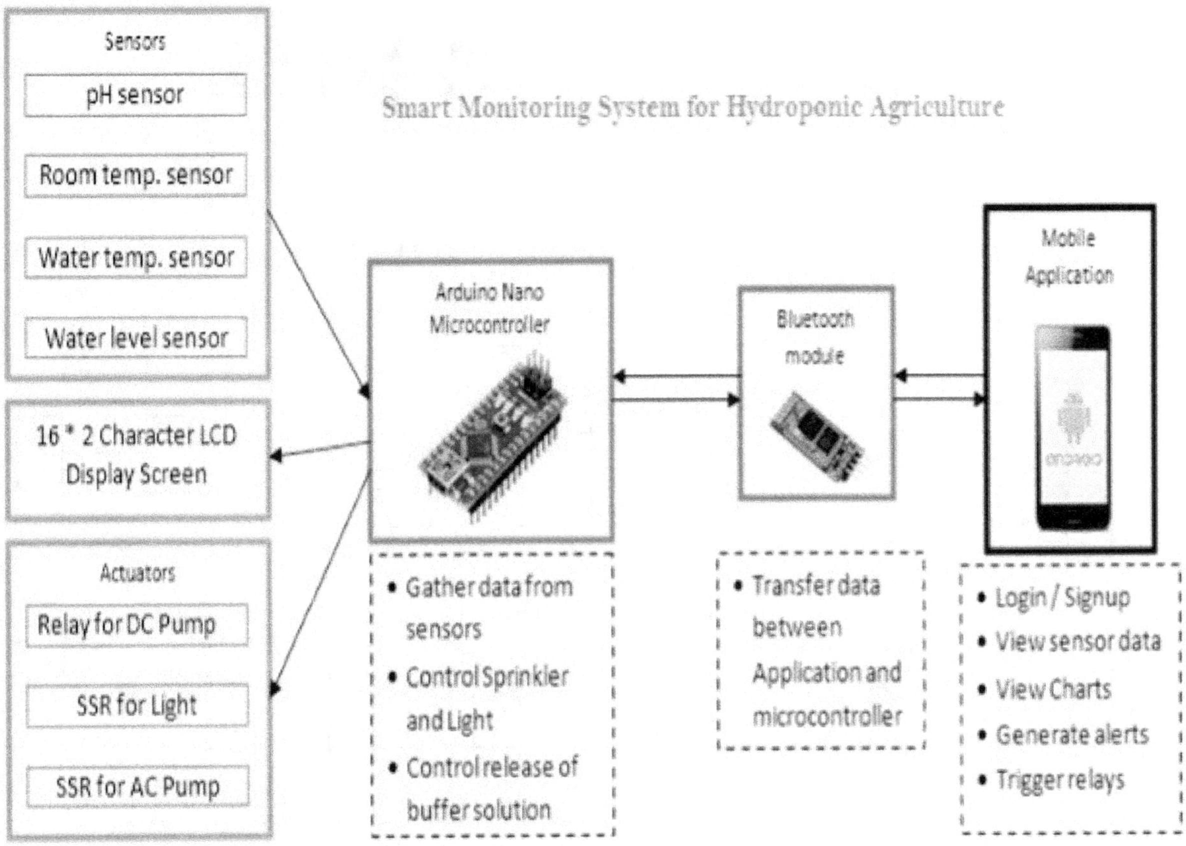

RESULTS AND DISCUSSIONS

The monitoring system has been developed and successfully integrated with the NFT hydroponics setup shown in figure 11.

LIMITATIONS

Although the developed project meets the initial project plan and requirements specification and has been positively tested for working as per the expectations, yet the system has some constraints that it needs to overcome in future for better performance. These constraints have been identified below.

1. Close range connectivity: Due to the implementation of Bluetooth module for data transmission between the hardware and the mobile application, the system is bound to a pre-defined close range for operation. In other words, remote monitoring capability is not present in the current model developed.

Figure 10. Screenshots of the mobile application showing positive testing for Graph activity for plotting the variations in the water and room temperature readings

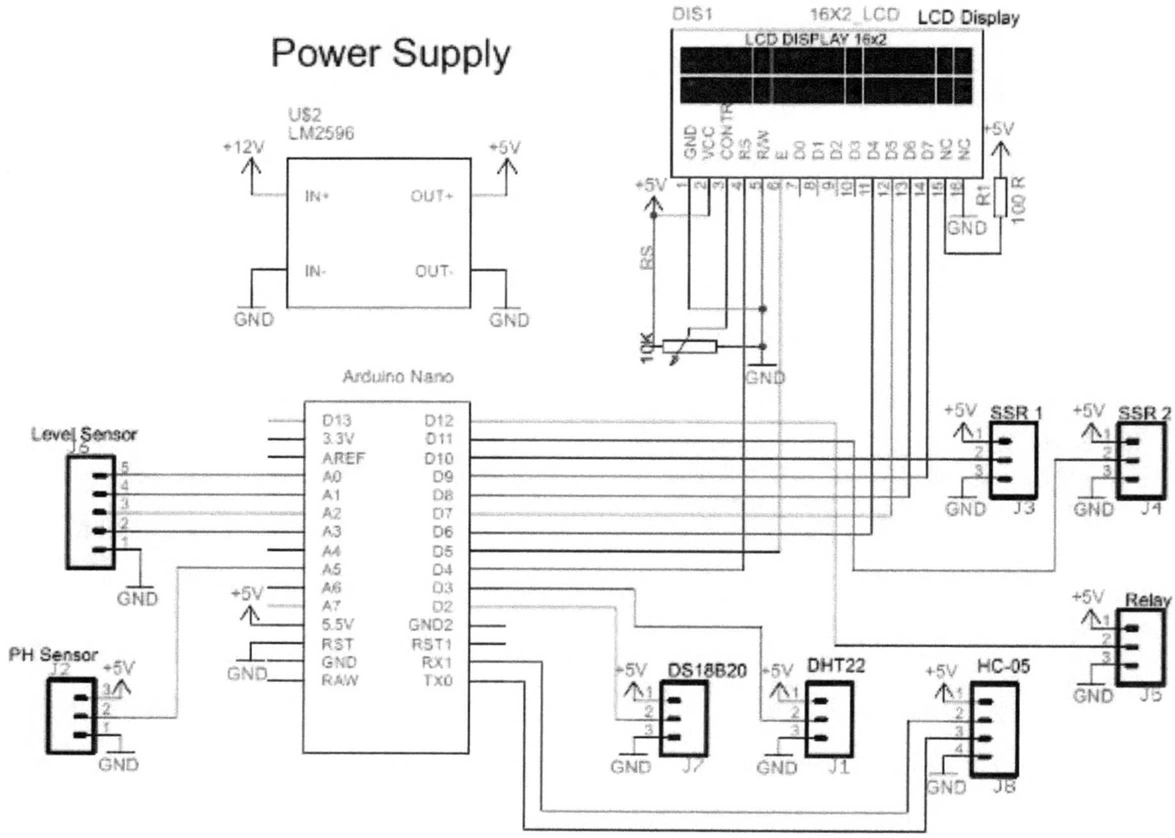

2. Partly autonomous: The control of the setup parameters is partially automated only in the sense that it needs the user to trigger the actuators by clicking corresponding buttons in the mobile application. The system isn't fully automated as it cannot trigger the actuators on its own even when it is sensing alerts for critical values.
3. Pre-defined critical values for parameters: The critical values for generating alert notifications have been hard coded into the mobile application's program i.e., it is specified by the developer and cannot be changed dynamically during runtime. Different crops have different pH and temperature requirements, but the project doesn't have the feature to individually identify the crops in the setup and adjust the critical values accordingly. Rather the average value specified in the program is used for checking critical limits.
4. No feature for analysing plant growth: Although the parameters being monitored have been strategically selected on the basis of their significant role in the growth of plant in a hydroponics environment, the plant growth itself cannot be monitored by the system. The project scope has no parameters specified for the system on the basis of which plant growth can be tracked and analysed in a scheduled manner.

Figure 11. Crops showing significantly higher growth and better health due to integration of smart monitoring and control system

Table 3. Comparison of existing applications (available on Google Play Store) and solution developed

	Existing Applications	Developed Solution
Type	Mobile applications	Mobile application integrated with sensors to implement IoT-based system
Features	• Calculation of pH, EC and nutrient requirements for the plant growth based on crop. • Logging and planning of events during the crop growth cycle.	• Real-time monitoring of parameter changes in the setup through sensors. • Visual analysis of variations in parameters through graphs. • Generation of alert notifications in case of rapid/ critical change in parameters. • Calculation of pH and EC requirements. • Triggering relays for controlling parameter changes.
Setup Control	Completely manual	Partially automated

CONCLUSION

Authors have identified hydroponics to be a feasible and promising alternative to overcome the shortcomings of traditional farming methods, particularly in the Indian context. The research works and current innovations being carried out across the globe to enhance this technique by automating it through its integration with the field of Information technology. The solution developed has been successful in monitoring the parameters of the hydroponic setup available and has helped in bringing out better outcomes in terms of plant growth and better planning of activities involved in the crop cycle. Further this system can be used to carry out a comparative study of the results in crop yield, health, and nutrition values between two hydroponic setups, one integrated with the solution i.e., a smart setup and one without it i.e., a regular setup.

REFERENCES

Andaluz, V. H., Tovar, A. Y., Bedón, K. D., Ortiz, J. S., & Pruna, E. (2016). Automatic control of drip irrigation on hydroponic agriculture: Daniela tomato production. *2016 IEEE International Conference on Automatica (ICA-ACCA)*, 1-6. 10.1109/ICA-ACCA.2016.7778389

Changmai, T., Gertphol, S., & Chulak, P. (2018). Smart Hydroponic Lettuce Farm using Internet of Things. *2018 10th International Conference on Knowledge and Smart Technology (KST),* 231-236.

Crisnapati, P. N., Wardana, I. N. K., Aryanto, I. K. A. A., & Hermawan, A. (2017). Hommons: Hydroponic management and monitoring system for an IOT based NFT farm using web technology. *2017 5th International Conference on Cyber and IT Service Management,* 1-6. 10.1109/CITSM.2017.8089268

Helmy, M. G., Mahaidayu, A., Nursyahid, T. A., Setyawa, & Hasan, A. (2017). Nutrient Film Technique (NFT) hydroponic monitoring system based on wireless sensor network. *2017 IEEE International Conference on Communication, Networks and Satellite (Comnetsat)*, 81-84.

Hydroponic Vegetable Production – Guide(2017Department of Agriculture, Forestry and Fisheries, Republic of South Africa.

Lenord Melvix, J. S. M., & Sridevi, C. (2014). Design of efficient hydroponic nutrient solution control system using soft computing-based solution grading. *2014 International Conference on Computation of Power, Energy, Information and Communication (ICCPEIC)*, 148-154.

Manju, M., Karthik, V., Hariharan, S., & Sreekar, B. (2017). Real time monitoring of the environmental parameters of an aquaponic system based on Internet of Things. *2017 Third International Conference on Science Technology Engineering & Management (ICONSTEM)*, 943-948.

Nishimura, T., Okuyama, Y., Matsushita, A., Ikeda, H., & Satoh, A. (2017). A compact hardware design of a sensor module for hydroponics. *2017 IEEE 6th Global Conference on Consumer Electronics (GCCE)*, 1-4. 10.1109/GCCE.2017.8229255

Pal, S. (2016). *Growing Soil-Less with Hydroponics: An Introduction to Innovative Farming at Home*. The Better India.

Pandey, R., Jain, V., Pandey, K. S. R., & Singh, K. P. (2009). *Hydroponics Agriculture: Its Status, Scope and Limitations*. Division of Plant Physiology, Indian Agricultural Research Institute.

Peuchpanngarm, C., Srinitiworawong, P., Samerjai, W., & Sunetnanta, T. (2016). DIY sensor-based automatic control mobile application for hydroponics. *2016 Fifth ICT International Student Project Conference (ICT-ISPC)*, 57-60. 10.1109/ICT-ISPC.2016.7519235

Ruengittinun, S., Phongsamsuan, S., & Sureeratanakorn, P. (2017). Applied internet of thing for smart hydroponic farming ecosystem (HFE). *2017 10th International Conference on Ubi-media Computing and Workshops (Ubi-Media),* 1-4.

Sholto, D. (1975). *Hydroponics: The Bengal system*. Oxford University Press.

Siregar, B., Efendi, S., Pranoto, H., Ginting, R., Andayani, U., & Fahmi, F. (2017). Remote monitoring system for hydroponic planting media. *2017 International Conference on ICT For Smart Society (ICISS), Tangerang*, 1-6.

Umamaheswari, S., Preethi, A., Pravin, E., & Dhanusha, R. (2016). Integrating scheduled hydroponic system. *2016 IEEE International Conference on Advances in Computer Applications (ICACA)*, 333-337.

Yolanda, D., Hindersah, H., Hadiatna, F., & Triawan, M. A. (2016). Implementation of Real-Time Fuzzy logic control for NFT-based hydroponic system on Internet of Things environment. *2016 6th International Conference on System Engineering and Technology (ICSET),* 153-159.

Compilation of References

Rajesha & Gupta. (2018). Microfinance and Poverty Reduction in India. *Globus An International Journal of Management & IT, 9*(2), 1-6.

Yadav, L., Devi, S., Vaidh, N., & Sharma, S. (2020). Psychological, Social and Economic Effects Of COVID-19 Pandemic. *Cosmos Journal of Engineering & Technology, 10*(1), 1–2.

Kumar. (2017). Demonetization in India: Impact on the Economy. *Globus An International Journal of Management & IT, 9*(1), 1-4.

Mard, F. (2017). The effects of intellectual property rights protection in the technology transfer context on economic growth: The case of developing countries. *Journal of Innovation Economics & Management, 23*(2), 33–57. doi:10.3917/jie.023.0033

Muzaka, V. (2013). Intellectual Property Protection and European 'Competitiveness'. *Review of International Political Economy, 20*(4), 819–847. doi:10.1080/09692290.2012.724436

Glass, A. J., & Saggi, K. (2002). Intellectual Property Rights and Foreign Direct Investment. *Journal of International Economics, 56*(2), 387–410. doi:10.1016/S0022-1996(01)00117-9

Smarzynska, B. K. (2004). Composition of Foreign Direct Investment and Protection of Intellectual Property Rights: Evidence from transition Economies. *European Economic Review, 48*(1), 39–62. doi:10.1016/S0014-2921(02)00257-X

Schneider, P. H. (2005). International Trade, Economic Growth and Intellectual Property Rights: A Panel Data Study of Developed and Developing Countries. *Journal of Development Economics, 78*(2), 529–547. doi:10.1016/j.jdeveco.2004.09.001

Singh, S. (2015). Innovation, Intellectual Property Rights and Competition Policy. *Innovation and Development, 5*(1), 147–164. doi:10.1080/2157930X.2014.1003450

Sey, A., Lowe, B., & Poole, N. (2010). The Use of Intellectual Property Protection by Micro, Small, and Medium-Scale Enterprises: A Case Study of Ghana. *Enterprise Development & Microfinance, 21*(1), 67–83. doi:10.3362/1755-1986.2010.006

Sangwan. (2019). Innovation In Instructional Strategies & Design. *Globus Journal of Progressive Education, 9*(2), 1-3.

Adamson, K., Bliss, R., Shahab, R., Sengsavang, S., Craig, S., Rankin, V., & Sur, D. (2020, November). The SCOPE Intervention: Impact of a Social Care Optimization Pilot Initiative in the Emergency Department. *Health & Social Work, 45*(4), 284–288. doi:10.1093/hsw/hlaa021 PMID:33313754

Agarwal & Pundir. (2017). A Study of Personality Traits of B. Ed. Students. *Learning Community-An International Journal of Educational and Social Development, 7*(2), 127-131.

Agarwal, & Shiju. (2018). A Study on Content Generation for Internet Usage. *International Journal of Advanced Research and Development.*, *3*(2), 1380–1382.

Agarwal, N., & Kumar, P. (2009). Role of Information Technology in Education. In *AICT Sponsored National Conference on Information Integrity & Supply Chain Management Abstracts Proceeding.* Book World Publisher.

Agarwal, Sharma, & Tyagi. (2017). Role of Education in Meeting Challenges of Globalization. *Globus An International Journal of Management & IT*, *9*(1), 1-3.

Agarwal, N., & Kumar, P. (2009). Reflection on the new Innovations for maximizing the learning in Teacher of Mathematics. *International Journal Educational Herald*, *382*, 41.

Aguilar Pacas, G. (2020). Finanzas en familia y Coronavirus (COVID-19). *Realidad Empresarial*, (9), 51. doi:10.5377/reuca.v0i9.10070

Ahsan, K. M., Islam, M. S., Litan, M. M., & Huang, X. (2020). Cash Conversion Cycle Connection with Industrial Productivity and Volume. *Globus An International Journal of Management & IT*, *12*(1), 66–70.

Alexander, G. S. (2020). *What is the gig economy? Definition from WhatIs.com.* https://whatis.techtarget.com/definition/gig-economy

Ali, C. (2020). *The case of missing data on migrant workers deaths: The Free Press, 22nd September2020.* Indore Edition.

Amat, O. (2020). *La botella medio llena*. Profit Editorial.

Amity University, Dubai Campus, Institute of Electrical and Electronics Engineers, UAE Section, & Institute of Electrical and Electronics Engineers. (n.d.). *Abstract proceedings of International Conference on Computation, Automation and Knowledge Management (ICCAKM-2020) : 9th-10th January 2020.* Author.

Andaluz, V. H., Tovar, A. Y., Bedón, K. D., Ortiz, J. S., & Pruna, E. (2016). Automatic control of drip irrigation on hydroponic agriculture: Daniela tomato production. *2016 IEEE International Conference on Automatica (ICA-ACCA)*, 1-6. 10.1109/ICA-ACCA.2016.7778389

Anthony, B. Jr. (2021). Managing digital transformation of smart cities through enterprise architecture – a review and research agenda. *Enterprise Information Systems*, *15*(3), 299–331. doi:10.1080/17517575.2020.1812006

Arrow, K. J. (2003). *Uncertainty and the welfare economics of medical care (American economic review, 1963).* Duke University Press.

Atmanirbhar Bharat Abhiyan. (n.d.). Retrieved on June 25, 2021. https://www.investindia.gov.in/atmanirbhar-bharat-abhiyaan

Aylor, B., DeFauw, M., Gilbert, M., Knizek, C., Lang, N., Koch-Weser, J., & McAdoo, M. (2020). *Redrawing the map of global trade.* Boston Consulting Group. https:// www.bcg.com/publications/2020/redrawing-the-map-ofglobal-trade

Baldwin & Freeman. (2020). Supply Chain Contagion Waves: Thinking Ahead on Manufacturing 'Contagion and Reinfection' from the COVID Concussion. In *The COVID concussion and supply-chain contagion waves.* voxeu.org

Baldwin, R., & Tomiura, E. (2020). Thinking ahead about the trade impact of COVID-19. Economics in the Time of COVID-19, 59–72.

Balme, R. (1996). *Les politiques du néo-régionalisme: action collective régionale et globalisation.* Paris Economica.

Banxico. (2020). *Encuesta sobre las expectativas de los especialistas en economía del sector privado.* Recuperado de https://www.banxico.org.mx/publicaciones-y-prensa/encuestas-sobre-las-expectativas-de-los-especialis/encuestas-expectativas-del-se.html

Barbarosoglu, G., & Arda, Y. (2004). A two-stage stochastic programming framework for transportation planning in disaster response. *The Journal of the Operational Research Society*, *55*(1), 43–53. doi:10.1057/palgrave.jors.2601652

Basar, T. (2012). A Game Theoretic Approach to Decision and Analysis in Network Intrusion Detection. *Proceedings of the 42nd IEEE Conference on Decision and Control*, 90(5), 3-12.

Bayero, Ibrahim, & Safiyan. (2020). Effect Of Entrepreneurial Education And Attitude On Entrepreneurial Intention Among Graduating Students Of The Nigerian Universities: A Conceptual Framework. *Cosmos Journal of Engineering & Technology*, *10*(2), 1–12.

Beaverstock, J. V., Smith, R. G., & Taylor, P. J. (2000). World-City Network: A New Metageography? *Annals of the Association of American Geographers*, *90*(1), 123–134. doi:10.1111/0004-5608.00188

Bello, W. (2005). *Deglobalization: Ideas for a New World Economy*. Zed books.

Berumen, S. (2002). *Economía internacional*. Editorial Continental, Ciudad de México.

Bettencourt, L. M. A. (2019). *The digital transformation of metropolises*. Metropolis Observatory.

Bhargav, R., & Bhargav, R. (2020). A dignified period in an unprecedented era. *The Guardian*, p. 4.

Bhatia, G. (2020, Sept. 23). Devise a new labour law regime for gig economy workers. *The Hindustan Times*, p. 8.

Bidyadhar, P. (2020, Sept. 22). Child Labour in India. Around Odisha, p. 4.

Blecker, R. (1999). *Taming Global Finance: A Better Architecture for Growth and Equity*. Economic Policy Institute.

Bohra. (2011). Foreign Direct Investment in India's Service Sector: An Analysis. *Conference: Energizing Economies through Business and Technology Excellence, 4*(1), 23-30.

Botseva. (2020). Digital Transformation of Cities and Digital Transformation of Citizens. In *Economic Science, education and the real economy: Development and interactions in the digital age*. Publishing House Science and Economics Varna.

Brahma, M., & Gupta, R. (2018). Impact of National and International Institution on the Behavior of Indian Stock Market in Indian Economy. *International Journal of Creative Research Thoughts*, *6*(2), 833–838.

Brand, M. (2018). *Why Did Kodak Fail and What Can You Learn from its Demise? | by BRAND MINDS | Medium*. https://brand-minds.medium.com/why-did-kodak-fail-and-what-can-you-learn-from-its-failure-70b92793493c

Brar, D. S. K. (2017). Transforming Education System: A Futuristic Perspective. *Globus An International Journal of Management & IT*, *8*(2), 1–3.

Bremmer, I. (2013). *Every Nation for Itself. What Happens When No One Leads the World*. Portfolio / Penguin.

Brown, P. (2003). The opportunity trap: Education and employment in a global economy. *European Educational Research Journal*, *2*(1), 141–179. doi:10.2304/eerj.2003.2.1.4

Buckley, P. J. (2020). The theory and empirics of the structural reshaping of globalization. *Journal of International Business Studies*, *51*(9), 1580–1592. doi:10.105741267-020-00355-5 PMID:32836503

ca buxozypk. (2020). *Top Countries in the Gig Economy | Gigonomy*. https://gigonomy.info/top-countries-in-the-gig-economy/

Cabus, P. (2001). The Meaning of Local in a Global Economy: The 'Region's Advocacy of Local Interests' as a Necessary Component of Current Global/Local Theories. *European Planning Studies*, *9*(8), 1011–1029. doi:10.1080/09654310120093322

Cardona, J. F. (2020, Abril 22). *Finanzas personales*. Recuperado de https://www.youtube.com/watch?v=Jddhe_15OIQ

Cassis, Y. (2006). Capitals of capital – a history of international financial centres, 1780-2005. Cambridge.

Chandra, A. (2020). Working towards a single license, registration, and return regime. Academic Press.

Chandra, S. (2004). Small Industries Development Organization (SIDO) in Global perspective. *Laghu Udyog Samachar: Journal of Small-Scale Industries, 28-29*(12-2), 249-253.

Changmai, T., Gertphol, S., & Chulak, P. (2018). Smart Hydroponic Lettuce Farm using Internet of Things. *2018 10th International Conference on Knowledge and Smart Technology (KST),* 231-236.

Chaudhary. (2015). Globalization and Education. *Globus Journal of Progressive Education, 6*(1), 1-6.

Chaudhary. (2015). Globalization and Education. *Globus Journal of Progressive Education, 6*(1), 1–6.

Chiodi, A. (2020). Compás financiero personal. *Descubre las finanzas desde lo básico e intuitivo hasta su sorprendente lado humano y pon los números a tu favor*. CONDUSEF, Conduguía, Finanzas Personales. Recuperado de (https://www.condusef.gob.mx/documentos/299734_Conduguia_finanzas_personales_y_familiares2018.pdf

Chopra, S., & Peter, M. (2007). *Supply chain management, strategy planning & operation* (3rd ed.). Pearson Prentice Hall. doi:10.1007/978-3-8349-9320-5_22

Correia, S., Luck, S., & Verner, E. (2020). Fight the Pandemic, Save the Economy: Lessons from the 1918 Flu. The Economic Historian. economic-historian.com

Corsetti, G., & Marin, E. A. (2020). *A Century of Arbitrage and Disaster Risk Pricing in the Foreign Exchange Market.* CEPR Discussion Paper No. 14497.

Costello, T., & Prohaska, B. (2013). 2013 trends and strategies. *IT Professional*, *15*(1), 64–64. doi:10.1109/MITP.2013.5

Crawford, A., Humphries, S. A., & Geddy, M. M. (2015). McDonald's: A Case Study in Glocalization. *Journal of Global Business Issues*, *9*(1), 11–18.

Crisnapati, P. N., Wardana, I. N. K., Aryanto, I. K. A. A., & Hermawan, A. (2017). Hommons: Hydroponic management and monitoring system for an IOT based NFT farm using web technology. *2017 5th International Conference on Cyber and IT Service Management,* 1-6. 10.1109/CITSM.2017.8089268

Dasari, Sudhakar, Jigeesh, Nasina, & Prabhukumar. (2015). Analysis of Project Success Issues: The Case of a Manufacturing SME. *IUP Journal of Operations Management*, *14*(1), 32-38.

Davies, D., Jindal-Snape, D., Collier, C., Digby, R., Hay, P., & Howe, A. (2013). Creative learning environments in education—A systematic literature review. *Thinking Skills and Creativity*, *8*, 80–91. doi:10.1016/j.tsc.2012.07.004

Davis, S. (2020). *Emerging-Market Economies Face COVID-19 and a 'Sudden Stop' in Capital Flows.* Federal Reserve Bank of Dallas. Retrieved from https://www.dallasfed.org/research/economics/2020/0414

De Martino, R., Reid, M. H., & David, Z. (2006). Balancing localization and globalization: Exploring the impact of firm internationalization on a regional cluster. *Entrepreneurship and Regional Development*, *18*(1), 1–24. doi:10.1080/08985620500397648

Demand for work under MGNRGEA up by 40 percent. (2020). *The Pioneer*, p. 7. Available at https://www.dailypioneer.com/2020/india/demand-for-work-under-mgnrega-up-by-40---parl-told

Derudder, B., Taylor, P. J., Witlox, F., & Catalano, G. (2003). Hierarchical Tendencies and Regional Patterns in the World City Network: A Global Urban Analysis of 234 Cities. *Regional Studies, 37*(9), 875–886. doi:10.1080/0034340032000143887

Developing, Monitoring and Evaluation Office. (n.d.). Retrieved on June 24. 2021. https://niti.gov.in/development-monitoring-and-evaluation-office

Devi & Yadav. (2017). Artificial Intelligence Through Machine Learning. *Globus An International Journal of Management & IT, 9*(1), 1-3.

Dev, U. (2020). Re-Engineering Expert System Powered by Machine Learning. *Cosmos Journal of Engineering & Technology, 10*(1), 1–5.

Dew, J. P. (2016). Family Finances. In C. L. Shehan (Ed.), *Encyclopedia of Family Studies*. doi:10.1002/9781119085621.wbefs038

Dimmitt, N. J., Mohammed, J., & Moore, D. (2018). Innovative Approaches to Education: Increasing Creative Confidence and Critical Thinking Skills. *ICPESS (International Congress on Politic, Economic and Social Studies), 4*.

Dito. (2020). *Dampak pandemi Covid-19 terhadap perekonomian Indonesia*. Jurnal Benefita. Universitas Sumatera Utara.

Dodangh, J., Majid, M., & Nasehifar, V. (2010). Ranking of strategic plans in balanced scorecard by using electric method. *International Journal of Innovation, Management and Technology*.

Duque Sánchez, A. (2015). Estado de flujos de efectivo: Aplicación de razonamientos algebraicos y de la NIC 7. *Cuadernos De Contabilidad, 16*(40). Advance online publication. doi:10.11144/Javeriana.cc16-40.efea

Dweck, C. (2015). Carol Dweck revisits the growth mindset. *Education Week, 35*(5), 20–24.

Employee Tenure in 2020. (2020). www.bls.gov/cps

ENIGH. (2018). *Encuesta Nacional de Ingresos y Gastos en los Hogares*. Recuperado de https://www.inegi.org.mx/contenidos/programas/enigh/nc/2018/doc/enigh2018_ns_presentacion_resultados.pdf

Evans-Obinna, R. N. (2016). Entrepreneurship education for self-reliance and economic development in Nigeria. *International Journal of Vocational and Technical Education Research, 2*(2), 9–14.

Fahmi, I. (2016). *Teori dan paraktik pengambilan keputusan kualitatif dan kuantitatif*. Rajawali Pers.

Fiedrich, F., Gehbauer, F., & Rickers, U. (2000). Optimized resource allocation for emergency response after earthquake disasters. *Safety Science, 35*(1-3), 41–57. doi:10.1016/S0925-7535(00)00021-7

Figueroa Delgado, L. O. (2009). Las finanzas personales. Revista EAN. *Núm., 65*, 123–144.

Financial Times. (2020, Apr. 24). US Banks Pull Back from Lending to European Companies. *Financial Times*.

Fontaine, R. (2020). Globalization will look very different after the coronavirus pandemic. *Foreign Policy*. https:// foreignpolicy.com/2020/04/17/globalization-trade-war-aftercoronavirus- pandemic/

Friedmann, J. (1986). The World City Hypothesis. *Development and Change, 17*(1), 69–83. doi:10.1111/j.1467-7660.1986.tb00231.x

Galtung, J. (1976). Trade or development: Some reflections on self-reliance. *Economic and Political Weekly*, 207–218.

Ghai, Tyagi, & Gupta. (2020). Leveraging Technology for Robust Financial Facilities: A Comparative Assessment of BRICS Nations. In *ICCAKM 2020*. IEEE Xplore.

Ghai, R., Tyagi, M., & Gupta, R. (2020). *Leveraging Technology for Robust Financial Facilities: A Comparative Assessment of BRICS Nations. In ICCAKM 2020. IEEE Xplore.*

Gig (music) - Wikipedia. (n.d.). Retrieved February 9, 2021, from https://en.wikipedia.org/wiki/Gig_(music)

Gitman, L. J., & Zutter, C. (2016). Principios de administración financiera (décimo cuarta edición. ed.). Pearson.

Godfrey, P. (2003). *Toward a Theory of Economic Self Reliance (ESR).* Marriot School of Management. Brigham Young University.

Goel, A. N. (2008). A Global Change in Education through Information Technology and Communication. In Enterprises Information Systems & Technology. MacMillan Advanced Research Series.

Goel. (2008). A Global Change in Education through Information Technology and Communication. In Enterprises Information Systems & Technology. MacMillan Advanced Research Series.

Görmez, N., Köksalan, M., & Salman, F. (2010). Locating disaster response facilities in Istanbul. *The Journal of the Operational Research Society, 62*(7), 1239–1252. doi:10.1057/jors.2010.67

Goyal. (2020). *Govt has identified 12 sectors in which India can become self-reliant, global supplier*. https://www.outlookindia.com/newsscroll/govt-has-identified-12-sectors-inwhich-india-can-become-selfreliant-global-supplier-goyal/1842028

Gultom, D. R. (2009). *Pengukuran kinerja perusahaan dengan balanced scorecard: studi kasus pada perusahaan perkebunan negara III (Persero) Medan.* Universitas Sumatra Utara.

Gupta, R. (2008). Information Security: An Economic Perspective. In Business and Competitive Dynamics. Macmillan India Limited.

Gupta, R., & Kumar, P. (2013). Information Technology Business Value Assessment: A Case of State Bank of India. *Globus: An International Journal of Management & IT, 4*(2), 30-34.

Gupta, D. A. (2019). Making India Digital: Transforming Towards Sustainable Development. *Cosmos Journal of Engineering & Technology, 9*(2), 1–6.

Guthrie, C. P., & Nicholls, C. M. (2015). The Personal Budget Project: A practical introduction to financial literacy. *Journal of Accounting Education, Elsevier, 33*(2), 138–163. doi:10.1016/j.jaccedu.2015.04.002

Hadiwardoyo, W. (2020). Kerugian ekonomi nasional akibat PSBB. *Jurnal of Business and Entrepreneurship, 2.*

Hair, J. F., Anderson, R. F., Tatham, R. L., & Black, W. C. (2008). *Análisis Multivariante*. Editorial Pearson Prentice Hall.

Haizer, J., & Render, B. (2010). *Manajemen operasi.* Salemba Empat.

Hanssens, H., Derudder, B., Taylor, P. J., Hoyler, M., Ni, P., Huang, J., Yang, X., & Witlox, F. (2010). The changing geography of globalized service provision, 2000-2008. The Service Industries Journal. doi:10.1080/02642069.2010.503887

Harrschar-Ehrnborg, S. (2002): *Finanzplatzstrukturen in Europa: Die Entstehung und Entwicklung von Finanzzentren. Academic Press.*

Helmy, M. G., Mahaidayu, A., Nursyahid, T. A., Setyawa, & Hasan, A. (2017). Nutrient Film Technique (NFT) hydroponic monitoring system based on wireless sensor network. *2017 IEEE International Conference on Communication, Networks and Satellite (Comnetsat)*, 81-84.

Henry, H. M. (1973). Efficiency Is a Valid Goal: Improving the Management of Government/Industry Programs. *Management Review, 62*(8), 4–18.

Hines, C. (2000). *Localization—A Global Manifesto*. Earthscan.

Hines, C. (2003). Time to Replace Globalization with Localization. *Global Environmental Politics*, *3*(3), 1–7. doi:10.1162/152638003322469240

Hoffmann, A., & Otteby, K. (2017). Personal finance blogs: Helpful tool for consumers with low financial literacy or preaching to the choir? *International Journal of Consumer Studies*, *42*(2), 241–254. doi:10.1111/ijcs.12412

Hollensen, S., & Møller, E. (2018). Is "glocalization" still the golden way for Electrolux? Is there more to be done? *Thunderbird International Business Review*, *60*(4), 463–476. doi:10.1002/tie.21923

Hooghe, L. (Ed.). (1996). *Cohesion policy and European integration: building multi-level governance*. Oxford University Press.

How Does the Gig Economy Benefit Employees & Businesses? TSheets. (n.d.). Retrieved February 9, 2021, from https://www.tsheets.com/resources/gig-economy-employees

Huber, L. R., Sloof, R., & Van Praag, M. (2014). The effect of early entrepreneurship education: Evidence from a field experiment. *European Economic Review*, *72*, 76–97. doi:10.1016/j.euroecorev.2014.09.002

Hydroponic Vegetable Production – Guide(2017Department of Agriculture, Forestry and Fisheries, Republic of South Africa.

Ibarra, P., & Letamendia, F. (1999). Los movimientos sociales. In M. Caminal (Ed.), *Manual de Ciencia Política*. Tecnos.

INEGI. (2020). *Estimación oportuna del PIB trimestral*. Recuperado de https://www.inegi.org.mx/temas/pibo/

INEGI. (2020). *México en cifras*. Recuperado de https://www.inegi.org.mx/app/areasgeograficas/

INEGI. (2020). *Sistema de Cuentas Nacionales de México*. Recuperado de https://www.inegi.org.mx/temas/itaee/

Inglehart, R., & Norris, P. (2016) *Trump, Brexit, and the rise of populism: economic have-nots and cultural backlash*. HKS Faculty Research Working Paper Series RWP16-026.

International Society for Ecology and Culture. (1999). *From Global to Local—Resisting Monoculture, Rebuilding Community*. ISEC.

Jaiswal, S. (2016). Quality Assurance in Teacher Education. *Globus Journal of Progressive Education*, *6*(2), 1–4.

James, H. (2018). Deglobalization: The rise of disembedded unilateralism. *Annual Review of Financial Economics*, *10*(1), 219–237. doi:10.1146/annurev-financial-110217-022625

Jauch, L. R., & Glueck, W. F. (2004). *Strategic management and business policy* (9th ed.). McGraw-Hill.

Jayant. (2018). Impact of Agriculture and FDI Inflows in Different Sector. *Globus: An International Journal of Management & IT, 10*(1), 1-3.

Jha, S. (2020, Oct. 29). Gig workers to contribute for social security cover. Business Standard, p. 15.

Kaplan, R. S., & dan Norton, D. P. (2000). Balance scorecard, menerapkan strategi menjadi aksi. Terjemahan. Penerbit Erlangga.

Kaplan, R. S., & Norton, D. P. (2004). *Strategy maps: Convert intangible assets into tangible outcomes*. Harvard Business School Press.

Karunaratne, N. D. (2012). The Globalization Deglobalization Policy Conundrum. *Modern Economy.*, *3*(4), 373–383. doi:10.4236/me.2012.34048

Katz, J. A. (2003). The chronology and intellectual trajectory of American entrepreneurship education: 1876–1999. *Journal of Business Venturing*, *18*(2), 283–300. doi:10.1016/S0883-9026(02)00098-8

Keating, M., & Jones, B. (Eds.). (1985). *Regions in the European Community*. Oxford University Press.

Kelley, T., & Kelley, D. (2012). Reclaim your Creative Confidence. *Harvard Business Review*, *90*(12), 115–118. PMID:23227579

Kementrian Kesehatan Republik Indonesia. (2020). *Peraturan menteri kesehatan republik indonesia nomor 9 tahun 2020 tentang pedoman pembatasan sosial berskala besar dalam rangka percepatan penanganan corona virus disease 2019 (covid-19)*. Kemenkes RI.

Kenge & Khan. (2020). A Conceptual Study of The Supply Chain Management 4.0 Implementation Process. *Cosmos Journal of Engineering & Technology*, *10*(2), 1–5.

Kerzner, H. (1992). *Project management: A systems approach to planning, scheduling and controlling* (4th ed.). Van Nostrand Reinholdt.

Khanna, LaBresh, Kengelbach, Selikowitz, Argent, & Burke. (2018). *The $75 Trillion Opportunity in Public Assets*. Boston Consulting Group Report.

Khari, D., Sharma, V., & Agarwal, D. N. (2020). Effect of Pandemic COVID-19 on Economic Crisis and Health Issues Globally. *Cosmos Journal of Engineering & Technology*, *10*(1), 1–7.

Kirzner, I. M. (1997). Entrepreneurial discovery and the competitive market process: An Austrian approach. *Journal of Economic Literature*, *35*(1), 60–85.

Kumar, P. (2009). Convergence of Rural Marketing Strategies and Trends in Developing Economics. *Globus - An International Journal of Management and IT, 1*(1), 61-66.

Kumar, P., & Kapri, T. (2010). Web Content Management System. In Information and Communication Technology: Challenges and Business Opportunities. Excel Publishers.

Kumari & Kumar. (2015). A Study On Value Education Quality In Dynamic World. *Globus An International Journal of Management & IT, 7*(1), 1-3.

Kumar, P. (2009). Convergence of Rural Marketing Strategies and Trends in Developing Economics. *Globus An International Journal of Management and IT, 1*(1), 61–66.

Kumar, P., & Gupta, R. (2008). Information System's Security by using Matrices and Graphs. *Conference Proceedings on Information Security and Mobile Computing*, 62-66.

Kusiak, A. (2020). Resilient manufacturing. *Journal of Intelligent Manufacturing*, *31*(2), 269. doi:10.100710845-019-01523-7

Labour Law Reforms | Ministry of Labour & Employment. (n.d.). Retrieved February 11, 2021, from https://labour.gov.in/labour-law-reforms

Lakshmi, P. (2020, Sept. 22). The future of work. The Indian Express, p. 7.

Lalit, G. (2020, Nov. 9). Evaluation is key for good governance. The Avenue, p. 6.

Lang, T., & Heasman, M. (2003). *Food Wars: The Battle for Mouths*. Minds and Markets.

Le Galès, P., & Lequesne, C. (1998). *Regions in Europe*. Routledge.

Lenord Melvix, J. S. M., & Sridevi, C. (2014). Design of efficient hydroponic nutrient solution control system using soft computing-based solution grading. *2014 International Conference on Computation of Power, Energy, Information and Communication (ICCPEIC)*, 148-154.

Levitt. (1983). *The Globalization of Markets. Harvard Business Review Ohmae Kinichi (1988). Beyond national borders.* Kodansha International.

Li-Ying, J., & Nell, P. (2020). Navigating opportunities for innovation and entrepreneurship under COVID-19. *California Management Review*, *63*(1).

Lodree, E. J. Jr, & Taskin, S. (2008). An insurance risk management framework for disaster relief and supply chain disruption inventory planning. *The Journal of the Operational Research Society*, *59*(5), 674–684. doi:10.1057/palgrave.jors.2602377

López García, J. C. (2016). *Las finanzas personales, un concepto que va más allá de su estructura. Estado del arte periodo 2006-2016 en Pereira, EAFIT.* Tesis Digitales. Universidad EAFTI Facultad de Ciencias Administrativas, Programa de Maestría en Administración, MBA. Disponible en https://repository.eafit.edu.co/bitstream/handle/10784/11784/LopezGarcia_JuanCarlos_2017.pdf?sequence=2

López Salido, D. (2020). Tribuna invitada. Confinamiento, mercado laboral y finanzas familiares. In *Aspectos económicos de la crisis del COVID-19: Boletín de seguimiento no. 2* (pp. 4–8). FEDEA.

Lo, V., & Schamp, E. W. (2001). Finanzplätze auf globalen Märkten – Beispiel Frankfurt/Main. *Geographische Rundschau*, *53*(7/8), 26–31.

Lucas, C. (2003). Localization – an alternative to corporate-led globalization. *International Journal of Consumer Studies*, *27*(4), 261–265. doi:10.1046/j.1470-6431.2003.00317.x

Lüthi, S., Thierstein, A., & Goebel, D. (2010). Intra-firm and extra-firm linkages in the knowledge economy: The case of the emerging mega-city region of Munich. *Global Networks*, *10*(1), 114–137. doi:10.1111/j.1471-0374.2010.00277.x

Magazine, A. (2020). In labour codes, what changes for workers, hirers. *The New Indian Express*. Available at https://indianexpress.com/article/explained/govts-new-versions-of-labour-codes-key-proposals-and-concerns-6603354/

Make UK: COVID 19 Manufacturing Monitor. (2020, May). Author.

Malik. (2015). Impact of Emotional Intelligence on Job Satisfaction. *Globus Journal of Progressive Education*, *5*(2), 1–5.

Mander & Goldsmith. (Eds.). (1996). *The Case Against the Global Economy*. San Francisco: Sierra Club Books.

Manju, M., Karthik, V., Hariharan, S., & Sreekar, B. (2017). Real time monitoring of the environmental parameters of an aquaponic system based on Internet of Things. *2017 Third International Conference on Science Technology Engineering & Management (ICONSTEM)*, 943-948.

Maritz, A., Perenyi, A., De Waal, G., & Buck, C. (2020). Entrepreneurship as the unsung hero during the current COVID-19 economic crisis: Australian perspectives. *Sustainability*, *12*(11), 4612. doi:10.3390u12114612

McKibbin, W., & Fernando, R. (2020). The Economic Impact of COVID-19. *Economics in The Time of COVID-19*, 45-51.

McKinsey. (2009). *Building India: Accelerating Infrastructure Projects*. Author.

McLeod, J. R., & Schell, G. P. (2011). *Sistem informasi manajemen*. Salemba Empat.

McMichael, P. (2000). The Power of Food. *Agriculture and Human Values*, *17*(1), 21–33. doi:10.1023/A:1007684827140

Meheta, B. S., & Kumr, A. (2020, Oct. 1). *White collar Blues.* The Pioneer, p. 9.

Merki, C. M. (Ed.). (2005). *Europas Finanzzentren. Geschichte und Bedeutung im 20.* Jahrhundert.

Michael, H. (2020). *Dampak coronavirus terhadap ekonomi global.* Bank Indonesia. https://www.bi.go.id/id/publikasi/ekonomi-keuangan-kerjasama-

Mishra, S., & Soni, D. (2016). A Study on Technology, Thinking Styles, and Content of Education. *Cosmos An International Journal of Art & Higher Education, 5*(2), 1–4.

Miskiewicz, J., & Ausloos, M. (2010). Has the World Economy Reached Its Globalization Limit? Physica A, 389(4), 797-806. DOI: .physa.2009.10.029 doi:10.1016/j

Modi, P. K. (2015). A Study on Life Insurance Companies Related to Service Quality. *Cosmos An International Journal of Management, 4*(2), 7–9.

Mohammed, J., & Hatakka, M. R. H. (2016). Enhancing Multiple Thinking through the Engineering Design Process. *2016 ASEE International Forum.*

Mohammed, J. (2021). Introducing Entrepreneurship and Innovation in a Manufacturing Design Course. *2021 ASEE Virtual Annual Conference Content Access.*

Mulyadi & Setyawan, J. (2000). *Sistem perencanaan dan pengenalian manajemen* (2nd ed.). Jakarta: Salemba Empat.

Mulyadi. (2001). *Balanced scorecard alat manajemen kontemporer untuk memperlipatgandakan kinerja keuangan perusahaan.* Jakarta: Salemba Empat.

Nanda, K. (2021, Apr. 24). Growth-Oriented Plan needs nurture in current scenario. Free Press Journal, p. 6.

Nautiyal, A. (2015). Role of Life Insurance in India. *Cosmos An International Journal of Management, 5*(1), 1–3.

Navdeep. (2016). A Study On Changes in Learning and Teaching Process in Today Environment. *Globus An International Journal of Management & IT, 8*(1), 1-3.

Navdeep. (2017). A Study of ICT in Various Aspects in Quality Education. *Globus An International Journal of Management & IT, 9*(1), 1-4.

Naveen & Agarwal. (2016). Social Media & Academic Performances: An Empirical Analysis. *Cosmos An International Journal of Art & Higher Education, 5*(2), 5–7.

Nel, H. J. (2001). A project management approach to the implementation of development programmes within the local government sphere: An empirical analysis. *Development Southern Africa, 18*(5), 605–624. doi:10.1080/03768350120097450

Nilanjan, B. (2020). *Gig economy: Opinion: India's gig economy needs affirmative policy push, Government News, ET Government.* https://government.economictimes.indiatimes.com/news/economy/opinion-indias-gig-economy-needs-affirmative-policy-push/73121847

Nishimura, T., Okuyama, Y., Matsushita, A., Ikeda, H., & Satoh, A. (2017). A compact hardware design of a sensor module for hydroponics. *2017 IEEE 6th Global Conference on Consumer Electronics (GCCE)*, 1-4. 10.1109/GCCE.2017.8229255

Nitin, M. (2021, June 22). *Rethinking Fenestration.* The Pioneer, p. 11.

Norberg-Hodge, Merri[a]eld, & Gorelick. (2002). Bringing the Food Economy Home: Local Alternatives to Global Agribusiness. London: Zed Press.

Nurmi, P., & Paasio, K. (2007). Entrepreneurship in Finnish universities. *Education + Training*, *49*(1), 56–65. doi:10.1108/00400910710729884

Obeng, K., & Ugboro, I. (2008). Effective strategic planning in public transit systems. *Transportation Research*, *44*(3), 420–439. doi:10.1016/j.tre.2006.10.008

Overview of Labour Law Reforms | PRSIndia. (n.d.). Retrieved February 11, 2021, from https://www.prsindia.org/billtrack/overview-labour-law-reforms

Oviatt, B. M., & McDougall, P. P. (2005). Defining international entrepreneurship and modeling the speed of internationalization. *Entrepreneurship Theory and Practice*, *29*(5), 537–553. doi:10.1111/j.1540-6520.2005.00097.x

Ozdamar, L., Ekinci, E., & Kucukyazici, B. (2004). Emergency logistics planning in natural disasters. *Annals of Operations Research*, *129*(1-4), 217–245. doi:10.1023/B:ANOR.0000030690.27939.39

Pal, S. (2016). *Growing Soil-Less with Hydroponics: An Introduction to Innovative Farming at Home*. The Better India.

Pandey & Kumar. (2017). A Study on Crash Attacks with Functions Related to Hash. *Globus An International Journal of Management & IT, 9*(1), 1-3.

Pandey, R., Jain, V., Pandey, K. S. R., & Singh, K. P. (2009). *Hydroponics Agriculture: Its Status, Scope and Limitations*. Division of Plant Physiology, Indian Agricultural Research Institute.

Parr, J. B., & Budd, L. (2000). Financial Services and the Urban System: An Exploration. *Urban Studies (Edinburgh, Scotland)*, *37*(3), 593–610. doi:10.1080/0042098002131

Pasha-Zaidi, N., Afari, E., Mohammed, J., Cubero, S., Shoukry, A. M., & El Sokkary, W. (2015). Gender-based teams: Perceptions of team satisfaction and effectiveness among engineering students in the United Arab Emirates. *International Journal of Engineering Education*, *31*(4), 953–966.

Paul, R., & Elder, L. (2006). *Thinker's Guide to the Art of Socratic Questioning*. Foundation Critical Thinking.

Periodic Labour Force Survey (PLFS) Ministry of Statistics and Programme Implementation Annual Report Periodic Labour Force Survey (PLFS) Government of India Ministry of Statistics and Programme Implementationin GoIStats GoIStats Periodic Labour Force Survey (PLFS) Ministry of Statistics and Programme Implementation goistats. (2020). www.mospi.gov.inwww.mospi.gov

Peuchpanngarm, C., Srinitiworawong, P., Samerjai, W., & Sunetnanta, T. (2016). DIY sensor-based automatic control mobile application for hydroponics. *2016 Fifth ICT International Student Project Conference (ICT-ISPC)*, 57-60. 10.1109/ICT-ISPC.2016.7519235

Pickard, W. G. (2019). *The History and Future of the Gig Economy - Small Business Trends*. https://smallbiztrends.com/2019/11/the-history-and-future-of-the-gig-economy.html

Pooja, M. (2020, January). *Gig Economy – Shaping the Future of Work*. https://www.investindia.gov.in/team-india-blogs/gig-economy-shaping-future-work

Poon, J. P. H., Eldredge, B., & Yeung, D. (2004). Rank Size Distribution of International Financial Centers. *International Regional Science Review*, *27*(4), 411–430. doi:10.1177/0160017604267629

Porteous, D. J. (1999). The Development of Financial Centres: Location, Information Externalities and Path Dependence. In R. Martin (Ed.), Money and the space economy (pp. 95–114). Academic Press.

Pradhan & Anup. (2018). Problems Facing Indian Economy. *Cosmos An International Journal of Art & Higher Education*, *7*(1), 12–15.

Pradhan & Goel. (2017). A Study on Empowering Education and Globalization. *Globus Journal of Progressive Education*, *7*(2), 1–5.

Praveen Kumar, K. (2014). A Study On Cloud Computing. *Cosmos Journal of Engineering & Technology*, *4*(2), 1–3.

Premand, P., Brodmann, S., Almeida, R., Grun, R., & Barouni, M. (2016). Entrepreneurship education and entry into self-employment among university graduates. *World Development*, *77*, 311–327. doi:10.1016/j.worlddev.2015.08.028

Princen, T. (2002). Distancing: Consumption and the Severing of Feedback. In T. Princen, M. Maniates, & K. Conca (Eds.), *Confronting Consumption*. MIT Press. doi:10.7551/mitpress/2097.003.0008

Program Management. (n.d.). Retrieved on June 20, 2021. https://www.pmi.org/learning/featured-topics/program

Pujawan, I. N. (2005). *Supply chain management*. Surabaya: Gundawidya.

Puneet, K. (2008). *A Comparative Study of Information System's Security by using Graphs*. In *Enterprise Information Systems & Technology*. MacMillan India Ltd.

Radha, A. (2015). Retailing: Emerging Challenges and Future Prospects In India. International Journal of Scientific Research and Management, 89(76), 6-13.

Rajah & Samar. (2021). *In India Economy Unlocking the Potential of the Gig Economy in India*. Academic Press.

Rajashekar, S. (2015). Agricultural Marketing of Products A Case Study of Haveri District. *Globus Journal of Progressive Education*, *5*(1), 1–2.

Ram. (2017). A Study on Teacher Performance Assessment for Quality Education. *Cosmos An International Journal of Art & Higher Education*, *6*(2), 21–23.

Ramarapu, S., Timmerman, J. E., & Ramarapu, N. (1999). Choosing Between Globalization and Localization As a Strategic Thrust for Your International Marketing Effort. *Journal of Marketing Theory and Practice*, *7*(2), 97–105. doi:10.1080/10696679.1999.11501832

Ranjan, S., Gupta, D. R., & Gupta, D. A. (2020). Artificial Intelligence in Financial Acumen: Challenges and Opportunities. *Cosmos Journal of Engineering & Technology*, *10*(1), 1–5.

Ranks, I. (2015, Aug. 26). 9th in Brookings Financial Inclusion Report Card Business. Standard, p. 4

Rao & Raja. (2018). Mutual Fund Industry and Market Scenario of India. *Globus An International Journal of Management & IT*, *9*(2), 1-3.

Ratten, V. (2020). Coronavirus and international business: An entrepreneurial ecosystem perspective. *Thunderbird International Business Review*, *62*(5), 629–634. doi:10.1002/tie.22161

Ravi Kumar, V. V. (2020, Oct. 28). *It's a matter of skills*. The Pioneer, p. 12.

Rawls, C., & Turnquist, M. (2010). Pre-positioning of emergency supplies for disaster response. *Transportation Research Part B: Methodological*, *44*(4), 521–534. doi:10.1016/j.trb.2009.08.003

Rebecca, H. (2020, December 10). *How COVID-19 Has Transformed The Gig Economy*. https://www.forbes.com/sites/rebeccahenderson/2020/12/10/how-covid-19-has-transformed-the-gig-economy/?sh=313143416c99

Report of Prime Minister's Task Force. (2010). *Micro Small and Medium Enterprises*. Government of India. Available at http://dcmsme.gov.in/final_report.pdf

Report, A. (2016-17). *Ministry of Micro, Small & Medium Enterprises, Government of India*. Available at https://www.msmedithrissur.gov.in/assets/uploads/downloadfile/Annual%20Report%202016%20-17%20of%20MSME-DI,%20Thrissur.pdf

Rituraj, T. (2020, June 6). States told to pace up distribution of free grains to migrants. *The Economic Times*, p. 7.

Riya, R. (2020). *India Lockdown: Most Affected Is Unorganized Sector; It Is 93% Of The Total Workforce, 41 Crore People Lack Economic Security - Inventiva*. https://www.inventiva.co.in/stories/riyarana/india-lockdown-most-affected-is-unorganized-sector-it-is-93-of-the-total-workforce-41-crore-people-lack-economic-security/

Robinson, J.P., Shaver, P. R., & Wrightsman, L.S. (1991). Criteria for Scale Selection and Evaluation. *Measures of Personality and Social Psychological Attitudes, 13*.

Robinson. (2004). A theory of global capitalism: Production class, and state in a transnational world. *International Journal on World Peace, 21*(2), 81-86.

Robinson, J. (2005). Urban geography: World cities, or a world of cities. *Progress in Human Geography, 29*(6), 757–765. doi:10.1191/0309132505ph582pr

Rodríguez-Raga, S. (2017). *Finanzas personales, su mejor plan de vida*. Bogotá: Universidad de los Andes, Facultad de Administración: Ediciones Uniandes.

Rojas-López, M. D., Maya-Fernández, L. M., & Valencia, M. E. (2017). Definición de un modelo para la planeación financiera personal aplicado al caso colombiano. *Revista Ingenierías Universidad de Medellín, 16*(31), 155–171. doi:10.22395/rium.v16n31a8

Ruengittinun, S., Phongsamsuan, S., & Sureeratanakorn, P. (2017). Applied internet of thing for smart hydroponic farming ecosystem (HFE). *2017 10th International Conference on Ubi-media Computing and Workshops (Ubi-Media)*, 1-4.

Sahamati - Collective of the Account Aggregator Ecosystem. (n.d.). Retrieved January 22, 2021, from https://sahamati.org.in/#

Salmeron, J., & Apte, A. (2010). Stochastic optimization for natural disaster asset prepositioning. *Production and Operations Management, 19*(5), 561–574. doi:10.1111/j.1937-5956.2009.01119.x

Sanju, V. (2020, Sept. 29). PM Modi's game-changing labour reforms to boost growth. *The Guardian*, p. 5.

Sarasvathy, S. D., & Venkataraman, S. (2011). Entrepreneurship as method: Open questions for an entrepreneurial future. *Entrepreneurship Theory and Practice, 35*(1), 113–135. doi:10.1111/j.1540-6520.2010.00425.x

Sarder, M. D., & Iqbal, G. (2013). Healthcare Service Modeling to Minimize Disruptions due to Natural Disasters. *Proceeding of the Annual Industrial & Systems Engineering Research Conference (ISERC)*.

Sassen, S. (1991). The global city. Academic Press.

Schamp, E. W. (2009). Das Finanzzentrum – ein Cluster? Ein multiskalarer Ansatz und seine Evidenz am Beispiel von Frankfurt/Rhein-Main. *Zeitschrift für Wirtschaftsgeographie, 53*(1-2), 1–2, 89–105. doi:10.1515/zfw.2009.0006

Schmidt, R. S., & Grote, M. (2005). *Was ist und was braucht ein bedeutender Finanzplatz?* Working Paper Series Finance and Accounting 150, Department of Economics, Johann Wolfgang Goethe-University Frankfurt.

Sengupta, A. (2013). Emergence of modern Indian retail: An historical perspective. *International Journal of Retail & Distribution Management, 36*(9), 689–700. doi:10.1108/09590550810890939

Sergio, R., Argollo, C., Gouvêa, C., Vânia, B., Mello, B., & Renata, A. (2012). Supply Chains in Humanitarian Operations: Cases and Analysis. *Procedia: Social and Behavioral Sciences*, *54*, 598–607. doi:10.1016/j.sbspro.2012.09.777

Seyf, A. (2001). Can Globalization and Global Localization Explain Foreign Direct Investment? Japanese Firms in Europe. *International Journal of the Economics of Business*, *8*(1), 137–153. doi:10.1080/13571510151075350

Shane, S., & Venkataraman, S. (2000). The promise of entrepreneurship as a field of research. *Academy of Management Review*, *25*(1), 217–226. doi:10.5465/amr.2000.2791611

Sharma, M. (2020, November 12). *Govt announces Atmanirbhar Bharat 3.0; claims COVID stimulus now worth Rs 29.8 lakh crore*. https://www.businesstoday.in/current/corporate/govt-announces-atmanirbhar-bharat-30-covid-stimulus-worth-rs-29-lakh-crore/story/421809.html

Sharma. (2017). Technology, E-Learning and Social Media with Reference to Academic Achievement. *Cosmos An International Journal of Art & Higher Education*, *6*(1), 7–8.

Sharma, A. (2014). A Study of Total Quality Management: Its Legacy, Importance and Implementation In Educational Institutes. *Globus Journal of Progressive Education*, *4*(2), 1–5.

Sharma, R. K. (2013). An Abstract of Quality Assurance in Higher Education: For World Class Institution. *Globus Journal of Progressive Education*, *3*(1), 1–5.

Sheu, J.-B. (2007). An emergency logistics distribution approach for quick response to urgent relief demand in disasters. *Transportation Research Part E, Logistics and Transportation Review*, *43*(6), 687–709. doi:10.1016/j.tre.2006.04.004

Shishir, S. (2020, Sept. 17). Govt clueless on number of jobs lost during pandemic. The Business Line, p. 1.

Sholto, D. (1975). *Hydroponics: The Bengal system*. Oxford University Press.

Singh, G., Gupta, R., & Agarwal, N. (2020). Economic Re-Engineering: Covid-19. *International Journal on Emerging Technologies, 114*, 1–5.

Singh, A. (2011). Foreign Direct Investment (FDI) In India Service Sector (A Study of Post Liberalization). *International Journal of Economic Research*, *2*(2), 10–18.

Siregar, B., Efendi, S., Pranoto, H., Ginting, R., Andayani, U., & Fahmi, F. (2017). Remote monitoring system for hydroponic planting media. *2017 International Conference on ICT For Smart Society (ICISS), Tangerang*, 1-6.

Solihin, I. (2009). *Pengantar manajemen*. Erlangga.

Solihin, I. (2014). *Pengantar bisnis*. Erlangga.

Somesh, J. (2020, Sept. 28). Six months on Migrants caught between hope and despair. Business Standard, p. 1.

Srivastava, S., & Singh, R. (2021). Exploring integrated supply chain performance in healthcare: A service provider perspective. *Benchmarking*, *28*(1), 106–130. doi:10.1108/BIJ-03-2020-0125

Sternberg, R. (2008). The WICS Approach to Leadership: Stories of Leadership and the Structure and Processes that Support Them. *The Leadership Quarterly*, *19*(3), 360–371. doi:10.1016/j.leaqua.2008.03.008

Studies, C., Cv, O., & Abadi, K. (2018). Analisis saluran distribusi kayu (studi kasus di cv. Karya abadi, Manado). *Jurnal EMBA: Jurnal Riset Ekonomi, Manajemen. Bisnis Dan Akuntansi*, *6*. Advance online publication. doi:10.35794/emba.v6i3.20444

Subhadra, C. (2020, Sept. 28). Unused rural funds hint migrant s may be back at work in cities. *The Hindustan Times*, p. 1.

Sudhakar, S. (2014). Growth of Retail Industry in India. *Globus An International Journal of Management & IT*, *6*(1), 1–4.

Swiss Economic Institute. (2014). *Press Release, KOF Index of Globalization: Switzerland no Longer Among the Top Ten*. Zurich: SEI. Available from: http://globalization.kof. ethz.ch/media/filer_public/2014/04/16/press_release_2014_en.pdf

Taylor, P. (2004). *World City Network: A global urban analysis*. doi:10.4324/9780203634059

The Associated Chamber of Commerce and Industry of India. (2020). *Gig economy national conference aligning consumer preferences: the way forward background note*. www.assocham.org

The Code on Social Security. (2020).

The Controller of Publications. (2020).

The Insolvency and Bankruptcy Code. (2017, September). *Chartered Secretary*, *47*(9), 6.

The Personal Data Protection Bill, 2018 Chapter I Preliminary. (n.d.).

The Pros and Cons of the Gig Economy. (2018). https://www.wgu.edu/blog/pros-and-cons-gig-economy1808.html

The top five advantages and disadvantages of gig economy workers revealed – Engage Employee. (2018). https://engageemployee.com/top-five-advantages-disadvantages-gig-economy-workers-revealed/

Thorik, S. H. (2020). Efektivitas pembatasan sosial berskala besar di indonesia dalam penanggulangan pandemi covid-19. *Jurnal: Hukum dan Keadilan, 4*(1).

Tjiptono, F. (2014). *Pemasaran jasa – prinsip, penerapan, dan penelitian*. Andi Offset.

Tomasini, R., & Van Wassenhove, L. N. (2004). *A framework to unravel, prioritize and coordinate vulnerability and complexity factors affecting a humanitarian operation*. Academic Press.

Tunggal, A. W. (2011). *Pokok-pokok performance measurement dan balanced scorecard*. Harvindo.

Tzeng, G., Cheng, H., & Huang, T. (2007). Multi-objective optimal planning for designing relief delivery systems. *Transp Res E*, *43*(6), 673–686. doi:10.1016/j.tre.2006.10.012

Umamaheswari, S., Preethi, A., Pravin, E., & Dhanusha, R. (2016). Integrating scheduled hydroponic system. *2016 IEEE International Conference on Advances in Computer Applications (ICACA)*, 333-337.

UN DESA. (2018). *The 2018 Revision of the World Urbanization Prospects*. Population Division of the United Nations Department of Economic and Social Affairs.

United Nations Conference on Trade and Development. (2020). *Trade Trends under the COVID-19 Pandemic*. United Nations.

United Nations Global Pulse & WFP. (2016). *Using financial transaction data to measure economic resilience to natural disasters*. Project Series, No. 24.

United Nations. (2018). *World Economic Situation and Prospects 2018* (Sales No. E.18.II.C.2). Author.

Van Bergeijk, P. A. G. (2010). *On the Brink of Deglobalization*. Edward Elgar. doi:10.4337/9781849805803

Van Wassenhove, L. N. (2006). Humanitarian aid logistics: Supply chain management in high gear journal of the operational research society. *The Journal of the Operational Research Society*, *57*(5), 475–489. doi:10.1057/palgrave.jors.2602125

van Winden, W., & de Carvalho, L. (2017). *Cities and digitalization*. Amsterdam University of Applied Sciences.

Veselovská, L. (2020). Supply chain disruptions in the context of early stages of the global COVID-19 outbreak. *Problems and Perspectives in Management, 18*(2), 490–500. doi:10.21511/ppm.18(2).2020.40

Vesper, K. H., & Gartner, W. B. (1997). Measuring progress in entrepreneurship education. *Journal of Business Venturing, 12*(5), 403–421. doi:10.1016/S0883-9026(97)00009-8

Villada, F., López-Lezama, J. M., & Muñoz-Galeano, N. (2018). Análisis de la Relación entre Rentabilidad y Riesgo en la Planeación de las Finanzas Personales. *Formación Universitaria, 11*(6), 41–52. doi:10.4067/S0718-50062018000600041

Wairdel, L. (2002). *Coffee with Pleasure: Just Java and World Trade*. Black Rose.

Wang, C., Wang, F., & Onega, T. (2021, April). Network optimization approach to delineating health care service areas: Spatially constrained Louvain and Leiden algorithms. *Transactions in GIS, 25*(2), 1065–1081. doi:10.1111/tgis.12722 PMID:34456609

Ways your business can benefit from the gig economy | Moonlyte. (2021). https://www.moonlyte.com/blog/56/Ways-your-business-can-benefit-from-the-gig-economy

Weitzman, M. (1998). Recombinant Growth. *The Quarterly Journal of Economics, 113*(2), 331–360. doi:10.1162/003355398555595

What is Gig Economy? Pros and Cons of GIG Economy explained, Is Indian Economy becoming GIG Economy? - YouTube. (2019). https://www.youtube.com/watch?v=qECRrrQu8y8&t=75s

What is Industry 4.0? | The Industrial Internet of Things | Epicor India. (n.d.). Retrieved February 7, 2021, from https://www.epicor.com/en-in/resource-center/articles/what-is-industry-4-0/

Wheelen, T. L., & Hunger, D. J. (2004). *Concepts in strategic management and business policy*. Prentice Hall.

Wilhelmina, Q., Joost, J., George, E., & Guido, R. (2010). Globalization vs. localization: Global food challenges and local solutions. *International Journal of Consumer Studies, 34*(3), 357–366. doi:10.1111/j.1470-6431.2010.00868.x

Witt, M. A., & Jackson, A. (2016). Varieties of Capitalism and institutional comparative advantage: A test and reinterpretation. *Journal of International Business Studies, 47*(7-2), 778-806.

Witt, M. A. (2019). De-Globalization: Theories, Predictions, and Opportunities for International Business Research. *Journal of International Business Studies, 50*(7), 1053–1107. doi:10.105741267-019-00219-7

World Health Organization (WHO). (2018). World Health Statistics 2018: Monitoring Health for the Sustainable Development Goal. Author.

Yadav, A.,, & Dwivedi, P. K. (2016). Model Based on the Utilization of Utilitarian Documentation. *Cosmos An International Journal of Management, 5*(2), 1–3.

Ye, M., Lu, W., Flanagan, R., & Chau, K. W. (2020). Corporate social responsibility "glocalisation": Evidence from the international construction business. *Corporate Social Responsibility and Environmental Management, 27*(2), 655–669. doi:10.1002/csr.1831

Yolanda, D., Hindersah, H., Hadiatna, F., & Triawan, M. A. (2016). Implementation of Real-Time Fuzzy logic control for NFT-based hydroponic system on Internet of Things environment. *2016 6th International Conference on System Engineering and Technology (ICSET),* 153-159.

Yulianti, A. (2020). *Knowledge management: learning organization di rs seri VIII.* http://mutupelayanankesehatan.net/sample-levels/19-headline/3437-keberlangsungan-usaha-rs-di-masa-covid-19-apakah-akan-menuju-new- normal-perspektif-learning-organization

Zapata Lambraño, G. C. (2020). *Manual de finanzas personales.* Tesis Digitales. Universidad Cooperativa de Colombia Facultad de Ciencias Económicas, Administrativas y afines programa administración de empresas. Medellín. Disponible en http://hdl.handle.net/20.500.12494/18393

Zehra, N. (2011). The Realist State and Deglobalization. Policy Perspectives, 2.

About the Contributors

Ruchika Gupta is a Professor and HOD (Management) at Amity Business School, Amity University Greater Noida Campus. She is having an academic experience over 17 years during which she has played multifaceted role being a teacher, trainer, mentor, and administrator as well. She is holding a Ph.D. with 3 Masters Degrees. Her research areas are diverse and focus on interdisciplinary research. She has presented and published business cases and research papers in national and international conferences/journals and has been granted 35 copyrights. She is also serving as Editor, Reviewer, and Advisory Board member of several Indexed Journals.

M. Affan Badar, PhD, CPEM is a Professor and former Chair of the Department of Applied Engineering and Technology Management at Indiana State University, USA. From 2016 to 2018, he was Professor and Chair of the Department of Industrial Engineering and Engineering Management at the University of Sharjah, UAE. He received a PhD Degree in Industrial Engineering from the University of Oklahoma in 2002, MS in Mechanical Engineering from King Fahd University of Petroleum and Minerals in 1993, and MSc in Industrial Engineering in 1990 and BSc (Hons) in Mechanical Engineering in 1988 from Aligarh Muslim University, India. Dr. Badar has published two book chapters and more than 80 articles in refereed journals and proceedings in the areas of quality, reliability, lean six sigma, economic analysis, coordinate metrology, health care, energy system design, and supply chain. He is a member of IISE, IEOM, ASEM, and ASEE.

* * *

Ekansh Agarwal is pursuing his business administrative course from NMIMS, Mumbai. He has done various engineering projects at National level. He contributed five research papers in reputed Journals and presented the papers in National & International Conferences. He is a life member of IETE, GE&RA, ISCA. His specialization is in Algorithm & Technological Innovation, E-Commerce, Managerial Prospective.

Abdul Sattar A. Al-Ausi, PhD, Professor & Dean, American University in the Emirates, UAE. He has a good number of research publications to his credit on various subjects. He has the experience of participating & organizing, FDP, seminars, and conferences.

Anna Liza R. Alfonso an experienced Delivery Room and Breastfeeding Advocate Nurse, who values dedication, service and excellence. A fulltime Faculty of the IN - FEU. Finished Doctor in Nursing Management in Trinity University of Asia. In the past, she worked as Supervisor of Delivery Room Department of DLSMC a tertiary Hospital and Lactation Nurse of this institution and work as Professor from different schools and Universities to share her knowledge and expertise.

Rita Ambarwati is a permanent lecturer in the Faculty of Business Law and Social Sciences, Muhammadiyah University of Sidoarjo, who teaches several subjects including industrial management, human resource management, marketing management, and marketing strategies. The fourth daughter of the couple Mr. H.Sudarso and Mrs. Hj. Sri Asmaningwati was born in Surabaya, April 7, 1980, who began her career as a banking practitioner in 2000 2012 and has been a trainer and operational management lecturer since 2017. The educational background of researchers include Bachelor of Management, Wijaya Putra University in Surabaya (graduated in 2003). S-2 Master of Technology Management, ITS 10 November Surabaya (graduated in 20I1), and S-3 Doctoral Program in Management, Brawijaya University in Malang (graduated in 2014). The author is involved in research and Community service both funded by Ristekdikti and an independent fund on the implementation of good governance in public government services.

S. K. Baral did his M. Com, LL. B, MBA, and Ph.D. (Awarded in the year 1999) from Utkal University, Bhubaneswar, Orissa. He has authored 18 books with most current, comprehensive and state-of-art analysis to fulfil the need of Commerce & Management students, professionals and executives working in related fields. He has been conferred with 20 National and International Awards. He has been associated as the Life Member of 17 prestigious Indian Organizations and as an active academician, he has been closely associated with several Indian and foreign Universities. He is the Chief Editor of the 'Splint International Journal of Professionals', a Quarterly Peer Reviewed International Journal, ISSN 2349 – 6045, published by Indianjournals.com, indexed and abstracted @ ProQuest, USA, J-Gate, Indian Citation Index and International Scientific Indexing. He has contributed 131 Research Articles in different referred National and International Journals to his credit and working as Professor, Department of Commerce, Faculty of Commerce & Management at Indira Gandhi National Tribal University (A Central University of Govt. of India), Amarkantak, Madhya Pradesh, India.

Sunil Kumar Chowdhary is an assistance professor in Information Technology in Amity University. He handled many responsibilities. He has research interest in System modeling, ICT, Distributed system. He has published several research papers in conferences & journals. He is Post Graduated in M.Tech (Computer Science)-2008, from IIT Guwahati and currently pursuing PhD. His teaching interest are Distributed Operating system, Advanced system administration, Linux, Programming, Networking, Concepts and applications of IT, Cloud computing, Management Information system.

Anjuli Deepak Gupta, M.Phill Economics, H.O.D. Convent of Jesus and Mary, Dehra Dun, India. She has a teaching experience of ISC for more than 20 years. She has many research papers to her credit. She has participated in many seminars and conferences.

Jocelyn Hipona has a PhD major in Educational Management and is currently enrolled for her second PhD major in Nursing Science from the Philippines. She is a registered nurse in her home country and has spent 10 years working in the nursing academe until she became engaged in research. She is involved in peer reviewing articles internationally. Her research interests are in nursing education, nursing science and technologies, and the advancement of nursing practice. She recently joined DOAJ editorial subcommittee that made her expand her scope in research and publications.

Montasir Islam is a Research Assistant at Illinois State University, USA. He is also a graduate student of Data Science and Management Analytics at the Department of Technology. Previously his research included topics on organizational innovation, startups and entrepreneurship.

Muhammad Irfan Khan is an Associate Professor and Chairperson, Department of Business Administration at Jinnah University for Women. He earned his PhD degree in Finance from the Iqra University, Pakistan. He has 14 years of work experience in Academia and 6 years experience in corporate sector. He has participated in international research conference as paper presenter and Session Chair. Currently he is serving as Reviewer in various nationally recognized as well as International Impact Factor Research Journals. He has published 15 research papers in national as well international research journals. He has also got publication of ONE book on the topic of Development Finance.

Doni Maryono was born in Blitar, March 03, 1981. Basic education was taken at SDN Sumberasri IV. Secondary education is taken at SMPN 2 Nglegok and SMAN I Blitar. S1 education in Business Management Study Program was completed at Muhammadiyah University of Sidoarjo completed in 2020. Now the author is completing his master's study in management at Muhammadiyah University of Sidoarjo. The author has worked since 2009 at the Sidoarjo Hospital until now, and in several hospitals in the Sidoarjo area.

Jaby Mohammed is an Assistant Professor of Technology at Illinois State University, where he teaches Six sigma and Parametric modeling. Jaby joined the technology department after working with Khalifa University, Purdue University, and Morehead State University. He had also worked as engineering faculty with Kentucky Governors Scholars Program for the years 2006-2012. Dr. Mohammed is a senior member of the Society of Manufacturing Engineers (SME) and Institute of Industrial Engineers (IIE). His area of research includes New Product development, human factors, six sigma, and Lean Manufacturing. He has conducted applied research in the area of laser cladding and rapid prototyping using DMD and SLS machines. His research had been sponsored by the Water furnace International, Kentucky science and engineering foundation (KSEF), a Technical assistance program from the state of Indiana (TAP), Institute of regional analysis, and public policy (IRAPP) at Morehead State University. He has published technical papers in handbooks, journals, and conference proceedings. He has mentored six graduate MS students on their thesis. His teaching interests are in the area of quality control, project management, and engineering education. Jaby holds a Ph.D. in Industrial Engineering from the University of Louisville, an MBA in operations management, and his bachelor's in mechanical engineering from the University of Kerala.

Muskan Nagi, PhD in Human Resource, Assistant Professor in Department of Administrative and Financial Sciences, Gulf University, Bahrain. She has nearly 10 research Scopus publication to her credit. She has the experience of participating in and organizing seminars and conferences.

Wilfredo D. Quijencio Jr. is an obstetrician-gynecologist, public health enthusiast, a registered nurse, registered midwife, licensed professional teacher and a Master of Arts in Nursing. He also finished his

Master of Public Health degree at the Institute of Community and Family Health. He shares his medical expertise as a regular fulltime faculty in the Institute of Nursing Department of Graduate Studies and Undergraduate Studies as well as in the Institute of Arts and Sciences Department of Medical Technology. At present he is one of the Chief Education Officer of Health Educators, Advocates and Leaders Philippines - HealPh.

Shiv Ranjan is Assistant Director, Executive Program, Amity University, Greater Noida Campus.

Surinder Sangwan is working as Associate Professor, NRS Govt College, Rohtak, Haryana, India. He has done various skills projects at National level. He contributed eight research papers in reputed Journals and presented the papers in National & International Conferences. He is associated with various International and National Bodies. His specialization is in Skill Mapping, English Literature and Communication.

Md. Sarder is a professor and chair of Engineering Technologies at Bowling Green State University. Prior to joining BGSU, he worked at the U.S. Air Force Academy as a distinguished research fellow and as an associate professor and graduate program director at the University of Southern Mississippi. Dr. Sarder has extensive teaching and research experiences in various areas of industrial & systems engineering predominantly in logistics transportation and supply chain management. He authored three books, four book chapters and over 85 scholarly articles. He was awarded more than $2.5M funding from various agencies including NSF and U.S. Department of Transportation. Some of his research projects include intermodal facility analysis, warehousing need assessment, reshoring and its impact on U.S. transportation & economy, and transportation modeling. He developed a BS program and an MS program in logistics, a research center on logistics trade & transportation, and numerous undergraduate and graduate level courses. Dr. Sarder's primary research areas include logistics transportation & distribution systems, supply chain modeling, optimization, lean, process improvement, and STEM education. He is actively involved with many professional societies including Institute of Industrial & Systems Engineers (IISE), Transportation Research Board (TRB), and American Society of Engineering Education (ASEE). He founded a division of Logistics and Supply Chain within IISE and he served as founding president of that division from 2011-2014. He served as a program chair and conference chair for several premier conferences in his discipline. He also served on editorial board for a number of journals including the editor in chief for the International Journal of Logistics and Transportation Research.

Sarah Sarder is a senior at Perrysburg High School. She has taken several AP courses and conducted research in the Healthcare area. She also worked at Mercy Hospital systems and is very passionate about her healthcare career.

Ramatu Ussif is a lecturer at the University of Education, Winneba, Department of Applied Finance and Policy Management. Ramatu holds a Ph.D. in Finance from Anadolu University, Eskisehir Turkey. She also holds a Postgraduate Diploma in Teaching and Learning in Higher Education (PGDTLHE) from the University of Education, Winneba. She holds a Master of Science Degree in Development Finance and a Bachelor of Science Degree in Banking and Finance from the University of Ghana. Ramatu also obtained two different diplomas in Project Management and Human Resource Management from the Institute of Commercial Management London-UK. Her research interest includes Technological Innovation, Financial Institutions, Financial Inclusion (Microfinance Institutions, Small and Medium Enterprises, Islamic Banking and Finance), Financial Regulations, Development Finance, Digital Finance, Micro and Macro Economics, and SGDs.

Hayri Uygun is a present working in Recep Tayyip Erdogan University, Rize, Turkey. He has 27 years of teaching and industry experience at various levels. He has attended many national and international conferences and seminars. He has published a couple of papers in National and International Journals and various books. He has attended various workshops and FDP's. He is a Managing Director & Editorial Board Member of Tradepreneur Global Academic Platform, Southampton, UK. Also Editorial Board Member of JSBT Journal Group. His research interest is in Teaching Areas are marketing, tourism marketing, public relation, and communication.

José G. Vargas-Hernández, M.B.A., Ph.D., Member of the National System of Researchers of Mexico and a research professor at University Center for Economic and Managerial Sciences, University of Guadalajara. Professor Vargas-Hernández has a Ph. D. in Public Administration and a Ph.D. in Organizational Economics. He has undertaken studies in Organisational Behaviour and has a Master of Business Administration, published four books and more than 200 papers in international journals and reviews (some translated to English, French, German, Portuguese, Farsi, Chinese, etc.) and more than 300 essays in national journals and reviews. He has obtained several international Awards and recognition.

Siddharth Varma is a professor at International Management Institute New Delhi. He is a Mechanical Engineer from University of Roorkee (now IIT Roorkee) with an MBA from Asian Institute of Technology Bangkok and an M Tech and Ph. D from Indian Institute of Technology New Delhi. His areas of interest are Operations Management, Supply Chain Management and Project Management. He has also been involved in training programs for prominent organizations like Indian Oil Corporation Ltd, Engineers India Ltd and Hindustan Zinc Ltd. He has been a regular member of expert committees set up by National Board of Accreditation for accreditation of management institutes in India.

Bhawna Yadav has served many educational institutions in India. She contributed ten research papers in reputed Journals and presented the papers in National & International Conferences. She is a life member of CTE and GE&RA. Her specialization is in Education, Psychology, Technology and Social Work.

Syed Imran Zaman is an Assistant Professor at Jinnah University for Women, one of Pakistan's leading women's university. He has five years of corporate experience in Pakistan Telecommunication Company Ltd. He completed his Ph.D. in 2018 from Southwest Jiaotong University, Chengdu, China. He is having five years of adjunct teaching experience in the Wuhan Summer School program. He has many international research publications to his credit in journals such as Asia Pacific Journal of Marketing and Logistics, International Journal of Finance and Economics, Emerging Markets Finance and Trade, International Journal of Emerging Markets etc., as well as attending international research conferences. He has supervised numerous final theses of bachelor and master level students.

Index

T

U

V

W

Premier Reference Source
Emerging GIS Applications for Emergency and Disaster Management

Premier Reference Source
Managerial Strategies and Green Solutions for Project Sustainability

Premier Reference Source
Comparative Approaches to Using R and Python for Statistical Data Analysis

Premier Reference Source
Solutions for High-Touch Communications in a High-Tech World

www.ingramcontent.com/pod-product-compliance
Lightning Source LLC
LaVergne TN
LVHW062155300926
849161LV00010B/2676
* 9 7 8 1 7 9 9 8 8 7 0 5 8 *